Listening

Listening: Processes, Functions, and Competency explores the role of listening as an essential element in human communication. The book addresses listening as a cognitive process, as a social function, and as a critical professional competency. Blending theory with practical application, *Listening* builds knowledge, insight, and skill to help the reader achieve the desired outcome of effective listening. This second edition introduces listening as a goal-directed activity and has been expanded to include a new chapter addressing listening in mediated contexts. Theory and research throughout the text have been updated, and the final chapter covers new research methodologies and contexts, including functional magnetic resonance imaging, aural architecture, and music.

Debra L. Worthington, Professor of Communication at Auburn University, is a past president of the International Listening Association. Reflecting her interest in listening research, she is the co-editor of *The Sourcebook of Listening Research: Methodology & Measures* (2017). Other research has examined factors affecting listening processes, including listening style and mobile technology.

Margaret E. Fitch-Hauser, Associate Professor Emeritus of Communication at Auburn University, is a past editor of the *International Journal of Listening* (Taylor & Francis). Her research has explored listening fidelity, information distortion, and the effect of schemata on the listening process. She has authored a textbook on business writing, multiple book chapters, case studies, and numerous scholastic papers.

Listening
Processes, Functions, and Competency

Second Edition

Debra L. Worthington, PhD
Margaret E. Fitch-Hauser, PhD

Routledge
Taylor & Francis Group

NEW YORK AND LONDON

Second edition published 2018
by Routledge
711 Third Avenue, New York, NY 10017

and by Routledge
2 Park Square, Milton Park, Abingdon, Oxon OX14 4RN

Routledge is an imprint of the Taylor & Francis Group, an informa business

First edition published by Pearson 2011

Library of Congress Cataloging in Publication Data
Names: Worthington, Debra L., author. | Fitch-Hauser, Margaret E., author.
Title: Listening : processes, functioning, and competency /
Debra L. Worthington, Ph.D., Margaret E. Fitch-Hauser, Ph.D.
Description: Second Edition. | New York : Routledge, 2017.
Identifiers: LCCN 2017019685 | ISBN 9781138229495 (hardback) | ISBN 9781138229501 (pbk.)
Subjects: LCSH: Listening. | Listening comprehension. | Listening–Social aspects.
Classification: LCC BF323.L5 W67 2017 | DDC 153.6/8–dc23
LC record available at https://lccn.loc.gov/2017019685

ISBN: 978-1-138-22949-5 (hbk)
ISBN: 978-1-138-22950-1 (pbk)
ISBN: 978-1-315-38920-2 (ebk)

Typeset in Times New Roman
by Out of House Publishing

Visit the eResource at: www.routledge.com/9781138229501

Contents

Acknowledgments

We would like to thank the many people who helped make this book possible. First, we would like to thank our family members, Don, Jerry, and Kathryn, for their patience and understanding as we spent time and energy on researching, writing, and editing this book. We would like to thank the many graduate students who aided us in our research as well as undergraduates who reviewed and gave us feedback on individual chapters. We would like to express our appreciation to our colleagues and the School of Communication and Journalism for their help in bringing this project to completion. Finally we'd like to thank everyone at Routledge/Taylor & Francis Group who contributed to bringing this project to fruition, and especially the reviewers of early drafts of the text and this second edition.

Preface

We went into the project of writing this book with the firm belief that listening is a critical life competency. Support for our belief can be found in the numerous business articles that are written about the importance of listening in various occupations. Even the American Medical Association has recognized the importance of listening by mandating listening training for future physicians. Unfortunately, however, listening is so embedded in our daily communication processes that few of us take the time to contemplate how it contributes (or detracts) from our ability to communicate effectively with others. Our primary motivation, as active researchers in listening processes, is to provide a vehicle to spur student awareness of and interest in listening as a critical communication competency and as a field of study.

As educators we know that today's college students are very pragmatic. Therefore, we address how listening can contribute to their future success in life as well as careers. Specifically, our text addresses the role and effect of listening in four selected academic and professional contexts. However, our text also has a significant theoretical focus. We provide a review of the progression of more than 70 years of listening research to provide an overview of theory and application. We believe it is important to understand what works but, more important, why it works. An understanding of theory will allow students to adapt their skills, not only in the areas covered in the text, but also in other situations, thus greatly extending their ability to apply skilled listening to a variety of personal and professional challenges.

As scholars, we have built upon the work of past researchers. We would like to dedicate this edition to one who influenced our work, Larry L. Barker: friend, mentor and scholar.

Organization of the Book

Our approach to this textbook provides a theory and research-based discussion of listening as a cognitive process, as a social function, and as a critical professional competency. To achieve the above goals, we have organized the text into three sections. The first section introduces foundational concepts, such as types of listening, as well as cognitive and individual-related factors that might affect listening processes. New to this section in our second edition is a dedicated chapter on mediated listening. The second section addresses social aspects of listening such as how it affects and is affected by the important relationships in our lives. The third section addresses listening in selected professional contexts, while the final chapter focuses on the future of listening: emerging contexts and research.

Pedagogical Features

Each chapter begins with a brief case study vignette based on a set of hypothetical students enrolled in a college listening course. Their interactions with each other and family members form the basis for examples and topic-specific discussions. Key concepts are identified in bold or italicized. At the end of each chapter is a list of key concepts, discussion questions, and additional readings and resources. Instructors can use the discussion questions as the basis for reading responses to assess comprehension and recall of material, to spark additional in-class discussion, or to assess students' ability to apply and critique concepts. *Think on it* boxes are located throughout the text, providing students with the opportunity to consider how a concept directly applies to them. Some boxes identify Internet sites where students can take self-tests associated with the personality or communication construct under discussion. Finally, each chapter is well supported by research as evidenced by extensive endnotes and bibliographies.

Part I

Listening as a Cognitive Process

1   Introduction and Overview

Walk into any Student Union on a college campus and you will find a group of students working on a project or discussing a class. Today, at a large table, we see a group involved in an intense discussion. They are all students in Professor Jackie Merritt's Listening class and just learned that they will be working together on a small group project writing and performing a skit about listening. Since this is the first week of school, they decided to meet so they could get to know each other better. Meet Ben Goleman, Tamarah Jackson, Nolvia Guetierez, Namii Kim, Carter Bishop, and Radley Monroe. Let's listen to part of their conversation.

Case Study 1.1 Introductions

*Well, since I appear to be the oldest in this group, why don't I get things started. As you know, I'm **Tamarah Jackson** and I really appreciate you agreeing to meet at this time. Since I work full time in the city's public safety department, I can only meet after five. I'm an only child and grew up surrounded by members of the Choctaw Nation since my dad is a tribal elder. My mom is a social worker and my dad is a plumber.*

*Hi Tamarah, I bet your background will add a lot to our class discussions about listening. I'm **Ben Goleman** and like Tamarah, I have some time constraints. I can't meet between sundown on Friday and sundown on Saturday. Friday evening my family observes Shabbat and then attends synagogue on Saturday. I'm a middle child, and my mother is a physician and dad is the VP of Human Resources at the auto plant here in town. He thought I picked a good class when I told him I was taking a listening class. He thinks it's a skill that can really help me in all aspects of life. I sure hope he's right – I hate the idea of just taking a class to get a grade.*

*I know what you mean. Some classes can be a real waste of time. But I think this one will be different. My name is **Carter Bishop**, and I'm a "second batch" kid. My parents had three girls and then fifteen years later I came along. They split up when I was four. My mom, sisters and I stayed here. Dad moved to Chicago and works for a PR firm there. Mom's an administrator in the Dean's office. I know both of my parents think listening is important. Just last week, when I visited my Dad, he talked about how important listening to his clients is to his success.*

*You're the youngest kid? I'm the oldest of four and my folks really seem to be zeroed in on me setting the bar for my sisters and little brother. I'm **Radley Monroe**. If you're from around here, you may have heard of my folks. Dad's the football coach at Mockingbird High. He was the first African American to get a graduate degree from State U. He also teaches math, so he's pretty smart. Mom's Scout Monroe, one of the anchors of the 6:00 o'clock news on Channel 10.*

*Wow, my parents never miss your mom's newscast. They will be so excited when I tell them that we are working on a project together. My name is **NaMii Kim** and as you have probably figured out, I'm Korean. My grandparents immigrated here in the 50s. My dad is the eldest of their children and the only boy. My grandparents love to talk about Korean traditions. It's pretty interesting most of the time. But sometimes they don't exactly approve of the "modern" ideas my brothers and I have, and since they live with us, we get an earful. My dad works at the auto plant as an accountant and business manager. And Ben, I think my dad knows your dad. My mother works at Merc's Department store. Let me know if you need anything, I can get a discount.*

*Well it looks like I'm last. I'm **Nolvia Guetierez**. I know what you mean, NaMii, about grandparents and their old-fashioned ideas. Mine came from Honduras and live next door to my family. But it actually has been a good thing. My dad had an accident a few years ago and now he's a paraplegic. Thank goodness my grandparents were there. They really helped while dad went through operations, therapy and all that stuff. My mom works as a pharmacist with Rex Drugs, and she really relied on them a lot to help my dad and to look after my brother and me.*

Introduction

As children, we are often praised and reinforced for speaking well. But how many of you were praised for "listening well?" For not interrupting? For being attentive? In school, you are assigned speeches to give, and you can even take speaking classes. However, it is unlikely that you have received formal listening training before now. At best, you were exposed to a unit of listening as part of another class you have taken – public speaking, interpersonal communication, music education, or perhaps a second language class.

Classes aren't the only way you've learned about communication. You've spent your life studying the communication behaviors of those around you, particularly the communication habits and behaviors of significant people, like your parents and friends. We tend to model our communication behaviors after those whom we observe. This holds true for listening as well. But just because you model your communication and listening on others in your lives, doesn't mean you can't learn a great deal more about useful and effective listening behaviors.

As scholars and consultants in the field of communication and listening, we feel that listening is not just a critical communication competency; it is an important life competency. As a listener, you receive information that helps you to reach personal goals and develop and support relationships. Business owners often report that one of the skills they value most is listening.[1] As consultants, we often hear them complain that they have a hard time finding employees who listen effectively.

Listening is Fundamental

The Importance of Listening Competency

One reason we believe listening is a critical life competency is because it is fundamental to all other communication competencies – speaking, writing, and reading. Of these competencies, listening is the first communication skill we acquire and use. In fact, you began to listen before you were born. Researchers have found that during the last trimester of a pregnancy, the fetus actively processes incoming auditory input, and can clearly distinguish between music, language, and other sounds.[2] Thus, at the very beginnings of human consciousness listening plays an important role.

Listening is also key to learning language.[3] In fact, "learning to speak a language is very largely a task of learning to hear it."[4] Infants are born with the ability to distinguish between every sound – consonants and vowels – necessary to produce any human language.[5] However, if infants do not hear certain sounds, they eventually lose the ability to easily reproduce it. By 12 months, children have learned the sounds and rules of their native language. So, an English speaking child distinguishes between and can articulate both "R" and "L," while a Japanese child does not. It is by listening that infants fine tune their brain to Swahili instead of Spanish, or to English instead of Egyptian. Infants, then, learn to understand and master language by simply listening to us talk. You'll notice that we said "listening to us talk." Emerging research in language development suggests that social interaction is a key component of language development. This emphasis on interaction may help explain why children with autism sometimes have difficulty with language; they prefer non-speech sounds over their mother's speaking.[6]

Learn more: Dr. Patricia Kuhl, a leading researcher in early language and bilingual development, provides a short TED talk on research in infant language development: www.ted.com/speakers/patricia_kuhl.

The understanding of oral language becomes the basis for learning how we comprehend and accurately read and write. In fact, reading comprehension is highly correlated with listening comprehension.[7] This finding is illustrated by how children learn to read by first listening to others read aloud (parents, teachers, babysitters), and then listening to the words as they themselves read aloud. By reading aloud, children can recognize (by listening to their own voice) and self-correct their pronunciation.[8]

Ultimately, your ability to "speak, read, write, and reason" are influenced by your listening ability.[9] As students, listening is fundamental to your personal and academic success.[10] Educator Joseph Beatty goes even further arguing that good listening is both an intellectual as well as a moral virtue because it is fundamental to understanding both yourself as well as others. It is only through good listening that you have the ability to "transform" yourself (and others). In other words, through listening you have the opportunity to "be all that you can be" and can help others do the same.

Think on it: Can you think of a time when listening led you to discover something new about yourself? How did you react? Do you think you would have learned this about yourself if you hadn't learned it by listening to others?

Listening Takes Time (Literally)

As the discussion and proposed skit at the beginning of this chapter suggests, listening is an important communication competency. But just how important is it? Of the many forms of communication – reading, writing, speaking, and listening – which is used the most?

Researcher Paul Rankin was the first to ask this question – in 1926. Results of Rankin's communication time study suggested that people in the early 20th century engaged in listening approximately 42% of their waking hours. Studies conducted since then have consistently supported Rankin's findings across a variety of populations and contexts. For example, research in the early 1970s showed that homemakers spent about 48% of their time listening, while business people spent 33% of their time listening.[11] Another study assessing how students, employees, and homemakers spent their communication time, found that 55% of that time was spent listening.[12] For business people, this percentage increases as they advance into management positions. Managers and executives report spending 60% and 75%, respectively, of their time listening.[13] Table 1.1 summarizes much of the time research that has been conducted over the past 70 years.

Table 1.1 Time Studies Showing the Percentage of Time in Various Communication Activities[a]

Year	Study	Population	Time listening	Time speaking	Time reading	Time writing	Time with media
1926	Rankin	Varied	0.42	0.32	0.15	0.11	
1971	Breiter	Homemakers	0.48	0.35	0.10	0.07	
1975	Weinrauch & Swanda	College students	0.33	0.26	0.19	0.23	
1975	Werner	Varied	0.55	0.23	0.13	0.08	
1980	Barker et al.	College students	0.53*	0.16	0.17	0.14	0.20*
1990	Vickers	College students	0.64*	0.22	0.08	0.07	0.31*
1999	Bohlken	College students	0.53	0.22	0.13	0.12	
2001	Davis	College students	0.34	0.31	0.12	0.10	
2006	Janusik & Wolvin	College students	0.24**	0.20	0.08	0.09	0.39
2008	Emanuel, et al.	College Students	0.55*	0.17	0.16	0.11	0.28*

[a] Adapted from Janusik & Wolvin (2009).
* Time spent listening to media is also included in total time spent listening.
** Time spent listening does not include time spent listening to or using the media.

When looking at the results presented in this table, notice the impact of media usage on the time spent listening. As indicated in Table 1.1, some studies included time spent listening to media in their calculation of the total percentage of time we spend listening. These studies were conducted before the advent of many of the computer and related communication technology commonly used today. To get an accurate picture of how much time you and your colleagues actually spend listening, we must look at the impact of your use of the Internet, e-mail, Snapchat, Facebook, Instagram, mobile phones and so forth. One time study reported in 2006 by listening scholars Laura Janusik and Andy Wolvin, measured media usage (including internet and e-mail) and looked at communication in specific settings such as work and family/friend time.[14] They concluded that, on average, we spend at least 50% of our day listening to either another person or to media. However, given the ubiquitous nature of media technology, they speculate that the figure may actually be higher. Another interesting finding emerging from the Janusik and Wolvin study is that use of technology has impacted how much time we interact face to face. Their research suggests that while overall communication time has increased, it appears that for the first time we spend less than 50% of our communication time speaking (20%) and listening (24%) to others. Listening associated with new media has apparently taken time from previous listening and speaking interactions. Importantly, Janusik and Wolvin's study indicates that we still spend more time listening in a face-to-face context than we do in any other communication activity.

A study done a couple of years after Janusik's and Wolvin's, found college students engaged in communication activities over 13 hours a day. As indicated in Table 1.1, of that 13+ hours, over 55% of the time was spent listening. The time spent listening interpersonally included listening to lectures, in face-to-face encounters, on the phone, and instant messages. Interpersonal listening accounted for just under 50% of total listening time. The remainder of listening time was spent listening to media, primarily television and music.

Taken as a whole, these studies indicate that you spend approximately half of your time communicating with others. And, you spend at least half of your communication time listening.

> ***Think on it:*** Time studies, such as those presented in Table 1.1, typically rely on self-report data. That is, they ask people to make estimates of how much time they engaged in specific communication activities (e.g., in the past hour, day, or week). What type of problems might arise when conducting such a study? How might these problems affect study results and our interpretation of them?

Clearly, listening plays a significant role in our intellectual and social development as well as being critical to effective communication. To get us started in our exploration of this critical competency, we first discuss definitions of listening and review models of listening. We, then, introduce a new model of listening that we use throughout this book, and finally we provide an overview of the topics covered in this text.

Defining Listening

Even though listening is one of the most important skills you can develop, scholars haven't always agreed upon just what constitutes listening competency. One early overview of definitions of listening was written by Ethel Glenn in 1989. In that article, she analyzed the content of 50 definitions of listening.[15] A more recent review was written by Professors Debra Worthington and Graham Bodie. In their *Sourcebook of Listening Research*, they present an historical overview as well as an analysis of multiple definitions of listening. Table 1.2 provides a sampling of listening definitions.

Glenn concluded her 1989 article by stating "[a] universal definition of listening from which operational guidelines may be established will not be easy to formulate."[16] Her observations presented a challenge to scholars around the world involved in listening research. After much discussion and debate, the members of the International Listening Association (ILA) adopted the following definition: Listening is ***"the process of receiving, constructing meaning from, and responding to spoken and/or nonverbal messages."***[17]

> ***Think on it:*** Looking at the definitions presented in Table 1.2, what do they have in common? How do they differ? How do they compare to the definition adopted by the members of the ILA? Do you think the ILA definition should incorporate any other elements? Given recent advances in technology would you suggest any changes to the ILA's definition?

Today, it is one of the most utilized definitions in both professional and academic listening publications. However, Worthington and Bodie, focusing on the role of defining listening in research studies, wrote, "We are not convinced that a single definition of listening is practical or even

Table 1.2 Definitions of Listening*

Author(s)	Date	Definition
Rankin	1926	…the ability to understand spoken language.
Barbe & Meyers	1954	…the process of reacting to, interpreting, and relating the spoken language in terms of past experiences and further course of action.
Brown & Carlson	1955	…the aural assimilation of spoken symbols in a face-to-face speaker audience situation, with both oral and visual cues present.
Barker	1971	…the selective process of attending to, hearing, understanding, and remembering aural symbols.
Lundsteen	1971	…the process by which spoken language is converted to meaning in the mind.
Kelly	1975	…a rather definite and deliberative ability to hear information, to analyze it, to recall it at a later time, and to draw conclusions from it.
Millar & Millar	1976	…three interwoven processes: (1) the physical reception of auditory stimuli, (2) the perception (symbolic classification) of the stimuli, and (3) the interpretation of the stimuli.
Wolff et al.	1983	…a unitary-receptive communication process of hearing and selecting, assimilating and organizing, and retaining and covertly responding to aural and nonverbal stimuli.
Wovin & Coakley	1988	…the process of receiving, attending to, and assigning meaning to aural stimuli.
Vasile & Mintz	1986	… an intellectual or active function that involves the mind, eyes, ears, and memory.
International Listening Association	1996	…the process of receiving, constructing meaning from and responding to spoken and/or nonverbal messages.
Bostrom	2011	…the acquisition, processing, and retention of information in the interpersonal context.

* See Glenn, 1989; Wolvin & Coakley (1996) and Worthington & Bodie (2017) for full citations.

desirable."[18] One reason they make this argument is that listening researchers still do not fully understand many of the underlying processes of listening (e.g., memory, comprehension, recall, etc.). They assert that trying to develop a single definition of listening may essentially be "putting the proverbial cart before the horse."

As you examine the definitions provided in Table 1.2, you'll notice that many suggest that listening is a multidimensional construct. Most typically, elements of these (and many other) definitions fall into three broad, yet complex categories: a) affective processes, which include aspects related to motivation and appreciation; b) behavioral processes, which generally focus on responding, including verbal and nonverbal feedback; and c) cognitive processes, which address attention, understanding, reception, and interpretation.[19] These elements are featured prominently in many listening models, including several outlined below.

Models of Listening

Most of you are probably familiar with basic communication models that address the sender, receiver, message, feedback, and noise. These elements are combined with various other characteristics in a multitude of models. Based upon these communication models, we have learned a great deal about constructing and sending messages. However, while you have spent much of your lives learning how to put together a message, this time is wasted if you don't also think about what happens when the other party receives it. Just as you are mindful about what goes into a message that you send, you need to be mindful of how incoming information is received and processed. To help us start down that road, we will first introduce the purpose behind model building, then look at several models of listening. The primary purpose of a **model** is to illustrate complex, abstract processes in such a way that you have a clear understanding of how the process works.

While many types of models exist, listening is most often portrayed using *process models*, which attempt to illustrate what happens in our minds as we listen. Process models serve a number of purposes for researchers.[20] They are *organizational*, illustrating the connections and rules between elements. Ideally, models also serve *heuristic, predictive,* and *measurement* functions. Put more plainly, they should give us ideas of what to research, make predictions of how components (or other concepts and elements) work together, and give us an idea of how best to measure listening processes. The primary purpose of models in most textbooks is organizational, and our model of listening (the WFH model) is no different.

However, before introducing our own model of listening, we need to look briefly at existing models. Following the work of early listening scholar, Belle Ruth Witkin, we divide these models into three broad areas: speech communication models, cognitive models, and speech science models.[21]

Speech Communication Models

Speech communication models look at listening within the context of a communication setting or as a communication specific skill. Essentially, these models go beyond traditional communication models to emphasize the skills and processes used to listen.[22] For example, models by Larry Barker, and Andy Wolvin and Carolyn Coakley highlight the role and importance of receiving information and assigning meaning to messages. Most general communication models at the time tended to ignore these aspects of communication.

Speech communication models are rooted in the early work of Ralph Nichols. Known as the "Father of Listening," Nichols' early research had a profound impact on how scholars viewed listening. Nichols' research motivated scholars to think of listening as a separate and identifiable aspect of communication. During this period, Nichols was mostly interested in listening as it related to the comprehension of lecture information. He constructed a test designed to tap listening comprehension of a lecture and compared the results with several standardized tests covering intelligence, social ease, and other mental and social variables. His results suggested that there are a number of elements impacting **listening comprehension,** including *cognitive factors* (e.g., intelligence, curiosity, inference-making ability, and ability to concentrate), *language-related factors* (e.g., reading comprehension, recognition of correct English usage, size of the listener's vocabulary, ability to identify main ideas), *speaker-related factors* (e.g., speaker effectiveness, audibility of the speaker, admiration for the speaker), *contextual factors* (e.g., interest in the subject, importance of the subject, room ventilation and temperature, listener's physical fatigue), and *demographic factors* (e.g., listener sex, parental occupation, high school academic achievement).

Looking at Nichols' research, you can see that he focused on the overall communication process. Importantly, while he began to isolate or separate listening from other communication elements, he still included the impact of the speaker. Thus, Nichol's approach still ultimately embeds listening in the sender–receiver mode.

One of the most important conclusions Nichols drew from his work was that "listening comprehension apparently involves a number of factors not operative in reading comprehension."[23] This statement suggested that listening was a separate receiving and information processing skill that qualitatively differed from other communication skills studied at that time (e.g., reading, writing, etc.). So even though he focused on the communication aspect of listening, he laid important groundwork for the next generation of listening scholars to use in their development of cognitive models.

Cognitive Models

Cognitive models emerged from the field of cognitive psychology. While these models are not listening specific, they do include in-depth analyses of two essential elements of listening – attention and memory. In general, these models tend to focus on getting a receiver's attention and then moving the incoming information into memory. With the exception of a memory based listening model introduced by Bob Bostrom and Enid Waldhart, the concept of listening wasn't included in most early cognitive models.[24] Listening scholars Bostrom and Waldhart felt that components of memory were essential to understanding the listening process. Perhaps the most important contributions of cognitive models are their emphasis on short-term and long-term memory and the function memory plays in listening. Eventually, scholars expanded cognitive models to include a variety of related elements, such as attention, comprehension, and inference-making, which are now considered key areas of interest to listening researchers.[25] Other cognitive and listening research has discovered that listening is related to inductive reasoning, verbal comprehension, memory, reading, cognitive complexity, and receiver apprehension.[26]

Laura Janusik has continued this line of research by going beyond just looking at related cognitive functions. She proposed a model of listening grounded in working memory (i.e., short-term memory). Her model addresses how we process information as well as how we store it.[27] Her research findings support claims that listening is a cognitive process. We discuss cognitive aspects of listening further in Chapter 3.

Speech Science Models

The third category of models that Witkin explored was speech science models or auditory processing models. These models focus greater attention on the physiological aspects of listening or hearing and the act of discriminating types of incoming stimulus. Through her research, Witkin identified a number of important auditory elements affecting listening, such as pitch/intonation and oral language processing.[28] While critics of these models suggest that they confuse the hearing process with listening (and we certainly don't want to do that), these models are important because they emphasize two critical aspects of listening – physical reception of the stimulus and the ability to discriminate among pieces of the stimulus. While knowing the physiology of listening is important, we must keep in mind that people who are profoundly deaf and those who have hearing disabilities are able to take in information and process it. This observation suggests that listening is much more than the physiological process of receiving and processing sound.

Current Listening Models

Recent models attempt to blend the three areas identified by Witkin. One of these models, Judy Brownell's **HURIER model,** includes elements of the cognitive and speech science perspectives.[29] The model looks at six interrelated processes:

- **H**earing – the accurate physical reception of sound. This element of the process includes focusing on the speaker, discriminating among sounds, and concentrating on the message.
- **U**nderstanding – listening comprehension or understanding the message. This element involves information processing and inner speech.
- **R**emembering – retaining and recalling information.
- **I**nterpreting – using the interaction context and knowledge of the other person to assign meaning to the message.
- **E**valuating – applying your own perspectives and biases to your interpretation.
- **R**esponding – appropriately responding to the message.

In the HURIER model, the above elements are situated in the context of the listening goal and the situation making it an interpersonally based model.

Other models are more contextually based. For example, the **Integrative Listening Model** (ILM), developed by Kathy Thompson and colleagues, is based on a specific definition of listening: "the dynamic, interactive process of integrating appropriate listening attitudes, knowledge, and behaviors to achieve the selected goals(s) of a listening event."[30] This model revolves around four stages:

- **Preparing to listen** – establishing listening goals ahead of time, analyzing the interaction context, and addressing potential listening filters.
- **Applying listening processes** – using distinctive components of listening – such as receiving, comprehending, evaluating, and responding – in ways that are appropriate for the specific listening setting.
- **Assessing listening effectiveness** – reflecting on one's listening performance by one's self and others.
- **Establishing future listening** – ongoing development of listening goals based on self-assessment and feedback.

The authors suggest that the stages are interrelated, discrete elements that uniquely contribute to the listening process. In addition to context, the ILM also emphasizes the importance of evaluating how well we listen.

The next model was developed to study cultural differences in listening. Professors Margarete Imhof of Germany and Laura Janusik of the United States developed a **systems model** of the listening process.[31] The Imhof–Janusik model explores the associations between three aspects of listening: presage, process, and product. *Presage* includes the interaction of context factors and the mental and motivational aspect of the listener, while *process* includes different courses of listening action. For example, listening for information and listening for relationship building are two very different things. Finally, *product* reflects the listening outcome that the listener seeks and achieves. It is important to remember that presage, process, and product interact and affect each other.

The Listening MATERRS Model

The above discussion of existing models of listening gives you a good idea of the breadth of perspectives of the listening process. We next introduce our model of listening – the Worthington Fitch-Hauser **Listening MATERRS Model**, whose primary elements include:

Mental stimulus
Awareness
Translation
Evaluation
Recall
Response
Staying connected and motivated

We will use this process model throughout the course of the book as we examine listening as a critical communication and life competency. As you can see, our model was designed to serve an organizational function. It provides a means of introducing key components of the listening process and, as seen in Figure 1.1, it provides a means of visualizing the possible relationships between them. While we recognize that listening occurs within a communication context, we feel it is important to focus on what happens from the point the listener becomes aware of a stimulus. This starting point is the beginning of the conscious process of listening and acknowledges that there are many sounds "out there" that we choose to ignore. Before reading about our model, take a moment to "***Think on it***."

Figure 1.1 Worthington Fitch-Hauser Model of Listening

Think on it: Have you ever thought about how noisy our world is? To test this premise, get everyone in the room to stop talking for 60 seconds. During this time of silence, count the number of sounds you can identify.

Worthington Fitch-Hauser Model of Listening: Listening MATERRS

Each of the interdependent elements of this model are illustrated and discussed below in the order presented in our acronym – Listening *MATERRS.*

We chose to illustrate our model using gears because we believe gears better reflect the interdependent nature of each element of the model. Once we receive the mental stimulus, our mind gets to work. Moreover, as seen with the arrows pointing in both directions, individuals can move between the elements as necessary to help achieve their listening goals.

Mental Stimulus

In many ways, listening is a sorting process. We hear a tremendous amount of material every day, but as you know, we can't listen to all of it. **Mental stimulus** occurs when you begin to actively *attend* to a physical noise or stimulus. You make a conscious decision to focus and "listen" to a particular input. Thus, you hear your name from across the room, someone raises their voice and speaks angrily, or you see a quick movement and direct your focus to that particular listening event. Thus, hearing is the physiological process, while listening involves *intentionality* on the part of the receiver. We hear a great deal, but attend to relatively little of it.

Awareness

Once you become fully aware of or intentionally listen to a sound or message, you can then say you have moved to **awareness**. Here, you engage in what can best be described as a mental sorting process, which means you have begun to listen more closely to the message or sound. Your decision to actively attend to a message is affected by any number of factors. One of these factors is **motivation.** If you are motivated by the subject matter, the situation, or the individual, you will find a way to focus and pay attention. Another factor, **cognitive load**, refers to the amount of information you are mentally processing at a given point in time.[32] For example, if you are experiencing a particularly high cognitive load, you may not be able to listen. The student who is worried about an exam, the woman driving and talking on mobile phone, and the dad with a child jumping up and down trying to get his attention will all have a higher cognitive load than the person who is sitting quietly focused on a presentation. The higher the cognitive load, the fewer mental resources you have available to listen. Although most of us like to think we can multitask, multitasking simply does **not** work well when it comes to really listening to others. As we will discuss later in the text, multitasking is directly related to cognitive load. The more activities you engage in, the greater your cognitive load.

Cognitive filtering can also affect your ability to listen. Cognitive filtering addresses your ability to filter out common noises like the ones you identified when you tried the 60 second exercise in the *Think on it* box above. During that brief time you "heard" any number of mental stimulus inputs. However, until that moment, you were probably unaware of them largely because you had no reason, or lacked motivation, to tune in to them. **Environmental factors** can also affect your ability to listen. These factors can be internal or external. For example, a loud radio, uncomfortable temperatures, being hungry, and worrying about something, can distract you from listening. Finally, cognitive filtering includes your **personal biases**. You may stop listening to a speaker because you think you have "heard it all before," because you personally dislike him, or you think she is too young to offer insight into your conversation. Your biases can have a tremendous impact on your choice to engage in the next aspect of our model – translation.

Think on it: Grammy award-winning violinist Joshua Bell, one of the world's premier violinists, participated in a study conducted by the *Washington Post*. Would the people of Washington, DC stop and listen as they passed through the L'Enfant Plaza, one of many subway stops in the city? Would they listen to a man who sells out concert halls and who owns and plays a $3.5 million dollar Stradivarius violin? Would you stop and listen? As you watch the video clips embedded in the *Washington Post*'s story, you can tell that for some people, his music did not register with them. These people do not appear to hear him at all. Other individuals are obviously aware of Bell's playing. They look over to him, but continue walking. A few people stop and put money in his violin case. Even fewer actually stopped and truly listened.

Reviewing the factors that may affect the first two levels of listening described above, what may be affecting their listening processes? Why would all the children who heard Bell play attempt to stop and listen, while their parents try to hurry them along?

A few individuals did stop and listen. What has to happen in terms of their listening in order for this to occur? Why would they stop? If you're interested in the explanations from individuals who heard Mr. Bell play that day, you can access the full article at the *Washington Post* website (www.washingtonpost.com). Gene Weingarten's article is titled "Pearls Before Breakfast."

Translation

Given sufficient motivation, you move from awareness to **translation**. At this level, the listener begins to recognize the basic components of the message. Here, language is processed, non-verbals are interpreted, and schemas are triggered. Three types of processing of information may occur – affective processing, rational processing, and dual processing.

Affective processing occurs when you primarily focus on the emotional elements of what you are hearing. Is the person upset? Or, does the message make you happy? Sad? Angry? Is it uplifting or depressing? Some contexts require that you primarily focus on affective processing. At those times, you are less concerned about whether a person's message makes sense and are more interested in determining how he or she is feeling. At other times, you may need to suppress your own emotions, and focus on fully understanding a message – grammar, logic, clarity, coherence, etc. At these times, you engage in **rational processing**. Rational processing occurs when you focus on the information itself and the logic of that information. In this type of processing you analyze, fairly objectively, the validity of the message and begin to connect it with what you have stored in your memory. You may also evaluate the credentials of the speaker and the appropriateness of the information for the situation. When you use your rational processing as a listener, you are assessing the information according to your individual understanding of the rules of logic. In other words, what seems logical to Ben, may not seem logical to Tamarah. Thus, it's important for you to remember that like all information processing, this type of reasoning is governed by individual experiences and education. Finally, you can combine the two types of processing and engage in what is called **dual processing**. At times, effective listening requires you to use both affective and rational processing to translate a message.

Evaluation

When you truly begin linking what you hear to what you know, you have moved to **evaluating** a message. This level involves the actual cognitive processing of the information. You use your schemas to aid in the interpretation of what you hear, to develop new mental models, and to categorize information. This level also includes value assessments. In judging the violin playing of Joshua Bell (see previous *Think on it* box), you may decide the music has a beautiful melody, too slow of a beat, or just isn't "your style." If you determine the information is important enough or novel enough, you are motivated to move to the next element in our model of listening – recalling.

Recall

Two important things happen at this point. First, you determine what gets stored in your memory. Second, you assess whether a message requires a response. In the context of this model, memory can be divided into two primary areas – working memory and long-term memory. **Working memory** is the information that is accessible to you during a listening event. Memory researchers would call this short-term memory (we discuss this further in Chapter 3). Working memory can be equated to short-term storage. It is where you place information while you decide what you are going to do with it.[33] For example, if you hear a professor say information is going to be covered on an exam, you will not only pay close attention, you will likely send the information to long-term memory. On the other hand, if you are engaging in a social conversation with the same professor, you will retain information just long enough to make an appropriate response, you may or may not send the information to long-term storage. **Long-term memory** is your storehouse of information. It contains all of the information you have learned in life. However, it is important to note that if you are not listening, information probably will never make it to long-term storage. Throughout the book, we discuss a number of factors that can affect your working and long-term memory.

Responding

At this level, you make decisions about how you will respond to the other party. Your internal response occurs at both the translation and the evaluation levels. When responding, you may decide against overtly responding to a message (i.e., ignore it), you may decide that a touch of the hand is enough, or you may verbally respond to the incoming message. Your decisions about responding are influenced by any number of factors – your knowledge of the topic, your history with that individual, the schemas stored in memory of what is appropriate in this particular type of situation, or your mood, at the time. For example, if the other person is emotionally upset, you use your "how to respond to sadness schema" to help you determine what the right response is. If you are going to reply verbally, at this point, you determine the best form and content for the message. Your memory of previous encounters will aid you in determining the best way to respond to a situation. A good listener will be aware of the entire message – words, emotions, and context – and will be able to react in a caring and appropriate manner.

Staying Connected (and Motivated)

Central to the entire listening process is staying connected and being motivated. Staying connected implies that the listening process is more than "in one ear and out the other." Listening is built around relationships you have with others. As you listen, you identify what you know about the other person, what you have learned from past interactions, what the person's nonverbal messages are, and what the context is. In addition, you continue to pull in additional information during each listening episode with the person, context, event, etc., and use it in your future interactions. You use this information to help build schemas and scripts to help guide your behavior in future interactions and in similar contexts (using long-term memory). Here, we focus on remaining engaged, truly listening to the other.

Motivation is of critical importance because it links each of the factors we have discussed. When receiving a mental stimulus, you must be motivated in some way to become fully aware of what you hear, and even more motivation is needed to translate and evaluate the stimulus. Essentially, motivation is the tie that binds all parts of the greater listening process.

Finally, another central element of the listening process is **personal bias**. As we mentioned above, your biases can affect not only your choice to actually listen, but likewise your decision to continue listening. Your biases also affect how you translate and evaluate what you hear, as well as what and how you remember what you attend to.

Overview of the Text

As we noted earlier, this textbook focuses on listening as more than just a critical communication competency, but also as a life skill. Consequently, you will find that many of the chapters cover the role and function of listening either in important settings we find ourselves in or within certain occupational areas.

The book is divided into three major sections. The first section of the text addresses the cognitive processes associated with listening. Chapter 2 introduces you to the different types of listening, the role of empathy, and the importance of listening across the life-span. It also examines the importance of listening competence, shows you how to measure your own listening competency, and concludes with a discussion of the importance of setting personal and professional listening goals. Chapter 3 addresses information processing issues, including the role of schemas and the impact of memory and recall have on listening. Chapter 4 focuses on individual differences that can affect our listening processes. In it, we explore listening style preferences, personality type, communication apprehension, as well as emotional IQ. This section ends with Chapter 5, which examines the impact that technologies have on our ability to be good listeners and explores the effect of technology on how we process information.

The second section of the text explores the social functions of listening. Chapter 6 examines the fundamental role listening plays in understanding ourselves, especially as related to daily conversations, conflict, and relationship building. Chapters 7 and 8 explore the impact listening has on specific relationships, including friendships, romance, and families.

The third section of the book looks at listening in specific contexts, such as organizations, health, education, and law. As students, you may find Chapter 9 particularly interesting as it addresses listening in the educational context. We explore connections between listening and topics such as learning and academic performance, teaching effectiveness, and note-taking. Chapter 10, the organizational chapter, explores the connection between listening and job satisfaction, and the importance of listening to customer satisfaction. Chapter 11 addresses listening and the health industry. We explore listening links to patient health, medical error, and patient satisfaction and compliance. Finally, Chapter 12 examines listening in the legal context. For example, we address listening theory and practice in the trial process, in attorney–client interviews, jury decision-making, and in alternative dispute resolution.

In Chapter 13, we conclude the book with a brief look at the "future" of listening, especially how new areas of listening research are contributing to our understanding of listening processes and listening competency.

Key Concepts

Model
Process Models
    Organizational function
    Heuristic function
    Predictive function
    Measurement function
Listening Models
    Speech Communication Models
        Listening comprehension
        Cognitive factors
        Language-related factors
        Speaker-related factors
        Contextual factors
        Demographic factors
    Cognitive Models
    Speech Science Models
    HURRIER Model
    Integrative Listening Model
    Systems Model
        Presage
        Process
        Product
Listening MATERRS Model
Mental Stimulus
    Intentionality
    Awareness
        Motivation
        Cognitive load
        Cognitive filtering
        Environmental factors
        Personal biases
    Translation
        Affective processing
        Rational processing
        Dual processing
    Evaluation

       Recall
           Working memory
           Long-term memory
    Response
    Stay connected
           Motivation
           Personal biases

Discussion Questions

1. Who are some of the significant people you believe have affected your communication and listening? What communication and listening skills and habits (good and bad) do you engage in that you can trace back to them?
2. Do you think your culture or ethnic background has affected how you listen? If so, how? If not, why not?
3. We cover three primary types of models – Speech Communication Models, Cognitive Models, and Speech Science Models. What commonalities do they share? What do these commonalities suggest about the process of listening? What differences do you see? What do these differences suggest about how researchers perceive listening?
4. The WFH Model of Listening introduces the idea of different types of processing as part of the translation process. When are you most likely to engage in affective processing? Rational processing? Dual processing?

Listening Activities

1. How do your communication and listening activities stack up against the studies described in Table 1.1? Chart your activities for a day, or two, or even a week. Do you spend more time on the computer? Talking face to face with friends? Using your cell phone? How do your findings compare with your friends? In a small group or with the entire class, average your findings together and compare them to those presented in Table 1.1.
2. Tinnitus (ringing in the ears) is one of the many factors that can affect listening. What are other hearing disabilities? Locate and interview someone with a hearing disability. How severe do they find the disability? How does it impact their life? Does it interfere with how they communicate with others? If yes, how do they compensate for it? If possible, also interview a friend or family member of the person with the hearing disability. Do they agree that their friend/loved one listens effectively?

Notes

1 Casserly, 2012; Worthington, 2014; Hansen & Hansen, 2007; Lloyd & Kennedy, 1997
2 Karmiloff-Smith, 1995; Wilkin, 1993
3 Vandergrift & Goh, 2009; Weiler, 2016
4 Nida, 1957, p. 53, as cited in Peterson, 2001
5 Moon, Lagercrantz, & Kuhl, 2013
6 Kuhl, 2011
7 Hyobin & Yusun, 2016
8 De Jong & van der Leij, 2002; Verhoeven & Van Leeuwe, 2008

9 Rubin & Morreale, 1996; Sandall, Schramm,& Seiber, 2003
10 Webb, Carey, Villares, Wells, & Sayer, 2014
11 Brieter, 1971; Weinrauch & Swanda, 1975
12 Werner, 1975
13 These statistics are presented in Krizan, Merrier, Logan, & Williams (2008), who did not provide citations for original studies.
14 Janusik & Wolvin, 2009
15 Glenn, 1989
16 Glenn, 1989, p. 29
17 International Listening Association, 2007
18 Worthington & Bodie, 2017
19 Halone, Cunconan, Coakley, & Wolvin, 1998
20 Deutsch, 1952
21 Witkin, 1990
22 Barker, 1971; Wolvin & Coakley, 1996
23 Nichols, 1948, p. 162
24 Bostrom & Waldhart, 1980
25 See, for example, Reed, Goolsby & Johnston (2014), who focused on measuring co-workers' perceptions of attention; Vandergrift, Goh, Mareschal, & Tafaghodtari (2006), and, Janusik & Keaton (2015), who both addressed individual memory and comprehension
26 See, for example, Beatty & Payne, 1984; Bodie & Villaume, 2003; Caffrey, 1953; Hyobin & Yusun, 2016; Sawyer, Gayle, Topa, & Powers, 2014
27 Janusik, 2005
28 Witking, Butler, &Whalen, 1977
29 Brownell, 2013
30 Thompson, Leintz, Nevers & Witkowski, 2004
31 The Imhof–Janusik model (2006) is based upon earlier work of Biggs (1999)
32 Kalyuga, 2009
33 For an excellent discussion of working memory and problems with poor working memory, see Klingberg, 2009.

Additional Readings

Holtgraves, T. M. (2002). *Language as social action: Social psychology and language use.* Mahwah, NJ: Erlbaum.
Johnson, A., & Proctor, R. W. (2004). *Attention: Theory and practice.* Thousand Oaks, CA: Sage.
Wolvin, A. (2010). *Listening and human communication in the 21st century.* Malden, MA: Wiley.

References

Barker, L. (1971). *Listening behavior.* Englewood Cliffs, NJ: Prentice-Hall.
Beatty, M., & Payne, S. (1984). Listening comprehension as a function of cognitive complexity: A research note. *Communication Monographs, 51,* 85–89.
Biggs, J. (1999). *Teaching for quality learning at university.* Buckingham, UK: Society for Research on Higher Education.
Bodie, G. D., & Villaume, W. A. (2003). Aspects of receiving information: The relationship between listening preferences, communication apprehension, receiver apprehension, and communicator style. *International Journal of Listening, 17,* 47–67.
Bostrom, R. N., & Waldhart, E. S. (1980). Components in listening behavior: The role of short-term memory. *Human Communication Research, 6,* 221–227.

Brieter, L. R. (1971). Research in listening and its importance to literature. In L. Barker (Ed.), *Listening behavior.* Englewood Cliffs, NJ: Prentice-Hall.

Brownell, J. (2013). *Listening: Attitudes, principles and skills* (5th ed.). Boston: Allyn & Bacon.

Caffrey, J. G. (1953). *Auding ability as a function of certain psychometric variables.* Unpublished doctoral dissertation, University of California, Berkley.

Casserly, M. (2012, December 10). The 10 skills that will get you hired in 2013. *Forbes.* Retrieved from www.forbes.com/sites/meghancasserly/2012/12/10/the-10-skills-that-will-get-you-a-job-in-2013/#7b57c34c664b.

De Jong, P., & van der Leij, A. (2002). Effects of phonological abilities and linguistics comprehension on the development of reading. *Scientific Studies of Reading, 6,* 51–77.

Deutsch, K. W. (1952). On communication models in the social sciences. *Public Opinion Quarterly, 16,* 356–380.

Glenn, E. (1989). A content analysis of fifty definitions of listening. *Journal of the International Listening Association, 3,* 21–31.

Halone, K., Cunconan, T. M., Coakley, C. G., & Wolvin, A. D. (1998). Toward the establishment of general dimensions underlying the listening process. *International Journal of Listening, 12,* 12–28.

Hansen, R. S., & Hansen, K. (2007). What do employers really want? Top skills and values employers seek from job-seekers. *Quintessential Careers.* Retrieved from www.quintcareers.com/job_skills_values.html.

Hyobin, A., & Yusun, K. (2016). Reading fluency and listening comprehension abilities as predictors of reading comprehension. *English Teaching, 71,* 3–24.

International Listening Association. (2007). Listen and make the connection. Janusik, L. (2005). Conversational listening span: A proposed measure of conversational listening. *International Journal of Listening, 19,* 12–30.

Janusik. L. A., & Keaton, S. (2015). Toward developing a cross-cultural metacognition instrument for listening in first language (L1) contexts: The (Janusik-Keaton) Metacognitive Listening Instrument. *Journal of Intercultural Communication Research, 44,* 288–306.

Janusik, L., & Wolvin, A. (2009). 24 hours in a day: A listening update to the time study. *International Journal of Listening, 23,* 104–120.

Kalyuga, S. (2009). *Managing cognitive load in adaptive multimedia learning.* Hershey, PA: IGI Global.

Karmiloff-Smith, A. (1995). *Beyond modularity: A developmental perspective on cognitive science.* Cambridge, MA: MIT Press.

Klingberg, T. (2009). *The overflowing brain.* New York: Oxford.

Krizan, A. C., Merrier, P., Logan, J. P., & Williams, K. S. (2008). *Business communication* (7th ed.). Mason, OH: Thomson.

Kuhl, P. K. (2011). Social mechanisms in early language acquisition: Understanding integrated brain systems supporting language. In J. Decety and J. T. Cacioppo (Eds.), *The Oxford handbook of social neuroscience* (pp. 649–667). New York: Oxford.

Lloyd, M. A., & Kennedy, J. H. (1997, August 28). Skills employers seek. Retrieved from PsychWeb www.psywww.com/careers/skills.htm.

Moon, C., Lagercrantz, H., & Kuhl, P. K. (2013). Language experienced in utero affects vowel perception after birth: A two-country study. *Acta Paediatrica, 102,* 156–160.

Nichols, R. (1948). Factors in listening comprehension. *Speech Monographs, 15,* 154–163.

Peterson, P. W. (2001). Skills and strategies for proficient listening. In M. Celce-Murcia (Ed.), *Teaching English as second or foreign language* (3rd ed., pp. 87–100). Boston: Heinle & Heinle.

Rankin, P. T. (1926). *The measurement of the ability to understand spoken language.* (Doctoral dissertation). ProQuest Dissertations and Theses database. (AAT 0004362).

Reed, K., Goolsby, J. R., & Johnston, M. K. (2014). Extracting meaning and relevance from work: The potential connection between the listening environment and employee's organizational identification and commitment. *International Journal of Business Communication, 53,* 1–17.

Rubin, R. B., & Morreale, S. P. (1996). Setting expectations for speech communication and listening. *New Directions for Higher Education, 96,* 19–29.

Sandall, N., Schramm, K., & Seiber, A. (2003). *Improving listening skills through the use of children's literature.* Chicago, IL: Saint Xavier University & SkyLight Professional Development Field-Based Masters Program. Retrieved from Eric. (ED No. 482002).

Sawyer, C. R., Gayle, K., Topa, A., & Powers, W. G. (2014). Listening fidelity among native and nonnative English-speaking undergraduates as a function of listening apprehension and gender. *Communication Research Reports, 31,* 62–71.

Thompson, K., Leintz, P., Nevers, B., & Witkowski, S. (2004). The integrative listening model: An approach to teaching and learning listening. *The Journal of General Education, 53,* 225–246.

Vandergrift, L., & Goh, C. (2009). Teaching and testing listening comprehension. In M. H. Long & C. J. Doughty (Eds.), *The handbook of language teaching* (pp. 395–411). Malden, MA: Wiley-Blackwell.

Vandergrift, L., Goh, C. C., Mareschal, C. J., & Tafaghodtari, M. H. (2006). The metacognitive awareness listening questionnaire: Development and validation. *Language Learning, 56,* 431–462.

Verhoeven, L., & van Leeuwe, J. (2008). Predictors of text comprehension development. *Applied Cognitive Psychology, 22,* 407–423.

Webb, L., Carey, J., Villares, E., Wells, C., & Sayer, A., (2014). Results of a randomized controlled trial of student success skills. *Society for Research on Educational Effectiveness.* Retrieved from http://files.eric.ed.gov/fulltext/ED562995.pdf.

Weiler, A. (2016, April 20). The heart of learning languages: Listening. *EFL Magazine.* Retrieved from www.eflmagazine.com/the-heart-of-learning-languages-listening/.

Weinrauch, J. D. & Swanda, R., Jr. (1975). Examining the significance of listening: An exploratory study of contemporary management. *The Journal of Business Communication, 13,* 25–32.

Werner, E. (1975). *A study of communication time.* Unpublished master's thesis. College Park: University of Maryland.

Wilkin P. E. (1993). Prenatal and postnatal responses to music and sound stimuli. In T. Blum (Ed.), *Prenatal perception learning and bonding* (pp. 307–329). Berlin: Leonardo.

Witkin, B. R. (1990). Listening theory and research: The state of the art. *Journal of the International Listening Association, 4,* 7–32.

Witking, B. R., Butler, K. G., & Whalen, T. E. (1977). Auditory processing in children: Two studies of component factors. *Language, Speech & Hearing Services in Schools, 8,* 140–154.

Wolvin, A., & Coakley, C. (1996). *Listening* (5th ed.). Boston: McGraw-Hill.

Worthington, D. L., & Bodie, G. D. (2017). Defining listening: A historical, theoretical and pragmatic assessment. In D. L. Worthington & G. D. Bodie (Eds.), *The sourcebook of listening.* (Chapter 1). Malden, MA: Wiley-Blackwell.

Worthington, R. E. (2014). *2014 Corporate recruiters survey report.* Graduate Management Admission Council/MBA Career Services & Employer Alliance. Retrieved from www.gmac.com/~/media/Files/gmac/Research/Employment-Outlook/2014-corporaterecruiters-final-release-3.pdf.

2 Listening

Types and Competencies

Case Study 2.1 Listening is Hard to Do

Man, I just heard the best lecture ever this morning. My mechanical engineering professor lectured on properties of ceramic materials – you know like the tiles on the original space shuttles. She made half of the class want to apply to the space program.

Oh, Carter, you are such a nerd! I don't see how you stay interested in technical stuff like that.

I was thinking about that question on my way here, Radley. Don't you think it's odd that I find it so easy to listen to lectures on ceramics or other materials of engineering, but have such a problem listening to my mom? You'd think that if I'm a good listener in class, I would be a good listener with her. Just yesterday my mom caught me not listening when she was telling me about my sister, Clara – you know the one who lives in Jackson Gap.

I know what you mean. Some information is just easier for me to listen to. Why is it that I have problems listening in music appreciation and none when I talk with your dad about his football team?

Listening as a Critical Communication Competency

As you know, we believe listening is both a critical communication competency and a critical life competency. However, identifying listening competencies has been the topic of significant disagreement of listening scholars. If you recall from the definitions and models of listening discussed in Chapter 1, the skill of listening involves many dimensions. As a **multi-dimensional skill**, listening competency necessarily involves a number of elements. If you consider the Listening MATERRS model, it is easy to see that it will take a number of different skills to be a competent listener. The multi-dimensionality of listening is also one of the reasons it can be difficult to be a good listener.

We begin the chapter with a brief overview of listening competencies. Next, we examine types of listening and their related contexts. We finish the chapter with a discussion of the importance of levels of listening as an additional component of listening types.

Listening Competency

The National Communication Association (NCA), the largest national organization for scholars in the field of communication in the United States, has identified a number of competencies that are listening focused.[1] NCA suggests that a competent listener should be proficient in at least two areas – literal comprehension and critical comprehension. **Literal comprehension** includes the ability to identify main ideas, supporting details, and the relationships among ideas. As a competent listener, one level of listening in which you want to develop skills is focusing on the *denotative* or literal meaning of the message. As seen in Case Study 2.1, Carter must use literal comprehension to understand his professor's lecture on ceramic materials. However, if he uses this same type of listening in his exchange with Radley, he will completely miss the intended meaning and may end up being offended. So, a good listener must also be able to listen beyond the literal message itself.

This leads us to the second area of competence: **critical comprehension**. Under critical comprehension, NCA suggests that a competent listener listens with an open mind. Listening with an open mind means that you are aware of your biases and recognize that everyone has a unique perspective. Listening with an open mind also indicates that you will provide feedback indicating your willingness to listen.

Think on it: Can you think of a time where you listened critically, when you should have listened literally (or vice versa)?

Critical comprehension also includes identifying the speaker's purpose and pattern of organization of the ideas. You should also be able to identify the speaker's bias and prejudice, and the impact of that bias and prejudice and the speaker's attitude. By focusing on these elements, you will be able to pick up the *connotative* meanings, or meanings that are intended rather than literally stated. So, when Radley refers to his friend as a "nerd," he isn't being literal, he is rather engaging in light banter. Since Carter can listen beyond the words and pick up the entire message in the context, he understands Radley's intended meaning.

While their exchange is rather simplistic, it doesn't take much imagination to apply the principles to truly important aspects of your lives. Clearly, competent listening involves much more than just taking in only the words themselves; it is a complex process we use to accurately assign meaning to incoming information. A truly effective listener must use a wide variety of knowledge sources, rapidly interpret incoming data, and make sense of the message.[2]

Separating general communication competencies from listening ones is difficult to do since communication and listening are so intertwined. In a recent study, listening scholar, Graham Bodie and his colleagues attempted to identify listening competencies.[3] While they identified a number of characteristics associated with perceived listening competency, ten traits appear to be key components. These traits, listed in Table 2.1, provide us with insight into the types of behaviors we should exhibit (verbally and nonverbally) if we wish to be considered a competent listener. As the receiving component of the communication process, listening is essential to the completion of the act of communication.

Table 2.1 Top Ten Traits Associated with Listening Competency

Attentiveness	Open mindedness
Understanding	Reflectiveness
Perceptiveness	Supportiveness
Empathy	Cooperativeness
Responsiveness	Alertness

One of the goals of communicating with others is to reach a shared understanding of a message. But, how do we know that the listener comprehends our message? Research in this area primarily focuses on the question, "How do we know a message was accurately received?" **Listening fidelity** explores the goodness of fit between what the receiver mentally processes and what the sender actually sends. It is defined as "the degree of congruence between the cognitions of a listener and the cognitions of a source following a communication event."[4]

In most listening focused fidelity studies, cognitions have been measured by the listeners' abilities to reproduce an orally presented geometric form (see Figure 2.1 for an example). In other words, this particular measurement of listening focuses on how well the receiver is able to reproduce the sender's message accurately.[5] Obviously, most of us aren't asked on a regular basis to reproduce a geometric figure being described to us. To clearly understand the importance of high fidelity listening, we need only to look at a common occurrence – following instructions. How many times have you started a class project only to find that you misunderstood the directions? Or, perhaps you were told how to access material online, but then found yourself later unable to do so? Yes, sometimes instructions can be unclear. But, if we are honest with ourselves, at least some of those misunderstandings are caused by our own poor listening skills. As you read the rest of this chapter, think about how each of the dimensions and types of listening discussed can help you be a higher fidelity listener.

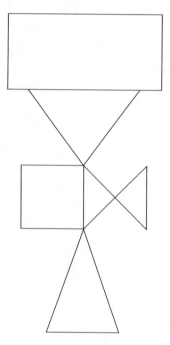

Figure 2.1 Example of Listening Fidelity Geometric Figure

As we turn to types of listening, we want to point out a shift in how listening scholars are beginning to approach this area. Early listening researchers typically categorized listening in different types (e.g., appreciative, critical). More recently, scholars have begun examining listening as a goal driven communication act.

Different types of listening reflect the different contexts you are in when you listen as well as the various outcomes you want from the encounters. Because you listen in many different contexts ranging from classroom lectures to intimate personal conversations, you listen to a wide variety of information that calls for different skills and levels of involvement. Therefore, you need a broad range of listening skills that will help you adapt to the shifts in listening demands you encounter. The following discussion of types of listening will introduce some of the critical listening skills you can use.

Types of Listening

If you are committed to high fidelity listening, you need to think about listening to all types of information. One way to cope with the variety of information and situations that you face is by realizing that listening is a multifaceted skill that you use to gather many types of information. That is, one size doesn't fit all when it comes to listening. Just as you would use different clubs to hit golf balls depending upon the conditions of the course, the length of the needed shot, and your goal, you also use a variety of "clubs" or types of listening. The question is why do we need so many "clubs" in our listening bag? The reason is that, as communicators, we have many communication and listening goals. We want to use the skill that best fits a specific goal.

For our initial discussion, we draw upon five types of listening introduced by Andrew Wolvin and Carolyn Coakley in their early listening text.[6] While they introduce them as types, they felt that each category represents different purposes of listening. In this respect, they reflect the idea of listening goals. Using a tree as a metaphor for listening, they made discriminative listening the root that feeds the tree, comprehensive listening the trunk that supports the branches, and critical, appreciative, and therapeutic listening as branches. We will talk about these types of listening as well as others.

Discriminative Listening

Wolvin and Coakley defined **discriminative listening** as "listening to distinguish aural and sometimes visual stimuli." In essence, it is the reception of the stimulus. If you don't physically receive the stimulus, you can't listen. When you engage in discriminative listening, you focus on whether a stimulus is worthy of paying attention to or not, how you should classify the sound (language, large truck, etc.), and detecting changes and nuances in a speaker's pitch, volume, rate, and language-related sounds. Discriminative listening also helps you determine a sound's source. Clearly, it is most closely related to the first element of the Listening MATERRS Model – mental stimulus.

This type of listening involves distinguishing between aural and other types of stimuli. In essence, discriminative listening is about being tuned into the variations and differences in the sounds and visual stimuli around you. Our world is filled with noises, both visual and aural. As you are reading this chapter, cars may be driving by, people may be talking in the hallway, the heating/air system may be switching on and off, or you may be following a friend's tweets. With all of this noise going on, how do you make the decision about what to pay attention to and which sounds to ignore? You make the decision by using discriminative listening.

Discriminative listening is also critical to our survival. When we pick up a sound, one of the first things we do is decide whether the sound is friend or foe. If we hear something that is threatening, our fight or flight instinct kicks in. Think about what you do when you are walking down a street and suddenly hear a loud horn honking. Chances are you jump a little or in some other way physically react to the unexpected sound. You will probably also look for the source of the horn. The purpose of your physical reaction is to help you get out of harm's way if you determine you are in danger.

Discriminative listening is so crucial to your survival that you develop this capability *in utero* and continue to develop it during the first few months of your life. As we noted in Chapter 1, research indicates that a fetus can distinguish between music, language and other sounds.[7] Measurement of heart rate and motor responses clearly shows a fetus can tell the difference in sounds – a sudden sharp noise elicits a different response than a Mozart sonata. This discriminative capability is also seen in a newborn's ability to distinguish its mother's voice from other female voices.[8] Another study found that the language processing centers of the infants' brains were developed to the point they could distinguish between male and female voices and distinguish between similar sounding syllables.[9] As early as four days old, babies are able to differentiate their mother's language from other languages.[10] In truth, your discriminative abilities may be at their peak early in your life. As we noted in Chapter 1, a child up to four months old can distinguish among all 150 sounds that make up human languages.[11] However, we quickly lose this ability as we gain more experience in the language or languages used around us.

Another way you use discriminative listening is to make sense out of human sounds. If you are flying on a crowded flight and hear the person sitting next to you make a sound, you will try to determine whether the person is talking or simply making a noise. If you notice the person's eyes are closed and his head is rolling forward, you will conclude that he isn't trying to talk to you. If, however, you notice that the person is looking at you, you will probably try to come up with an appropriate answer. As you learn a language, whether it is your native language or another one, you begin to learn the pattern of sounds associated with the language and then tune your ears to listen for those sounds so you can make sense of them.

One concept that helps clarify discriminative listening is **speech intelligibility**.[12] Speech intelligibility is "the amount of speech understood from the signal alone."[13] You use discriminative listening to pick up speaker affect and voice quality as well as the words themselves. **Speaker affect** relays emotion and is perceived by listening to the pitch, precision, and patterns of emphasis. It is what helps us to determine if someone is being sarcastic or is sad. Research by audiologists indicates that processing paralinguistic cues of this type is a parallel process to hearing the words. These findings led researchers to conclude that listeners have to work extra hard to decode speech that is different from what they are accustomed to hearing. To fully listen and understand someone, we must understand the words and the feelings behind them.

Unfortunately, this increased degree of difficulty can create a listening barrier. For example, both authors of this book have spent the majority of their lives in the southern part of the United States. Consequently, our ears are very accustomed to southern English. When we travel to other areas of the country, we sometimes have difficulty recognizing words because the sound structures are different. The same things occur when we travel internationally.

Think on it: If you aren't personally familiar with one, get with a friend who is fluent in another language. What are some of the sounds that don't "translate" well into English? Or, as in Chinese, a word whose meaning may change with a change in pitch? How can such differences affect how we listen and understand others?

Every language has its own sounds. While we are able to hear the nuances of southern US English, we have difficulty physically picking up (and producing) the nuances of a language like Korean. Discriminative listening is one key to learning another language as adults. Research by Professor Akiyo Hirai of the University of Tsukuba in Japan found a relationship between listening and proficiency in a second language. He concluded that proficiency in a second language is dependent upon the ability to process the spoken language, which we can only get through listening.[14]

Another challenge in discriminative listening is picking up words in a loud setting like a club or sports stadium.[15] This problem may be further compounded if you are particularly noise sensitive (discussed in Chapter 5).

Even though discriminative listening is physically receiving the stimulus, it is important that a listener doesn't use this first step in listening as an excuse not to listen. When you find yourself in a situation where you have difficulty hearing the speaker completely, you have listening choices. First, you can watch the nonverbals: the facial expressions, the body postures, and gestures. Based upon these visual elements as well as responses from other audience members who can hear, you can draw certain conclusions. Other options include moving to a place where you can hear or informing the speaker that you can't hear. The main lesson of this example is that even at the discriminative level, you have the responsibility to: 1) choose to attend to the stimulus (or not); and, if yes, 2) to make an effort to attend to the stimulus.

Just as in the example of a non-native language, discriminative listening also helps us distinguish between sounds in our own language. Many sounds are somewhat similar. For example, plosive sounds such as "p" and "b" take focus and concentration to distinguish in less than ideal conditions. The same can be said of distinguishing between "b" and "d." This problem can be extended even further as we think about how we pronounce certain words. For example, homonyms are words that sound alike (to, two, too). Only by listening to the context are we able to determine which word is being used. We have similar problems with words that aren't really homonyms, but are regionally pronounced alike. For example, pen and pin and aunt and ant are pronounced very similarly in many parts of the US. Good discriminative listeners will be able to distinguish between these similar sounds. They will also be able to identify underlying emotion, which may color the meaning (connotation) of a message.

As seen here, discriminative listening is crucial to our survival and forms a basis for our ability to understand the messages of others. While distinguishing stimuli is very important to listening, we must also be able to establish what the stimuli mean. We do this as we begin to listen comprehensively.

Comprehensive Listening

In comprehensive listening, our goal is to reach a level of listening fidelity that will allow us to assign meanings to a message that are as close as possible to what the sender intended. So, we must learn to focus on the words plus all of the appropriate nonverbal elements that accompany the words. It is at this level that we try to truly achieve communication fidelity. According to Wolvin and Coakley, **comprehensive listening** is "listening for understanding of the message."[16] In comprehensive listening then, we must pay attention to all of the information coming in: the words, the tone of voice and other paralinguistic cues, all nonverbal cues including facial expressions, and the interactive situation itself.

Consider what happens in the following scenarios:

- Ben overhears his parents talking after work. His father is talking about a confrontation he had with a disgruntled employee. As he gets into the details of the incident, his voice begins to sound angry.
- Tamarah is taking a 911 call. Her tone of voice remains calm and level as she asks the caller to calm down and tell her where the accident has occurred.

As a listener to the first situation, one could conclude that Mr. Goleman, Ben's father, is angry. One might even assume that he is angry with Mrs. Goleman because she is the person he is talking with. However, Ben is a good comprehensive listener who sees both parties in the interaction. He also takes into account the situation. Consequently, he is able to understand that his father is expressing frustration with events at work, not showing anger toward Mrs. Goleman.

In the second case, the person on the other end of the phone call could assume that Tamarah is uncaring. But, instead, the individual probably picks up the message to remain as calm as possible so the important information about the accident can be relayed.

Both of these cases illustrate the importance of assigning meaning to a message based on more than just the words themselves. In the previous section, we talked about the importance of a discriminative listener paying attention to speaker emotion or affect. A good comprehensive listener is able to interpret this affect and determine how it influences what the message really means.

Of course, it is also important for us to understand the words used to express the message. If we don't understand the words a speaker is using, we will have great difficulty assigning meaning to the message. Wolvin and Coakley suggest that one thing we can do to be better comprehensive listeners is to build our vocabularies.

In addition to assigning meaning to the message, comprehensive listening also involves storing the information into our memory banks. When we focus on what is being said, we process that information in such a way that we can store it in the appropriate place. One way we do this is by using schemas to make sense of information. Schemas are patterns we use to organize and make sense of information (we discuss schemas in more detail in Chapter 3). Thus, when you hear one of your friends start talking about his or her date last night, you listen with the expectation of hearing information that fits your "date story" schema. You will also store the information using that set of expectations.

Discriminative and comprehensive listening allows us to focus on, understand and remember information. However, we seldom simply just take information in; we also evaluate the stimuli in some way.

Critical Listening

The third type of listening described by Wolvin and Coakley is critical listening. Some listening scholars feel that this level of listening is the most significant.[17] It is in **critical listening** that we think about the message, make inferences, and evaluate both the speaker and the message.[18] This type of listening is important anytime we need to assess the value of information. It is perhaps most important when we are listening to information meant to persuade us.

One decision a listener should make when taking in a message concerns the type of information we are hearing. Is it factual or not? Whether listening to a newscast or to another individual, a competent critical listener will be able to distinguish between fact and information that isn't fact.

Let's take a quick look at the difference in the types of information. Case Study 2.2 presents an actual news story about a college student. Read over the article and see if you can distinguish information that is fact from information that is opinion.

Case Study 2.2 Distinguishing Facts from Opinion

Auburn Student Honored for Bravery
March 8, 2008
By AMY WEAVER

Daniel Brinson will probably never feel comfortable being regarded as a hero.

It's a title the Auburn University sophomore earned after he and a friend encountered a multiple-vehicle car accident on their way to the beach last fall. With some of the cars on fire, the pair jumped out of their vehicle and dashed to the scene. Brinson said it was clear they were too late for some, but then they heard voices.

One belonged to a young girl trapped in a car.

"There was no telling when the car was going to explode, but we had to get her out," said Brinson, an agriculture business and economics major.

As the weeks and months have passed since then, it's gotten easier for Brinson to talk about that day's events and that young girl. He still remembers how they had to break her legs to free her from the wreck and how her passenger friend wasn't as lucky. She died at the scene, he said.

"I saw that she was young and pretty," Brinson said, "And I knew it was more important for her to live and go on, than myself."

Congressman Mike Rogers heard the heroic tale of Brinson and Terrell Webb and shared it with his fellow legislators on the floor of the US House of Representatives back in January. On Monday, he presented Brinson with a certificate of commendation at AU's Samford Hall.

"Anytime we see extraordinary bravery, we should acknowledge it," Rogers said.

Perhaps Brinson's instincts as a former volunteer firefighter kicked in or it was just his inherent instinct to help others, but no matter what it was that drove him into that dangerous situation, he's glad he happened to be there and could do what he did.

"You can't pass burning cars and not stop," he said. "You just can't."

Since then, Brinson has learned more about the young girl whose life he saved, including how she had a young baby girl at home. She told the Brinson family how someone was looking out for her that September day and how she was meant to live her life for that little one.

News like that melts Brinson's big heart and puts a big grin on his face.

The last time he talked to her, he said he learned that she had started rehabilitation and is even enrolled at Southern Union State Community College.

Reproduced with permission from the Opelika Auburn News.

Even in a news story not all information is factual. A good listener will be able to distinguish what type of information is forthcoming.

Another aspect of competent critical listening is the ability to recognize discrepancies between verbal and nonverbal messages. In fact, this aspect of critical listening can help us be more sensitive to cultural differences in our multicultural society and can help us detect whether the speaker is being truthful. A good critical listener knows that the vast majority of a message is contained in the nonverbal behavior of the speaker.[19] Several studies support this point. For instance, Susan Timm and Betty Schroeder found a relationship between cultural sensitivity and training in listening and nonverbal communication.[20] It seems that people who learned to listen and focus on the nonverbal aspects of the message are more aware of and accepting of cultural differences. This finding suggests that if you are sensitive to the subtleties of the relationship between verbal and nonverbal messages, you will probably also be more aware of and open to cultural differences. Another study, conducted in a medical clinic, found that effective clinical leaders were good at reading nonverbal communication.[21] One of the participants in the study equated paying attention to nonverbal communication (e.g., eye contact body language) to reading a book.[22]

Other research suggests that when there is a discrepancy between the verbal and the nonverbal, we should believe the nonverbal.[23] A good critical listener needs to understand the impact of nonverbal messages on the overall perception of the meaning of the message. Early research by Dale Leathers tells us that we respond to inconsistent messages in one of three ways.[24] First, we attempt to determine the literal meaning of the inconsistent message. Second, we try increasing our level of concentration and search for any overlooked clues that will help us clarify the message. Third, we may withdraw from our interaction with the sending party. The upshot of this research is that inconsistency between verbal and nonverbal messages is disruptive to a relationship and to an interaction. Consequently, a good critical listener needs to be aware of possible explanations about why the inconsistency exists.

Reasons for Inconsistent Messages. People who send inconsistent messages seem to do so for a number of reasons.[25] One reason is that the sender may not be clear as to his or her intent. If we don't really know what we want to accomplish by sending a message, it will be difficult for us to be truly consistent in all aspects of our message. Think about it. If you have a fight with a sibling or close friend, your first meeting after the fight is probably going to be filled with inconsistent messages. Part of you wants to apologize; part of you may want to continue the disagreement. It will take a bit of give and take between you and the other party before you establish in your own mind what your exact purpose is.

A person might also have conflicting intentions in sending a message. Think about one of your favorite teachers. If that person has a reputation of being both tough and fun, it's possible that he or she sends out inconsistent messages at times. Keep in mind that these inconsistencies aren't signs of deception; they are signs of, to some extent, mixed motives.

Another reason messages might be inconsistent is when there is a disconnect between what is being said and what the individual actually means. At one level, a perceptive listener will be able to detect the hesitation in the speaker's voice or see the slumped shoulders that indicate that the individual's heart isn't behind the words. At another level, some discrepancies are more difficult to detect because the other party is trying to deceive. Looking at a positive example, think about a time when you have attempted to keep a secret from someone you care about. It might have been about a surprise party or a really exciting gift. If the other person was very perceptive, he or she probably picked up signs of deception in your face, speech, voice, or body as you tried to conceal the truth.[26]

A fourth reason someone might display inconsistent messages is because the information is unpleasant. Most of us will attempt to soften unpleasant news. One way we do so is to use softer, more supportive nonverbals. So the message may be bad, but we use nonverbal behavior to take part of the sting out of the message.

We also will use our nonverbal behavior to protect ourselves from being perceived in a negative light. The best example of this explanation of inconsistent messages is the experience of giving a speech. Most of us feel at least some level of anxiety when we get up in front of a class or meeting to deliver a speech. However, we also want to appear confident. When our goal and our emotions clash, we are more than likely to send some inconsistent messages.

The types of listening covered up to this point have all focused on taking in information and processing it. However, listening can also be a pleasurable activity. The next type of listening addresses listening for pleasure.

Appreciative Listening

Wolvin and Coakley define **appreciative listening** as "listening for sensory stimulation or enjoyment."[27] According to another listening scholar, Anthony Clark, appreciative listening "occurs when a perceptive listener derives pleasure or satisfaction from the form, rhythm, and/or tone of aural stimuli."[28] It is worth our while to look at a couple of the elements to which Clark refers. Clark suggests that a perceptive listener is someone who is sensitive to the aesthetic elements of spoken and/or musical qualities. If you think about it, there are some voices that we appreciate more than others. Most of us find actor James Earl Jones' (the voice of Darth Vadar in the *Star Wars* movies and Mufasa in the movie *The Lion King*) voice pleasant and rich, while we find the voice of comedian Gilbert Gottfried irritating and painful at times. He gave voice to Iago in *Aladdin* and plays Trevor in *The Comedian*.

> Want to hear these voices for yourself? Visit the following links: http://bit.ly/JEJones and http://bit.ly/GGAladdin.

The pleasure or satisfaction element refers to our physical or emotional response to sound. For example, think about the classic movie, *Jurassic Park*. The sounds produced by the little dinosaurs are "cute" and non-threatening, much like sounds we associate with baby animals of any kind. However, when the large dinosaurs or the T. Rexes come on the screen, the sounds they produce are intended to generate fear and anxiety, so they are loud and harsh. We also respond emotionally to other elements of sound such as form, the structure of the parts of a stimulus; rhythm, the flow of the stressed and unstressed parts of the stimulus; and tone, the quality of a voice or sound.

Just as we respond in emotional ways to sound, appreciative listening probably helps us tune in to the emotional content of a message. Music educator and researcher, Frank Dias, reports that when listeners are actively engaged in listening to music, they experience heightened affective responses.[29] It makes sense to extrapolate that the same effect happens when we engage in conversation. Musician and composer Jean François Mathieu would likely agree. He believes that appreciative listening makes people better leaders. When we are aware of and can appreciate the role sound plays in shaping our lives, we may be more cognizant of how voices and other sounds in a setting shape our impressions and thus realize how important it is to maintain awareness of what we sound like when we communicate with others.[30] According to Mathieu, we can learn to be better listeners through appreciative listening. From the viewpoint of this composer and jazz musician, listeners can:

- (re)discover the joy of listening
- tame the fear of listening
- use their memories to recall sounds that made them feel good, or boost their energy
- gain more awareness about their own emotions
- develop concentration and better focus
- experience and develop comprehensive and critical listening.

To learn more about Mathieu's perspective, see his interview below.

Appreciative Listening: Listening Lessons

Jean François Mathieu
Musician/Composer
Geneva, Switzerland

One crucial lesson is to prepare to listen. By setting aside individual biases of what music should sound like, you're more likely to enjoy the concert. Another lesson is listening for components of the music or message. For example you should listen for the use of rhythm and be aware of the impact of changes. The same is true of volume. You also want to listen for themes, repetition, and melody – whether listening to conversation or music.

There are similarities between music and the spoken word that affect how we interpret a message. Specifically, elements like tone, silence and articulation are important. A dark voice affects you differently from a warm voice. Silence can create suspense or give the listener time to absorb the message.

Appreciative listening will make you more aware of the elements of a message as well as the intent and impact of the sounds of the message.

Appreciative listening should help us become more enlightened and expand our mind as we learn to appreciate a wider variety of sounds. Appreciative listening is critical if we are going to expand our ability to understand and accept cultures other than the one in which we grew up. Every civilization and culture uses a language made up of varying sounds and produces musical sounds unique to that culture. Music is an important aspect of a civilization or culture because it is often an expression of spiritual joy.[31] Being good appreciative listeners requires us to keep an open mind to these expressions of joy.

Think on it: How do you react when you hear music that doesn't conform to the eight note scale you may have learned in music appreciation class? Listen to traditional music from Korea, Thailand, Kenya, or any other non-Western country. Compare that music to a Bach fugue. What are the specific differences you notice?

Therapeutic Listening

The final type of listening Wolvin and Coakley introduced is therapeutic listening. This term is sometimes used interchangeably with supportive listening and empathic listening. While they share many qualities, we briefly distinguish between them before moving to a more in-depth discussion of empathic listening. **Empathic listening** takes place when we listen to understand the thoughts, feelings and beliefs of the speaker – it is other focused.[32] With empathic listening, we seek to comfort and provide emotional support for another. When the listening goal is to be supportive of another person, the listener tries to be optimistic, truthful, attentive, and understanding. They exhibit these characteristics both verbally and nonverbally.[33] In essence, supportive listeners "respond to the emotional needs of distressed others."[34]

When empathic listening occurs between close friends and family, it is often referred to as **supportive listening**. Supportive listening can, however, occur in our interactions with others. For example, you may visit with a co-worker when you face a difficult situation at work. To understand supportive listening better, we draw upon a simple typology developed by Bill Arnold to help us gain a clearer picture of how this type of listening differs from other, non-supportive types of listening.[35] Using a traffic light analogy, the first type of listening in **Arnold's Typology of Listening** is **red listening**. Red listening doesn't involve much listening. Red listeners tend to ignore the needs of the other person and instead focus on his or her own needs. The second of the Arnold listening categories is **yellow listening**. Yellow listening is characterized by a tendency to judge or evaluate what is said. This type of listening is often accompanied by a "yes, but" or "let me tell you how to fix it" type of approach. With yellow listening, we listen to the message and respond from our perspective without really thinking about whether we truly address the needs of the other party. **Green listening** is true, supportive listening, the type that involves listening to the person from where they are, not where we want them to be. Green light listening means you withhold judgment and don't unnecessarily shift away from the other person's concerns or needs. In essence, green listening is empathic listening.

> ***Think on it:*** Can you think of examples of Red, Yellow, and Green listening you have experienced in the last month? Can you think of examples of each color in your own listening behavior?

Empathic listening that occurs in formal helping situations is typically described as **therapeutic listening**. We typically think of counselors and mental health professionals engaging in the type of listening. Supportive listening and therapeutic listening may sound quite similar. However, when the goal of listening is to "just listen" and withhold the impulse to fix the situation or to give advice, it is therapeutic. Wolvin and Coakley suggest that five skills are essential to therapeutic listening: *focusing attention, demonstrating attending behaviors, developing a supportive communication climate, listening with empathy,* and *responding appropriately*. All of these skills keep the focus on the other person and away from the listener who serves the function of supporter and listener. The role of the therapist, then, is to reflect back to the speaker to help him or her work through the problem.

Empathic Listening

Certainly, being empathic is an important part of listening. Michael Nichols, a family therapist, argues that empathy is the "essence of good listening," noting that it is "part intuition and part effort, it is the stuff of human connection."[36] He goes on to say that "listening is the art by which we use empathy to reach across the space between us. Passive attention doesn't work."[37] A bit later in his book, *The Lost Art of Listening*, he says that listening often "takes a deliberate effort to suspend our own needs and reaction" and to control "the urge to interrupt or argue."[38]

Before we continue, it is important to establish that ***empathy*** – feeling "with" someone, is qualitatively different from ***sympathy*** – feeling "for" someone. Focusing on a receiver-based definition, we define *empathy* as a process by which we emotionally connect with others. When we empathize with someone we use our perceptions of how that person feels to help us determine how we should respond. This definition implies we can identify and share emotions with others by being empathic listeners.

In Case Study 2.3, notice that the doctor is able to understand how Mr. Gutierrez feels and is consequently able to respond appropriately.

Case Study 2.3 Mr. Gutierrez and Dr. Kyle

Nolvia remembers the day she and her father met with the doctor after his accident. When the doctor told him that he would be a paraplegic and need a motorized wheel chair, Mr. Gutierrez began to cry. The doctor sat down in a chair, took Mr. Gutierrez's hand in hers and looked him straight in the eye. In a soft, clear voice Dr. Kyle told him the following: *Your mental ability is better than mine. However, your body has been damaged. I want you to be able to live a fulfilling life, see your children grow up, and become fully re-engaged in life. I can't heal your body, but this chair will give you the ability to actually be with your children and watch their activities, not just stay in a bed and hear about them.*

The history of focusing on empathic listening can be traced to the work of Carl Rogers, a psychotherapist. Rogers is credited with developing a client-centered style of listening that he used in therapy and taught to a new generation of therapists. We paraphrase Neil Friedman's explanation of Rogers' approach to listening: The primary role of the listening response is to acknowledge clients' feelings and experiences and encourage them to build on and continue communicating them with the therapist. The therapist must go beyond simply repeating or paraphrasing a client's words. Words are not feelings. The listening therapist's responses are attempts to make concrete the thoughts, feelings, and experiences of the client so that they are more recognizable to the client and so that they can aid in reaching the ultimate goal of the therapeutic encounter and for the client.[39]

Empathy is important to listening in that it affects our responses to speakers. If you are highly empathic, you are more likely to provide comforting responses to the speaker – whether it is a friend or stranger. Your response manifests itself in at least three ways.[40] For example, imagine for a moment that your best friend has just broken up with her significant other. On one level, you engage in **empathic responsiveness.** Essentially what happens is that you take on the emotions being felt by your friend – you feel "with" him. He is sad and upset, so you begin feeling sad and upset too. After all, he's a good friend. Second, you may engage in **perspective taking.** Perspective taking refers to your ability to put yourself in your friend's shoes. Of course, this is easier to do if you, too, have been in a serious relationship. However, it is not necessary for you actually to have had the same or a similar experience. What is required is that you be able to *imagine* yourself in his place.

> ***Think on it:*** Think about how you react when someone shares confidences with you. Do you attempt to understand without judgment? Do you look for solutions to the other person's problem? Are you taking steps to be empathic or are you simply nodding?

The last way you may manifest an empathic response is in terms of **sympathetic responsiveness**. This concept is considered a relatively new aspect of empathy. It reflects our traditional definition of sympathy where we feel "for" someone else. When you engage in sympathetic responsiveness you also feel other emotions that are in keeping with the situation. You may feel concern for your friend, while at the same time you are angry at the "evil" former significant other. So with empathic responsiveness, you would feel sad and upset reflecting his feelings of sadness and being upset at the break-up, but with sympathetic responsiveness, you would feel other related emotions that would reflect your "emotional concern" for your friend.[41] Of course, this example presents a situation with your friend being upset about a break-up. He could just as easily be happy over receiving an "A" on his chemistry exam or getting promoted at his job.

Factors Affecting Empathy. Empathy seems to be influenced by a number of factors. One of them is the **gender** of the individual. Men's and women's listening skills differ in several ways. How much of these differences are biological and how much is learned is still debated by researchers. In the area of empathy, we do know that as young as one year, boys and girls differ in how they react to someone who has supposedly injured themselves: girls generally react with more empathy and greater distress than little boys.[42]

Empathy and how empathically responsive we are appears to be related to sociability as well. Even at six months of age, girls tend to display a more social nature than boys, initiating more social interactions, engaging in turn taking, and developing more expressive language, including broader vocabularies. Thus, at a very young age, your little girl cousin has many of the elements needed to be empathic – a greater focus on nonverbals, broader language skills, and a disposition to respond to the hurt of others. One school of thought suggests that parents respond to these characteristics by expressing more positive emotions to their daughters as well as using a greater variety of emotional words. However, when interacting with their sons, mothers behave differently. For example, they often over-exaggerate the faces they make to their sons. In other words, when expressing surprise or fear, mothers exaggerate their nonverbals. As a result, mothers may make it more difficult for boys to learn the more subtle nonverbal cues. For whatever reason, as adults, men tend not to be as adept at picking up subtle emotional cues from others. We explore sociability in more detail in Chapter 4.

Another factor that influences empathy is **culture**. Of course, cultural differences play a large role in gender differences. Differences in emphases in cultural conformity, display rules (what emotions are appropriate for men/women to display or present to others), socialization by parents, peers, and others can affect how we respond empathically. For example, if you grow up in a family where conformity and rule-following was both expected and enforced, and where crying was frowned upon, you may find it difficult not only to express your own emotions, but also to listen as others express theirs. Think of expressing empathy as a skill that you just have not had much practice with. You may feel awkward and think to yourself, "What am I supposed to do?"

In terms of the larger cultural context, Western cultures such as the United States tend to share a cultural belief that women are more emotional than men.[43] While there does appear to be at least a small biological difference in empathy and sociability of male and female infants, the culture you grow up in has a major impact on how you use empathy in your interactions with others. In Western cultures, women are more likely to express prosocial emotions such as empathy, happiness, and joy. In addition, it is acceptable for women to express emotions such as fear and sadness. If you are from a culture similar to the United States, you know that men are not encouraged to express those types of emotions publicly. Men, in contrast, are more likely to express "powerful" emotions such as anger and pride.[44] As a result, when it comes to empathic and sympathetic responsiveness, women in Western cultures appear to have an advantage in terms of both biology and cultural learning.

But do these differences hold true for men and women in non-Western cultures? Research by Agneta Fischer and Antony Manstead provide us with a partial answer to this question.[45] These researchers examined the data from approximately 3000 surveys that had been administered to men and women from 37 countries across five continents. Some of the countries included in the survey were Botswana, Brazil, China, Finland, India, Israel, Malawi, New Zealand, Poland, and the United States. The researchers were interested in how men and women from these different cultures compared in their intensity, duration, and nonverbal expressions of their emotions. *Intensity* refers to the strength or level of an emotional response, *duration* refers to the overall time a respondent reported an emotion lasting, and *nonverbal expression* refers to the behavioral expression of an emotion (e.g., laughing, crying, yelling, withdrawing from others). Their analysis found that, in general, women from *all* the countries surveyed reported more intense emotions, which were longer in duration. Survey responses also indicated that the women were more overtly expressive of their emotions.

However, before you begin adjusting your current view of men and women, you need also to be aware of the cultural differences that Fischer and Manstead found. For example, they discovered that the behaviors of men and women from individualistic cultures differ from those in collectivistic cultures. **Individualistic cultures**, like the United States, emphasize individual expression, self-reliance, autonomy, and independence, which led its members to value "being yourself" or "expressing yourself." As a result, social ties in individualistic cultures are looser than those in collectivistic cultures, such as China or Japan. **Collectivistic cultures** value meeting social and group norms and respecting others of the group. In keeping with these differences, the research indicated that gender-specific display rules were associated more with individualistic cultures than with collective cultures. What this means is that women and men differed more in how they displayed their emotions (intensity, duration, and overtness) if they were from an individualistic culture, while the sexes were more alike if they were from a collectivistic culture. Thus, the rules of our individualistic culture lead women to value emotional expressiveness more than men do, and they give women the freedom to be more expressive. In fact, it is a cultural expectation.

Coming back to our discussion of empathy, it appears then that women have an "empathic edge." Any empathic responsiveness they are born with is culturally reinforced, particularly in individualistic cultures. As a result, women have more practice at empathy resulting in a better ability to respond empathically to others. In the United States, both men and women view women as more empathic listeners than men. Some evidence suggests that women listen more to relationship information over fact-based information and prefer discussing topics associated with relationships and personal experiences. Subsequently, they are more likely to gain a listener's trust and be privy to more intimate self-disclosures.[46] As noted in Chapter 1, one of the bases of empathic listening is knowledge and understanding of the other person.

This is not to say that men cannot or will not respond empathically! As you will be learning later in the text, a number of other factors affect how empathic we are with others, including how well we know them, how closely we can identify with them, as well as how skilled we are at establishing a supportive listening climate. In addition, we will be learning how our verbal and nonverbal skills affect others' perceptions of how empathic we are. Whether male or female, it is a good idea to assess your "empathic-ness," so you can determine if you need to hone this particular listening skill.[47]

In this section, we have distinguished between empathy and sympathy and explored several factors associated with it. We explore the relationship of empathy and listening in more detail in Chapter 4, expanding on related characteristics and introducing active-empathic listening.

Up to this point we have focused on types of listening. Related to types of listening is the notion of levels of energy and intensity we need to use as we listen.

Levels of Listening

Another aspect of being a competent communicator and listener is knowing how much listening effort you need to expend in any given context. As a listener you find yourself in situations where you need to identify the purpose of the exchange and respond appropriately. At other times, you need to engage in the very deepest of critical listening or empathic listening. For example, greeting someone you meet in the hallway calls for a different level or intensity of listening than does listening carefully to a lecture on molecular biology or to a friend talk about an emotionally charged event. In other words, you have different needs and outcome goals depending on the nature and purpose of the interaction. Erik Van Slyke, managing director of Solleva Group, identified six levels of listening that provide a guide for us to use as we determine how deeply we need to listen.[48]

The first level identified by Van Slyke is **passive listening**. This type of listening is one in which we sit quietly while another person talks. However, sitting quietly doesn't mean we are engaged in the listening process. Passive listening has also been referred to as marginal listening because the receiver hears words but is easily distracted and allows his/her mind to wander.[49] If we are guilty of passive listening, more than likely, we are engaging in very low fidelity listening because we only catch a few phrases or words. We are aware that the other person is talking, but we don't expend enough energy to truly comprehend what the individual is saying. We probably all have to admit that we have on occasion engaged in this type of behavior. Unfortunately, most of us believe that if someone sits quietly while they are talking, the other person must be listening. This is a mistake many speakers (and teachers) make.

Chances are all of us use passive listening when we engage in certain levels of multitasking. For example, when you listen to music while you drive, you are probably using passive listening. In this case, this level of listening allows you to stay focused on what is important, driving safely. In contrast, if you attend a concert, you will use deeper level of listening since you are at the event specifically for the music.

Van Slykes' second level of listening is responsive listening. He identifies responsive listening as making acknowledgments, either verbal or nonverbal, that we are listening. We would prefer to call this **responding listening** because all we are doing is going through the motions of listening and making "listening noises" rather than truly engaging our listening brain. This type of listening behavior has the potential to damage a relationship because we remain disengaged as communicator but send the false message that we are paying attention and listening. In truth, we probably aren't really listening at all to the other person. This level of listening is probably only useful for purely social situations like exchanging greeting as we pass someone in the hall or other setting. Even in this situation, responding listening can lead to inappropriate responses. Have you ever said hello to someone and had them respond, "fine thank you?" This interaction is a classic example of responding listening. The listener relied on a social schema (or expectation) that says greetings follow this pattern or script:

> *Hello, how are you?*
> *Fine, thank you. And you?*
> *Fine, thanks.*

Because the listener was using responding listening, he or she didn't actually hear what was said. If this happens in a greeting, typically no harm is done. However, if this problem occurs during an important discussion, much damage can be done. (Social schemas are discussed more fully in Chapter 3.)

The third level of listening is selective listening. **Selective listening** occurs when we engage our brains and only listen for things that support what we believe, think, or support. In essence, it is listening with an agenda. Van Slyke suggests that this is the type of listening we use when we argue or debate. When we use this type of listening, we tend to exhibit the following behavior. When we hear something that catches our attention, we will interrupt and deliver an evaluative response in the form of a statement or question. According to Van Slyke, the rest of the time we are only partially engaged or busy thinking about our responses and listening for those points where we can interrupt. Unfortunately, we don't gather the information we really need to understand what the other person wants. Instead, we remain focused on what we want. If we continue to use this type of listening behavior, our efforts will make the situation worse because the other person will probably grow to resent us for our lack of awareness.

With certain modifications, however, aspects of selective listening can be useful in situations where we are trying to diagnose something and keep an open ear and open mind to what the individual is saying. For example, when we are engaged in a conversation with someone who seems to be rambling, we can listen for opportunities to get the person back on track. We can attend to what he or she is saying, while listening for cues that link the information we hear to the purpose of the discussion. Caring health care providers will engage in this type of listening as they try to diagnose what is wrong with a patient. This type of listening is called **attentive listening**. Van Slyke says that while attentive listening is listening with an agenda, it includes probing and inquisitiveness. More importantly, we engage our analytical mind as we attend to the other party's message. An attentive listener will respond with evaluative questions that guide the responses of the other person. For example, your instructor might ask a question that guides you into admitting you chose to go to a party rather than study for a test. The following quotation gives us an example of the perception of attentive listening:

> *One of the most powerful tools at our disposal is the ability to listen. Not only does active listening make those around you feel vested in the conversation; it also provides you valuable time to process and prepare our comments.* [50]

While the author of the above remark refers to "active" listening, what he is really referring to is attentive listening. Notice that the focus of the listening in the quote is the listener.

Attentive listening, like the previous levels we have discussed, is from the perspective of the listener. It doesn't focus on what the other person needs or wants from us, we instead focus on what we need from the other person. For example, the caring health care provider needs information that pertains to the person's ailment, so she will listen for facts and data and ignore any emotional content. Unfortunately, sometimes the very information we need is in the emotion.

The level at which we shift away from our own interests and turn to the needs of the other party is truly active listening. **Active listening** involves using all of our listening capabilities. It is total sensory listening. What this means is that we listen with not only our ears, but also with our eyes and the rest of our senses. So, we listen to the paralinguistic aspects of the message, we focus on the facial expressions and the body language, and we listen to the patterns of silence. We truly listen with an open mind that isn't hindered by our expectations or agenda.

Active listeners respond with reflective responses that provide feedback to the other party. A reflective response helps verify the listener's understanding of what the other person is saying and encourages that person to continue. An example of a reflective response can be seen in the following scenario.

Case Study 2.4 Nolvia's Frustration

Nolvia: *I am having such a hard time getting my grandparents to understand what is expected of me by my teachers. They ...*

Radley: *It sounds like you're kinda frustrated with how your grandparents are reacting to you going to college.*

Nolvia: *That's not the half of it, they don't understand just how different things are for me than things were for them in Honduras. They don't understand the pressure.*

Radley: *Oh boy, generational and cultural differences. Do you have any ideas about what you are going to do next?*

If you really examine the above example, notice that Radley paraphrases what Nolvia is saying. This use of *paraphrasing* shows that he is truly listening to what Nolvia is saying as well as the affect, or feelings, she is expressing.

Reflective listening engenders confidence in the listener on the part of the speaker. Consequently, reflective listening tends to boost the self-esteem of the listener because we have been willing as listeners to accept that the other person has particular feelings and ideas. In other words, we can accept the fact the other person has particular feelings, but we may not accept the justifications of those feelings from that person's perspective. According to Van Slyke, active listening "allows us to accept the message, but we do not have to understand or accept the messenger."[51]

The last level of listening identified by Van Slyke is **empathic listening**. Like the type of listening by the same name we discussed earlier, this level of listening involves "listening with the intent to accept and understand the other person's frame of reference."[52] The purpose shifts from gathering information to understanding and accepting the other person's feelings. So, as Carl Rogers suggests, we must separate the person from the problem and accept the value of the person.

©Jeff Stahler/Distributed by Universal Uclick for UFS via CartoonStock.com

Summary

Clearly listening is much more than "just a single communication skill." Instead, it is a multi-faceted skill that involves a great deal of awareness and sensitivity to the other parties in an interaction. As you think back about the types of listening discussed in this chapter, you will see that they are connected with the Listening MATERRS Model presented in the first chapter. In discriminative listening your mind is awakened to and becomes aware of the stimulus. In comprehensive listening you translate or make sense of the message as well as recall it later. Critical listening allows you to evaluate the information, while appreciative listening allows you to respond to the pleasure aspects of a stimulus. To be responsive to people, we use therapeutic and empathic listening. If we use the appropriate type of listening, we will stay connected with the other party.

In essence, to be a truly effective listener, we must make strategic choices about what type of listening is needed and what depth of listening is needed in every listening situation. Our decisions will be based on the context we find ourselves in, our relationship with the other person, and our assessment of the needs of the other party.

Key Concepts

Multi-dimensional skill
Literal comprehension
    Denotative meaning
Critical comprehension
    Connotative meaning
Listening fidelity
Types of listening
    Discriminative listening
        Speech intelligibility
        Speaker affect
        Message inconsistencies
    Comprehensive listening
    Critical listening
    Appreciative listening
    Therapeutic/Supportive listening
    Arnold's Typology of Listening
Empathic listening
    Empathy versus sympathy
    Empathic responsiveness
    Perspective taking
    Sympathetic responsiveness
Factors affecting empathy
    Biological sex
    Culture
Van Slykes' Levels of Listening
    Passive listening
    Responding listening
    Selective listening
    Attentive listening
    Active listening
    Reflective listening responses

Discussion Questions

1. In the chapter we discussed the importance of discriminative listening to survival. Have you had a time when discriminative listening helped you avoid an accident? What are behaviors we engage in today that may interfere with this type of listening?
2. Think back on a time when someone's verbal message was inconsistent with their nonverbals. Which of the sources of message inconsistencies may explain the discrepancy between what was said and how it was said?
3. Do you agree that "women appear to have an empathic edge?" Are women more empathic or do men express empathy differently? How can men express caring and empathy in culturally acceptable ways? To women? To other men?

Listening Activities

1. Listen to a recording of different dialects. You can listen to dialects from across the country and around the world at the following website: http://web.ku.edu/~idea. Can you tell what the person is saying? Try listening to computer generated voices. Check out the following resources or you can Google for other voices: www.saffas-voice.co.uk/animated-voices.php; http://en.wikipedia.org/wiki/Speech_synthesis; www.cereproc.com/products/voices.
2. Play the audio (not video) of the speeches of political candidates or other famous speakers. (Try the following website for a great selection: www.presidency.ucsb.edu; http://millercenter.org/scripps/archive/speeches.) What biases, prejudices, or attitudes do you hear evidenced in the words? Try doing the same while listening to news stories. Can you identify biases of the announcer or commenter? What about the network? Finally, why do you think we asked that you listen to the audio without the video of the political speech you listened to?
3. Prior to beginning, divide into groups of five or six. Each group should write a script of a short interaction that a person might typically face (asking for directions; friend in crisis; little sister with hurt knee; meeting a classmate for the first time, etc.). Spend about 10 minutes developing the script from greeting to farewell. Identify the topics discussed, then identify the appropriate type of listening to use. Be prepared to role play your script and be ready to discuss the type of listening as well as the depth of listening needed.

Notes

1 National Communication Association, 1998
2 Graham, 2006
3 Bodie, Pence, Rold, Chapman, Lejune, & Anzalone, 2015
4 Mulanax & Powers, 2001, p. 70
5 Fitch-Hauser, Powers, O'Brien, & Hanson 2007
6 Wolvin & Coakley, 1996
7 Wilkin, 1991; Lecanuet, Granier-Deferre, & Busnel, 1988
8 Hepper, Scott, & Shahidullah, 1993
9 Yuhas, 2013
10 Mehler, Lambertz, Jusczyk, & Amiel-Tison, 1986
11 Kuhl, 1991
12 Evitts & Searl, 2006
13 Keintz, Bunton, & Hoit, 2007, p. 223
14 Hirai, 1999
15 Fontan, Tardieu, Gaillard, Woisard, & Ruiz, 2015
16 Wolvin & Coakley, 1996, p. 211
17 Goss, 1982
18 Goss, 1982
19 Mehrabian, 1971
20 Timm & Schroeder, 2000
21 Ennis, Happell, & Reid-Searl, 2013
22 Ennis et al., 2013, p. 816
23 Leathers, 1997
24 Leathers, 1997
25 Leathers, 1997
26 Ekman, 1985
27 Wolvin & Coakley, 1996, p. 363

28 Clark, 1989, p. 4
29 Diaz, 2015
30 Matheau, 2016
31 Klein & Ackerman, 1995
32 Bodie, Gearhart, Denham, &Vickery, 2013
33 Bodie & Jones, 2012
34 Keaton, Bodie, & Keteyian, 2015, p. 482
35 Carkhuff, 1960
36 Nichols, 2009, p. 10
37 Nichols, 2009, p. 74
38 Nichols, 2009, p. 74
39 Friedman, 2005, p. 222
40 Richendoller & Weaver, 1994
41 Emotional concern is discussed by Davis, 1980, 1983 and Stiff et al., 1988.
42 Brody, 2000
43 Fischer & Manstead, 2000
44 Fischer & Manstead, 2000
45 Fischer & Mantsead, 2000
46 Gender differences have been addressed by many researchers including Bassili (1970), Solomon (1998); Richardson (1999); Borisoff & Merrill (1991).
47 See Drollinger, Comer, & Warrington (2006) for a discussion of an empathy scale
48 Van Slyke, 1999
49 Comer & Drollinger, 1999
50 Michel, 2006
51 Van Slyke, 1999, p. 108
52 Van Slyke, 1999, p. 108

References

Bassili, J. (1970). Emotional recognition: The role of facial movement and the relative importance of the upper and lower areas of the face. *Journal of Personality and Social Psychology, 37,* 249–258.

Bodie, G., Gearhart, C., Denham, J., & Vickery, A. (2013). The temporal stability and situational contingency of active-empathic listening. *Western Journal of Communication, 77,* 113–138.

Bodie, G. D., Pence, M., Rold, M., Chapman, M. D., Lejune, J., & Anzalone, L. (2015). Listening competence in initial interactions II: Applying trait centrality to discover the relative placement of listening competence among implicit competency theories. *Communication Studies, 66,* 528–548.

Bodie, G., & Jones, S. (2012). The nature of supportive listening II: The role of verbal person centeredness and nonverbal immediacy. *Western Journal of Communication, 76,* 250–269.

Borisoff, D., & Merrill, L. (1991). Gender issues and listening. In D. Borisoff & M. Purdy (Eds.), *Listening in everyday life: A personal and professional approach* (pp. 59–85). Lanham, MD: University Press of America.

Brody, L. R. (2000). The socialization of gender differences in emotional expression: Display rules, infant temperament, and differentiation. In A. Fisher (Ed.), *Gender and emotions: Social psychological perspectives* (pp. 24–47). Cambridge, UK: Cambridge University Press.

Carkhuff, R. (1960). *Helping and human relations.* New York: Holt, Reinhart & Winston.

Clark, A. J., (1989). *Appreciative listening.* Paper presented to the annual meeting of the International Listening Association, Atlanta, GA.

Comer, L. B., & Drollinger, T. (1999). Active empathetic listening and selling success: A conceptual framework. *Journal of Personal Selling and Sales Management, 19,* 15–29.

Davis, M. H. (1980). A multidimensional approach to the study of empathy. *JSAS Catalog of Selected Documents In Psychology, 10,* 85.

Davis, M. H. (1983). Measuring individual differences in empathy: Evidence for a multidimensional approach. *Journal of Personality and Social Psychology, 44*, 213–236.

Diaz, F. (2015). Listening and musical engagements: An exploration of the effects of different listening strategies on attention, emotion, and peak affective experiences. *Update, 33*(2), 27–33.

Drollinger, T., Comer, L. B., & Warrington, P. T. (2006). Development and validation of the active empathic listening scale. *Psychology & Marketing, 23*, 161–180.

Ekman, P. (1985). *Telling lies: Clues to deceit in the marketplace, politics, and marriage.* New York: Norton.

Ennis, G. Happell, B., & Reid-Searl, K. (2013). The importance of communication for clinical leaders in mental health nursing: The perspective of nurses working in mental health. *Issues in Mental Health Nursing, 34*, 814–819.

Evitts, P. M., & Searl, J. (2006). Reaction time of normal listeners to laryngeal, alaryngeal, and synthetic speech. *Journal of Speech, Language, and Hearing Research, 49*, 1380–1390.

Fischer, A. H., & Manstead, A. S. R. (2000). The relation between gender and emotion in different cultures. In A. Fisher (Ed.), *Gender and emotions: Social psychological perspectives* (pp. 71–96). Cambridge, UK: Cambridge University Press.

Fitch-Hauser, M., Powers, W. G., O'Brien, K., & Hanson, S. (2007). Extending the conceptualization of listening fidelity. *The International Journal of Listening, 12*, 81–91.

Fontan, L., Tardieu, J., Gaillard, P., Woisard, V., & Ruiz, R. (2015). Relationship between speech intelligibility and speech compression in babble noise. *Journal of Speech, Language, and Hearing Research, 58*, 977–986.

Friedman, N. (2005). Experiential listening. *Journal of Humanistic Psychology, 45*, 217–238.

Goss, B. (1982). Listening as information processing. *Communication Quarterly, 30*, 304–307.

Graham, S. (2006). Listening comprehension: The learner's perspective. *System, 34*, 165–182.

Hepper, P. G., Scott, D., & Shahidullah, S. (1993). Newborn and fetal response to maternal voice. *Journal of Reproductive and Infant Psychology, 11*, 147–153.

Hirai, A. (1999). The relationship between listening and reading rates of Japanese EFL learners. *The Modern Language Journal, 83*, 367–384.

Keaton, S., Bodie, G., & Keteyian, R. (2015). Relational listening goals influence how people report talking about problems. *Communication Quarterly, 63*, 480–494.

Keintz, C. K., Bunton, K., & Hoit, J. (2007). Influence of visual information on the intelligibility of dysarthric speech. *American Journal of Speech-Language Pathology, 16*, 222–234.

Klein, L., & Ackerman, D. (Writers). (1995). *Mystery of the senses. Hearing.* L. Klein (Producer/Director) and P. Jones (Series Producer). *NOVA miniseries.* Boston: WGBH.

Kuhl, P. K. (1991). Perception, cognition, and the ontogenetic and phylogenetic emergence of human speech. In S. Brauth, W. Hall, & R. Dooling (Eds.), *Plasticity of development* (pp. 73–106). Cambridge, MA: MIT Press/Gradford Books.

Leathers, D. B. (1997). *Successful nonverbal communication: Principles and applications* (3rd ed.). Boston: Allyn & Bacon.

Lecanuet, J. P., Granier-Deferre, C., & Busnel, M. (1988). Fetal cardiac and motor responses to octave-band noises as a function of central frequency, intensity and heart rate variability. *Early Human Development, 13*, 269–283.

Matheau, J. (2016, April 4; May 2). Personal correspondence.

Mehler, J., Lambertz, G., Jusczyk, P., & Amiel-Tison, C. (1986). Discrimination de la langue maternelle par le nouveau-né. *Comptes-rendus de l'Académie des Sciences de Paris, 303*, Série III, 637–640.

Mehrabian, A. (1971). *Silent messages.* Belmont, CA: Wadsworth.

Michel, C. (2006). Hallmarks of enlightened leadership. *US Naval Institute Proceedings, 132*, 96.

Mulanax, A., & Powers, W. G. (2001). Listening fidelity development and relationship to receiver apprehension and locus of control. *International Journal of Listening, 15*, 69–78.

National Communication Association. (1998). Speaking and listening competencies for college students. Retrieved from www.natcom.org/NCA/files/ccLibraryFiles/FILENAME/000000000085/College%20 Competencies.pdf.

Nichols, M. P. (2009). *The lost art of listening* (2nd ed.). New York: Guilford.

Richardson, J. L. (1999). Women lead in style. *Transportations & Distribution, 40*, 78–82.

Richendoller, N. R., & Weaver, J. B. III. (1994). Exploring the links between personality and empathic response style. *Personality and Individual Differences, 17*, 303–311.

Solomon, C. M. (1998). Women are still undervalued: Bridge the parity gap. *Workforce, 77*, 78–86.

Stiff, J. B., Dillard, J. P., Somera, B., Kim, H., & Sleight, C. (1988). Empathy, communication, and prosocial behavior. *Communication Monographs, 55*, 198–213.

Timm, S., & Schroeder, B. (2000). Listening/nonverbal communication training. *International Journal of Listening, 14*, 109–128.

Van Slyke, E. (1999). *Listening to conflict: Finding constructive solutions to workplace disputes.* New York: AMACOM.

Wilkin, P. E. (1991). Prenatal and postnatal responses to music and sound stimuli – A clinical report. *Canadian Music Educator (Research Edition), 33*, 223–232.

Wolvin, A., & Coakley, C. (1996). *Listening* (5th ed.). Boston: McGraw-Hill.

Yuhas, D. (2013, July 1). Infants are born to talk. *Scientific American.* Retrieved from www.scientificamerican.com/article/infants-born-to-talk.

3 Listening and Information Processing

Case Study 3.1 Carter's Dilemma

Say Carter, why are you looking so bummed?

Hi, Ben. I just sat through a lecture by a guest speaker and I seem to have forgotten everything. I know that my professor is going to ask test questions over the presentation. I sure thought I was paying attention.

What was the lecture about?

It had to do with nanotechnology and the latest discoveries in that area. Going into the presentation, I didn't know what nanotechnology was, and I sure don't know now. I wish I'd read up on the topic before the lecture. Maybe then …

As the receiving aspect of communication, listening involves much more than simply receiving the messages sent by the sender. As you saw in the listening models in Chapter 1, it involves all of the complexity associated with receiving, interpreting, storing, and recalling information. By understanding how you take in information and process it into meaningful, usable, even memorable information, you should be able to make strategic choices as a listener that will help you more accurately process incoming stimuli or come closer to high fidelity listening.

As you remember from the basic listening model presented in Chapter 1, the first thing that must happen for listening to occur is that the message must be physically received. This step is physiological. The appropriate receptor center, whether it be audio, visual, or some other sensation, receives the signal. A series of electrochemical responses occur, sending information to your brain and your brain registers the physical reception of the stimulus. However, as we have previously pointed out, just because you physically receive the signal, doesn't mean that you consciously recognize or process the stimulus. You are surrounded by sights and sounds that you either ignore or simply don't notice. For example, think about your dorm room or your apartment. Chances are your roommates or other occupants of the dorm or complex are going about their own business. Whatever they are doing probably makes some noise. Unless the noise is exceptionally loud or unusual, or you are particularly noise sensitive, you probably "tune it out" and don't let it interfere with your reading this chapter. In other words, you physically receive the sound but you have learned not to listen to it. This example is an excellent way to point out that being an effective listener involves a large dose of choice by you, the listener. That is, listening begins when we make the conscious decision to pay attention to incoming information. This chapter focuses on what happens to the information once you choose to listen.

Receiving and Processing Information

As you read in the first chapter, listening, as defined by both ILA and NCA, is an active, conscious communication act. Much of this activity occurs within your information processing system. The model of intrapersonal processing in Figure 3.1 illustrates how you process information when you receive it. Clearly, this discussion is biased toward listening and isn't intended as a comprehensive review of either information or cognitive processing. However, you will learn enough about these two areas to have a good understanding of the importance of the cognitive aspects of the listening process. To help illustrate the internal listening process, we present the intrapersonal information flow (IIF) model, which is adapted from an early model of intrapersonal processing developed by early listening scholars Deborah Roach, Larry Barker, and Margaret Fitch-Hauser.[1] The IIF model illustrates the fundamental elements of cognitive processing that occur during the listening process. The model provides a visual illustration of what happens as information enters our conscious awareness, passes through our perceptions and is perceived, used, or stored for future usage.

The model presents an overview of conscious and subconscious processing. The following discussion will examine each of the model parts and focus on how they work together.

External stimuli are signs, signals, or any other stimulus transmitted by sources other than the receiver and picked up through the senses. In the listening process, the two senses most used are hearing and seeing. Stimuli, picked up subconsciously or consciously, become information that is transmitted to the central nervous system and the appropriate receptor centers in the brain.

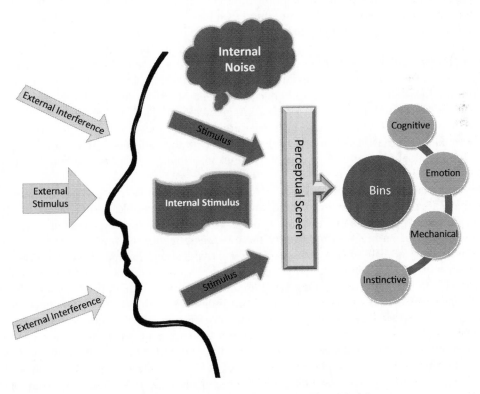

Figure 3.1 Intrapersonal Information Flow Model

External interference is noise that makes it difficult or impossible to perceive or identify external stimulus. Examples include the temperature of a room, a train rumbling by, or a competing conversation. In other words, external interference is anything in the surroundings of an interaction that hinders you from focusing on the desired stimulus.

Internal stimuli are nerve impulses received by the brain as a result of your own physiological or emotional state. Hunger is an example of a physical internal stimulus, while thoughts are examples of a cognitive internal stimulus, and a feeling of joy is an emotional stimulus. Sometimes internal stimuli interfere with our listening. In the case study at the beginning of the chapter, Carter's confusion about the topic and his distress about not understanding may be generating a great deal of internal distraction. This distraction then interferes with his ability fully to attend to the speaker's presentation. Anytime internal stimuli prevent us from listening, they become internal noise.

Internal noises as stimuli within the person can take many forms. They might occur at a subconscious level, such as a vague feeling of discomfort that occurs when someone stands too close to us. They might also be at a more conscious level, such as being distracted in class because you can't remember if you hit "submit" when uploading your homework assignment.

Reception is the neural reception of the stimulus. When you register the noise of the train rumbling by, whether you pay attention to it or not, you have received the sound. However, if that reception doesn't capture your attention, you will quickly dismiss the sound without registering its presence. For you truly to listen, you must recognize that you have received the stimulus. In essence, you have to choose to attend to the stimulus that you have received.

Perceptual screens are psychological filters that affect how you perceive the stimulus. Using the example of the train once again, we can illustrate how different experiences can affect how one perceives the sound. If you associate the sound of a train as something fun and adventuresome, you perceive the sound to be non-threatening or even pleasant. Also, if you live by a train track, you perceive the sound as something ordinary and probably don't waste any cognitive energy focusing on its rumble. In other words, you ignore it. If you have had a bad experience with a train, such as knowing someone who has been involved in a train wreck, you might perceive the sound to be threatening. Perceptual filters can also take the form of stereotypes about people. This type of perceptual filter will be discussed in greater detail later in this chapter.

Once information flows into the mental structure described above, you begin to sort it so it can be processed appropriately. According to the IIF model, information goes to one of four distinct areas. In the model, these areas are depicted as four information categories or bins – emotional, mechanical, instinctive and cognitive.

The **emotional bin** includes attitudes, values and beliefs that guide how you live your life. These three things form the predispositions used when responding to people, events, places or objects. *Beliefs* are your "perceptions of the real world."[2] You act on these perceptions or observations as if they were true and real. Consequently, these beliefs influence the way you perceive information as a listener and will influence the decisions you make about the information. *Attitudes* refer to your view of whether something is "good" or "bad."[3] Values differ. *Values* reflect your view of what "ought" to be.[4] Thus, your values form the core of the way you think things should be; beliefs reflect your views of the way things are, while attitudes signal how much or how little you like something. (It is possible to have a neutral or ambiguous attitude if there are elements you like or dislike about something or someone.) If, for example, you are concerned about plastic pollution, that concern likely indicates that you *value* our environment and caring for it and that you *believe* the use of single use plastics like plastic grocery bags is a threat to the environment. As a result, you might have a positive attitude toward banning the use of plastic bags by stores. Working together, these three constructs may lead you to write to your state senator in support of a new bill banning the production and use of these bags. The combination of values, attitudes and beliefs provides the foundation of your emotional processes. As you can see in our plastics pollution example, if you strongly support a position on an issue, your attitudes, values, and beliefs will affect how you listen to messages related to it. When you hear a message that supports your point of view, you will probably pay attention and participate in the interaction. On the other hand, when you hear a message that disagrees with your point of view, you might find yourself subject to internal stimuli (discussed above) that could interfere with your ability to listen fully. In such cases, you might spend your energy coming up with counter arguments or simply disagreeing rather than remaining open to actually listening to the message. If you find yourself doing that, remember that you can choose to bypass your biases and listen to messages that are contrary to your beliefs.

The **mechanical bin** of the IIF model addresses learned behaviors. Included in this type of processing are those everyday tasks that seem to take little cognitive effort on your part. Many of these tasks are behaviors that are habitual or everyday things that you do without really thinking about how to do them. For example, if you know how to play a piano, you don't have to think much about how to strike the keys. When you first learned how to drive, you consciously went through the process of identifying what you needed to do. However, after a few times of getting behind the wheel, starting the car, fastening your seatbelt, putting the car in gear, putting your foot on the accelerator, and so forth, you likely no longer really think about these aspects of the driving process. The knowledge has become automatic, almost encoded into your muscles. More recent research indicates that some of this processing might become programmed behavior or muscle memory.[5] This programing is so thorough that the muscle system seems to retain the memory and use the appropriate reaction when you encounter a stimulus again.[6]

> *Think on it:* Can you think of other tasks or behaviors that you engage in that would fall into the mechanical bin? What differentiates them from the other four areas we discuss?

Nobel Prize winner Eric Kandel found that repeated stimulation of sensory neurons in cells strengthened and created new synaptic connections that lead to long-term memory of appropriate reactions.[7] Even though Kandel looked at physical reactions, you can extrapolate from those results to other behaviors as well. For example, if you are accustomed to engaging in the same behaviors every time you are asked to listen to information, that response might become so automatic, or habitual, that you no longer engage the conscious aspects of cognitive functioning necessary for you to truly listen (or pay attention) to the information. If you are in a class where the professor presents everything in the same manner, such as using three PowerPoint slides for every topic, you might stop focusing on the content after the third or fourth time.

The **instinctive bin** includes the physiological functioning of the human system. You don't have to think about how to sneeze, you just sneeze when your nose becomes irritated by some element such as perfume or pepper. The instinctive function also includes the functioning of the five senses through which you receive external stimuli. It is in this capacity that the instinctive function has an effect on listening.

The **cognitive bin** is associated with thought and the active processing of information. Included at this level are functions such as the interpretation and storage of information. Here, we briefly introduce three important factors that influence our cognitive processing – memory, priming, and framing. Later, we will address schema formation, which also plays a significant role in cognitive processing and listening.

The type of memory that seems most relevant to listening is working memory.[8] **Working memory** can be defined as the *active* contents of memory, where we select, temporarily store, then manipulate and use relevant information to carry out complex cognitive tasks to achieve our personal goals at a moment in time.[9] Working memory, then, is the information base that you use as you listen. Importantly, it is believed to influence what we pay attention to and can be affected by distractions.[10] Interestingly, distractions that are similar to what is in our working memory at a particular time are more distracting to us than unrelated information.

As you can see, the content of working memory can help you listen better or it can present challenges to the effectiveness of your listening. Listening scholar Laura Janusik suggests that working memory serves us in two important ways – the processing of information and information storage. These two functions are necessarily affected by the short-term and long-term feature of working memory.[11]

Associated primarily with the brain's frontal lobe, **short-term working memory** has a direct effect on attending. Using this aspect of memory, you move information from reception to cognitive interpretation. If you think of the Listening MATERRS Model presented in Chapter 1, short-term working memory helps you navigate between the awareness, translation, and evaluation functions as you process incoming mental stimuli. It also helps you incorporate new information into what you already know by allowing you to retrieve appropriate information from your long-term memory. In essence, short-term working memory becomes the recall link in the Listening MATERRS Model. It is important to keep in mind that in working memory you will find information that you actively pay attention to as well as that which you choose either to ignore or simply don't recall. For example, if the incoming stimulus (either external or internal) is deemed unimportant, you dismiss it.

Part of a listener's challenge is that only a limited amount of information can be held in the focus of attention at any given time. If too much competing information is going on, such as when

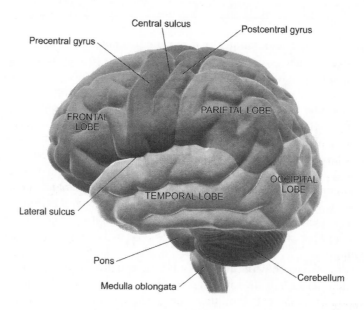

Figure 3.2 Lateral View of the Brain
Source: Bruce Blaus

you send and receive text messages during lectures, you might lose critical information. However, if you decide the information might possibly be important, you either use it or send it on to other levels of memory. In situations where you don't pay attention to a thought or piece of information, you lose it very quickly. Have you ever had a thought that popped up and before you had a chance to express that thought, it evaporated into thin air? Chances are that you delayed too long in attending to that piece of information.

The cognitive function also includes **long-term memory**. Your memories of language, events that have happened to you, the lessons you learn in school and other information are all stored in your long-term memory. Recent research indicates that our busy lifestyles and attempts to multi-task may inhibit the movement of information to long-term memory. However, you can help your memory in two ways. First, scholars in Britain and the US found that brief periods of rest help us when we take in new information.[12] Specifically, people who took a break after receiving information are better able to recall that information at a later time than those who undertook another task immediately after hearing it. It seems that integrating new information into our memory takes a little time. Second, get plenty of sleep as it appears that one of the primary times that we solidify new information in our memories is while we sleep.

Think on it: Have you ever taken a three hour class? Had several classes back to back? Or, had a meeting that went several hours? Is it easy to remember the material or hard? Do you remember the main points? What about details? Did the teacher or leader allow for "brain breaks" (i.e., time for you to process the information? Imagine you're in a three hour meeting. How often would you need to take a break to allow your brain to process material and/or move it into long-term memory? How long do you think the break would need to be?

The long-term aspect of working memory goes beyond the ability to store and recall. It also includes your ability to *use* that recalled information. So, your logical reasoning capacities as well as your abilities to synthesize and analyze information and consequently assimilate information are all part of the cognitive function. It takes all of these activities for you to comprehend and understand both the obvious and the more subtle meanings of events, messages, or feelings. To understand most incoming information, you need to be able to access the information you have stored in long-term memory.[13]

Exactly what information you access is, in part, affected by priming and framing. **Primes** are clues embedded in a message that signal how the information should be interpreted. For example, if Eleanor says to you that she wants to discuss an opportunity, the word, "opportunity," will influence how you interpret the message that follows. Your interpretation will be based on your knowledge of the term, your experiences with things labeled "opportunities" and your reaction to those experiences. The prime helps you decide what to focus on or attend to in the message. As seen in the previous example, the prime was a single word. However, it can also be a phrase or idea and may be visual as well as auditory.

Primes are part of how a message is framed. Framing involves a speaker highlighting some aspects of a subject thus shaping the listener's interpretation.[14] Therefore, we can conclude that **frames** function in two ways. First, they are a literal aspect of the message, and they act as "cognitive structures that guide information processing."[15] Second, the way in which a message is framed will promote a particular view, evaluation, solution, and so forth. As you can see, how a message is framed affects individual perception. The effect of message framing has been examined in a number of areas including news presentation and health communication. One area of health communication research addresses the effectiveness of gain-framed and loss-framed messages. Psychologist Alexander Rothman and his colleagues write that "*Gain-framed statements* can refer to both good things that will happen and the bad things that will not happen, whereas *loss-framed statements* can refer to bad things that will happen and good things that will not happen."[16] A simple example illustrates the difference between these two types of framing: "If you floss, you will enjoy fresh, minty breath" is a gain-framed statement, while "If you don't floss, you will have bad breath" is a loss-framed statement.[17] Findings from this research indicate that presenting the same information with slight differences in wording has a profound impact on how the listeners respond. In general, people exposed to a gain-framed message tend to be less willing to risk the bad outcome (i.e., bad breath).[18] Thus, frames, or how the message is worded, can affect how you process an incoming message by leading you to focus on specific information or by enhancing the importance of a particular part of a message.[19]

Message frames can affect multiple aspects of a message.[20] As a listener, one of your listening goals, therefore, might be to identify the speaker's frame or frames. A recent research article stated that "the way we frame things linguistically influences the way we conceptualize social matters such as political attitudes, and moral and causal reasoning."[21] The scholars go on to say that framing shapes the way we perceive people, events, situations and basically the world. As a responsible listener, you want to develop your comprehension and analytical skills to distinguish the bias reflected in the frame from the information.

Along with priming and framing, how you receive, access, and store information in your memory is also affected by your use of schemas and scripts. Schemas and scripts are often thought of as patterns of information that you have learned to expect. Because of their importance to listening and information processing, they are addressed separately in the following section.

While we have discussed your emotional, mechanical, instinctive and cognitive bins separately, it is important to realize that they work with each other as you process information and stimuli. For example, information is processed simultaneously, such as when you jump when a spider drops from the ceiling. This instinctive response will also be affected by your level of like (or dislike) for spiders.

As you look at the model (Figure 3.1) of how we receive, screen, and process information, you can see what occurs internally as you listen. It is important to note that when this model is placed into the framework of interpersonal interactions, it helps you understand why listening is truly a complex process. Not only are you going through the process, so are all of the other parties involved in an interaction. To help explain further what happens internally when you listen, we next address the impact of schema on the listening process.

Schemas and Information Processing

One way to better understand how listening and information processing are tied together is to learn more about how information is perceived and processed. Drawing on research from communication, psychology, and other areas, we use schema theory to help unravel the mystery of what happens as you make sense of the messages you receive as a listener.[22] More specifically, we will examine the effect of schemas on attending, perceiving, and recalling information. However, before we address these areas, you need to understand what a schema is. A **schema** is a cognitive structure consisting of representations of some defined area (e.g., person, place, or thing). These structures contain general knowledge, including expectations about relationships among the attributes as well as examples and expectations about how those attributes function. This knowledge helps you identify what a stimulus is as well as making sense of it. In essence, you develop scripts or templates that you use to understand the world around you. **Scripts** address the sequence of actions associated with a particular event.[23]

Schemas and scripts start developing at an incredibly young age. In fact, some researchers feel that we can develop schemas even before we are born, and certainly while still infants.[24] One of the early ways we experience schemas is in our expectations for how the information is "supposed to be" presented. For example, if your professor were to say the following phrase, "Once upon a time," you would have little difficulty in taking up the thread of the story. You would almost automatically continue with information about a damsel in distress who has evil relatives, and who is ultimately rescued by a handsome prince. You can fill in the rest of the story because you use schematic processing, or an information processing system using schema(s). As a child, your schema for this type of story was developed as you heard stories, such as Cinderella, that use this plot line. Our fairytale example reflects one of the many types of schemas that can develop. When you think of such stories, Cinderella likely reflects what you typically think of as a script. However, we also use scripts for events that occur in our everyday life. For example, you have a script for the sequence of events that occurs when you go to your typical college class (i.e., find your seat, get your books/materials ready, silence your mobile phone, stop talking when the professor begins speaking). Schemas and scripts are drawn from our experiences, and the stronger those experiences and the more frequently we repeat them, the stronger these schemas and scripts tend to be. If you know several people in college who are really into computers and are rather "geeky," you might develop a schema for IT people that you take with you when you begin working after graduation. Thus, when you experience information being structured in the same way, events occurring in the same way, or interact with groups of people in the same way repeatedly, you begin to establish and strengthen your schemas.

Figure 3.3 The Princess and Curdie
Source: James Allen

> ***Think on it:*** Do you believe it is possible for infants to develop schema in utero? If so, what type of schema might they develop? If not, when do you think early schema develop and what form might they take?

As seen in the Cinderella example, you use your schema for narratives to help you first identify what the subject is – a fairytale. In addition, you will fill in the story with expectations about what is "supposed to be" in the story. In this capacity, schemas and scripts also function as maps for perceiving incoming information.[25] Not only do they influence what you pay attention to, they also act as units of knowledge that help organize what you "know" about the world around you. In essence, they guide you in determining what information is worthy of attention, and that which can be ignored.

Schemas and Attending

Once you decide to attend to something, your schema for that subject triggers a set of expectations for the incoming information. Our previous discussion demonstrated that many of our social interactions are based on narratives. Consequently, how you handle narrative information will have a profound effect on how you listen, beginning with whether you truly pay attention to what the other person is saying. Seminal research by Roger Schank and Robert Abelson suggests that narrative information that evokes one of the story lines in your story bank may cause you to rely on a script rather than paying attention to the details of the incoming information.[26] So, if you recognize the "baseball game won by a walk-off home run" script, you might focus more on what *you* want to say about your favorite baseball team or player than you do on the actual message. Another possibility can occur when you recognize what the story is about. With this recognition you are steered toward listening to specific aspects of the story, particularly those that resonate with you. In essence, the schema helps you prioritize information so that you focus your energy on that which is most important to you. In essence, the schema helps you prioritize information.

Schemas and Perceiving

Not only do schemas impact what we attend to and how, they also affect the way information is perceived. They do this, in part, by directing our attention to particular aspects of incoming messages. Working in conjunction with priming and framing, schemas help us track information as it comes in and provides a basis for predicting what will be said next. We will examine several ways in which schemas affect our perceptions, including our expectations for how information should be structured or organized; the effect of our attitudes, values and beliefs on schemas; how we handle contradictory information, and the influence of several common social schemas.

Structural Expectations and Schemas. As seen in our fairytale example, one of our expectations is that information is supposed to be structured or organized in a pattern that is appropriate to and in keeping with the triggered schema.[27] Just as you put together a puzzle by fitting the pieces together, you fit different parts of a message together until you have something that makes sense to you. There are times when we are faced with an incomplete story. In such cases, you can use a schema to help you fill in the blanks of the missing information. Because this is often done unconsciously, it is not unusual for you to "remember" details that you filled in as if they were true and real.[28] For example, most of you have an established morning routine. If part of that routine is carrying coffee with you to class, you "remember" picking up the travel mug that morning when in reality you didn't. You may convince yourself that you left the mug on the bus because you have a clear memory of picking it up on the way out the door. If so, you will be quite surprised when you return home and discover that your memory of carrying your coffee with you was inaccurate.

A study conducted with lists of words illustrates the power of schema on memory. The researchers presented lists with high and low associative strength.[29] The high associative list contained words that one could associate with a concept or another word. For example, one list contained sit, seat, recliner, swivel, rocking, as well as other related words. Upon recalling the lists, individuals "remembered" the object the words were associated with (i.e., chair), even though the word wasn't on the original list. The lesson for listeners is that schemas can distort our memory.

Effect of Values on Schemas. We introduced attitudes, beliefs, and values earlier in the chapter and so won't review them again here. Suffice to say, another way that schema affects how you perceive information is the importance that you associate with it. The more incoming information is associated with schemas that are linked to strong values, beliefs or attitudes you hold, the more motivated you will be to focus your attention on it. And, as you will see in the next section, it can affect what information you choose to move from working memory to long-term memory.

Schemas do impact how messages are processed, particularly when the information contradicts your expectations. People respond to **contradictory information** in one of several ways. They can discount or suspend the information, or they can re-evaluate their schema and change it. **Discounting** information means that you basically ignore it. For example, you may convince yourself that the information is unimportant, that your friend had a good reason for being late, and so on. **Suspended information** is left in a type of cognitive limbo. It is significant enough for you to make note of, but you may not be sure what to do with it. In such cases, you may *tag* the piece of information or the experience. However, one tag will rarely lead someone to adjust or **re-evaluate a schema.** Generally speaking, the stronger the schema, the more tags will be needed to change it. Thus, if you have a schema of your best friend as a warm and caring person, he or she will likely have to engage in a number of negative events or actions before you will reconfigure your schema to include the contradictory information. Tagging information that is out of synch with a schema is quite common. We can also tag information and use it when we are developing new schemas. Typically, it takes repeated encounters to establish a working schema. However, there are occasions when it might take only one event to form or adjust a strong schema. For instance, your favorite food may quickly become your least favorite, if you develop food poisoning after eating it.

Think on it: Have you ever changed an established schema? Did you change it after tagging one significant piece of information, or did it change as the result of tagging several separate pieces of information?

Types of Schema. Schemas also affect the way we perceive people, relationships, and events. **Social schemas** reflect our expectations about how the social world operates.[30] These schemas include how we organize our knowledge about people, self, social roles and events. Other names associated with this type of schemas are prototypes, stereotypes, and scripts. Like all schemas, social schemas help us fill in missing information and ignore irrelevant information.

People schemas affect how we perceive individuals.[31] We often use these schemas to help us categorize people, so we can better understand them or make decisions about their credibility. One aspect of people schemas is personality. If you think about it, when you meet someone for the first time, you often classify that person as an introvert or extravert (I-E). You then use this assessment to make assumptions about that person based on the expectations triggered by your use of your I-E schema. If you feel that extraversion is a positive personality trait, you will perceive individuals classified as extraverts in a positive manner and consequently be more willing to listen to them.

Research has shown that listeners also form impressions about and evaluate people using physical attributes, such as age, racial and ethnic backgrounds, physical appearance, and even the sound of their voices.[32] For example, a great deal of research has indicated that regional dialects and foreign accents greatly affect the perceptions of a speaker's status, intelligence, wealth, competence, friendliness and kindness.[33] Many of the schemas based on these elements fall into the category of stereotypes. *Stereotypes* as schemas contain value-laden attitudes and beliefs. Listeners hearing a speaker with an Asian accent may well rate the speaker on dimensions such as leadership and social status based solely on the stereotypes the accent elicits in their schema bank.

The above example illustrates another important aspect of people schemas. When you meet or hear someone for the first time, you tend to assess that person based on your experiences with others whom you feel are similar to him or her. Unfortunately, when you have little or no experience with a particular group, your stereotypes are often based on what you hear other people say or media representations of that group. If your only exposure to Buddhism and Buddhists is dramatic depictions of monks in martial arts movies, your schema about that group will reflect what you see in those movies and have little to do with the real values of followers of that religion. Consequently, when you encounter a real Buddhist monk, your internal and external reaction to that individual will probably reflect the expectations established by that fiction-based schema. Likewise, if you grow up in households where certain groups are either revered or vilified, your stereotypes will more than likely reflect those values and attitudes. It is important to realize, however, that schemas are merely temporary representations of information. As we noted previously, while schemas help you process information on many levels, they are malleable and can change with new experiences. Only the strongest ones are difficult to change.

Context also influences how you perceive an individual. Calling upon your **event schemas** (expectations governing what we expect events to be like), you make assessments about the appropriateness of someone's behavior. For example, if you go to a boxing match and hear someone in the crowd yell, "knock him out," you don't think much about what the person has said. After all, that type of comment is expected in that setting. However, if you are walking down a sidewalk in your favorite shopping area and hear the same phrase yelled out, you will probably start looking around in alarm and think that something is wrong. As you can see, schemas are used to decode messages.

Self-schema can be considered an aspect of people schema. Your self-schema is your cognitive representation of yourself in various contexts. Your self-concept is central to this schema, which is made up of your self-descriptions and traits you hold as important to your identity. So, if you picture yourself as family centered, that idea is part of your self-schema. However, self-schema is also context based. The schema you have for yourself when you are at a party with friends is probably different than the one you have when you attend a religious service with your family. The various aspects of your self-schema help you decide how to act in which setting.

Gender schema is another sub-category of people schema. Gender schemas are cognitive representations of traits, attitudes, behaviors, occupations, and other information associated with maleness and femaleness (not to be confused with biological sex).[34] These schemas, like all other schemas, affect how you interpret information and make inferences and predictions. Interestingly, your gender schemas seem to influence your assessment of a person, particularly in situations when you know little about him or her as an individual.[35] Gender schema are culturally defined and develop at an early age.[36] However, this doesn't mean that the individual is simply a passive recipient of societal expectations about gender roles. More recent thinking suggests that we actively participate in the process of the social construction of gender roles. So, as you look around and see that more than 50% of the members of your class are women, you will think that the women in the class value education and will be pursuing careers upon graduation. In fact, less than 60 years ago, people joked about women going to college in pursuit of a MRS degree. College was treated as a dating service, where women met future husbands, careers were secondary to having a family. While many of you (male and female) will meet your future spouse while at college, few people today would think your primary purpose for attending school was to gain a spouse.

> ***Think on it:*** As we noted in the text. Many of our schemas are culturally based. Over the last decade gender has received considerable attention, both socially and scientifically. It is, arguably, one of the fastest changing schema. What are some of the events that have led to these changes? What other types of schema do you feel are experiencing a similar rapid change?

Occupational schemas are yet another type of people schema. These schemas might work alongside your gender schemas. For example, you might think that fire fighters are supposed to be men or that kindergarten teachers are supposed to be women. However, the reality of both of those occupations is that both men and women choose to enter them. Other elements of occupation schema include the trustworthiness, types of duties expected, and amount of money associated with the job. A 2016 survey in Australia rated nurses as the most ethical and honest profession, followed by doctors and pharmacists.[37] A similar study in Canada found nurses and farmers to be the most respected professions and politicians and car salespeople the least respected in the same year.[38] In the United States, a 2015 Gallup poll identified nurses, pharmacists, physicians, high school teachers and police officers as the top five most honest and ethical occupations.[39]

The differences in the results of these polls indicate that the culture in which we live has an impact on the schema that we have. Although we don't always think of Canada, Australia, and the United States as being different cultures, we have only to look at one element of the occupation schema, trust, to find cultural difference and similarities.

Culture and Schema. When schema theory was first introduced in 1932 by Fredrick Bartlett, he argued that culture affects schema in two ways. First, it affects the content and structure of any schema we form. This, in turn, influences how we use schemas to make sense of information, events, people, and other things we encounter. One way to illustrate this is to look at the folklore of any culture. For example, by listening to the traditional folk tales of many Native American tribes, we can identify a reverence for nature and the belief that we coexist with all creatures. This reverence is part of the cultural schema of how people treat the land and animals as well as how they would interpret certain events. A Native American schooled in the traditions of the culture may watch a show about deer hunting from the perspective of thankfulness that Mother Earth provides for her children. In contrast, someone who grew up in a culture that values hunting for the experience and the trophy might focus on the number of points on the antlers of the deer. Although these perspectives are very different, they are simply ways of perceiving the world based upon environment and culture. A good listener will take these cultural differences into account when interpreting incoming information from the two individuals.

> ***Think on it:*** Can you identify any culturally shared memories? What about culturally shared memories that you have learned were untrue?

A contributing factor to the strength of cultural schemas is the shared nature of cognitive representations. In other words, group members rely on schemas when remembering actual events.[40] This reliance often results in a group-held schema that is inconsistent with actual events. These errors reflect the common knowledge, beliefs, and shared mental models of a group. Notably, group members can have great difficulty correcting this type of memory error, particularly if the schema is strong.

As we noted earlier, your expectations about a culture are based on your exposure to it. That exposure can be direct or indirect. One group of researchers testing the effects of cultural exposure on schema building, used an indirect method, teaching elementary students a unit on a culture different from their own (e.g., Spain, China). When the students were tested over their own culture and the other culture, their responses to the questions about the new culture clearly reflected the impact of the instructional unit.[41] This finding suggests that the instructional unit on culture helped the students establish a schema for that particular culture and that they used the schema to understand and remember the information.

Another source of information about culture is media. A Canadian study revealed that television food and dining advertising reflects different schemas for various cultures.[42] The study found that the ads examined often conformed to stereotypes. Among the stereotypes the study revealed: White people belong to a nuclear family, Asians are unemotional overachievers, and Black people are blue-collar employees. If someone is only exposed to media portrayal of stereotypes, his or her schemas would be skewed in the direction portrayed. Fortunately we have other sources of information about culture. Direct experience, such as interacting with people from another culture or traveling to other areas or countries, can affect individual schemas as well.

> ***Think on it:*** Schemas established via direct means often tend to be stronger than those established indirectly. Following 9/11, many people experienced profound changes to their schemas of the Middle East, Arab-Americans, and terrorists and terrorism. Can you think of a time when an indirect exposure or experience significantly affected a schema you hold?

When you hear cultural information or see visual evidence of cultural or ethnic background, you will more than likely use that information to process verbal and nonverbal messages.[43] As the example of the Buddhist monk earlier in the chapter illustrates, your perceptions of individuals are based upon what you believe or think you know about a group. Any cultural bias, good or bad, will impact how you perceive the credibility of a person and how you translate information from that source. Many years ago, two 13 year olds became pen pals, one from South Australia and one from Texas. The first letter the Australian wrote asked about Indians and cowboys in Texas. Her schema about Texas, or any western state in the United States, was largely based upon the television shows and movies that she had seen. She was very surprised to learn that her new friend lived in a town and went to school just like she did. When she visited the United States for the first time, she experienced for herself what the country and the people were really like.

Listeners need to be aware of the impact of schemas on how they perceive both the source of information and the information itself. As we discussed in Chapter 1, your perceptions are screens through which you filter information. Many of your perceptual filters consist of schemas that you have about different topics and people. However, schemas are malleable and dynamic. Recent research has shown that increased knowledge and experience will adjust your schemas.[44] A good listener will remain open to such experiences.

Schemas and Memory

In addition to influencing what you attend to and how you perceive many types of information as a listener, schemas also affect the memory stage of listening by helping us identify information that should be stored or forgotten, organize information in our memories, and aid us in recalling information.

Memory Storage and Recall. Schemas help you decide when a message is complete and ready to be stored in memory, or when you need to keep a category open until you gain sufficient information to formulate a working schema. They help you decide what information is important and what is not, and they help you determine what should be transferred from short-term to long-term memory.

In essence, the very way you perceive the information affects how you store and recall any message. Schema consistent information fits the expected categories of a schema. Most research has shown that schema consistent information is more readily and accurately remembered over time, while schema inconsistent information tends to fade from the memory.[45] More recent research, however, indicates schema inconsistent memory might be resistant to decay if the receiver is required to recall the inconsistent information several times over a relatively brief period of time. This is particularly true if the schema inconsistent piece is significantly different from what was expected, thus leading you to remember it because of the extreme disparity.[46] Schema consistent information is frequently distorted in the form of false recollections. We are prone to "remember" objects or actions consistent with our schema for an event that either were not actually present or didn't occur.[47]

A category of information that does succumb to decay, however, is schema irrelevant information, or information that has no relationship to the schema itself. Information that the professor of your class had pasta Alfredo for lunch would probably be irrelevant to your schema, therefore, not worthy of taking up space in your memory.[48]

Suspended information, information that doesn't readily fit a schema, might also be held in memory until either you get enough information to form the foundation of a new schema or you can link it to one of your existing categories. Remember Carter in the case study at the start of the chapter? He doesn't remember what the speaker said because he doesn't have a foundation of knowledge about the subject, nanotechnology. As he continues his studies, he will build a foundation that will allow him to integrate increasingly complex concepts into his knowledge structures.

Finally, contradictory information might be held as a tagged memory, until a sufficient number of tags lead you to adjust or change your existing schema. Previous research indicates that information that is inconsistent with or contradicts schemas tends to be forgotten more quickly than that which is schema consistent.[49] When this is factored in along with the overall strength of a schema, you can see how difficult it can be for a single tag to lead to a change in a schema. It might be easier for us to discount the information in such cases.

Memory and Organization. In addition to schemas focusing your attention on information that is consistent or inconsistent with expectations, they also help organize information in memory in such a way that it can be recalled. For example, research shows that information about people (people schema) is stored in a different category than information about objects.[50] When storing information about people, you often call upon stereotypes and categorize them by race and sex.[51] In addition, schemas associated with important values, beliefs, and attitudes tend to be ranked higher, this ranking makes them more available to us. As a result, they are easier to recall and more likely to be utilized when processing incoming information.

Our schema-based expectations also affect how we organize information. For example, as we described earlier, you expect certain elements to be present in a narrative. As you listen to the information, you store elements of it in the appropriate categories. For example, if the friend says that a group went to the beach and rented a place, you will probably store the information in the following manner: {A group of friends (you might remember the names)} {vacationed on a beach} {rented a place}. You will break the information down into logical units, separating people from actions and places. When you recall the information, you might recall that your friends (you would say their names) rented either a condo or a house on the beach. Using your schema, you know that people who rent places don't stay in hotels; they either rent a house or some type of condominium. When you reconstruct the story, you reconstruct it based upon your schema and add the element of the condo.

This illustration also points to a potential source of ***schema-based distortion*** to your memories. In our earlier example of the missing coffee mug, we pointed out that when information is missing from an original narrative, your memories tend to fill in the missing pieces.[52] There might not be much of a consequence for not remembering a coffee mug (except perhaps being groggy in class), but misremembering information can play a more serious role in other aspects of life. For example, let's say you are the witness to a bank robbery. You overhear the robber demanding money. When later being interviewed by police, you might "remember" a weapon being used to threaten the bank employees. Visualizing a weapon would be consistent with most schemas about bank robberies. Consequently, you may "remember" that detail even though it was not part of the actual robbery.[53]

It is safe to say that schemas have an effect on human memory. They affect what we remember as well as how well we remember. As a listener, you can use schemas to focus your attention on the important elements of incoming messages. You can also examine your preconceptions about a person, event, or any other type of information to determine if schemas are distorting information as you reconstruct it.

Schema and Listening

As the discussion about the impact of schema has indicated, the way we process information has a strong effect on us as listeners. Schemas contain knowledge about a subject, script or person.

They affect how you process information and they guide your behavior.[54] As we conclude this chapter, we believe it is important to note that schema theory is only one theory of information processing. There are others. Individuals interested in human information processing can find a rich collection of theories and research in cognitive psychological literature. We chose to discuss schema because of the breadth and depth of the theory. Schema theory helps explain what listeners do with information in several ways.[55] First, schema theory clearly shows that human information processing is dynamic. In other words, listeners actively seek to make connections in their minds. Schemas help prioritize information based on what is relevant or irrelevant for the purpose at hand. Consequently, listeners use schemas to decide whether to assign importance (relevance) to incoming information and actually attend to that message. In addition, listeners will incorporate new material they encounter into their information banks if they deem the information important and relevant. The connections listeners make between new information and their existing schemas are influenced by all of their life experiences. This conclusion makes sense if you consider that your schemas are also dynamic and are adjusted as you experience and learn new things.

The second way that schema theory explains what happens to information during the listening process is to account for the effect of culture on how listeners structure schema and subsequently interpret information. As listeners make connections between pieces of information, they are guided by the values, world views, and assumptions of the culture in which they grew up. This suggests that listeners need to be aware of their own cultural values while keeping an open mind to the cultural values of others. Being open to the cultural values of others helps listeners more accurately understand what the speaker is saying and intending.

The third way that schema affect listening is by providing a means to incorporate the context of the listening event. Schemas help listeners make sense of the world around them. Sometimes, making sense of a situation is very easy because an interaction or event goes the way the schematic script says it should go. However, often, things happen in such a way that listeners have to search for ways to interpret what is happening. This might occur when listeners find themselves in situations that call into question their existing beliefs (i.e., their version of truth or their expectations about the way things are supposed to be). For example, many people were surprised when Donald Trump won the 2016 US presidential election, while others had difficulty processing the idea that thousands of people in West Virginia and Flint, Michigan, could not drink water from their taps because of contaminated water supplies. Events like these force many listeners to reshape their schema as they process the events and the messages.

The fourth way that schemas affect listening is assisting in the understanding of conversations and listener perceptions. As noted above, part of the effect of conversations comes in the transmission of cultural values. Conversations reveal the frames, story themes, and the words used to explain the world around us.

Finally, schema theory might also explain, in part, why we are sometimes selective in our listening. As we discussed earlier in this chapter, a lot of stimuli are competing for our attention. Adam Gazzaley and Larry Rosen assert in their book, *The Distracted Mind*, that selectivity is crucial to goal attainment. "Selectivity can be thought of as the 'spotlight' in our cognitive control toolkit. It enables fine-tuning of processing across all sensory domains..."[56] By using our various schemas relevant to our goal(s) at any given moment, we will choose to focus on things that will help us attain that goal. Thus, when you are deeply engrossed in reading this chapter and using your information processing schemas, you ignore the sounds of your roommate's television. (You are ignoring it, aren't you?)

Summary

Research into how individuals process information and the effect of schemas on information processing and memory continues. Each new discovery helps us better understand the link between the way we perceive, process, store and recall information and the communication act of listening. Our perceptions color our listening behavior and one of the principal components of our perceptions is our life-time collection of schemas. As you have seen in this chapter, any number of factors can influence how we process information. In the next chapter we explore a number of individual differences that affect how we process information and form schemas. In Chapter 5, we explore the impact of technology on how we perceive and process information.

Key Concepts

Intrapersonal Information Flow Model
  External stimuli
  External interference
  Internal stimuli
  Internal noise
  Reception
  Perceptual screens
  Emotional bin
  Values, beliefs, attitudes
  Mechanical bin
  Instinctive bin
  Cognitive bin
  Short-term memory
  Long-term memory
  Working memory
  Primes
  Framing
Schemas
  Schema
  Scripts
  Tagging
  Discounting information
  Suspending information
  Re-evaluating schemas
  Social schema
  People schema
  Self schema
  Stereotypes
  Event schema
  Gender schema
  Occupational schema
  Culture schema
  Memory distortion

Discussion Questions

1. Going back to Chapter 1, how would our information processing model be integrated within or contribute to the WFH Model of Listening?
2. Our information processing includes several prominent concepts (e.g., external and internal stimuli). However, no model can account for every potential input. Can you think of any additional aspects of communication that could or should be included in our model?
3. In this chapter we discussed several common schemas (e.g., people, event, gender). Can you think of any other common schemas that people may hold that likely affect their listening processes?
4. Make a list of five particularly strong schemas that you hold. How are they associated with your values? Your beliefs and attitudes? How might these schemas affect your ability to listen effectively (and fairly) to others when interacting on these topics?

Listening Activities

1. Imagine that you are teaching a class. You want to encourage students to attend. In small groups, develop two messages to encourage attendance. One message should emphasize gain-framing, while the other loss-framing. Present your messages to your class. Which messages do you believe will be most effective? Why?
2. Listen to two political speeches, preferably on opposite sides of an issue. Identify framing words or phrases that are designed to shape your perception of the message.
3. Write a brief summary of what you know about the following groups. Include what type of exposure you have had to each group (e.g., personal experience, read about them, saw them on televisions). Identify your biases. How likely is it that these biases will impact how you listen to someone in each category?

Girl Scouts	Professors
Boy Scouts	Fire fighters
Asians	Pilots
New York City residents	Medical doctors
Christians	Buddhists
Dutch	Irish
South Africans	Brazilians

4. In groups of three to five individuals, using your summaries from the previous activity, compare your responses to others in your class. What similarities and differences do you find? What underlies or is the source of the similarities you hold? The differences you have?
5. Review two to three of your favorite advertisements. What type of schemas are they trying to invoke? What related values and attitudes are triggered?

Notes

1 Roach, Barker, & Fitch-Hauser, 1987
2 Goss, 1982
3 Breckler & Wiggins, 1992; Petty & Cacioppo, 2012
4 Petty & Cacioppo, 2012

5 Kandel, 2004
6 Sharples, Stewart, & Seaborne, 2016
7 Kandel, 2004
8 Baddeley, 2003; Janusik, 2007
9 Ungerleider & Courtney, 2016
10 Olivers & Eimer, 2011
11 Ericsson & Kintsch, 1995
12 Dewar, et al., 2012
13 Was & Woltz, 2007
14 Entman, 1993; Reali, Soriano, & Rodriguez, 2016
15 Hoffner & Ye, 2009, p. 189
16 Rothman, Bartels, Wlaschin, & Salovey, 2006, p. S202
17 Chaurand, Bossart, & Dehomme, 2015; See Rothman et al., 2006, for other examples of gain-framed and loss-framed health messages.
18 Rothman et al., 2006
19 D'Angelo, 2002
20 Chaurand et al., 2015
21 Reali, et al., 2016
22 Beals, 1998; Memelink & Hommel, 2006; Mazzocco, Green, & Brock, 2007
23 Schank & Abelson, 1977
24 See, for example, Karmiloff-Smith, 1995
25 Fitch-Hauser, 1984
26 Schank & Abelson, 1995
27 Freeman & Martin, 2004
28 Fitch-Hauser, 1984
29 Betts & Hinsz, 2013
30 Clemans & Graber, 2016
31 Hosoda, Sonte-Romero, & Walter, 2007
32 Hosoda, et al., 2007
33 See Hosoda, et al., 2007, for a summary of related research.
34 Bem, 1983; Martin & Halaverson, 1981; Frawley, 2008
35 Chang & Hitchon, 2004
36 Bem, 1987; Clemans & Graber, 2016
37 Roy Morgan Research, 2016
38 Hampel, 2016
39 Gallup, 2016
40 Betts & Hinsz, 2013
41 Erwin, 1992
42 Baumen & Ho, 2014
43 Brown, Smiley, Day, Townsend, & Lawton, 1977
44 Janicik & Larrick, 2005
45 Rice & Okun, 1994; Frawley, 2008, Chang & Hitchon, 2004
46 Yamada & Itsukushima, 2013; Koppel & Berntsen, 2014
47 Yamada & Itsukushima, 2013
48 Tuckey & Brewer, 2003
49 Tuckey & Brewer, 2003
50 Kuethe, 1964
51 Frawley, 2008; Chang & Hitchon, 2004
52 See Fitch-Hauser, 1984
53 Research into eyewitness accounts and testimony supports this example (e.g., work by Elizabeth Loftus and her colleagues).

54 Frawley, 2008
55 For a discussion, see Beals 1998 Gazzaley & Rosen, 2016, p. 36.
56 Gazzaley & Rosen, 2016, p. 36

Additional Readings

Albarracín, D., Johnson, B. T., Zanna, M. P., & Kumkale, G. T. (2005). *The handbook of attitudes*. Mahwah, NJ: Erlbaum.

Frawley, T. J. (2008). Gender schema and prejudicial recall: How children misremember, fabricate, and distort gendered picture book information. *Journal of Research in Childhood Education, 22*, 291–303.

Green, B. A. (2010). Understanding schema, understanding difference. *Journal of Instructional Psychology, 37*, 133–145.

References

Baddeley, A. D. (2003). Working memory and language: An overview. *Journal of Communication Disorders, 36*, 189–208.

Baumann, S., & Ho, L. (2014). Cultural schemas for racial identity in Canadian television advertising. *Canadian Sociological Association, 51*, 152–169.

Beals, D. (1998). Reappropriating schema: Conceptions of development from Bartlett and Bakhtin. *Mind, Culture, and Activity, 5*, 3–24.

Bem, S. (1983). Gender schema theory and its implications for child development: Raising gender-aschematic children in a gender-schematic society. *Signs, 8*, 598–616.

Bem, S. (1987). Gender schema theory and the romantic tradition. In P. Shaver & C. Hendrick (Eds.), *Review of personality and social psychology* (Vol. 7, pp. 251–271). Newbury Park, CA: Sage.

Betts, K., & Hinsz, V. (2013). Strong shared representations promote schema-consistent memory errors in groups. *Group Processes & Intergroup Relations, 16*, 734–751.

Breckler, S. J., & Wiggins, E. C. (1992). On defining attitude and attitude theory: Once more with feeling. In A. R. Pratkanis, S. J. Breckler, & A. G. Greenwald (Eds.), *Attitude structure and function* (pp. 407–427). Hillsdale, NJ: Erlbaum.

Brown, A., Smiley, S., Day, J., Townsend, M., & Lawton, S. (1977). Intrusion of a thematic idea in children's comprehension and retention of stories. *Child Development, 48*, 1454–1466.

Chang, C., & Hitchon, J. C. B. (2004). When does gender count? Further insights into gender schematic processing of female candidates' political advertisements. *Sex Roles, 51*, 197–208.

Chaurand, N., Bossart, F., & Delhomme, P. (2015). A naturalistic study of the impact of message framing on highway speeding. *Transportation Research Part F, 35*, 37–44.

Clemans, K., & Graber, J. (2016). Young adolescents' gender, ethnicity-, and popularity-based social schemas of aggressive behavior. *Youth & Society, 48*, 303–317.

D'Angelo, P. (2002). News framing as a multiparadigmatic research program: A response to Entman. *Journal of Communication, 52*, 570–888.

Dewar, M., Alber, J., Butler, C., Cowan, N., & Sala, S. (2012). Brief wakeful resting boosts new memories over the long term. *Psychological Science, 23*, 1–6.

Entman, R. M. (1993). Framing: Toward clarification of a fractured paradigm. *Journal of Communication, 43*, 51–58.

Ericsson, K. A., & Kintsch, W. (1995). Long-term working memory. *Psychological Review, 102*, 211–245.

Erwin, B. (1992). *The effect of culturally related schemata and instruction using thematic units on comprehension*. Paper presented to the 14th World Congress on Reading, Maui, HI.

Fitch-Hauser, M. (1984). Message structure and recall. In R. Bostrom (Ed.), *Communication yearbook 8* (pp. 378–392). Beverly Hills, CA: Sage.

Frawley, T. J. (2008). Gender schema and prejudicial recall: How children misremember, fabricate, and distort gendered picture book information. *Journal of Research in Childhood Education, 22*, 291–303.

Freeman, A., & Martin, D. (2004). A psychosocial approach for conceptualizing schematic development. *Cognition and Psychotherapy* (2nd ed., pp. 221–256). New York: Springer.

Gallup. (2016). Honesty/Ethics in Professions. Retrieved from www.gallup.com/poll/1654/Honesty-Ethics-Professions.aspx.

Gazzaley, A., & Rosen, L. (2016). *The distracted mind: Ancient brains in a high-tech world.* Cambridge, MA: The MIT Press.

Goss, B. (1982). *Processing communication,* Belmont, CA: Wadsworth.

Hampel, E. (2016, June). Nursing, farming are the most respected profession in Canada: Insights west survey. *Business Vancouver.* Retrieved from www.biv.com/articles/2016/6/nurses-farmers-are-most-repected-professions-cana.

Hoffner, C., & Ye, J. (2009). Young adults' responses to news about sunscreen and skin cancer: The role of framing and social comparison. *Health Communication, 24,* 189–198.

Hosoda, M., Stone-Romero, E., & Walter, J. (2007). Listeners' cognitive and affective reactions to English speakers with standard American English and Asian accents. *Perceptual and Motor Skills, 104,* 307–326.

Janicik, F., & Larrick, R. (2005). Social network schemas and the learning of incomplete networks. *Journal of Personality and Social Psychology, 88,* 348–365.

Janusik, L. A. (2007). Building listening theory: The validation of the conversational listening span. *Communication Studies, 58,* 139–156.

Kandel, E. (May, 2004). *The storage and persistence of memory.* Address delivered to the Symposia on Brain and Mind functioning. Columbia University. Retrieved from http://c250.columbia.edu/c250_now/symposia/brain_and_mind.html.

Karmiloff-Smith, A. (1995). Annotation: The extraordinary cognitive journey from fetus through infancy. *Journal of Child Psychology, 36,* 1293–1313.

Koppel, J., & Berntsen, D. (2014). The cultural life script as cognitive schema: how the life script shapes memory for fictional life stories. *Memory, 22,* 949–971.

Kuethe, J. (1964). Pervasive influence of social schemata. *Journal of Abnormal and Social Psychology, 68,* 248–254.

Martin, C., & Halaverson, C. (1981). A schematic processing model of sex typing and stereotyping in children. *Child Development, 52,* 1119–1134.

Mazzocco, P. J., Green, M. C., & Brock, T. C. (2007). The effects of a prior story-bank on the processing of a related narrative. *Media Psychology, 10,* 64–90.

Memelink, J., & Hommel, B. (2006). Tailoring perception and action to the task at hand. *European Journal of Cognitive Psychology, 18,* 579–592.

Olivers, C. N., & Eimer, M. (2011). On the difference between working memory and attentional set. *Neuropsychologia, 49,* 1553–1558.

Petty, R., & Cacioppo, J. (2012). *Communication and persuasion: Central and peripheral routes to attitude change.* New York: Springer-Verlag.

Reali, F., Soriano, T., & Rodriguez, D. (2016). How we think about depression: The role of linguistic framing. *Revista Latinamericana de Psicologia, 48,* 127–136.

Rice, E., & Okun, M. (1994). Older readers' processing of medical information that contradicts their beliefs. *Journal of Gerontology, 49,* 119–128.

Roach, D., Barker, L., & Fitch-Hauser, M. (1987). Origins, evolution, and development of a systems-based model of intrapersonal communication. *Information and Behavior, 2,* 197–215.

Rothman, A., Bartels, R., Wlaschi, J., & Salovey. (2006). The strategic use of gain-and loss-framed messages to promote healthy behavior: How theory can inform practice. *Journal of Communication, 56,* s202–s220.

Roy Morgan Research. (2016). *Nurses still easily most highly regarded – followed by doctors, pharmacists & engineers.* Roy Morgan Image of Professions Survey. Retrieved from http://roymorgan.com/findings/6797-image-of-professions-2016-201605110031.

Schank, R. C., & Abelson, R. P. (1977). *Scripts, plans, goals and understanding.* Hillsdale, NJ: Lawrence Erlbaum.

Schank, R. C., & Abelson, R. P. (1995). Knowledge and memory: The real story. In R. S. Wyler (Ed.), *Knowledge and memory: The real story* (pp. 1–85). Hillsdale, NJ: Lawrence Erlbaum.

Sharples, A., Stewart, C., & Seaborne, R. (2016). Does skeletal muscle have an 'epi'-memory? The role of epigenetics in nutritional programming, metabolic disease, aging and exercise. *Aging Cell, 15,* 603–616.

Tuckey, M. R. & Brewer, N. (2003). How schemas affect eyewitness memory over repeated retrieval attempts. *Applied Cognitive Psychology, 17,* 785–800.

Ungerleider, L., & Courtney, S. (2016). Working memory. In D. W. Pfaff & N. D. Volkow (Eds.), *Neuroscience in the 21st century* (2nd ed., pp. 2679–2695). New York: Spring.

Was, C. A., & Woltz, D. J. (2007). Reexamining the relationship between working memory and comprehension: The role of available long-term memory. *Journal of Memory and Language, 56,* 86–102.

Yamada, R., & Itsukushima, Y. (2013). The effect of schema on recognition memories and subjective experiences for actions and objects. *Japanese Psychological Research, 55,* 366–377.

4   Individual Differences in Listening Processes

Case Study 4.1 Troubles

NaMii Kim walked into class and slumps into a chair next to Ben.

Ben: *You look beat. Anything you would like to talk about?*

NaMii: *No, I'm fine.*

Ben: *Are you sure? I might be able to help.*

NaMii: *I'm really fine.* NaMii thinks to herself: I wish Ben would leave me alone, I've got to figure out what to do about my Grandmother.

Ben: *Hey, I was just trying to be nice.* Ben thinks to himself: I thought we were becoming real friends. Friends help each other out.

A few minutes later, Nolvia walks into the room and sits next to Ben.

Ben: *Are you ready for your presentation today? Personally, I can't wait. I love public speaking.*

Nolvia: *You are warped. Who actually wants to give a speech?*

Ben: *Well, I'd rather give a speech, than work in a small group any day. No offense.*

Nolvia (laughs): *None taken.*

Ben: *I still can't believe you chose to do a group project instead of an individual one in your Interior Design class. How's it going anyway?*

Nolvia (grimaces): *Slow. My classmate Sharee and I can't seem to get our act together. She is driving me crazy. I just don't understand what the problem is. I've never had a problem working in a group before. Maybe you can help me. You see …*

As you have learned in earlier chapters, how you listen can be affected by a number of things – your attitude when listening, your motivation to listen, the context of the listening setting, and, of course, individual differences. We also introduced types of listening, and examined how cognitive processes related to schemas can affect our processing of incoming messages. In this chapter, we look at how individual differences can affect how we listen. We'll be examining a number of concepts, from the following areas:

- personality traits
- personality type
- listening style
- empathy
- communication apprehension
- cognitive complexity

Why Study Individual Differences?

To put it simply, we don't know as much as we should about how physical and psychological differences between people may (or may not) affect their listening processes and listening ability.[1] While early listening scholars were more interested in defining listening and identifying listening skills, research over the past 20 years has increasingly explored the role of individual differences.[2] One reason for this interest is that a number of personality and psychological constructs appear to be biologically based. Research in this area led to the rise of a new approach to studying communication – **communibiology**.[3] Many of the researchers studying this area argue that "personality and communication are inherently intertwined."[4] They believe that our communication behaviors are, in part, influenced by biology.

At the heart of this debate is the question of how much of our listening ability comes from our temperament or personality (nature), and how much is learned (nurture)? Communibiologists argue that there is a robust body of research in areas such as neurobiology, psychobiology, psychological temperament, and personality, suggesting that some aspects of our personality (those believed to be genetically driven) do affect how we interact with others. For example, Michael Beatty and James McCroskey studied the relationship between interpersonal communication and temperament.[5] They note that a variety of communicative attributes have been associated with "inherited neurobiological processes" such as temperament (e.g., communicator style, empathy, extraversion). Researchers in temperament and personality often discuss the relationship between temperament type, personality, and social behavior, including communication preferences, miscommunication, and conflict, while others have explored neurologically based differences associated with types of communicators.[6]

Exploring Personality Traits

For our purposes, we first need to understand what makes up personality. Researchers often divide personality into two broad categories – temperament and personality. Temperament refers to personality traits we may possess. **Traits** are "enduring personal qualities or attributes that influence behavior across situations."[7] The underlying assumption of the study of temperament is that our personality traits should "meaningfully differentiate" us from others. In other words, people with different traits, such as introverts and extraverts, should systematically differ from one another.

Arnold Buss and Richard Plomin's theory of personality distinguishes temperament in terms of broad personality dispositions.[8] **Temperament** is generally considered that part of the personality that is "inborn." Essentially, then, temperamental traits form the biological basis of our personality and are believed to be inheritable.[9] In other words, there's a good chance your temperament is derived in part from one or both of your parents, your grandparents, and so forth. It's one of the reasons that people may say, "you're just like your mother (or aunt, or uncle, or grandfather)." Temperament is also believed to be quite stable.[10] Thus, your introverted five-year-old cousin is likely to grow up to be an introverted 20-year-old adult.

Traits are also believed to be motivational in nature. Again, this does not mean that you are genetically programmed to behave in a certain way. It does, however, suggest that you may be predisposed to act (or not act) in a certain way.[11] In addition, some traits such as communication and receiver apprehension appear to have a broader influence on your behaviors than others. In general, temperament addresses the expressive behavior that a person brings to a role or situation (e.g., introverted, extraverted, empathic).[12] For example, in our case study at the beginning of this chapter, Ben may be an extravert – someone who is generally out-going and animated when meeting new people. Yet, his temperament does not pre-determine that he's going to be happy and outgoing with every new person he meets. In fact, as you saw, he wasn't overly happy with NaMii's response to his friendly overtures.

Personality States versus Traits

Obviously, your interactions with your parents, siblings, cousins, and friends influence your behavior. Your personality necessarily reflects these influences. Thus, your personality is also a product of your social environment – the people and environment all individuals come in contact with. Researchers often use the term character or **state** when discussing the impact that the external environment may have upon us.[13] For example, your general temperament traits can often be discerned shortly after birth (i.e., happy baby, grumpy baby, etc.), while your personality state develops as you grow into adulthood. Personality states, then, are those parts of your personality that are shaped by your experience with your environment and the people within it.

A full discussion of the communibiological approach is beyond the scope of this book. What is important to keep in mind is that temperamental traits are considered to be relatively stable over the course of your life and that they are generally consistent across situations. Thus, temperamental traits may influence (but not determine) how you communicate with others. Table 4.1 summarizes the differences between temperament and personality.

Our traits and states have obvious implications for the elements of the Listening MATERRS Model. Individual differences may affect how you translate, evaluate, and respond to a message. We begin our examination of individual differences with a review of personality type and its potential effects on how we listen.

Table 4.1 Comparing Personality Traits and States

Traits	States
Inborn/Inherited	Learned
Stable	Adaptive
Stylistic-driven	Content-driven
Is a predisposition	Is situational

Personality Type

The interest in personality and temperament has been significantly influenced by the development and introduction of the Myers–Briggs type indicator (MBTI).[14] While it has received some criticism,[15] the MBTI remains one of the best known and most used personality inventories.[16] Its developers, the mother–daughter team of Isabel Myers and Katherine Briggs, believed that many of the differences we see in people have to do with the "the way people prefer to use their minds."[17] The descriptions associated with the Myers–Briggs typology reflect the underlying cognitive or mental functions associated with each of the four areas composing the MBTI.[18]

Undoubtedly, some of you have had the opportunity to take the Myers–Briggs type indicator. For those of you who have not, the measure centers around four bi-polar preferences – extraversion/introversion, thinking/feeling, sensing/intuiting, and judging/perceiving. It is important to keep in mind that these distinctions are on a continuum. So, for example, you could be a strong thinker, a strong feeler, or fall somewhere in between. Myers and Briggs believe that our preferences indicate two very important things about us. First, they reveal how we perceive or view things around us; second, they draw attention to how we evaluate or draw conclusions about these perceptions.

Ultimately, your preferences in these four areas reflect the communication patterns and behaviors you use with others as well as the tools you use to accomplish personal goals.[19] We next look at each of the four dimensions and then discuss their relationship to listening.

Learn more: Are you interested in knowing your own personality type? David Keirsey has developed a personality test – the Keirsey temperament sorter – that you can take. While the MBTI and KTS don't measure exactly the same types, research suggests there is a relationship between the two. The KTS is available in his 1998 book, *Please Understand Me II,* published by the Prometheus Nemesis Book Company. A short version is offered online at his website: www.keirsey.com.

Here's a website offering a version of the MBTI: www.onlinepersonalitytests.org/mbti.

Extraversion or Introversion

The easiest way to think about extraversion and introversion is to view it as a source of personal energy.[20] Individuals who are strong Extraverts tend to be outgoing, action-oriented, and social. They enjoy spending time with others and find it easy to communicate with them. Extraverts become "energized" through their contact with others and may experience a "power drain" if they experience too much quiet or seclusion. Thus, the friend who is an "Energizer Bunny" at parties and is animated when working in groups is likely a strong Extravert. On the other end of the continuum are Introverts. These people prefer solitary pursuits. Unlike what is portrayed in the cartoon below, they can and do enjoy interacting with others. However, they generally find working in groups or being in crowds tiring. They experience a power drain if they socialize with others for too long. Essentially, Introverts need time alone in order to recharge their mental batteries. In addition, they need time for contemplation and thought. Please note, however, that this does not necessarily mean that Introverts avoid working in groups or dislike parties. As a friend of ours once said, "Introverts are not party poopers, but they often get pooped by the party."

When communicating with others, Extraverts have been described as "quick to speak and slow to listen," while Introverts are "quick to listen and slow to speak."[21] This distinction is important for several reasons. For example, Extraverts tend to unload their feelings as they feel them, while Introverts tend to bottle their emotions up. Eventually, however, the Introvert will have to let those emotions out, and they may do so quite explosively.

Another important communication difference between Introverts and Extraverts is that Extraverts have a tendency to work out or solve problems "out loud." If you tend to talk out

loud to yourself when you are thinking a problem through, then you are likely an Extravert. Strong Introverts tend to do just the opposite. Remember, they like to contemplate things, so they tend to "think before they speak." As a result, they will mull over and process information until they reach a decision; then, they are ready to discuss it. These differences can lead to communication misunderstandings in a couple of ways. It's easy to see that Introverts and Extraverts can operate very differently when responding to a message. For example, drawing upon our Listening MATERRS Model, Introverts will tend to want additional time to translate and evaluate information.

In our case study at the beginning of the chapter, Ben is trying to draw NaMii into a conversation about what is bothering her. However, NaMii, resists. Thus, Ben, the Extravert, is trying to get NaMii to discuss the issue, while NaMii, the Introvert, refuses. Ben may interpret or translate her behavior as a sign of avoidance and feel hurt by what he perceives to be NaMii's unwillingness to open up to him. On the other hand, NaMii is thinking long and hard on her problem. As an Introvert, she feels the need to think more deeply about the problem before she is comfortable discussing it. Contrast NaMii and Nolvia in our case study. Nolvia is certainly more extraverted than NaMii. She immediately voices her discontent with her classmate to Ben.

Miscommunication between Introverts and Extraverts can occur in other ways as well. For example, if during the remodel on the Goleman home, Mrs. Goleman was musing (aloud) on the type of door she wanted, her contractor, an Introvert, may take her comments as a definite decision. The Goleman's may find themselves living with a sliding glass door to their patio (instead of the French doors Mrs. Goleman actually wanted). As seen here, you need to keep in mind the effect these communication differences can have on your interactions when working with others who score differently than you on the Introvert–Extravert continuum.

Sensing or Intuiting

This dimension is particularly important to how you perceive and learn things. It has been described as the method by which people become "aware of things, people, events or ideas [including] information gathering, the seeking of sensation or of inspiration, and the selection of the stimulus to be attended to."[22]

Sensors tend to be quite practical and pragmatic. As a result, they are more interested in the "here and now" and are less interested in addressing hypothetical futures. Sensors trust their own senses and personal experiences, relying on their senses and experiences to aid them in assessing their perceptions. It's no surprise then that Sensors tend to develop strong observational skills and that they are generally quite good at retaining and recalling details.[23] In fact, Sensors are particularly known for being detail oriented.

Intuitors, in contrast, are more abstract in their thinking. As a result, they tend to be more imaginative than practical. They place greater trust in their intuition and imagination than in their senses. In other words, they will sometimes rely on a personal insight or a "hunch" when deciding a course of action rather than searching out facts or evidence as the Sensor would. However, the downside is that Intuitors are often not as good as Sensors in focusing on current events or paying attention to details. On a positive note, Intuitors have a better ability to address potential futures or courses of action.[24]

> ***Think on it:*** Based on the description of Sensors and Intuitors, who might have a better working memory? Long-term memory? How might this affect their ability to recall information?

Arguably, this dimension is a primary source of communication problems.[25] Usually, when working on a project, Sensors and Intuitors will tend to be interested in different things. For example, imagine that Sharee and Nolvia have been working on their joint interior design project for about a month. Sharee is currently focusing on how they can adapt the William Morris style into the next phase of the project, the living room, while Nolvia is choosing the final accessories for the sunroom, the current phase of the project. Thus, Sharee, the Intuitor, is focusing on the "big" picture and planning the next stage of the project, while Nolvia, the Sensor, is focusing on the details necessary to complete the current stage. When drawing on each other's strengths, Intuitors and Sensors can accomplish great things. Intuitors have the vision, while Sensors have the follow-through. However, these same qualities can cause communication difficulties. For instance, Nolvia can become frustrated with Sharee when Sharee continually tries to shift their conversation away from deciding the final details of the sunroom to possibilities for decorating the living room. What Sensors and Intuitors are interested in, how they approach problems, and what they perceive to be immediate and important, can differ substantially. Such differences can affect a number of listening processes, including awareness and recall.

Thinking or Feeling

This dimension addresses how people make decisions about what they have perceived. Thus, it includes "decision-making, evaluation, choice, and the selection of the response after perceiving the stimulus."[26] Not surprisingly, it has important implications for evaluation, the fourth element in the Listening MATERRS Model.

Rationality is at the core of this dimension of the MBTI. However, Thinkers and Feelers employ "rationality" in very different ways. For example, Thinkers have strong analytical skills. They like focusing on the technical aspects of problems. In addition, they value logic, truthfulness, and criticism as well as objectivity, justice, and fairness. When making decisions, they analyze things in terms of causes and effects, and logic guides their behaviors and actions.[27]

Feelers differ markedly from Thinkers. Feelers have a higher need for affiliation or belonging. As a result, they value sympathy, empathy, and harmony. When making decisions, Feelers are more subjective, weighing the relative merits of alternatives.[28] One reason for this is that Feelers rely on "attending to what matters to others" and "an understanding of people."[29] Thus, they tend to consider what the human impact of their decision will be. When working with others, Feelers value tactfulness because it is related to being sympathetic and empathic, two qualities they value highly. This communication behavior also reflects a Feeler's need for maintaining harmony with others.

Needless to say, Thinkers and Feelers value very different things. Thinkers will listen for causes and effects as well as for facts and evidence they believe will assist them in making a logical, objective, and fair decision. In addition, when engaging in discussions, Thinkers stress truthfulness and criticism – two aspects that they value highly. However, this tendency can cause them problems when working with Feelers, who value tactfulness and harmony. Feelers often do not understand why a Thinker is being, what appears to them, very blunt and critical. At the same time, a Feeler's need for inclusion can sometimes lead to miscommunication. In a quest to maintain harmony with others, they may use ambiguous, vague, or euphemistic language, which allows greater listener discretion when interpreting incoming messages but can leave Thinkers frustrated.

As noted above, Feelers pay more attention to the human element of a message. They focus on relationships and are usually quite aware of the values and attitudes of others. Importantly, Feelers listen for information to help them determine the best alternative, not in terms of objectivity, but in terms of its human cost. Finally, in discussions with Thinkers, Feelers may not understand that they need to provide evidence to support their claims. It is not enough for Ben to say, "You don't care about me," when speaking to his Thinker girlfriend, Susan. Ben needs to provide Susan with specific reasons (e.g., "You work all the time" or "You've canceled our last three dates"). Logical arguments with clear support will carry more weight and be more convincing for Susan when listening to Ben.

Judgment or Perception

This final dimension addresses how we utilize time. Judgers value time and using it effectively. As a result, it is not unusual for them to push others for decisions. In addition, effectively using time includes organizing and planning a schedule. Judgers who experience a lack of structure in their daily lives may actually experience a great deal of stress. For example, when taking a class where there is a lot of free-wheeling discussion, Judgers may feel uncomfortable. They prefer classes with a clear agenda. In other words, they like classes where the instructor writes a key word outline on the board (or uses PowerPoint) so that they can clearly follow what is being discussed. Judgers also value work before play and subsequently are often seen as having a strong work ethic. For example, Judgers will want to complete a project before taking time out of their day to go have "fun." When Ben tells his girlfriend Susan that he'll be happy to go out on Saturday night *if* he finishes his English homework, he may be a Judger.

Perceivers are curious, flexible, and like keeping their options open. However, Perceivers quickly learn that keeping their options open can sometimes mean a delay in making decisions and/or completing projects. It is this aspect of a Perceiver's personality that often drive Judgers crazy. They don't understand why Perceivers aren't like them – looking for closure by making a final decision. However, Perceivers often hold off on decisions because they are searching for new or additional information. Finally, Perceivers view structure very differently than Judgers. Too much structure prevents them from being spontaneous and doesn't allow them to integrate play or periods of relaxation throughout their day (e.g., text friends, surf the net, take a short walk). As a result, Perceivers experience stress when faced with too much structure in their daily lives. Perceivers dislike living a scheduled life because it prevents them from acting on new opportunities.

Differences in this personality dimension can affect our lives significantly. For example, when communicating with others, both Perceivers and Judgers will focus on gathering additional information and ideas. However, Judgers will focus on information that helps them to reach the closure they desire, while Perceivers will interpret the same information as just another step along the way to making a decision. Thus, how Judgers and Perceivers listen and what they attend to can differ markedly.

Finally, understanding our Judging–Perceiving personality type can be important to job satisfaction. We can see its effect in a true-life example. Suzanne, who graduated with a Master's in Business, took a good-paying position as a project manager with a respected firm in town. The job required her to manage her time constantly; there were lots of meetings with vendors and employees. Subsequently, she had little personal free time at work. Within six months, she dreaded every morning and even called in sick to avoid having to go to work. Suzanne was a Perceiver working at a job that would have been better suited for someone who is a Judger. Eventually, Suzanne quit her job and started her own business, which allowed her great personal flexibility. Today, she is a successful small business woman.

> ***Think on it:*** Have differences in personality affected your communication with others? What happened? How might knowledge about personality differences help you in future communication with others?

Whether an Extravert or Introvert, Sensor or Intuitor, Thinker or Feeler, or a Judger or Perceiver, our personality type can significantly affect our personal and professional interactions with others. If we understand ourselves and others, we will be able to communicate better. Going back to our case study above, if Ben had understood that he was an Extravert and that NaMii was an Introvert, he would have had better insight into the best method of listening and communicating with her, and he would probably not have gotten offended by her lack of disclosure.

In Table 4.2, we summarize important attributes associated with each type. Now that you know more about these personality differences, review the different aspects of our Listening

MATERRS Model. How might these differences manifest themselves and affect each of the elements in the model?

Table 4.2 Summary of the Myers–Briggs Type Indicator Types

Extravert: Outgoing; speaks then thinks; sociable; likes groups.	**Introvert:** Private; thinks before speaking; reflective; prefers working alone.
Sensor: Focuses on details; factual; practical; realistic; present-focused.	**Intuitor:** Focuses on the big picture; theoretical; becomes bored with facts or details; future-focused.
Thinker: Task-oriented; logical; objective; analytical; detached; values truthfulness.	**Feeler:** People-oriented; values harmony, empathy, and tactfulness.
Judger: Well-organized; prefers structure; likes clear deadlines.	**Perceiver:** Flexible; spontaneous; dislikes deadlines.

Listening Style

As we noted earlier, the context or situation can affect both how we listen and how we respond. For example, when listening to your two-year-old sister, you may be more patient trying to understand what she is saying. In contrast, you may become frustrated with an IT instructor who doesn't provide a clear and precise explanation of the differences between Spark and Hadoop.

Listening Style as Habitual Listening

While listening scholars have studied and written about the individual nature of listening for quite some time, it was not until relatively recently that researchers Kittie Watson and Larry Barker identified specific individual listening style preferences.[30] A short time later, Watson and Barker, along with listening scholar James Weaver, developed the Listening Styles Profile (LSP-16), a measurement designed to identify our individual preferences. Specifically, Watson, Barker, and Weaver identified four listening styles or individual preferences – people, action, content, and time. They suggest these styles reflect the "who, how, where, when and types" of information people most enjoy listening to. They view listening styles as listening "habits" that are particularly evident when listeners were faced with novel situations.[31] This perspective suggests that listening styles are a trait. Their concept of listening style was typically presented and discussed as if one's style would be a listener's primary way of listening in most situations.

The idea of individual listening style preferences generated much research in the listening field. One reason is that individual differences like this appeal to researchers and the public in much the same way as our interest in personality. We tend to enjoy gaining insight into ourselves, especially when that insight can be presented in relatively straightforward ways. How many online "personality" tests have you taken? Do you know what Game of Thrones character you are? However, research findings are only as good as the measurements that are used. Without getting overly technical, researchers using the LSP-16 began noticing that the scale was unreliable. In the simplest terms, statistically, each time a person completed the LSP-16, the score should be similar (i.e., reliable). Unfortunately, this was not always the case with the LSP-16. If a measurement is unreliable, then you have to be distrustful of researching findings using that measure. Such was the case with the LSP-16.

Below, we present the revised Listening Styles Profile. Prior to our discussion of the different types of listening, please complete the scale and note your score for each of the types.

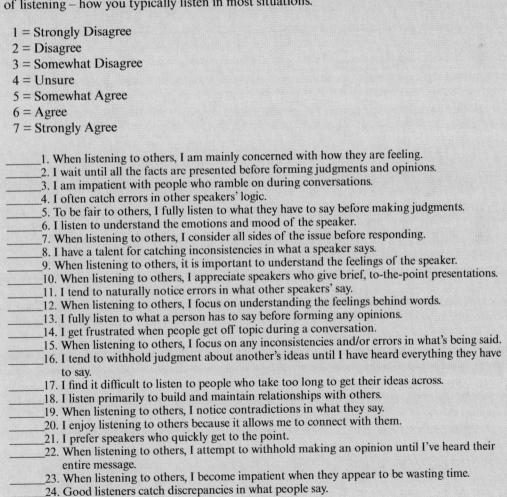

Scale 4.1 The Listening Styles Profile Revised (LSP-R)*

Below are several items that reflect how people describe themselves as a listener. We would like you to assess how each statement applies to you by marking your level of agreement/ disagreement with each item. The stronger you disagree with a statement, the lower the number you will choose. The stronger you agree with a statement, the higher the number you will use. Please do not think of any specific listening situation but of your general ways of listening – how you typically listen in most situations.

1 = Strongly Disagree
2 = Disagree
3 = Somewhat Disagree
4 = Unsure
5 = Somewhat Agree
6 = Agree
7 = Strongly Agree

_____1. When listening to others, I am mainly concerned with how they are feeling.
_____2. I wait until all the facts are presented before forming judgments and opinions.
_____3. I am impatient with people who ramble on during conversations.
_____4. I often catch errors in other speakers' logic.
_____5. To be fair to others, I fully listen to what they have to say before making judgments.
_____6. I listen to understand the emotions and mood of the speaker.
_____7. When listening to others, I consider all sides of the issue before responding.
_____8. I have a talent for catching inconsistencies in what a speaker says.
_____9. When listening to others, it is important to understand the feelings of the speaker.
_____10. When listening to others, I appreciate speakers who give brief, to-the-point presentations.
_____11. I tend to naturally notice errors in what other speakers' say.
_____12. When listening to others, I focus on understanding the feelings behind words.
_____13. I fully listen to what a person has to say before forming any opinions.
_____14. I get frustrated when people get off topic during a conversation.
_____15. When listening to others, I focus on any inconsistencies and/or errors in what's being said.
_____16. I tend to withhold judgment about another's ideas until I have heard everything they have to say.
_____17. I find it difficult to listen to people who take too long to get their ideas across.
_____18. I listen primarily to build and maintain relationships with others.
_____19. When listening to others, I notice contradictions in what they say.
_____20. I enjoy listening to others because it allows me to connect with them.
_____21. I prefer speakers who quickly get to the point.
_____22. When listening to others, I attempt to withhold making an opinion until I've heard their entire message.
_____23. When listening to others, I become impatient when they appear to be wasting time.
_____24. Good listeners catch discrepancies in what people say.

Calculate Your Score

Carefully enter your response for the corresponding item below and total your score for the column. Your total for each listening type can range from 6 to 42.

1.	2.	3.	4.
6.	5.	10.	8.
9.	7.	14.	11.
12.	13.	17.	15.
18.	16.	21.	19.
20.	22.	23.	24.
Relational Listening Section Score:	*Analytical Listening Section Score:*	*Task-Oriented Listening Section Score:*	*Critical Listening Section Score:*

* Reprinted with permission. Bodie, Worthington, & Gearhart, 2013
Note: For self-evaluation purposes, high scores range from 35 to 42; low scores range from 6 to 15.

Listening Style as a Situational Demand

Professor Worthington, one of the authors of your text, along with Professors Graham Bodie and Christopher Gearhart, studied the problems with the original Listening Styles Profile (the LSP-16). Specifically, their study findings suggested that the original LSP-16 needed to be significantly revised and that how we conceptualize listening style needed to be rethought. Their research, along with that of other listening scholars, has resulted in an increased emphasis on the effect of individual goals in listening contexts. Thus, while the early research into listening styles suggested we were creatures of habit whose listening reactions were relatively constant across listening contexts, today we emphasize how the "goals that listeners have when engaged in situations... [call upon] them to be a particular kind of listener."[32] Here, we introduce you to the revised view of listening style, which, like the original LSP-16, also includes four listening orientations – relational listening, analytical listening, critical listening, and task-oriented listening.

Before we begin describing each style, we previously asked you to complete the LSP-R. Some of you may have a clear primary listening style, while others of you may have scored highly on several styles or perhaps none. At this point in time, the research does not clearly suggest what differences may result if you have no or more than one primary listening style. It does, however, tell us that you will vary your style with your listening goal and provides us with an idea of one's listening attitudes and behaviors when enacting that style.

If a situation calls upon you to be a **Relational listener**, you will be more concerned with, have a greater awareness of, and be responsive to the feelings and emotions of those you are interacting with. You will draw upon your view of the situation and your relationships with others to determine if an emphasis on relational listening is required, and if it is, to what extent it should be emphasized. Not surprisingly, this style of listening is central to establishing and sustaining interpersonal relationships. Thus, when Simone first meets Ella, she may engage in relational listening, especially if she wants to develop a friendship. Is she happy? Upset? Sad? These listeners will generally let the speaker know they are interested in and concerned about the speaker's emotional state. Relational listening shares many characteristics with the original People listening style introduced in the LSP-16. Looking back at the Myers–Briggs Typology, you probably are not surprised to discover that Feeling has been associated with relationally oriented listening.[33]

As we learned, Feelers are more interested in the human dimension of a decision rather than the technical aspect of problems.[34] Other studies have found this listening style positively associated with empathy, sympathy, and conversational sensitivity.[35]

When engaging in **Analytical listening**, our goal is to focus on the speaker's entire message, then form a judgment. Analytical listeners prefer to listen systematically and will work to take into account the perspectives of others.[36] This willingness to remain objective when listening suggests that they may be able to more effectively evaluate the information being presented by others. While additional work is needed, some studies suggest that this listening style may be associated with the Myers–Briggs type, Thinking.[37] Just as Thinkers prefer to be logical, objective and fair, so do these listeners.

Critical listening is a tendency to evaluate and critically assess messages for accuracy and consistency. If a situation calls upon you to use this listening style, you will pay particular attention to errors and inconsistencies in the conversation. Recent research found critical listening associated with an individual's need for cognition and need to evaluate (i.e., thinking about and evaluating information). These findings also likely explain why early studies reported that individuals who engage in critical listening enjoy the challenge of complex information and pay particular attention to how speakers support their claim.[38]

When engaging in **Task-oriented listening** we are driven by two concerns: 1) the amount of time we have available to listen, and 2) a preference for interacting with speakers who can manage to stay focused and on-topic. There is some evidence that when listeners are driven by time considerations, they may engage in a more socially callous listening style, which is hallmarked by less empathy and increased verbal aggressiveness.[39] Taken together, these characteristics may lead task-oriented listeners to interrupt the speaker in order to hurry the conversation along. They also may tell the speaker how much time they have available for listening or discourage speakers they perceive to be wordy or rambling. Previous research found time-oriented listening to be associated with the MBTI type, Thinking – the dimension that addresses how we make decisions. As we saw above, Feelers focus on the effect decisions have on the people involved, while Thinkers are more interested in the technical aspects of a problem. It is believed that Feelers are more willing to take the time needed to understand the human dimension of a problem. Thinkers, in contrast, may acknowledge the human cost, but only as one aspect of the greater issue being addressed. For instance, if the Student Government Association is considering funding a controversial initiative, the Feelers in the group may want to spend more time discussing the response the decision will get from students, parents and alumni. Thinkers will acknowledge this aspect of the decision. However, the public reaction is only one issue of many they will need to address when making the final decision.

You will notice that when we asked you to complete the LSP-R scale earlier, you were instructed to avoid thinking of a specific listening context. Imagine yourself in the following listening situation: You've just been asked to review a detailed report by your boss. You have to complete the review in one hour, when a colleague steps in to discuss a personal problem. Now, complete the LSP-R a second time. Did your scores differ appreciatively? What if you had two weeks to complete the report? Would it affect how you listen?

Think on it: Looking back at our case study, can you determine which listening style Ben, NaMii, or Nolvia may be utilizing?

What recent research has found is that individuals rarely utilize one primary listening style. In fact, 50% of the study participants either reported having high scores (e.g., scores of 35 and higher) in multiple styles or reported no primary style at all (i.e., low scores across all types) (e.g., 15 or lower).[40] This same study found that people will switch their primary listening style depending on the nature of the conversation. Specifically, you will adjust your listening style based on the amount of three elements of an interaction: *depth, empathy*, and *perspective taking*.[41] Depth refers to how intimate, personal, and superficial a conversation is. We discussed empathy and perspective-taking in depth in Chapter 2. For example, your LSP-R score may suggest your primary listening style is relational, which requires you to utilize a certain level of empathy. In contrast, when listening to a lecture you may engage in task-oriented or critical listening.

An understanding of listening styles is important because it is likely that we develop "listening frameworks for common interpersonal functions and situations (i.e., social support)…"[42] When faced with the demands or goals of a particular situation, we will use that framework to help us determine the listening style and/or behavior we should employ. Put another way, we pull up relevant cognitive schemas to help us make stylistic and behavioral choices of how to listen (and act) in a particular context.

Empathy

By now, you are familiar with a number of elements related to empathy. As you learned in Chapter 2, empathy is an important aspect of relational listening and is central to building relationships with others. We distinguished between empathic responsiveness (the ability to feel "with" others) and sympathetic responsiveness (feeling "for" someone). Here, we expand on the relationship between empathy and listening with a broader examination of active-empathic listening.

Active-empathic Listening

Over the last few years, a number of listening researchers have studied active-empathic listening (AEL). Research into AEL suggests that it is a trait, but how it is enacted can be affected by the situation. It was first examined in a sales context and later to more general social contexts.[43] In the sales and marketing context, researchers found the combination of listening and empathy to be associated with more effective sales people.[44] Later in the text, we address its role in other contexts such as interpersonal communication and supportive communication.[45]

Before we explore this further, take a moment to complete the self-report version of the AEL scale.

Scale 4.2 The Active-Empathic Listening Self-Report Scale

Instructions: Using the following scale, please indicate how frequently you perceive these statements to be true about yourself in the line provided beside each item:

1	2	3	4	5	6	7
Never/Almost never true						*Always/Almost always true*

_____1. I am sensitive to what others are not saying.

_____2. I am aware of what others imply but do not say.

_____3. I understand how others feel.

_____4. I listen for more than just the spoken words.

_____5. I assure others that I will remember what they say.

_____6. I summarize points of agreement and disagreement when appropriate.

_____7. I keep track of points others make.

_____8. I assure others that I am listening by using verbal acknowledgments.

_____9. I assure others that I am receptive to their ideas.

_____10. I ask questions that show my understanding of others' positions.

_____11. I show others that I am listening by my body language (e.g., head nods).

Calculate Your Score

Please record your response to each item by its respective number. Total the score for each item in each column, then calculate your overall AEL score.

1. _____	5. _____	8. _____
2. _____	6. _____	9. _____
3. _____	7. _____	10. _____
4. _____		11. _____

Sensing: _____ + *Processing:* _____ + *Responding:* _____ = _____

Total AEL Score

Reprinted with permission: Bodie (2011). Note: You will have a self-score for each dimension of the AEL as well as a grand total score. Grand total scores range between 11 and 77. Sensing and Responding scores can range from 4 to 44, while Processing can range from 3 to 33. For self-evaluation purposes, high scores are in the top 20% of the possible points and low scores fall into the bottom 20% (e.g., above 62 and below 25 for totaled scores).

Active-empathic listening combines the techniques of active listening with the personal connection of empathy. It encompasses both cognitive and behavioral elements as reflected in its three dimensions: sensing, processing, and responding.[46] *Sensing* is characterized by a listener's ability to identify the relational elements of speech. *Processing* includes many elements of the Listening MATERRS Model, specifically: attention, comprehensions, receiving and interpreting. You will notice these elements are primarily cognitive in nature. *Responding* addresses verbal and nonverbal feedback, and thus focuses on behavioral elements, such as asking clarifying questions and generally signaling the listener is attending to the conversation.[47] Active-empathic listening is characterized by a sensitivity which allows the listener to take in and respond appropriately to the social environment and the emotions of the people involved in the interaction.[48] It is positively associated with emotional intelligence and negatively associated with emotional control. Put another way, these individuals tend to be emotionally sensitive (i.e., can accurately sense and perceive their personal/interpersonal situation).[49] Most importantly, studies have demonstrated that individuals engaging in this type of listening are viewed as more conversationally effective and seen as more competent communicators.[50] Interestingly, studies also suggest it can be beneficial in business contexts. For instance, clients often perceive sales people who engage in active-empathic listening as more trustworthy.[51] It is unclear, however, if this finding also applies to romantic or similar relationships.

You likely can see the advantages of active-empathic listening. In Case Study 4.1, if Ben had noticed Namii was introverted in their interactions, he wouldn't have pushed her to tell him what was bothering her. Do you remember Case Study 2.1 in Chapter 2 about Nolvia's father? His physician, Dr. Kyle had obviously been listening to Mr. Gutierrez's concerns about being a paraplegic as a result of his accident. Her nonverbal and verbal response shows that she was paying attention to Mr. Gutierrez's words as well as his emotions. She felt "with" him and addressed what was important to him – being involved in his children's lives.

Sociability

One area in which people appear to differ in their ability to show empathy is in the area of **sociability**. People who are highly sociable are adept at expressing sympathetic responses to others and believe it is important to try to engage in perspective-taking (seeing things from others' point of view). In contrast, individuals who are more egocentric generally do not demonstrate signs of either empathic or sympathetic responsiveness.[52] Both types of responsiveness are expressed verbally and nonverbally. Listeners high in empathy are often quite skilled at picking up on cross-cues (when a person's words and nonverbals conflict with each other). As seen in our Case Study, Ben easily determined that NaMii was upset about something. Individuals high in empathy rarely need such obvious cues, as presented in our case study, to determine someone is "not fine." They are the ones who can often tell something is not right, even when the other person is doing their best to hide the fact. In other words, they are very good at picking up on subtle nonverbal cues. As we mentioned in Chapter 2, one reason empathy and sociability are believed to occur together is that highly empathic individuals also tend to be highly sociable. Sociability encourages you to interact with others and in turn, the interactions provide empathic individuals with numerous opportunities to hone their verbal and nonverbal skills. Thus, sociability has implications for all elements of the Listening MATERRS Model, but especially awareness, translation, and response.

Differences in sociability may also help explain why people differ in empathic perspective taking. As you may recall from Chapter 2, empathic perspective taking refers to your ability to place yourself in someone else's shoes – to understand things from their perspective.

Scale 4.3 Conversational Sensitivity Scale

Using the following scale, how much would you say each of the following statements reflects you and the way you communicate? Indicate your level of agreement using the following scale on the line provided by each item:

1	2	3	4	5
Strongly Disagree				*Strongly Agree*

_____1. I often find myself detecting the purposes or goals of what people are saying in their conversations.

_____2. I think I can remember conversations I participate in more than the average person.

_____3. I have the ability to say the right thing at the right time.

_____4. I'm not very good at detecting irony or sarcasm in conversations.*

_____5. I can often tell when someone is trying to get the upper hand in a conversation.

_____6. I would enjoy being a fly on the wall listening in on other people's conversations.

_____7. Compared to most people, I don't spend much time inventing "make-believe" conversation.*

_____8. I'm usually the last person in a conversation to catch hidden meanings in puns and riddles.*

_____9. I often notice double meanings in conversations.

_____10. I'm terrible at recalling conversations I had in the past.*

_____11. If people ask me how to say something, I can come up with a number of different ways of saying it.

_____12. Often in conversations, I can tell whether the people involved in the conversation like or dislike one another.

_____13. I'm often able to figure out who's in charge in conversations.

_____14. Conversations are fascinating to listen to.

_____15. I like to think up imaginary conversations in my head.

_____16. I often have difficulty paraphrasing what another person said in a conversation.*

_____17. I often have a sense that I can forecast where people are going in conversations.

_____18. If you gave me a few moments, I could probably easily recall a conversation I had a few days ago.

_____19. I'm very good at coming up with neat ways of saying things in conversations.

_____20. I can tell in conversations whether people are on good terms with one another.

_____21. Most of the time, I'm able to identify the dominant person in a conversation.

_____22. I really enjoy overhearing conversations.

_____23. I often make up conversations in my mind.

_____24. In conversations, I seem to be able to often predict what another person is going to say even before he or she says it.

_____25. I have a good memory for conversations.

_____26. I am good at wording the same thought in different ways.

_____27. I can often tell how long people have known each other just by listening to their conversation.

_____28. In group interactions, I'm not good at determining who the leader is in the conversation.*

_____29. I'm less interested in listening in on others' conversations than most people.*

_____30. I often hear things in what people are saying that others don't seem to notice.

_____31. I can often remember specific words or phrases that were said in past conversations.

_____32. In virtually any situation, I can think of tactful ways to say something.

_____33. I'm not very good at figuring out who likes whom in social conversations.*

_____34. I often find hidden meanings in what people are saying during conversations.

_____35. I can often understand why someone said something even though others don't see that intent.

_____36. Many times, I pick up from conversations little bits of information that people don't mean to disclose.

Calculate Your Score

To obtain a total CS core, all items are summed, producing a score that ranges from 36 and 180.

To determine your subscale scores, you will need to *first reverse code items* with an asterisk beside them. For example, if you put a 1 for this item, you should change it to a 5, 2 becomes 4, 3 remains a 3, etc. After reverse coding relevant items, subscale scores are obtained by computing the *average* of item responses, producing seven scores that each range between 1 and 5.

Meaning	Memory	Alternatives	Affinity	Power	Enjoyment	Imagination	Interpretation
1.	2.	3.	4.	5.	6.	7.	8.
9.	10.	11.	12.	13.	14.	15.	16.
17.	18.	19.	20.	21.	22.	23.	
24.	25.	26.	27.	28.	29.		
30.	31.	32.	33.				
34.							
35.							
36.							
/8 =	/5 =	/5 =	/5 =	/4 =	/4 =	/3 =	/2 =

For dimensional scores, average your scores for each column.

Reprinted with permission: Daly, Vangelisti, & Daughton (1987)

Conversational Sensitivity

People who are more empathic also tend to be more conversationally sensitive.[53] **Conversational sensitivity** refers to how attentive and responsive you are to your conversation partners. It is composed of several dimensions. These dimensions and their descriptions are presented in Table 4.3.

People who are highly sensitive are particularly good at picking up cues during social interactions. For example, if you are high in conversational sensitivity, you will tend to enjoy conversing with others more than those who score lower in conversational sensitivity. Let's assume for a moment that Ben is high in conversational sensitivity. If the conversations in Case Study 4.1 continued, Ben will probably be the one who not only notices that NaMii continues to appear anxious, but he will also retain or remember more about the conversation. If Nolvia is less conversationally sensitive, she will not only remember less, she will likely take the conversation at face

Table 4.3 Dimensions of Conversational Sensitivity

Detecting Meaning: The ability to recognize underlying and/or multiple meaning in our conversations with others.

Conversational Memory: How well we remember the content of a conversation.

Conversational Alternatives: The ability to select from a range of words and phrases (i.e., conversational flexibility).

Perceiving Affinity: The ability to evaluate how much conversational members like, are attracted to, and/or their affiliations with one another.

Detecting Power: The ability to recognize power dynamics/relationships between members of a conversation.

Conversational Enjoyment: How much enjoyment we get from participating in or listening to conversations with others.

Conversational Imagination: The level to which one engages in imagined conversations.

Interpretation: The ability to paraphrase and recognize underlying meaning and other nuances in a conversation, such as sarcasm, irony, etc.

---

value and, subsequently, will miss some of the implied dynamics that occur during the conversation. For example, she will likely be less aware of nonverbal cues which, as we noted above, often tell us a lot about the emotional state of the speaker.

As you can see, empathy is made up of several components that are in turn related to other emotion-related concepts. The next individual difference we discuss – Emotional Intelligence – is also related to empathy, but focuses more on your awareness of specific emotions and your knowledge of how they can affect our interactions.

Emotional Intelligence

Individuals who are conversationally sensitive are likely to have a higher emotional "IQ." Actually known as emotional intelligence or EI, trait-emotional intelligence is a relatively new concept introduced by John Mayer and Peter Salovey.[54] The theory is quite popular with researchers in a variety of areas including management, psychology, communication, and counseling. There is some disagreement among researchers about if, and how, we should distinguish between trait-EI (inborn/natural emotional intelligence) and ability-EI (learned emotional intelligence).[55] No matter the viewpoint (inborn or learned), EI has important implications for how we listen and communicate with others.

Salovey and his colleagues describe **emotional intelligence** as "the ability to perceive and express emotions, to understand and use them, and to manage them to foster personal growth."[56] They contend that emotions can inform your decision-making in four basic ways. First, *EI helps you to identify or perceive emotions* – your own as well as the emotions of others. They argue that this perception, also known as **emotional awareness**, can go beyond people to encompass all kinds of things including your pets, the arts, and your home, as well as other objects or events. For instance, Radley's parents are avid folk art collectors. When a neighbor asked them why they bought a particular piece, they said, "It's a fun piece and we love the colors." With this dimension of EI, it's important that we have the ability to identify the emotions involved – both yours and others'.

Second, *emotion can be used to facilitate thought.* Salovey and others believe that emotions can help you to focus your attention and to process information more rationally.[57] Thus, your emotions can assist you in solving personal problems, can be used to encourage creativity at work, and can lead to more flexible and adaptive communication with others. For example, in our case study, if NaMii believes she has offended Ben, she may assess her options for making up with him (e.g., apologize, defend her actions) by how she thinks Ben will respond (angrily, sympathetically, etc.).

Third, it is important for you to **understand emotions.** Of course, you use emotions to communicate concern or excitement to others. While this dimension seems straight forward, it is at the core of empathy. However, Salovey and his colleagues note that this function of EI includes both the ability to understand emotional information and the ability to understand how our emotions can change or morph over the course of a relationship. If you have had the opportunity to take an interpersonal or relational communication course, you are aware that relationships are dynamic (constantly changing and evolving). Necessarily, the emotions you experience over the course of the relationship will vary in both type (e.g., attraction, friendship, love, disappointment, hate) and intensity (e.g., weak to strong). What sets this aspect of EI apart is the emphasis on how emotions affect the changes that occur over the course of a relationship. It addresses (and emphasizes) the great variety of emotional or feeling states people can experience.[58]

The final dimension of EI addresses how you **manage emotion.** An important part of this dimension is simply being open to feelings – both your own and others'. For example, you have to be willing to recognize when you are sad, but also when you make someone else sad. Another aspect of this dimension involves being able to regulate your feelings and assist others in doing the same. When you've had a bad day, you can use any number of strategies to cheer yourself up. Some people head for the movies. Others will call a friend and talk things through. Still others may eat chocolate. All of these strategies help you manage your emotions. You can do similar things for the other people in your lives. Oftentimes, you can simply provide a willing ear and listen with an open attitude. Most friends appreciate and rightly expect you to be an attentive listener in both good times and bad. People who are particularly adept in this area of EI always seem to know just what to say and when to say it so that you end up feeling inspired or happier. Finally, Salovey and his colleagues argue that this aspect of EI leads to self-actualization (i.e., personal understanding and growth). Essentially, the more you know about and understand emotions, the better you understand yourself, and the better you can communicate with others.

Learn more: Dr. Petrides directs the London Psychometric Laboratory in the Department of Psychology at University College London. It is home to the trait emotional intelligence research program. He has made several versions of his Emotional Intelligence Scale available to the public. If you are interested in learning about your own E-IQ, you can visit his website at: www.psychometriclab.com.

Dr. Reuven Bar-On, a world-renowned researcher in Emotional Intelligence, writes, "…people who are emotionally and socially intelligent are able to understand and express themselves, to understand and relate well to others, and to successfully cope with the demands of daily life."[59] Research by Dr. Bar-On and others shows that EI can impact our physical and mental health, as well as school and work performance, and the overall quality of our social interactions.[60] EI is essential to the listening process because it highlights the importance of emotions when interacting and listening to others. As you can see, you need to be aware of your own emotions and how they can affect or color your listening. For example, in our earlier example of Nolvia and Sharee's design project, it is understandable that Nolvia would be angry at Sharee for being late to work on their project, leaving her to meet a project deadline alone. However, when Sharee does arrive, Nolvia's anger may prevent her from fully listening to her reason for being late. Nolvia may also not want to hear anything Sharee has to say about the project as they complete the final touches together. In this case, Nolvia would be displaying low EI competency because she would not recognize how her anger is getting in the way of completing the project.

If, on the other hand, Nolvia can see that Sharee is upset and she acknowledges that fact (as well as the fact she is none too happy herself), she can use this knowledge and what she knows about Sharee to make judgments about which section of the project would be best for her to work on. For example, should Sharee be working on editing, a detail-oriented job? Or, would it be better for her to do something more global like choosing artwork? It depends on how Nolvia think Sharee's emotions will affect her work. Will her task distract her from her emotions or will her emotions be too distracting for detail work? Of course, she can and should apply the same emotional evaluation to herself.

Here, we have only briefly introduced the topic of emotional intelligence. As you can see, it is related to our model of listening in several ways. How aware are you of your own and other's emotions? And, how might you translate and evaluate them? Of course, it can affect how you respond as well. It is easy to see its application to interpersonal communication, and, as seen in the example above, that it also has organizational and business applications. Later in the text, when we address relational and organizational listening, we will readdress this topic.

Communication Apprehension

Another area of individual differences addresses the anxiety or apprehension you experience when communicating with others. Importantly, excessive apprehension can affect how effectively and appropriately you communicate with others. Ideally, you should be higher in approach predispositions and lower in avoidance predispositions. **Approach predispositions** refer to communication behaviors which lead you to interact comfortably with others, while **avoidance predispositions** make you feel uncomfortable. Communication and receiver apprehension fall into the latter category. When you are comfortable both in expressing yourself to others and in receiving information from them, you are likely more skilled at identifying and adapting to cues from others and generally will have and display greater poise and composure when dealing with them.[61] As a result, you are more likely to achieve your personal and professional goals.

Communication apprehension (CA) refers to the anxiety we feel when communicating with others. Not surprisingly, CA has been associated with general social anxiety.[62] While we can talk about general communication apprehension which may occur across situations, communication researchers also discriminate between the types of apprehension we feel in different communication contexts – interpersonal, small group, meeting, and public speaking.[63] Communication apprehension has a variety of sources.[64] First, some people experience a **generalized anxiety**. This type of feeling is often considered trait or personality based. The public speaker who engages in negative thinking, "I can't do this. I'm going to faint," would be said to be expressing a trait-based predisposition or motivation (to avoid public speaking whenever possible). Other scholars suggest that we can also learn apprehensive behavior. Thus, Nolvia's attitude toward public speaking may be due to a bad experience (e.g., she blanked when giving a speech on Kipling to her high school English class). She is experiencing **conditioned anxiety** – most likely manifesting itself as sweaty palms, hyperventilating, or nausea.

Recent research suggests that communication apprehension is heritable.[65] This genetic predisposition and its apparent association with general social anxiety means that some people tend to feel more anxious as they enter into a communication situation. Their anxiety leads them to focus a great deal of attention on how others will judge their communication competence. The problem is that even when people have the motivation and the necessary skills to communicate with others, anxiety can still get in the way. Imagine a baseball player at the World Series. The very fact that he's playing in the World Series suggests that he has a lot of skill and knowledge about how to be a good baseball player. Presumably anyone who would ever make it to the World Series would be highly motivated to do a good job (i.e., turn in a skilled performance). Have you ever seen a professional athlete in the World Series, Super Bowl, Olympics, etc. do a bad job? Why did that happen? Simply put, a lot of anxiety can interfere with a performance, even when there is a lot of ability, skill, motivation, and knowledge. Unfortunately, communication apprehension has been associated with reduced communicative abilities or skills.

Importantly, individuals experiencing high levels of CA often have difficulty achieving personal and professional goals. For example, the high CA person and the low CA person will differ in terms of their **social relations** and **conversational skills** as well as in **nonverbal leakage**.[66] In terms of overall social skills, individuals with low CA tend to be less shy, making it easier for them to establish friendships. In addition, they are more likely to date a variety of people, to take on group leadership positions, be more appreciative of a multicultural world, and to be more adaptable and less conformist.[67] In contrast, those high in CA tend to view themselves as less attractive, are more likely to avoid blind dates, and have greater difficulty in developing friendships. They also have poorer conversational skills, as evidenced by a greater number of non-fluencies (e.g., umms, you knows, etc.), longer silences, and increased speech repetitions. They are often unskilled at initiating or controlling conversations and can find it difficult to interrupt others. Finally, high CAs tend to have more nonverbal leakage. Think of the behaviors anxious people engage in. Thus, for example, NaMii appears stiff and tense, looks away, fidgets, and may physically distance herself from others. You can often recognize anxious individuals by the "vibes" they give off.

Intuitively, communication apprehension would appear related to how you listen, and research supports this connection. As noted earlier, high levels of anxiety interfere with your ability to perform any task, and listening is no different. Often when you become too focused on your "communicative performance," you forget or ignore the importance of listening to others. Even when you do try to listen, your anxiety can affect your ability to translate, evaluate, or recall a message.

Other types of anxiety have been studied as well. We cover one additional type of anxiety, Informational Reception Apprehension, when we discuss Conversation and Conflict in Chapter 6. Drawn from early work in receiver apprehension, informational reception apprehension affects our ability to receive information, including processing, interpreting, and dealing with an "information rich" environment.[68] Now, we turn to our final individual difference – cognitive complexity.

Cognitive Complexity

Cognitive complexity is important because it affects how we process information and how we form schemas. As you learned in Chapter 3, information processing and schemas are important in determining how we perceive and interpret incoming messages. Whether a personality trait or not, cognitive complexity has been identified as underlying a variety of communication-related skills and abilities affecting our perception as well as our message generation and reception.[69] In addition, research suggests that listening comprehension and memory are related to people's cognitive complexity. Thus, it is important for us to examine the effect individual differences in cognitive complexity may have on how we communicate with others.

Cognitive complexity addresses how you perceive the incoming message, organize it, and then use it to interpret the communication event. When looking at differences in cognitive complexity, we look at the number of constructs you are able to use or develop.[70] For example, individuals who are lower in cognitive complexity may describe Ben as a white male, majoring in Media Studies, who has one brother and one sister, while someone who is more cognitively complex may describe Ben as all of these things, as well as funny, friendly, and gregarious. As you can see, one way that individuals differ in cognitive complexity is that they are better able to identify a number of descriptors (also called elements or constructs) to apply to Ben Goleman. The ability to provide complex, detailed descriptions is often a sign someone is more cognitively complex. In addition, those high in complexity will often use more abstract descriptions. In our previous example, the first description is very concrete – white, male, with siblings, while the more "complex" description provides greater detail using more abstract terminology.

Think on it: Write a detailed paragraph about your best friend in high school. Write another paragraph about a classmate who wasn't a member of your circle. How do the two descriptions differ in detail and thoroughness?

Keep in mind, however, that cognitive complexity is not necessarily related to how smart someone is! It is more of an expert-novice distinction.[71] People who are experts have more abstract and better developed cognitive schemas. Subsequently, they will have more links among the elements composing their schemas (in this case, of Ben) and the ways in which they mentally organize those elements will be more complex.[72] However, someone who is cognitively complex about cats may be less so about dogs or computers or plumbing. Just as you are not experts on every topic, you are not cognitively complex in every area (or domain). Applied to how you interact with others, cognitive complexity provides you with a way of differentiating people in terms of their "social information-processing capacity."[73] Thus, you may be cognitively complex in your interpersonal relationships. Just as with other areas of expertise, interpersonal cognitive complexity is based upon knowledge, interactions, and experience with others. The resulting schemas can affect your communication in several ways. For example, cognitive complexity is believed to be associated with social perception skills including empathic perspective-taking.[74] It follows then that if you are more cognitively complex, you may be better able to understand how someone, such as a friend, is feeling.[75]

Cognitive complexity can affect your interpersonal interactions in other ways as well. People who tend to engage in **polarization** are believed to be less cognitively complex. For example, they tend to see people in bipolar dimensions – smart/stupid, mean/nice, etc. Not surprisingly, this limited perception colors how they view others. Individuals who are more complex will move beyond the concrete and begin to focus greater attention on more abstract levels of information such as psychological data and how it fits in with their concrete data – confident, secure, happy, etc. At this level, you would begin assigning causes or reasons for why Ben does a particular thing (e.g., snap at us, help with Habitat for Humanity). The ability to do this is called **person-centeredness.** Cognitively complex individuals are more likely to be person centered, tailoring their messages to match the person they are interacting with. Someone who is less complex may have more trouble doing this, especially with those they do not know very well. As a result, they may have greater difficulty differentiating between people or seeing each person as a unique individual.

At the same time, cognitively complex listeners respond more favorably to highly person-centered comforting messages.[76] These types of messages explicitly acknowledge and confirm the feelings of the listener, clearly express and provide reasons for those feelings, as well as show how the feelings fit and reflect the situation. In contrast, low person-centered messages typically deny, criticize, and/or challenge the listener's feelings. Senders using low person-centered messages are also more likely to tell receivers how to act and/or feel. While all receivers rate highly person-centered messages as more helpful, individuals high in interpersonal cognitive complexity give these messages even higher ratings. A primary reason for these differences is that highly cognitive individuals are believed to process such messages more deeply than their less complex counterparts.

Similarly, cognitively complex individuals are better able to process messages that contain multiple goals.[77] These goals may be related to the needs of the speaker, involve the relationship of the interactants, involve saving face, etc. For example, if Nolvia wants to borrow her parent's car (an instrumental goal), she may not want them to think of her as unable to manage her own life (saving-face) because she wants to be viewed as independent (relationship goal). Complex messages require a greater depth of processing. Notably, sophisticated, multi-goal messages are generally more effective than less sophisticated messages with all types of listeners, no matter how cognitively complex they may be. However, the more cognitively complex listener will gain more from the more nuanced complex message and respond more favorably to it, in contrast to their less complex counterparts. Thus, if her parents are more cognitively complex, they will be better able to gain the needed information and fully process it (and hopefully loan Nolvia their car). As noted earlier, cognitive complexity affects a variety of social perception skills, which in turn are related to our listening skills and ability.[78] For example, those who are cognitively complex have a larger, better defined cognitive system through which to interpret others' actions. As a result, they not only have a greater ability to generate several different motives or reasons for the behavior, but they are also better at generating multiple costs or benefits tied to those actions.

In addition, cognitively complex individuals are better able to reconcile incoming information that does not fit or conform to their schema for a person, place, etc. For example, let's assume for a moment that Tamarah tends to be quiet and does not say much during class discussions in her public speaking class. Ben, who's in the class with her, may develop an initial schema of her that is founded on communication apprehension. How confident will Ben think she will be? Will he think she will make an "A" or a "C" on her speech? When Tamarah gives her first major speech, she astounds Ben (and probably a lot of her classmates) by delivering a confident, well-supported, dynamic presentation. Now Ben has to adjust his original schema of Tamarah. If Ben is low in complexity, he may engage in polarization and simply substitute one schema (e.g., she's shy or apprehensive) for another (e.g., she's outgoing or is not apprehensive). However, if he is more cognitively complex, he will differentiate between the two situations (class discussion and speech making) and how Tamarah acts in each.

Think on it: Looking back at the discussion of Emotional Intelligence, how might EI be related to high versus low cognitive complexity?

Looking back at our listening model, you can see that cognitive complexity is related to Awareness, Translation, Retention, and Response. There is some debate among researchers about whether cognitive complexity is motivational (trait-like) or situational (state-like). Generally speaking, researchers are divided on the question of whether cognitive complexity is a personality trait.[79] Those who argue against it being a personality trait contend that it is not "motivational" in nature – that it doesn't predispose us to act in a particular way. We, however, tend to agree with scholars who have linked it to schema development and information processing – it is not so much related to intelligence as it is related to the level of expertise we have in a particular area (e.g., a best friend, a class mate, an instructor, wine, mushrooms, cats, dogs).

Build your skills: You can actually work at developing your cognitive complexity by broadening the topics or domains in which you are cognitively complex. How? Be curious! Expose yourself to new ideas. Read books and newspapers, research topics online. Watch or listen to programs that give you more than a 30-second spot of coverage on a topic. Ask your friends questions! This advice is particularly true for "opinionated" topics. It's not enough to know the facts about your political candidate or support for your belief or value, you should also learn as much as you can about the opposing side. Only then can you truly understand a person, topic, or issue. The more you know, the more developed your schemas become, and the more cognitively complex you will be.

Summary

As we finish our review of individual differences, there are several things we should consider. While these individual differences in listening have been associated with several personality and temperament traits, how much do differences actually direct your listening behavior? Watson and Barker, the scholars who researched listening style preferences, argue that we adapt our listening style to fit a situation. However, as you saw above, the different listening styles have been associated with concepts that are generally considered traits. It is true that most of these associations are small or moderate in nature. However, they do suggest that there may be a link between personality and our listening attitudes and behaviors? Thus we conclude this chapter asking a question that we posed at its beginning: "Is it nature or is it nurture?" What has the greatest impact on our listening abilities and skills? What do you think? What do your classmates think?

Key Concepts

Communibiology
Personality
    Temperament
    State versus Trait
MBTI Types
    Introversion and Extraversion
    Sensing and Intuiting
    Feeling and Thinking
    Judgment and Perception
Listening Style (LSP-16)
Listening Style (LSP-R)
Empathy
    Active-Empathic Listening
    Sociability
Conversational Sensitivity
Emotional Intelligence
    Emotional Awareness

Communication Apprehension
  Approach and Avoidance
  Generalized versus Conditioned Anxiety
  Social Relations
  Conversational Skills
  Nonverbal Leakage
Cognitive Complexity
  Polarization
  Person-centeredness

Discussion Questions

1. The LSP-R outlines several types of listening we may engage in depending on the context. Where do you feel you are most likely to use each of the types of listening? How does time or your relationship with the other person affect the style you choose?

2. We all experience communication apprehension on occasion. What types of situations tend to make you feel the most anxious? How does your apprehension affect your listening ability? What techniques can you use to help lessen your anxiety? Improve your listening?

3. On what topics, or with what individuals, would you say that you are cognitively complex or not? Why? Or why not?

Listening Activities

1. For 30 seconds each class member should write down as many alternative words or synonyms as they can for the color purple. Next, class members should gather into small groups based on their gender identity. In a three minute period, groups should first combine their individual brainstorming efforts, then try to come up with even more terms. Which individuals listed the greatest number of words? Who provided the most "sophisticated" list? What does this suggest about cognitive complexity on this topic?

2. After reading the different descriptions of the MBTI, write down which type you believe you are. Next, have two to three friends or family members read the descriptions. See if they agree with your personal assessment. If available, complete the Kiersey Temperament Sorter or the Myers–Briggs Indicator and see if you and your friends matched your scored types.

Notes

1 Bostrom, 1990
2 Bodie & Villaume, 2003; Chesebro, 1999; McCroskey, Daly, Martin, & Beatty, 1998; Pence & Vickery, 2012; Weaver, Watson, & Barker, 1996; Worthington, 2003
3 McCroskey, et al, 1998
4 Daly & Bippus, 1998
5 Beatty & McCroskey, 1998
6 See also, Bates, 1989; Bouchard, 1993; Kagen & Snidman, 2004; Lewis, 2008; Myers & McCaulley, 1985; Keirsey, 1998; O'Donnell, Falk, & Lieberman, 2015; and Worthington, 2003
7 American Psychological Association, 2002
8 Buss & Plomin, 1975
9 See Strelau, 1998, p. 35; Heck, et al., 2009

10 See Strelau, 1991

11 Gartstein & Rothbart, 2003

12 Buss & Plomin, 1975, p. 7.

13 For a more in-depth discussion of the terms trait and state and their relationship to measurement, see Daly & Bippus,1998. See also, Harkness, 2009

14 Keirsey, 1998

15 Carol Craig (Craig, n.d.) of the Center for Confidence and Well-being, a Scottish non-profit organization, offers a good summary of criticisms of the MBTI: http://bit.ly/MBTIreview.

16 Thompson & Ackerman, 1994

17 Myers & McCaulley, 1985

18 Myers & Myers, 1980, p. 1

19 Keirsey, 1998, p. 26

20 Myers & McCaulley, 1985, p. 13

21 Keirsey, 1998, p. 331

22 Myers & McCaulley, 1985, p. 12

23 Myers & McCaulley, 1985, p. 12

24 McCaulley, 1990

25 Keirsey, 1998

26 Myers & McCaulley, 1985, p. 12

27 McCaulley, 1990, p. 183

28 McCaulley, 1990, p. 183

29 Myers & McCaulley, 1985, p. 12–13

30 Watson & Barker, 1992; Watson et al., 1995

31 Imhof, 2004

32 Bodie, Worthington, & Gearhart, 2013, p. 86; see also Bodie & Worthington, 2010

33 Worthington, 2003

34 Myers & McCaulley, 1985

35 Weaver & Kirtley, 1995; Chesebro, 1999

36 Bodie, Gearhart, et al., 2013

37 Worthington, 2003

38 Keyton & Rhodes, 1994, p. 59

39 Keaton, Bodie, & Keteyian, 2015

40 Gearhart, Denham & Bodie, 2014

41 Gearhart et al., 2014.

42 Gearhart et al., 2014, p. 680.

43 Comer & Drollinger, 1999; Drollinger, Comer & Warrington, 2006; see Bodie, 2011 and Bodie et al., 2013, for scale development in social contexts

44 Comer & Drollinger, 1999; Drollinger et al., 2006

45 Bodie, 2011; Bodie & Jones, 2012; Bodie et al., 2014

46 see Keaton, 2017, for a review and critique

47 Gearhart & Bodie, 2011; Bodie, Gearhart, et al., 2013

48 Keaton, 2017

49 Gearhart & Bodie, 2011

50 Bodie, 2011

51 Ramsey & Sohi, 1997

52 Richendoller & Weaver, 1994

53 Daly, et al., 1987

54 Salovey & Mayer, 1990; Mayer & Salovey, 1997; Petrides & Furnham, 2000, 2001

55 Van Der Zee & Wabeke, 2004

56 Salovey, Mayer, Caruso, & Lopes, 2003, p. 251

57 Salovey et al., 2003, p. 253

58 Smith, Ciarrochi, & Heaven, 2008
59 Bar-On et al., 2007, p. 4
60 See Bar-On et al., 2007, for a summary of EI research findings
61 Dillon & McKenzie, 1998
62 Beatty, Heisel, Hall, Levine, & LaFrance, 2002
63 McCroskey, Beatty, Kearney, & Plax, 1985
64 McCroskey, et al., 1998
65 Beatty, McCroskey, & Heisel, 1998; Shimotsu & Mottett, 2009; Wahba & McCroskey, 2005; Wrench, Brogan, McCroskey, & Jowi, 2008
66 McCroskey, et al., 1998
67 Blume, Balwin, & Ryan, 2013; McCroskey, et al., 1998
68 Wheeless, 1975; Wheeless & Schrodt, 2001; Wheeless, Eddleman-Spears, Magness, & Preiss, 2005
69 Burleson & Caplan, 1998
70 Beatty & Payne, 1981
71 Burleson & Caplan, 1998
72 See Burleson & Caplan, 1998; Daly, Bell, Glenn & Lawrence, 1985; Ericsson & Smith, 1991; Fiske & Taylor, 1991; Hoffman, 1992
73 Burleson & Caplan, 1998
74 Burleson & Caplan, 1998
75 Beatty & Payne, 1981
76 For a brief review, see Burleson, 2011
77 For a brief review, see Burleson, 2011
78 Burleson, 1987
79 Burleson, & Caplan, 1998

Additional Readings

Bar-On, R., Maree, J. G., Elias, M. J. (Eds.). (2007). *Educating people to be emotionally intelligent.* Westport, CT: Praeger.

Beatty, M. J., McCroskey, J. C., & Valencic, K. M. (2001). *The biology of communication: A communibiological perspective.* Cresskill, NJ: Hampton.

Matthews, G., Zeidner, M., & Roberts, R. D. (2002). *Emotional intelligence: Science and myth.* Cambridge, MA: MIT Press.

Horwitz, B. (2002). *Communication apprehension: Origins and management.* Albany, NY: Thomson.

Boren, J. P., & Veksler, A. E. (2011). A decade of research exploring biology and communication: The brain, nervous, endocrine, cardiovascular, and immune systems. *Communication Research Trends, 30,* 1–31.

Brommelje, R., Houston, J. M., & Smither, R. (2003). Personality characteristics of effective listeners: A five factor perspective. *International Journal of Listening, 17,* 32–46.

References

American Psychological Association. (2002). Psychology Matters. APAOnline Glossary. [From R. J. Gerrig & P. G. Zimbardo. *Psychology and Life, 16/e* Published by Allyn & Bacon, Boston. Copyright (c) 2002 by Pearson Education.] Retrieved from www.psychologymatters.org/glossary.html.

Bar-On, R., Maree, J. G., & Elias, M. J. (Eds.). (2007). *Educating people to be emotionally intelligent.* Westport, CT: Praeger.

Bates, J. E. (1989). Concepts and measures of temperament. In G. A. Kohnstamm, J. E. Bates, & M. K. Rothbart (Eds.), *Temperament in childhood* (pp. 3–26). NY: Wiley.

Beatty, M. J., Heisel, A. D., Hall, A. E., Levine, T. R., & LaFrance, B. H. (2002). What can we learn from the study of twins about genetic and environmental influences on interpersonal affiliation, aggressiveness, and social anxiety? A meta-analytic study. *Communication Monographs, 69,* 1–18.

Beatty, M. J., & McCroskey, J. C. (1998). Interpersonal communication as temperamental expression: A communibiological paradigm. In J. C. McCroskey, J. A. Daly, M. M. Martin, & M. J. Beatty (Eds.), *Communication and personality* (pp. 41–67). Cresskill, NJ: Hampton Press.

Beatty, M. J., McCroskey, J. C., & Heisel, A. D. (1998). Communication apprehension as temperamental expression: A communibiological paradigm. *Communication Monographs, 65,* 197–219.

Beatty, M. J., & Payne, S. K. (1981). Receiver apprehension and cognitive complexity. *Western Journal of Speech Communication, 45,* 363–369.

Blume, B. D., Baldwin, T. T., & Ryan, K. C. (2013). Communication apprehension: A barrier to students' leadership, adaptability, and multicultural appreciation. *Academy of Management Learning & Education, 12,* 158–172.

Bodie, G. D. (2011). The Active-Empathic Listening Scale (AELS): Conceptualization and evidence of validity within the interpersonal domain. *Communication Quarterly, 59,* 277–295.

Bodie, G. D., Gearhart, C. C., Denham, J. P., & Vickery, A. J. (2013). The temporal stability and situational contingency of active-empathic listening. *Western Journal of Communication, 77,* 113–138.

Bodie, G. D., & Jones, S. M. (2012). The nature of supportive listening II: The role of verbal person centeredness and nonverbal immediacy. *Western Journal of Communication, 76,* 250–269.

Bodie, G. D., Jones, S. M., Vickery, A. J., Hatcher, L., & Cannava, K. (2014). Examining the construct validity of enacted support: A multitrait-multimethod analysis of three perspectives for judging immediacy and listening behaviors. *Communication Monographs, 81,* 495–523.

Bodie, G. D., Vickery, A. J., & Gearhart, C. C. (2013). The nature of supportive listening, I: Exploring the relation between supportive listeners and supportive people. *International Journal of Listening, 27,* 39–49.

Bodie, G., & Villaume, W. A. (2003). Aspects of receiving information: The relationship between listening preferences, communication apprehension, receiver apprehension, and communicator style. *International Journal of Listening, 17,* 47–67.

Bodie, G. D., & Worthington, D. L. (2010). Revisiting the Listening Styles Profile (LSP-16): A confirmatory factor analytic approach to scale validation and reliability estimation. *International Journal of Listening, 24,* 69–88.

Bodie, G. D., Worthington, D. L., & Gearhart, C. C. (2013). The revised Listening Styles Profile (LSP-R): Development and validation. *Communication Quarterly, 61,* 72–90.

Bostrom, R. N. (1990). *Listening behavior: Measurement and application.* NY: Guilford.

Bouchard, T. J. (1993). Genetic and environmental influence on adult personality: Evaluating the evidence. In J. Hettema & I. J. Deary (Eds.), *Foundations of personality* (pp. 15–44). Norwell, MA: Kluwer Academic.

Burleson, B. R. (1987). Cognitive complexity. In J. C. McCroskey & J. A. Daly (Eds.), *Personality and interpersonal communication* (pp. 305–349). Newbury Park, CA: Sage.

Burleson, B. R. (2011). A constructivist approach to listening. *The International Journal of Listening, 25,* 27–46.

Burleson, B. R., & Caplan, S. E. (1998). Cognitive complexity. In J. C. McCroskey, J. A. Daly, M. M. Martin, & M. J. Beatty (Eds.), *Communication and personality* (pp. 41–67). Cresskill, NJ: Hampton Press.

Buss, A. H., & Plomin, R. (1975). *A temperament theory of personality development.* NY: John Wiley & Sons.

Chesebro, J. L. (1999). The relationship between listening styles and conversational sensitivity. *Communication Research Reports, 16,* 233–238.

Comer, L. B, & Drollinger, T. (1999). Active empathetic listening and selling success: A conceptual framework. *Journal of Personal Selling & Sales Management, 19,* 15–29.

Craig, C. (n.d.). Criticism of the MBTI. Centre for Confidence and Well-Being. Retrieved from www.centreforconfidence.co.uk/resources.php?pid=335.

Daly, J. A., Bell, R. A., Glenn, P. J., & Lawrence, S. (1985). Conceptualizing conversational complexity. *Human Communication Research, 12,* 30–53.

Daly, J. A., & Bippus, A. (1998). Personality and interpersonal communication: Issues and directions. In J. C. McCroskey, J. A. Daly, M. M. Martin, & M. J. Beatty (Eds.), *Communication and personality: Trait perspectives* (pp. 1–40). Cresskill, NJ: Hampton.

Daly, J. A., Vangelisti, A. L., & Doughton, S. M. (1987). The nature and correlates of conversational sensitivity. *Human Communication Research, 14*, 167–202.

Dillon, R. K., & McKenzie, N. J. (1998). The influence of ethnicity on listening, communication competence, approach, and avoidance. *International Journal of Listening, 12*, 160–171.

Drollinger, T., Comer, L. B., & Warrington, P. T. (2006). Development and validation of the active empathetic listening scale. *Psychology & Marketing, 23*, 161–180.

Ericsson, K. A., & Smith, J. (Eds.). (1991). *Toward a general theory of expertise: Prospects and limits.* NY: Cambridge University Press.

Fiske, S. T., & Taylor, S. E. (1991). *Social cognition* (2nd ed.). NY: McGraw-Hill.

Gartstein, M. A., & Rothbart, M. K. (2003). Studying infant temperament via the Revised Infant Behavior Questionnaire. *Infant Behavior and Development, 26*, 64–86.

Gearhart, C. C., & Bodie, G. D. (2011). Active-empathic listening as a general social skill: Evidence from bivariate and canonical correlations. *Communication Reports, 24*, 86–98.

Gearhart, C. C., Denham, J. D., & Bodie, G. D. (2014). Listening as a goal directed activity. *Western Journal of Communication, 78*, 668–684.

Harkness, A. R. (2009). Theory and measurement of personality traits. In J. N. Butcher (Ed.), *Oxford handbook of personality assessment* (pp. 150–162). New York: Oxford University Press.

Heck, A., Lieb, R., Ellgas, A., Pfister, H., Lucae, S., Roeske, D., Pütz, B., Müller-Myhsok, B., Uhr, M., Holsboer, F., & Ising, M. (2009). Investigation of 17 candidate genes for personality traits confirms effects of the HTR2A gene on novelty seeking. *Genes Brain Behavior, 8*, 464–472.

Hoffman, R. R. (1992). *The psychology of expertise: Cognitive research and empirical findings.* NY: Springer-Verlag.

Imhof, M. (2004). Who are we as we listen? Individual listening profiles in varying contexts. *International Journal of Listening, 18*, 36–46.

Kagan, J., & Snidman, N. (2004). *The long shadow of temperament.* Cambridge, MA: Belknap.

Keaton, S. A. (2017). Active-empathic listening scale. In D. L. Worthington & G. Bodie (Eds.), *The sourcebook of listening: Measures and methodology.* (pp. 161–166). Malden, MA: Wiley.

Keaton, S. A., Bodie, G. D., & Keteyian, R. V. (2015). Relational listening goals influence how people report preferring to talk about problems. *Communication Quarterly, 63*, 480–494.

Keirsey, D. (1998). *Please understand me II.* Del Mar, CA: Prometheus Nemesis.

Keyton, J., & Rhodes, S. (1994). The effects of listener preference styles on identifying sexual harassment. *Journal of the International Listening Association, 8*, 50–79.

Lewis, R. J. (2008). *Neural characteristics of affectionate communicators: Trait affection and asymmetry in the prefrontal cortex.* (Master's Thesis). UMI Number: 1454917.

Mayer, J. D., & Salovey, P. (1997). What is emotional intelligence? In P. Salovey & D. Sluyter (Eds.), *Emotional development and emotional intelligence: Implications for educators* (pp. 3–31). NY: Basic Books.

McCaulley, M. H. (1990). The Myers–Briggs type indicator: A measure for individuals and groups. *Measurement and Evaluation in Counseling and Development, 22*, 181–195.

McCroskey, J. C., Beatty, M. J., Kearney, P. & Plax, T. G. (1985). The content validity of the PRCA-24 as a measure of communication apprehension across communication contexts. *Communication Quarterly, 33*, 165–173.

McCroskey, J. C., Daly, J. A., Martin, M. M., & Beatty, M. J. (1998). *Communication and personality: Trait perspectives.* Cresskill, NJ: Hampton.

Myers, I. B., & McCaulley, M. H. (1985). *Manual: A guide to the development and use of the Myers–Briggs Type Indicator.* Palo Alto, CA: Consulting Psychologists Press.

Myers, I. B., & Myers, P. B. (1980). *Gifts differing.* Palo Alto, CA: Consulting Psychologists Press.

O'Donnell, M. B., Falk, E. B., & Lieberman, M. D. (2015). Social in, social out: How the brain responds to social language with more social language. *Communication Monographs, 82*, 31–63.

Pence, M. E., & Vickery, A. J. (2012). The roles of personality and trait emotional intelligence in the active-empathic listening process: Evidence from correlational and regression analyses. *International Journal of Listening, 26*, 159–174.

Petrides, K. V., & Furnham, A. (2000). Gender differences in measured and self-estimated trait emotional intelligence. *Sex Roles, 42,* 449–461.

Petrides, K. V., & Furnham, A. (2001). Trait emotional intelligence: psychometric investigation with reference to established trait taxonomies. *European Journal of Personality,15,* 425–448.

Ramsey, R. P., & Sohi, R. S. (1997). Listening to your customers: The impact of perceived salesperson listening behavior on relationship outcomes. *Journal of the Academy of Marketing Science, 25,* 127–137.

Richendoller, N. R., & Weaver, J. B. (1994). Exploring the links between personality and empathic response style. *Personality and Individual Differences, 17,* 303–311.

Salovey, P., & Mayer, J. D. (1990). Emotional intelligence. *Imagination, Cognition, and Personality, 9,* 185–211.

Salovey, P., Mayer, J. D., Caruso, D., & Lopes, P. N. (2003). In S. J. Lopez & C. R. Snyder (Ed.), *Positive psychological assessment: A handbook of models and measures.* (pp. 251–265). Washington, DC, US: APA.

Shimotsu, S., & Mottett, T. P. (2009). The relationships among perfectionism, communication apprehension, and temperament. *Communication Research Reports, 26,* 188–197.

Smith, L., Ciarrochi, J., & Heaven, P. C. L. (2008). The stability and change of trait emotional intelligence, conflict communication patterns, and relationship satisfaction: A one-year longitudinal study. *Personality & Individual Differences, 45,* 738–743.

Strelau, J. (1991). *Explorations in temperament.* NY: Plenum.

Strelau, J. (1998). *Temperament: A psychological perspective.* NY: Plenum.

Thompson, B., & Ackerman, C. (1994) Review of the Myers–Briggs type indicator. In J. Kapes, M. Mestie, & E. Whitfield (Eds.), *A counselor's guide to career assessment instruments* (3rd ed., pp. 283–287). Alexandria, VA: American Counseling Association.

Van Der Zee, K., & Wabeke, R. (2004). Is trait-emotional intelligence simply or more than just a trait? *European Journal of Personality, 18,* 243–263.

Wahba, J. S., & McCroskey, J. C. (2005). Temperament and brain systems as predictors of assertive communication traits. *Communication Research Reports, 22,* 157–164.

Watson, K. W., & Barker, L. L. (1992). Comparison of the ETS national teacher examination listening model with models used in two standardized tests. *International Journal of Listening, 6,* 32–44.

Watson, K. W., Barker, L. L., & Weaver, J. B., III. (1995). The listening styles profile (LS-16): Development and validation of an instrument to assess four listening styles. *International Journal of Listening, 9,* 1–13.

Weaver, J. B., III, & Kirtley, M. D. (1995). Listening styles and empathy. *Southern Journal of Speech Communication, 60,* 131–140.

Weaver, J. B., III, Watson, K. W., & Barker, L. L. (1996). Individual differences in listening style: Do you hear what I hear? *Personality and Individual Differences, 20,* 381–387.

Wheeless, L. (1975). An investigation of receiver apprehension and social context dimension of communication apprehension. *Communication Education, 24,* 261–268.

Wheeless, L. R., Eddleman-Spears, L., Magness, L. D., & Preiss, R. W. (2005). Informational reception apprehension and information from technology aversion: Development of a new construct. *Communication Quarterly, 53,* 143–158.

Wheeless, L. R., & Schrodt, P. (2001). An examination of cognitive foundations of informational reception apprehension: Political identification, religious affiliation, and family environment. *Communication Research Reports, 18,* 1–10.

Worthington, D. L. (2001). Exploring juror listening processes: The effect of listening style preference on juror decision making. *International Journal of Listening, 15,* 20–35.

Worthington, D. L. (2003). Exploring the relationship between listening style preference and personality. *International Journal of Listening, 17,* 68–87.

Wrench, J. S., Brogan, S. M., McCroskey, J. C., & Jowi, D. (2008). Social communication apprehension: The intersection of communication apprehension and social phobia. *Human Communication, 11,* 409–429.

5   Listening in a Mediated World

Case Study 5.1 What do You Mean I'm not Listening to You?

Our group is meeting at Tamarah's house working on their project. In front of everyone is a mobile device of some description.

NaMii: *Oh no, I just noticed we all have our smartphones on the table and I think everyone has checked something on the phone at least once. We just talked about this in class.*

Carter: *You're right, NaMii. Hey, Ben, are you checking the game score or are you Googling something about the project?*

Ben: *Carter, you sound like my dad. It bothers him anytime someone picks up a tablet or a smart phone when he's talking. He doesn't realize I can listen to him and text you at the same time.*

Carter: *Yeah, right. That explains the text you sent me the other day! What is the score? Ben, are you with us?*

Ben: *I'm more than with you. I was checking my email and, yes, it was project related. I just got a reply from Professor Bodie and he is willing to talk with us about how technology is affecting how we listen. He has some time in an hour.*

Carter: *An hour? We haven't finalized our questions! And we've got to set up where we'll interview from. Tamarah, what's the password for your Wi-Fi? Can we borrow your dining room?*

It seems that our world is getting increasingly noisy. But, as our model in Chapter 1 and our case study above illustrates, noise goes beyond sound vibrations hitting our ears. It also includes environmental and mental distractions that affect all of our listening senses. Unfortunately, we are rarely aware of the impact that noise and distractions have upon our ability to listen well. This is particularly true when it comes to media use. Technology presents many opportunities, but it also can negatively impact our listening. In this chapter, we explore the effect of various media on our listening processes.

Noise Sensitivity

We discussed a number of individual differences in Chapter 4. We saved noise sensitivity for this chapter because it is so closely tied to this topic. When we think about noise, it is easy to think about it as a physical sensation. The Centers for Disease Control and Prevention estimates about 15% of the US population lives with constant noise. Tinnitus (TINitus), or ringing in the ears, is a medical problem that some people experience. But even for these individuals, some are more bothered by the noise in their head than others. Unfortunately, tinnitus is not very well understood. While it has been associated with some drugs (e.g., aspirin regime) and some physical injuries (soldiers and others who have been close to bomb blasts), doctors still do not completely understand why one person develops tinnitus, while others do not. Tinnitus is not to be confused with noise sensitivity.

Learn more: If you or someone you know has tinnitus, you can learn more about the condition, its causes, and possible treatments from the American Tinnitus Association: www. ata.org. Founded in 1971, ATA has worked on a global level to help find a cure for tinnitus by bringing together patients and researchers, health care professionals and others to create alliances and fund medical research.

The phrase **noise sensitivity** is pretty much self-explanatory. *Noise*, one of the most examined of our auditory reactions, has been referred to in any number of ways. It may be a sound that is unpleasant or loud, disturbing or annoying. Just as beauty is in the eye of the beholder, noise is in the ear of the hearer. What is annoying to you (water dripping) may be ignored or has no impact on your best friend. Noise sensitivity includes both a *stimulus* (the annoying sound) and a *psychological reaction* (this sound annoys me).[1] Early studies of noise sensitivity focused on the annoyance associated with different types of transportation modes, such as airplanes, railways, car and truck traffic, as well as noise associated with some types of factories and other types of manufacturing.[2]

Concern over the noise pollution caused by mobile devices has grown over the last decade. Today there are building materials specially designed to block or reduce mobile phone pollution.[3] As you can imagine, theatre and concert hall owners are particularly interested in such developments. Of course, other areas are designated as quiet spaces (e.g., libraries, doctor offices). Even cities have attempted to address mobile phone noise. The New York City Department of Environmental Protection's *Guide to New York City's Noise Code* discusses keeping mobile phone conversations "to a minimum in public spaces, especially confined areas like public transit," while the township of West Bloomfield suggests residents keep their mobile phone ringer at its lowest volume to reduce noise pollution.[4]

When we discuss noise, we are not only concentrating on loud noises, such as a car with speakers blasting, construction noises and the like, we also are addressing background or what is known as low-level noise. Low-level noise, whether in your home, at work, or in your school, can be quite distracting and disrupt your concentration. Health-wise, it can increase general stress levels and make other illnesses worse, including heart-related diseases, migraines and stomach ulcers. It may also result in lower dopamine availability in our prefrontal cortex, which in turn, may affect higher brain functions, including those related to memory.[5]

Noise sensitivity is believed to be a stable personality trait, such that those higher in sensitivity typically react more strongly to perceived noise.[6] Thus, if you are sensitive to noise, you will become aware of an annoying sound sooner than your less sensitive friends.[7] You will also tend to rate the sound more negatively than they will.[8] These two facts are true no matter the actual noise level.[9]

Think on it: Are there repetitive sounds in your daily life that you no longer attend to? People who live in the city may not hear sirens, while those who live on a beach may not hear waves. Do you hear noises at a friend's home or apartment that they do not seem to hear? Are they surprised when you point them out?

George Luz, a research psychologists with Luz Social and Environmental Associates, notes that if you are hypersensitive to noise, you may have a more *active orienting response* or reflex.[10] This response harks back to our days as hunter-gatherers, when hearing something new or strange resulted in heightened senses, and a flight-fight response. While today the focus is typically not on survival, we still actively orient to new sounds. However, we become accustomed to a sound through a process called *habitation.* For instance, most people who live by train tracks eventually no longer "hear" trains that go by. However, if you are noise sensitive you may find it difficult to tune out repeated sounds such as this or other intermittent audio sounds.[11] In fact, continued exposure typically does not result in habitation. Noise sensitivity does have some serious physiological and psychological responses, such as difficulty focusing or concentrating and increased errors when completing tasks.[12] Physiological responses include increased anxiety and blood pressure, changes in heart rate, depression, and problems sleeping.[13]

Tangential research suggests that highly noise sensitive individuals may focus so much internal attention on the offending noise that it interferes with their ability to attend to communication and social cues, making it more difficult to engage in social roles and behaviors effectively.[14] While not directly studying noise sensitivity, Communication Professor Christopher Gearhart found that sensitive individuals process information more deeply, which may result in a cognitive backlog, particularly when they experience multiple or particularly intense stimuli. Thus, your noise sensitive friend, when attending a large and noisy party, may experience cognitive overload, be distracted, and not as responsive to your conversation with him. He may pause longer, have difficulty listening, and be less adept at reading your verbal and nonverbal cues.

You may already have an idea if you are noise sensitive or not. If you can sleep through barking dogs, the neighbor's stereo, or a steadily dripping sink, you are probably not that noise sensitive. Of course, this does not mean that you ignore such sounds all the time. Anxiety about classes or a relational break-up may make you more sensitive than usual to the noises around you, particularly when trying to sleep. Remember, noise sensitivity is a general personality trait. While the Noise Sensitivity Scale presented in this chapter will give you some idea of your general sensitivity, bear in mind that your sensitivity may change with context. If you are from a small town, traffic noises may be particularly bothersome when visiting a large city.

Noise sensitivity is only one thing that may affect mediated listening. Sensitivity to any type of distraction can have a serious effect on our ability to listen. Closely related to the concept of noise sensitivity is **listening effort** (i.e., the "cognitive resources allocated for speech recognition").[15] This concept is related to cognitive load, which we discussed in Chapter 1. The demands made on cognitive resources by internal and external noise results in fewer mental resources for recall, affects the mental rehearsal necessary for memory, and impacts our capacity to scan the environment. All of these processes are necessary for quality listening.

Scale 5.1 Weinstein's Noise Sensitivity Scale (WNSS-21)

Instructions: Below are a number of statements addressing individual reactions to noise. After reading each statement, please circle the number that best represents your level of agreement with the statement. For each item please use the following scale:

1	2	3	4	5
Strongly Disagree				Strongly Agree

1. I wouldn't mind living on a noisy street if the apartment I had was nice. 1 2 3 4 5

2. I am more aware of noise than I used to be.* 1 2 3 4 5

3. No one should mind much if someone turns up his or her stereo full blast once in a while. 1 2 3 4 5

4. At movies, whispering and crinkling candy wrappers disturb me.* 1 2 3 4 5

5. I am easily awakened by noise.* 1 2 3 4 5

6. If it's noisy where I'm studying, I try to close the door or window or move someplace else.* 1 2 3 4 5

7. I get annoyed when my neighbors are noisy.* 1 2 3 4 5

8. I get used to most noises without much difficulty. 1 2 3 4 5

9. It would matter to me if an apartment I was interested in renting was located across from a fire station.* 1 2 3 4 5

10. Sometimes noises get on my nerves and get me irritated.* 1 2 3 4 5

11. Even music I normally like will bother me if I'm trying to concentrate.* 1 2 3 4 5

12. It wouldn't bother me to hear the sounds of everyday living from neighbors (footsteps, running water, etc.). 1 2 3 4 5

13. When I want to be alone, it disturbs me to hear outside noises.* 1 2 3 4 5

14. I'm good at concentrating no matter what is going on around me. 1 2 3 4 5

15. In a library, I don't mind if people carry on a conversation if they do it quietly. 1 2 3 4 5

16. There are often times when I want complete silence.* 1 2 3 4 5

17. Motorcycles ought to be required to have bigger mufflers.* 1 2 3 4 5

18. I find it hard to relax in a place that's noisy.* 1 2 3 4 5

19. I get mad at people who make noise that keeps me from falling asleep or getting work done.* 1 2 3 4 5

20. I wouldn't mind living in an apartment with thin walls. 1 2 3 4 5

21. I am sensitive to noise.* 1 2 3 4 5

Reprinted with permission. Weinstein (1978).

Items marked with an asterisk (*) should be reverse coded prior to scoring (i.e., 5 = 1, 4 = 2, 2 = 4, 1 = 5). After reverse scoring, total your score for all items. Scores range from a low of 21 to a high of 105. For self-evaluation purposes, high scores range from 80 to 105, low scores range from 21 to 45.

Note: For a description of item revisions, a critique of the Weinstein Noise Sensitivity scale and a description of related findings associated with noise sensitivity, see Worthington, 2017.

While electronic devices expand our listening opportunities, they also present communication and listening challenges. We next explore the effect of such devices on mediated social interactions.

Mediated Social Interactions

As social media platforms such as Facebook and Twitter gained popularity, both the public and researchers often viewed social media and social interactions as interchangeable concepts. However, University of Kansas Professor Jeffrey Hall disagrees. As he writes, "the social processes of meaning-making and relationship maintenance are central functions of media in general."[16] However, the degree and quality of the *social* experience users have will differ based on the level of interactivity of a particular platform (e.g., Facebook, FaceTime, Instagram). In a nutshell, he argues that social media is not the equivalent of social interaction. This distinction is important as early research in social media often equated use of a platform with interaction. For example, some studies addressing loneliness treated face-to-face (F2F) interactions as the same as, say, Facebook interactions. Hall says such an equivalence is "as misleading as [making] comparisons between people watching and having a conversation."[17]

Instead, Hall argues that mediated social interactions must reflect what sociologist Irving Goffman described as a privileged **focused social interaction**. Focused social interactions require that the conversational partners acknowledge each other as a unique individual. Thus, waving to a friend across a parking lot or Liking a Facebook post do not qualify as a focused social interaction. These types of routine interactions are more impersonal and are typically studied in relation to schemas, scripts or the roles we play. Put another way, you would wave to any friend across the parking lot, whether Celeste, Robert, or Margarete. If you work at a restaurant, your interaction with customers while taking an order would not qualify either.

Focused social interactions are further defined by the relationship ties we have with someone. Close relationships ties are hallmarked by stability over time, as well as the ability to recognize and recall the unique qualities of an individual. Many of your Facebook friends are probably friends and family, but many others are likely acquaintances. In fact, one estimate suggests that most people are in a close relationship with only about 20% of their Facebook "Friends."[18]

Thus, *focused social interactions* require that both you and the other person acknowledge a shared relationship, that conversational exchanges occur, and that both of you focus attention on the exchange. **Mediated social interactions** also require these elements. The only difference is that the conversation is facilitated by the use of technology. We can compare various technologies based on the dimensions of synchrony, social presence and reach. **Synchrony** addresses time delays that may occur. F2F and Google Hangouts conversations are *synchronous*; email is *asynchronous*. Skyped and F2F conversations also have greater **social presence** than email. Social presence refers to connectedness we feel with others. The greater the level to which a medium conveys social cues (e.g., eye contact, tone of voice, immediacy, etc.), the greater its social presence. Finally, a medium's **reach** reflects the number of people who can and/or do receive a message. You may use ooVoo (a synchronous platform) to arrange a video chat with all four of your brothers (reach) to learn how much they agree with the idea of your Father's surprise birthday party (social presence). Needless to say, chat programs are best able to meet the conditions for mediated social interactions.

Notably, most individuals recognize that their social media use does not qualify as social interactions. In fact, one recent study reported that participants reported approximately 98% of their social interactions did not involve social media. When they did, the interactions typically involved chatting (although posting on one another's walls was sometimes included). Dr. Hall notes that text-based chatting also meets the definition of social interactions and can lead to "digital intimacy" as well as affinity seeking and relationship maintenance. However, actions such as liking, re-tweeting, re-posting and re-gramming were not viewed as social interactions and did not contribute to feelings of relatedness. Perhaps the most important implication of his work is that it supports arguments "that social interaction is likely to take place with relational intimates for the purpose of conversation." While all social interactions engendered feelings of relatedness, general social media use did not.

Mobile Devices

Addressing the growth of digital technology and its consequences, Professor Sherry Turkle argues that as technology communications have grown, we rely on them more and on people less.[19] People and relationships can be messy. Her research suggests that as people, particularly adolescents, spend greater time with technology, their ability to empathize and deal with the complexity of conversations and relationships diminishes. Not only did teachers in her study report lower empathy levels in their adolescent students, but also that the children seemed to have a reduced ability to develop close relationships. Teenagers feels awkward with their still developing conversational skills – it is easier to deal with others at a distance, such as using texting or Facebook postings. They avoid synchronous social interactions, which means they have fewer opportunities to improve their conversational skills. It is these social interactions that teach us empathy and lead us to develop closer, more intimate friendships, and eventually romances. In extreme cases, some people become unwilling to put in the effort that a F2F conversation requires.

Of course, these findings can also be applied to adults. How often do children compete with a tablet or smartphone for their parents' attention? How do friends keep a conversation going if their peers are checking Instagram? How do we solve problems and build working relationships when our colleagues email us rather than working with us directly. Politically, we search for those who think the same as we do, to avoid potential conflicts. Conversations, the cornerstone of both democracy and business, are as Dr. Turkle puts it, "good for the bottom line." We may have conflict, but conversations also have the potential to generate positive solutions. In our private lives, they "build empathy, friendship, love, learning, and productivity." The good news is that Professor Turkle believes that as we come to terms with the cultural changes introduced by computers, smartphones and other digital technologies, we have a better understanding of what technology can and cannot do for us. As she concludes, conversation is "the most human – and humanizing – thing that we do."[20]

Not surprisingly, one of the fastest growing areas of listening research addresses the myriad of ways technology and media affect us. Arguably, the most significant technology in our daily life is the mobile phone. Mobile phones have fundamentally altered the way we communicate with others.[21] Today, we expect instant access to family and friends. You carry on mobile conversations while in line at the grocery store, at dinner with friends, and as you move from one class to another. In this respect, they have both expanded and contracted our world. Today, when you sit waiting for a class to start, you may be watching a YouTube video or texting someone. As a result, you're not communicating with those around you. So, while you can reach out and "touch" someone across the country or around the world, you may not be getting to know those sitting next to you in class. Your world becomes smaller when you lose the opportunity to interact and communicate with new others in your world. The fact is that most of us communicate with a small, select group of individuals on a daily basis. When we focus almost exclusively on our mobile devices, we miss meeting the person who could be our new best friend, study partner, or spouse. Of course, the mobile phone is only one of many new technologies that you have grown up with. The question, however, is how mobile devices and related media affect our interactions with others.

From a listening perspective, you have likely noticed that when you're on the phone it is often difficult to focus on those around you. When you focus on the **absent other** (the person on the other end of the connection) rather than those around you, **caller hegemony** occurs.[22] The caller, or absent other, becomes your immediate focus and priority, often to the detriment of your conversations with friends or family.[23] As we saw in our case study at the beginning of the chapter, we can experience problems listening when we use our mobile phones to media multitask (e.g., checking Pinterest, texting others, etc.) while in a social interaction with others. Referencing our Listening MATERRS Model, we see problems arise in multiple areas, but particularly with attention and recall. Media multitasking can also affect our social and psychological wellbeing. As we outlined above, multitasking pulls on a number of cognitive resources. Frequent media multitasking during F2F conversations is typically viewed negatively. In general, multitaskers are seen as having less self-control, being less socially successful, and have lower feelings of being understood and accepted by peers.[24] One reason for these findings is that focused social interactions are needed to build relationships and understanding between individuals. The constant interruption of attending to texts, tweets and Reddit postings interferes with the relationship building process. You are not truly *listening* to your friends' description of her bad day at work or his recent date, which negatively affects your relationship and also reduces feelings of closeness and understanding, for both you and them. Importantly, self-control, social success and understanding all contribute to our psychological wellbeing. Thus, regulating your behavior (i.e., checking a text or retweeting later) can positively benefit your relationships at work, with friends and with family. Think about it. How do you feel when your friend puts his mobile phone away (especially without looking at who just texted)? What does it say about how he values you? The interaction? Synchronous social interactions are a key element to building meaningful relationships and maintaining good mental health.[25] As communication activities, these interactions provide greater immediate feedback, more focused conversation, and build interpersonal relationships.

Now, we are not saying that mobile devices are evil and that you should put them away whenever someone walks into your room or at every lunch with friends (although personally, we think it's a good idea). The fact is that mobile devices can actually contribute to social interactions that are more entertainment oriented.[26] For example, using your tablet or smartphone to talk or chat with someone while watching the same program can be fun and contribute to a positive social experience. Similarly, using a device to look up and share past sports scores or information on a player while jointly watching a game, snapchatting with friends while at a concert, or posting photos to Kik and then chatting with friends are ways to expand the immediate conversation and joint activity. What is important is making deliberate decisions about how and when to use technology, given the context, the people involved, your relationship with them, and the type and nature of the conversational topic.

A Cautionary Comic For Writers

I AM GOING TO GET *SO* MUCH WRITING DONE TODAY!

BUT FIRST, I'LL JUST CHECK E-MAIL ONE MORE TIME...

Check e-mail.

Follow link in e-mail.

Find great blog post, decides to forward it to a friend.

Also tweets about it.

Friend loves it, asks about getting together for coffee.

Oh, and on Facebook, too!

Checks calendar. Notices an upcoming event she forgot about!

While on Twitter, notices some other interesting tweets...

While on Facebook, catches up on reading posts...

Doublechecks dates on Web. While on Web, realizes she wanted to research other attendees...

Discovers a fab blog for writers! Figuring this is work-related, she reads recent posts...

Posts happy birthday msgs

Discovers one of her FAVORITE authors is going to be there. And the author has a new book! Must buy this book right away...

Notices her RSS feed is SO messy! Spends "just a minute" cleaning it up...

Someone responds to her FB post with funny story that makes her LOL

Friend she hasn't heard from in a while sends her a msg...

Oh darn. Book is sold out. Goes to search for other online bookstores...

Amused, she responds with a related funny story...

Suddenly remembers she forgot to phone a non-FB friend on her birthday...

SO great to hear from this friend again! Won't take more than a few minutes to shoot back a reply...

Comes across photo of cookbook whose cover makes her hungry. Mmm, time to find food...

Great post inspires her to start a list of her career goals and time management list...

Sadly, someone takes her story the wrong way and is offended. Damage control needed...

Horrified, she immediately writes a long e-mail to send to her friend...

Tries to print list but printer cartridge is running low! Goes to office supply site...

FIVE HOURS LATER...

ACK! WHERE DID THE TIME GO?!?

Case Study 5.2 How to Succeed in Business?

Mr. Goleman has invited Ben to lunch. Let's listen in to part of their conversation.

Mr. Goleman: *How is your project going for the listening class?*

Ben: *It's going okay. We just had a meeting. For students studying listening, I don't know that we are practicing what we're learning. It seems like every time we got any momentum, someone gets a text or has to check email. It slows us down.*

Mr. Goleman: *Knowing when to put away your smartphone is important. Last week I interviewed a young man just older than you. He was applying for a job in customer service. Would you believe, he texted throughout the interview? On paper he had all the qualifications we were looking for, but his actions weren't professional. The funny thing is that when I called him and told him he didn't get the job, he was surprised. I pointed out to him that attention to detail and to the person in front of him was an important part of the job and that his actions during the interview suggested that he would find it difficult to be detailed-oriented.*

Ben: *You called him and told him he didn't get the job?*

Mr. Goleman: *I usually have my assistant send an email, but I felt the young man needed to know why. He reminded me of you!*

Ben: *Okay, I get the point. The phone's going in my pocket right now.*

The young man Mr. Goleman interviewed thought he could fully participate in the interview and take care of whatever business he was texting about. Unfortunately, like most people who try to multitask, he missed crucial information, such as how irritated Mr. Goleman was getting. We introduce multitasking in the next section below. As we do, consider how our discussion applies to events in Case Studies 5.1 and 5.2.

Media Supported Multitasking

Think of your average day. Did you text your mom while at lunch with friends? Check WhatsApp during a class presentation? Answer your roommate's questions while studying? (We hope you do not text and drive!) These are just few ways we multitask during our average day.

It seems that today everyone is constantly trying to do more in what seems to be less time. In actuality, you may have less time than your predecessors. It is our observation that the demands on students today has increased significantly. To get into the "right" school or get the "right" job, you may feel pressure to be involved in multiple student groups, participate in (typically) unpaid internships, and volunteer at a variety of community organizations. And, if that wasn't enough, we bet that many of you are working part-time (if not full-time) in order to help pay for college. It is no wonder that you may feel overwhelmed at times. All of this pressure may lead us to engage in multitasking. The problem is that as we attempt to "save" time, we actually end up wasting it. Here's why.

The Multitasking Brain

Despite all that you may have heard, our brain is not wired or structured to multitask. In comparison to other animals, human brains have a very large prefrontal cortex. Our prefrontal cortex takes up almost one-third of our total cortex. In comparison, this vital part of the brain takes up about 4–5% of the average cat or dog and around 15% in monkeys. By now, you are probably thinking, so what? As Earl Miller, Professor of Neuroscience, explains, our prefrontal cortex is the part of the brain that provides the "executive control" process which helps us switch and prioritize tasks. The larger the prefrontal cortex, the greater the cognitive flexibility. As Dr. Miller noted, "We can do a couple of things at the same time if they are routine, but once they demand more cognitive process, the brain has a severe bottleneck."

Learn more: If you'd like to test your ability to focus and multitask, try two online interactive tests presented by the *New York Times*. Both were published in the June 6, 2010 online edition. The easiest way to locate them is to Google the following two titles:
   1. *Test How Fast You Juggle Tasks*, and 2. *Test Your Focus.*

In some factories, line workers sort two types of parts at the same time. But, is this activity multitasking? Situational awareness expert Dr. Richard Gasaway says, "… The answer is yes… and no. Or better yet… it depends." He goes on to note that "If you are performing one or more tasks that do not require conscious thought, you are multitasking at the subconscious level of neural processing." However, in most cases, we do not multitask well, particularly if we are engaged in more than one task requiring **conscious thought**. For instance, you will be unable to actively listen to a dinner conversation while trying to send someone step-by-step directions to your restaurant. Although it appears that you are engaging in multitasking, in actuality, you are engaging in **switch-tasking** – or single tasking very, very quickly. As psychiatrist Dr. Edward Hallowell describes it, "Multitasking is shifting focus from one task to another in rapid succession. It gives the illusion that we're simultaneously tasking, but we're really not… you have to keep in mind that you sacrifice focus when you do this."[27] In social interactions, switch-tasking increases one's cognitive load making it difficult, if not impossible, to listen.

If we look at what occurs mentally when we engage in a task, we can see how the cognitive and listening loads increase. When you do something, your brain goes through two stages of *executive control*. In the first stage, you engage in *goal shifting* and in the second stage, *rule activation*. Goal shifting occurs when you say, "I'll focus on this, rather than that." Once this occurs, rule activation occurs as you pull up all the rules and elements associated with completing that task.[28] For example, if you check email at work, you have to pull up the steps involved in checking email, any social rules associated with the task, etc. Now, imagine trying to complete two tasks at the same time. Your brain does not hold all the information for each task simultaneously. It switches between one (listening attentively to your boss) to the other (reviewing a training manual). These types of interruptions have been termed *work fragmentation*. Work fragmentation occurs when there is a break or interruption in a continuous work task.[29]

Switching between the two may take only a second, but in actuality it is longer because your brain begins to slow down in an effort to process both tasks properly. What makes these interruptions even worse is that it takes on average 25 minutes to return to the original task.[30] This occurs because, as we saw in our previous cartoon, we typically will move on to other short tasks before returning to the original one. Thus, prior to returning to your training manual, your conversation with your boss may have sparked an idea that you followed up on with an email. While online, you checked other emails and perhaps checked to see how your Twitter post was trending. When you finally do return to the training manual, you'll have to remember exactly where you were. It is not unusual in such cases for you to go back and re-review previously examined material, which further slows down your work day.[31] Thus, when we engage in switch-tasking, we essentially jump from one thing to another, we may be interrupted by others, or we may interrupt ourselves, and we lose valuable time and energy. The same holds true when engaging in tasks at home or at school. No matter the context, we end up increasing our stress levels as well as the odds of making errors. But wait! There are more downsides of switch-tasking.

The Downsides to Switch-tasking

If the above discussion was not enough to convince you that multitasking has negative consequences, we list several additional reasons. Which of these do you find most convincing?

1. **Critical listening is reduced.**[32] In order to be able to analyze and critically evaluate, we need to understand and process a message fully. Needless to say, if we miss large chunks of the message, we won't be able to evaluate it very well.
2. **Productivity goes down.** If time is money, then switch-tasking costs us a bundle. A study by Professor David Meyer, of the University of Michigan's Brain Cognition and Action Laboratory, found that productivity goes down as much as 40%.[33] Basex, an IT research and consulting firm, estimates the interruptions and distractions associated with switch-tasking costs workers 2.1 hours of productivity every day, while Intel, the computer company, estimates that large companies lose up to $1 billion a year in employee productivity – just to email overload![34]
3. **Creativity is diminished.** Creativity takes focus and concentration. The more tasks you add, the less efficient your brain is causing it to shut down energy draining programs such as creativity.
4. **Wise decision-making is restricted.** When our mind is overloaded, it becomes much harder for us to assess the true consequences of our actions. The result? We send a snarky message, when we normally would not. We take an unethical short cut at work.
5. **Memory is impaired.** As the number of tasks increases, the ability of our mind to focus on and remember details decreases. It becomes more difficult to move material into our short-term memory, much less long-term memory. There is also robust literature describing the negative effects of switch-tasking on learning.
6. **Performance slows and errors increase.** In a recent study, computer science professors Brian Bailey and Joseph Konstan report that not only did interrupted workers have twice the number of errors than those who were not interrupted, they took as much as 27% longer to complete the task. They also found it harder to return to the task after being interrupted.[35]
7. **Stress and annoyance rises.** In the same study, Professors Bailey and Konstan also found that individuals who were interrupted while in the middle of a task were twice as anxious and reported increased levels of annoyance ranging from 31% to 106% over their counterparts who were not interrupted.
8. **Empathy dwindles.** When we are overloaded with information from trying to do too many things at once, we are less empathic. Switch-tasking taxes the brain to such an extent that we are unable to consider the feelings of others. Basically, we are less likely to register the nonverbal cues of others, and subsequently, miss clues that let us know how they are feeling – all information we need for high fidelity listening.[36]

As you can see from the list above, switch-tasking affects almost all elements of our Listening MATERRS Model – mental stimulus to translation and recall to staying connected. If switch-tasking has so many negative consequences, then why do we do it?

Why do we Switch-task?

While there are many reasons for why we switch-task, four key ones are:

1. **Overburdened schedules**. We are doing more and more within the same time schedules. The resulting stress leads us to try to do multiple things at one time.
2. **Emotional satisfaction**. Doing multiple things at the same time makes us feel efficient.
3. **We want to model others**. Others seem to be able to multitask quite well. It looks amazing. We want to be like them, so we put more pressure on ourselves. Spoiler alert – they probably aren't doing as well as you think they are.
4. **Fear of missing out**. We have access to so much information that some people are afraid that something amazing will happen while they are disconnected or away from their devices. We know of one reporter friend who, when he wakes up in the middle of the night, compulsively checks Twitter for breaking news.

Learn more: Did you know that dopamine production goes up with Twitter, Internet and other online media use? It is one reason that some people become addicted to their mobile device or internet use. You can read more about these topics here: http://bit.ly/whyweareaddicted

The Exceptions

Okay, there are exceptions to every rule and switch-tasking is no different. We introduce you to two. First, approximately 2% of people can actually switch-task quite well. Professor Worthington has given training seminars on this topic and in all her seminars only one person (a female state court judge in Illinois) actually could multitask well. Even she, however, would not qualify as a Supertasker. Research into switch-tasking suggests that the brains of supertaskers work differently from our own.[37]

Learn more: Are you one of the 2% of people who are Supertaskers? Find out by taking the following test developed by Dr. David Strayer, a Professor of Psychology at the University of Utah: http://bit.ly/SuperTaskerTest.
 You can read more about his research in this *New Yorker* article: http://bit.ly/NewYorkerMultitaskMasters.

The second exception occurs in our subconscious brain. The subconscious brain has an advantage over the conscious brain – it actually can switch-task, in part, because many tasks we engage in are outside our conscious awareness. You can drive and talk to a passenger, bike at the gym while reading a novel, walk and chew gum. Have you ever driven home and not remembered part of the drive? This is certainly not the safest way of driving, but your subconscious awareness allowed you to drive while you mind was elsewhere. You are able to do this because you have driven for several years. Until the physical aspects of driving entered the realm of muscle memory (discussed in Chapter 3), you had to think about the whole process of driving. Remember the first time you got behind the wheel of a car to drive with your driving instructor?

Strategies to Reduce Switch-tasking

While there is a lot of research on the perils and downsides of multitasking, there is little on how to reduce our switch-tasking tendencies – besides "stop." We reviewed any number of suggestions and below present several of what we consider the best:

- Chart your habits
- Use batch processing
- Engage in block timing
- Develop a single browser tab habit
- Take a break

First, you have to have some idea of what and how you use media. **Charting your habits** will reveal your media usage. Do you check your email while watching television? Regularly have 15 browser windows open? Constantly check text messages while at dinner with friends? When and where do you switch-task the most? This knowledge is the first step to getting control over your attentional habits.

Many people feel they must immediately respond to a text, posting or email. However, as we described above, doing so can actually cost you time. So what else can you do? Try batch processing. According to Joshua Leatherman, Director of Marketing and Sales Development for SEI, an information technology company, "**Batch processing** is the grouping of similar tasks that require similar resources in order to streamline their completion."[38] At the same time, prioritize these tasks, working on the one that is most important. Imagine that you have been hired to handle the social media for a small retail company. You determine that you need to make five Facebook postings each week. You could do one a day *or* you could do all five in one morning and schedule them to be released throughout the week. The advantage of doing them all in one day is that you are familiar with everything you are writing and shouldn't need to go back and review previous posts. You may discover something that doesn't work for one post is a great fit for another. Well, you get the idea. You can improve on this idea by using **block timing.** Block timing refers to blocking out dedicated periods of time to work on a task or project *and* sticking to it! So, each Monday morning from 8 a.m. to noon, you work on your Facebook postings. In order for this suggestion to be successful, you have to work with people who are willing to respect your time (family, friends and colleagues). If you block out Thursday afternoon to study what you have learned that week in your listening class, it is not helpful if your roommate pops in several times to ask you questions. Table 5.1 presents one method of block timing, the Pomodoro technique. Leatherman notes that it can take one to three weeks of hard work for you to begin to realize the benefits of this method of task management. Why Pomodoro? The technique's Italian creator, Francesco Cirillo, used a pomodoro (tomato)-shaped kitchen timer while developing the procedure. Some people find this technique rather rigid. Keep in mind that you can, and should, adapt it to your personal predispositions. Try working 45 minutes instead of 25 minutes on more complex projects, or take an extended break after five or six pomodoros.

Table 5.1 The Pomodoro Technique

1. Plan and prioritize the tasks that need to be completed by writing them down.
2. Set a timer for 25 minutes and devote that time to a task or to a group of similar tasks.
   - Larger tasks can be broken into multiple blocks or "pomodoros," and smaller tasks (responding to email, returning phone calls, etc.) can be grouped into a single block.
   - After completing each Pomodoro, you put an "X" next to it and mark the number of times that you were distracted.
3. Take a 5 minute break.
4. Begin another block of time or "pomodoro."
5. After completing 4 pomodoros, take an extended 20 minute break.

Most of you will have a job at some point in your life that includes significant time working on your computer. The problem is that the computer screen tends to monopolize our attention. One suggestion is to keep the number of browser tabs open to a minimum – ideally engage in **the single browser tab habit**. Not doing so causes any number of problems. For example, we're guessing that at some point you've been working on a paper or assignment, had multiple webpages or articles open, and essentially got lost flipping between the tabs. In other words, you found a great piece of information you want to reference in your article, but when you try to go back to it, you have to move through multiple tabs to find it. This is a waste of your valuable time. Similarly, leaving Facebook or similar social media sites open and readily available encourages us to click over and see what has been posted in the last five minutes. Do you really need to check Twitter or Instagram that often?

Finally, if you're a serious multitasker, you may want to try pulling the plug. Purposely, leave the mobile phone in your office when going to that meeting. Better yet, put it away for a day or a weekend. Professor Worthington sets an example for her students and colleagues by never carrying her phone to class or meetings. *We are not anti-technology.* We are, however, great advocates of strategic use of technology. It can be used in positive, proactive ways – ways that can benefit and strengthen our social ties. We do, however, have to be self-aware so that technology does not negatively affect our professional and personal relationships.

Computers, Television, and Music

Computer-Mediated Communication

Computer-mediated communication (CMC) is the focus of another growing body of research. The long-term effects of CMC on communication and listening behaviors are still unclear. What we do know is that it plays an important function in our professional, educational, and personal lives. As early as 1995, the former Chairman of the MIT Media Laboratory and founder of One Laptop One Child, Nicholas Negroponte, predicted that email would eventually approach, if not surpass, the voice as the primary means of interpersonal communication.[39] Think about your own daily lives. When you think of your interactions on Instagram, texting, and regular email interactions, how much time do you actually spend directly communicating with others? What if you take away classroom communications?

If you attend a webinar, you may be either at your own desk or in a room with other people from your organization. You look at what amounts to a television screen and watch either talking heads or PowerPoint slides. You know other people in other organizations may be "attending" the same webinar. If you have a question or comment, you probably have to type it in or go to a microphone. Under these conditions, listening is challenging. While we, as trainers, appreciate the cost effectiveness of the technique, we also struggle to be responsive to the attendees of such an event.

There are important differences between CMC and F2F interactions. Whether asynchronous or synchronous, mediated interactions differ from that which occurs in real time. Case Study 5.3 outlines one of the problems that may occur during a television interview. While it may appear to be synchronous, in actuality it is asynchronous.

Case Study 5.3 The Interview

Radley: *Hi Mom.*

Ms. Monroe: *Radley! What brings you to the station?*

Radley: *Stan Green, the Arts and Entertainment critic agreed to let me interview him about appreciating various kinds of music. I'm writing a report for a class.*

Ms. Monroe: *Is it for your listening class?*

Radley: *Yes. I wanted to get a critic's point of view on appreciative listening when you really don't like a genre.*

Ms. Monroe: *Have you thought of looking at the challenges on air reporters have when they do an interview? Especially one with a person via a live feed.*

Radley: *What kind of challenges?*

Ms. Monroe: *Well, last week in my story on new building codes, I interviewed Jason Anderson from the building association in Washington. The feed was live, but he forgot about the one second satellite delay. This means that it takes a second for him to hear my question, another second for me to hear his response. The problem was he thought the delay was a pause. He heard the "pause" and thought I wanted him to continue speaking. I had to stop and remind him of the satellite delay. Not my finest interview. It's only a one second delay, but it can make listening difficult.*

Television

In addition to time delays, there are other challenges in listening to television. Another area of research in mediated communication addresses how we process commercials. Viewers and listeners tend to find **compressed advertisements** – advertisements with faster speaking rates and fewer pauses – more interesting, more persuasive, and easier to remember. Other research suggests that slower speaking rates in advertisements allow listeners to focus on specific facts, while higher rates lead listeners to develop more global impressions of a message or speaker. In a study testing the effect of speaking rate on the effectiveness of radio advertisements, Professor Christopher Skinner and his colleagues concluded that ad designers should keep the goal of the ad in mind when making decisions about how much the speaking rate of an ad should be compressed. For example, if the goal is to teach a consumer a step-by-step process, then a slower rate may be needed. This advice may be especially pertinent for designers of Public Service Announcements and other health messages. Faster rates are fine when the goal of the ad is to establish or alter a listener's general opinion of a product, person, or event, etc.[40]

Other research examines the effect of media on schema formation and how those schemas can influence message processing. For example, one legal study by Kimbelianne Podlas found that when individuals who are heavy viewers of syndicated court programming, like Judge Judy or Judge Mathis, are called for jury duty, they expected judges to act similarly.[41] In other words, these viewers believed that judges were opinionated and that they voiced these opinions. The fact is that judges are instructed to act in exactly the opposite way of these television judges. The Model Code of Judicial Conduct instructs judges to avoid expressing any biases or prejudices via their oral communication or nonverbals. Thus, most judges tend to be silent unless one of the parties asks for a ruling or something occurs in the courtroom that must be addressed. How do you think these viewers interpret silence during actual legal proceedings? Podlas's research suggests that jurors who watch syndicated court television programs tend to interpret silence as agreement.

> **Think on it:** What are the courtroom implications for schemas based on television programs such as *Law & Order*, *Bull*, or *Judge Judy*?

Schemas about courtroom proceedings are not the only perceptions affected by television viewing. Attitudes toward money, family, health, sex and sexual behaviors have also been studied. Have any of you watched reality dating programs? Have you ever considered how such programming may affect your view of dating and dating behaviors? Of sex and sexual behaviors? One study by Eileen Zurbriggen and Elizabeth Morgan found that heavy viewers of programming such as *The Bachelor* were more likely to hold gender stereotypical views and beliefs of dating and dating relationships.[42] They were also more likely to see dating as an adversarial activity. Zurbriggen's and Morgan's findings held true for both men and women and held particularly true for individuals who report watching the programming primarily with the goal to learn dating techniques rather than for entertainment purposes. If you think about the highly sexual nature of many of these types of programs, you may not find the researchers' results very surprising. The compressed nature of the program (an evening or even a week of activities compressed to 50 minutes or less of programming) results in a high concentration of sexually suggestive activities and content (e.g., kissing, groping, stripping, suggestive dancing, language). As you can see, this type of programming and other mediated messages (YouTube videos, song lyrics, advertising, movies, etc.) can have a significant effect on our personal schemas (e.g., gender, occupational, etc.), which, in turn, affect how we listen to and process messages.

Music

Most of you likely use a mobile device to listen to music. One of the advantages is that people can listen to their music (or audio books, etc.) without disturbing others. Unfortunately, some people tend to listen to their music at a volume that can actually lead to hearing loss. Loud noises actually damage or kill the sensory cells within our ears that are necessary to our hearing.[43] Importantly, even a short exposure to a loud noise can injure our hearing, particularly when concentrated through headphones or earbuds, as is often the case when listening to music. In some cases, a loud noise can lead to immediate hearing loss and/or the development of tinnitus (e.g., explosion, siren, gunshot). In other cases, the damage accumulates over time (e.g., using earbuds, concert performances, target shooting, leaf blowers). Typically, we associate hearing loss with the elderly. However, in a recent publication, researchers from Massachusetts Eye and Ear found that college-aged subjects were evidencing symptoms of *cochlear synaptopathy*. Those with this condition, which is also known as "hidden hearing loss," have difficulty understanding speech in noisy environments such as bars, loud restaurants, and sporting events.[44] The amount of damage you receive is related to your distance from the sound source as well as how long you are exposed. Basically, you should avoid exposure to loud noises, particularly those that occur close to you or that last for an extended period of time (e.g., standing near the speakers while at a concert or a bar for any length of time). It is also recommended that you use hearing protection when using loud tools (e.g., leaf blowers, skill saws).

Learn more: You can learn more about the cause and effects of noise induced hearing loss at the National Institute on Deafness and Other Communication Disorders website: www. nidcd.nih.gov/health/noise-induced-hearing-loss.

Okay, so we started off with a negative. But, if you keep the volume under control, there are a number of positive outcomes when listening to music. First, it has a number of medical benefits. Previous research has found that music-related therapy is beneficial for both adults and children, but is particularly effective with children. One recent review of studies published between 1980 and 2015 (i.e., a meta-analysis) that focused on children up to 18 years old, found that patients who listened to music experienced a significant reduction of pain, anxiety and distress.[45] Importantly, this review included studies in a variety of health contexts and patients with a variety of diagnoses (e.g., hospitals, clinics, fear of needles, chronic illness, autism). If listening to music does help reduce pain and anxiety, it also makes it easier for medical personnel and patients to interact. Redirecting our attention to the music, relaxes us, taking our minds off of the immediate pain of a medical procedure or the anxiety we feel (at least to some degree). Musical beats can help patients with Parkinson's disease and other neurological disorders to walk and synchronize their movements more effectively. It may also help delay the onset of dementia and help these patients remember better.

Of course, music can make tasks more fun and energizing, especially disagreeable tasks. At the gym? A Zumba class will be more fun, you will exercise harder and faster when listening to upbeat music. Cleaning the house? Dancing your way through the dusting distracts you from a dull task. Of course, you may want something with a slower beat at your yoga class. For some people, listening to music while working actually makes them more creative because they are using different cognitive functions. We do offer the following caveat, some tasks require greater concentration and you may need to choose your music strategically. When we asked our students about their music habits, one student told Professor Worthington that she plays movie soundtracks at work. Her work requires a lot of writing and she finds lyrics distracting. In other words, something that was supposed to be in the background began pulling on her attention and cognitive resources, negatively affecting her concentration. (Hint: think multitasking here.) And, as we'll see in the next section, listening to music can help us learn.

Listening, Learning, and Technology

We probably don't need to tell you that listening is important to learning. In fact, we spend an entire chapter on this topic later in the text. Here, we point out several ways in which mediated listening can positively affect listening and learning. For example, computer programs are used to help small children improve their listening skills. One such program, **Phonomena,** helps children with language problems. The computer game, developed by Dr. David Moore of Oxford University, teaches children to differentiate better between phonemes, like the "i" in the word bit and the "e" in the word "bet." Moore's computer game has them first listen to the original phoneme, then pick one word from several that that sounds most like the phoneme they first heard (rather like an audio-based multiple choice test). Similar activities have long been available for children, but they are typically presented in either a written format and thus rely on children "hearing" the sound in their head or having an adult read off the phonemes and have the child choose among those provided. If the adult has a problematic pronunciation (i.e., dialects and accents), it can make identification more difficult for children. The game format of these "listen and learn" computer programs tends to be well received by children (and adults). Similar training programs have been used to help children with other listening-related problems such as auditory processing disorder. This disorder makes it difficult for a child to process sounds, particularly when in noisy areas such as restaurants, gyms, or ball games. Importantly, these types of listening-based training programs appear to have long-term, positive results.[46]

Computers are used in other ways to improve listening skills. Foreign language teachers utilize **computer-assisted language learning** (CALL) to enhance student listening skills. In a study conducted at Mohamed Kheider University in Algeria, Professor Hassina Nachoua examined the effect of using a CALL system with first year students. Professor Nachoua reported that while using the CALL system did enhance student listening skills, the improvement was mediated by a student's computer skills. In Algeria, many students are unfamiliar with computers and so they have a larger learning curve – they are learning both a new technology and a new language.[47]

Other types of learning are helped through the use of other mediums. You've likely had a teacher use movies or other video clips to illustrate concepts in his or her class. If you've taken a second language class, your instructor may have used movies (with or without subtitles) to help reinforce classroom lessons and increase language comprehension. Research in this area indicates that the use of movies like this is an effective way for second language learners to improve their listening ability. Importantly, most students reported enhanced listening skills, increased vocabulary, a greater understanding of foreign culture, and that the technique reduced anxiety and was generally fun.[48]

While the above examples point out the positives of using technology in the classroom, there are some downsides. Numerous studies have pointed out that using laptops, smartphones, and tablets in the classroom have a negative impact on learning. Students who use laptops during lectures score lower exam grades than their peers who do not.[49] Students typically don't just take notes, they also check emails, shop online, or do work for other classes. The obvious result of this switch-tasking is that they attend less to lecture content, which then negatively affects their comprehension. As the saying goes, "If you don't listen to the lecture, you won't know what you know, nor what you don't know." It is well established that our attentional resources are limited and multitasking in the classroom seriously affects our attention. In fact, one study estimated that students multitask for approximately 42% of their class time.[50] However, there is an additional factor you may be unaware of. Even if you personally do not use a laptop in the class, or you use one and you work hard to stay focused and on task, you may still be at a disadvantage. Have you been in a class where students are allowed to use their laptops? Were you distracted by the movie the person in front of you was watching or the Pinterest postings the person to your right was making? If so, you've experienced another major downside of this type of classroom multitasking – it affects the comprehension of both the user and those around them.[51]

If you do use a laptop in class to take notes, you may not be listening critically. It seems that students who take notes on a computer tend to transcribe rather than process the lecture. In contrast, students who take notes in long hand tend to listen more critically to a lecture, have better long-term recall of the information, and perform better on tests over both factual and conceptual questions.[52]

Referencing back to our discussion of social interactions, when given a choice, students enrolled in face-to-face (F2F) classes appear to prefer class discussions that occur in the classroom over those conducted online. These students were not completely opposed to computer-based tasks, but noted a number of advantages of F2F classroom interactions.[53] These advantages become even more important when faced with complex learning topics. They include:

- reduced misunderstanding and enhanced understanding
- improved collaboration and idea development
- increased spontaneity
- immediate feedback, and
- better and faster explanations.

You might notice that the advantages are closely related to elements of listening. Students have to stay engaged in the interaction and can get immediate responses to ideas and questions.

Finally, we address the impact of listening to music while learning. The question is, "Does listening to music negatively affect learning processes?" Yet again, the answer is "Yes," "No," and "It depends."[54] If you are lucky, you are one of the 8% of people who are not affected by background noise at all. You are able to tune out music, people talking, and the television when concentrating on a task. If you aren't a member of this group, it may be that your *habitude* enables you to neutralize the negative effects of irrelevant sounds on learning. In other words, over time, you may adapt to the sounds so that it doesn't affect your learning. If you aren't a member of the lucky 8%, you need to be aware of the potential effect music and other sounds may have on your learning.

Several studies suggest that "silence is golden" when studying. Students who study in silence (i.e., no music, no television, etc.) performed best on cognitive tasks. Other studies suggest that sounds that are irrelevant to a task negatively affect performance, comprehension and recall. These irrelevant sounds typically have significant acoustical variations. Much of what we hear fits in this category, including TV sound effects, speech and the majority of music we listen to. In fact, it includes music we like as well as that we dislike. Sounds and music with little acoustic variation have less of an impact on our learning. Other studies suggest that music with lyrics can be particularly problematic when reading or reviewing written material because of the dueling nature of the semantic information being received from both reading words and hearing words. Essentially, you're asking the same part of your brain to engage in processing two streams of similar information at the same time. Thus, some people will find listening to music with lyrics problematic. These findings help explain why Professor Worthington's student (described above) found it difficult to listen to music with lyrics while at work.

In general, consider the level of acoustical variation if you must have some type of background noise: Silence is better than music; music (with little acoustic variation) is preferred to television. If you listen to music, try "quiet" music such as soundscapes or instrumental works. Finally, if you are getting ready to take a test or perform another task, try listening to music beforehand. We know that many instructors won't let you listen to music while taking a test, but listening to music prior to the exam creates a state of "arousal" that is believed to make us more alert and receptive. Thus, repetitive jobs that tend to be less interesting, but that require significant concentration (e.g., assembly line workers or quality-control operators) benefit from upbeat music (without lyrics).[55]

Summary

As seen in this chapter, media can affect our listening in a number of ways – both positively and negatively. Because of the ubiquitous nature of mobile devices, we will return to this topic throughout the book, including our discussions of family and friends and organizations and health. What is clear from this discussion is that listeners are constantly challenged to match best listening practices to the particular listening situation.

Key Concepts

Noise sensitivity
Listening effort
Focused social interaction
Mediated social interactions
Synchrony
Social presence
Absent other
Caller hegemony
Conscious thought
Multitasking/Switch-tasking
   Executive control
   Goal shifting
   Rule activation
Work fragmentation
Switch-tasking
   Effects
   Causes
   Strategies to reduce it
Computer-mediated communication
Compressed advertisements
Cochlear synaptopathy
Phonomena
Computer-assisted language learning (CALL)

Discussion Questions

1. Assuming you are on Facebook, how many "Friends" do you have? How many of these individuals would you classify as close friends or family? Compare your numbers to those of your classmates. Do some people have more Friends than others? What are the advantages and disadvantages of having a smaller number of Friends versus a large number? Are you selective in who you friend? Why or why not?
2. How might you place the following media – short message services, texting, Facebook chat, instant messenger, Instagram, email, FaceTime, ooVoo, Tango, Twitter, Skype – on continuums for the three dimensions of mediated social interactions: synchronous/asynchronous, high/low social presence, and small/large reach. Be sure to provide a justification for your assessment.

3. In this chapter, we discussed the disadvantages of engaging in media multitasking. Do you always constantly engage in media multitasking? At selective times? What might lead you to put away your mobile device and concentrate on a synchronous social interaction?

4. On a scale of 1 (very unresponsive) to 5 (very responsive), rate your responsiveness to music. For example, if you find it difficult to sit still when any type of music is going, you might rate yourself a five. Why did you rate yourself this way? What are the implications for how you manage everyday tasks at work? At home?

Listening Activities

1. We discussed the impact of computer-mediated technology on how we listen. How do your instructors feel about mobile phones and computer use in the classroom? How do you feel when a mobile phone buzzes or rings in class? What about computer use? How does it affect listening in the class? Individually or in a small group, design a class policy for media use.

2. Choose a task (one that you estimate will take 60 minutes is best). It can be working on a project, researching for a paper, etc. Set an alarm to go off every 10 minutes while you work. Chart your media use. Did you stay on task? How distracting did you find the alarm. Did you go immediately back to work? Did knowing an alarm would go off make a difference?

3. As a class, declare a "Phone-free Day." For 24 hours, avoid texting, phoning, InstaGraming, etc. anyone (you may want to let friends and family know this in advance). Journal about your experiences three to four times over the course of the day. How difficult did you find it to do? What actions did you take to help yourself be successful? Did you cheat?

4. Retailers and others often use music strategically. Over the course of a week, keep a log of places where you hear music. What type of music is being played? Why might the store or organization make that music choice?

Notes

1 Mulgrew, 2013
2 Marks & Griefahn, 2007; Ouis, 2002
3 Research on research (r2), 2005
4 New York City Department of Environmental Protection, 2014, p. 7; Charter Township of West Bloomfield, 2014
5 Rugg & Andrew, 2010
6 Job, 1999
7 Miedema & Vos, 1999
8 Mulgrew, 2013; Zimmer & Ellermeier, 1999
9 Heinonen-Guzejev, et al., 2007; Nordin, Ljungberg, Claeson, & Neely, 2013
10 Luz, 2005
11 Gearhart, 2012
12 Aron, 1996; Aron & Aron, 1997; Smith & Stansfeld, 1986; Smith, 2003
13 See, for example, Fyhri & Klacboe, 2009; Heinonen-Guzejev et al., 2007; Mulgrew, 2013
14 Aron, 1996; Aron & Aron, 1997; Gearhart, 2012
15 Picou, Ricketts, & Hornsby, 2011, p. 1416
16 Hall, 2016, pp. 1–2
17 Hall, 2016, p. 2
18 Manago, Taylor, & Greenfield, 2012
19 Turkle, 2011, 2015

20 Turkle, 2015, p. 3
21 Seward, 2013
22 Hopper, 1992
23 Gergen, 2002
24 Shan, Wang & Prabu, 2016
25 Shan et al., 2016
26 Shan et al., 2016
27 Halloway, 2006, as cited in Tugend, 2008
28 Rubinstein, Meyer, & Evans, 2001
29 Mark, Gonzalez, & Harris, 2005; Arora, González, & Payne, 2011
30 Mark, et al., 2005; Arora, et al., 2011
31 Yeung & Monsell, 2003
32 Ophir, Nass, & Wagner, 2009
33 Rubinstein, Meyer, & Evans, 2001
34 As cited in Robinson, 2010
35 Bailey & Konstan, 2006
36 Sigman, 2012
37 See Konnikova, 2014, for an easy to read review of research in this area
38 Leatherman, 2014
39 Negroponte, 1995
40 Skinner et al., 1999
41 Podlas, 2001
42 Zurbriggen & Morgan, 2006
43 National Institute on Deafness and Other Communication Disorders, 2015
44 Liberman, Epstein, Cleveland, Wang, & Maison, 2016
45 Kim & Stegemann, 2016
46 Loo, Rosen, & Bamiou, 2016.
47 Nachoua, 2012
48 Safranj, 2014
49 Sana, Weston, & Cepeda, 2013
50 Kraushaar & Novak, 2010
51 Sana, Weston, & Cepeda, 2013
52 Mueller & Oppenheimer, 2014
53 An & Frick, 2006
54 Johnston & Williamson, n.d.; Full citations can be found in the original publication.
55 Fox & Embry, 1972; Wise, Hausknecht, & Zhao, 2014

Additional Readings

Thompson, W. F. (2015). *Music, thought, and feeling: Understanding the psychology of music.* New York: Oxford.

Gazzaley, A., & Rosen, L. D. (2016). *The distracted mind: Ancient brains in a high-tech world.* Cambridge, MA: MIT Press.

Logie, R. H., & Gilhooly, K. (Eds.). (2017). *Working memory and thinking.* East Sussex, UK: Psychology Press.

Worthington, D. L., Keaton, S., Imhof, M., & Valikoski, T.-R. (2015). Impact of noise sensitivity on mobile phone attitudes and behaviors. *Mobile Media and Communication, 4,* 3–18.

References

An, Y-J., & Frick, T. (2006). Student perceptions of asynchronous computer-mediated communication in face-to-face courses. *Journal of Computer-Mediated Communication, 11,* 485–499.

Aron, E. N. (1996). *The highly sensitive person*. New York: Broadway.

Aron, E. N., & Aron, A. (1997). Sensory-processing sensitivity and its relation to introversion and emotionality. *Journal of Personality and Social Psychology, 73*, 345–368.

Arora, A., González, V. M., & Payne, S. J. (2011). The social nature of work fragmentation: Revisiting informal workplace communication. *The Ergonomics Open Journal, 4*, 23–27.

Bailey, B. P., & Konstan, J. A. (2006). On the need for attention-aware systems: Measuring effects of interruption on task performance, error rate, and affective state. *Computers in Human Behavior, 22*, 685–708.

Charter Township of West Bloomfield. (2014). Types of Pollution. Retrieved September 16, 2014 from www.twp.west-bloomfield.mi.us/departments/Pollution.cfm.

Fox, J. G., & Embry, E. D. (1972). Music—an aid to productivity. *Applied Ergonomics, 3*(4), 202–205.

Fyhri, A., & Klacboe, R. (2009). Road traffic noise, sensitivity, annoyance and self-reported health – A structural equation model exercise. *Environment International, 35*, 91–97.

Gearhart, C. C. (2012). *Communicating while stimulated: The effects of sensory-processing sensitivity on behavior and relationships* (Doctoral dissertation). Louisiana State University and Agricultural and Mechanical College.

Gergen, K. (2002). The challenge of absent presence. In J. E. Katz & M. Aakhus (Eds.), *Perpetual contact: Mobile communication, private talk, public performance* (pp. 227–241). Cambridge, MA: Cambridge University Press.

New York City Department of Environmental Protection. (2014, June). Guide to New York City's noise code. Bureau of Environmental Compliance. Retrieved from www.nyc.gov/html/dep/pdf/noise_code_guide.pdf.

Hall, J. A. (2016). When is social media use social interaction? Defining mediated social interaction. *New Media & Society*, 1–18. Advance online publication.

Heinonen-Guzejev, M., Vuorinen, H. S., Mussalo-Rauhamaa, H., Heikkila, K., Koskenvuo, M., & Kaprio, J. (2007). The association of noise sensitivity with coronary heart and cardiovascular mortality among Finnish adults. *Science of the Total Environment, 372*, 406–412.

Hopper, R. (1992). *Telephone conversation*. Bloomington, IN: Indiana University Press.

Job, R. F. S. (1999). Noise sensitivity as a factor influencing human reaction to noise. *Noise & Health, 1*, 57–68.

Johnston, H., & Williamson, R. (n.d.). Music listening and learning interference. Oregon GEAR UP. Retrieved from http://oregongearup.org/sites/oregongearup.org/files/research-briefs/musiclearning.pdf.

Kim, J., & Stegemann, T. (2016). Music listening for children and adolescents in health care contexts: A systematic review. *The Arts in Psychotherapy, 51*, 72–85.

Konnikova, M. (2014, May 7). Multitask masters. *The New Yorker*. Retrieved from www.newyorker.com/science/maria-konnikova/multitask-masters.

Kraushaar, J. M., & Novak, D. C. (2010). Examining the effects of student multitasking with laptops during the lecture. *Journal of Information Systems Education, 21*, 241–251.

Leatherman, J. (2014, June 4). How to use batching to become more productive. LinkedIn. Retrieved from www.linkedin.com/pulse/20140604120709-30659934-how-to-use-batching-to-become-more-productive.

Liberman, M. C., Epstein, M. J., Cleveland, S. S., Wang, H., & Maison, S. F. (2016). Toward a differential diagnosis of hidden hearing loss in humans. *PLoS ONE* (11): e0162726.

Loo, J. H. Y., Rosen, S., & Bamiou, D.-E. (2016). Auditory training effects on the listening skills of children with auditory processing disorder. *Ear & Hearing, 37*, 38–47.

Luz, G. A. (2005). Noise sensitivity rating of individuals. *Sound and Vibration Magazine, 39*, 14–17.

Manago, A. M., Taylor, T., & Greenfield, P. (2012). Me and my 400 friends: The anatomy of college students' Facebook networks, their communication patterns, and well-being. *Developmental Psychology, 48*, 369–380.

Mark, G., Gonzalez, V. M., & Harris, J. (2005, April). No task left behind? Examining the nature of fragmented work. *Proceedings of the 2005 Conference on Human Factors in Computing Systems*, Portland, Oregon.

Marks, A., & Griefahn, B. (2007). Associations between noise sensitivity and sleep, subjectively evaluated sleep quality, annoyance, and performance after exposure to nocturnal traffic noise. *Noise & Health, 9*, 1–7.

Miedema, H. M. E., & Vos, H. (1999). Demographic and attitudinal factors that modify annoyance from transportation noise. *Journal of the Acoustical Society of America, 105*, 3336–3344.

Mueller, P. A., & Oppenheimer, D. M. (2014). The pen is mightier than the keyboard: Advantages of long-hand over laptop note taking. *Psychological Science, 25*, 1159–1168.

Mulgrew, J. (2013). Exploring noise sensitivity: Cardiac correlates of noise sensitivity and the auditory evoked orienting response. (Unpublished master's thesis). Auckland University of Technology, Aukland, New Zealand.

Nachoua, H. (2012). Computer-assisted language learning for improving students' listening skill. *Procedia – Social and Behavioral Sciences, 69*, 1150–1159.

National Institute on Deafness and Other Communication Disorders. (2015, May 15). Noise-induced Hearing Loss. Retrieved from www.nidcd.nih.gov/health/noise-induced-hearing-loss.

Negroponte, N. (1995). *Being digital.* New York: Knopf.

Nordin, S., Ljungberg, J. K., Claeson, A. S., & Neely, G. (2013). Stress and odor sensitivity in persons with noise sensitivity. *Noise Health, 15*, 173–177.

Ouis, D. (2002). Annoyance caused by exposure to road traffic noise: An update. *Noise & Health, 4*, 69–70.

Ophir, E., Nass, C. I., & Wagner, A. D. (2009). Cognitive control in media multitaskers, *Proceedings of the National Academy of Sciences, 106*, 15583–15587.

Picou, E. M., Ricketts, T. A., & Hornsby B. W. Y. (2011) Visual cues and listening effort: Individual variability. *Journal of Speech, Language, and Hearing Research, 54*, 1416–1430.

Podlas, K. (2001). Please adjust your signal: How television's syndicated courtrooms bias our juror citizenry. *American Business Law Journal, 39*. Retrieved from www.allbusiness.com/legal/837058-1.html.

Research on research (r2). (2005). Cell phone noise pollution. Retrieved from http://digitalunion. osu.edu/r2/node/15.

Robinson, J. (2010, Feb. 10). Tame the E-mail beast. *Entrepreneur.* Retrieved from www.entrepreneur.com/article/204980.

Rubinstein, J. S., Meyer, D. E. & Evans, J. E. (2001). Executive control of cognitive processes in task switching. *Journal of Experimental Psychology: Human Perception and Performance, 27*, 763–797.

Rugg, M. & Andrew, M. A. (2010). How does background noise affect our concentration? *Scientific American.* Retrieved from www.scientificamerican.com/article/ask-the-brains-background-noise.

Safranj, J. (2014). Advancing listening comprehension through movies. *Procedia: Social and Behavioral Sciences, 191*, 169–173.

Sana, F., Weston, T., & Cepeda, N. J. (2013). Laptop multitasking hinders classroom learning for both users and nearby peers. *Computers & Education, 62*, 24–31.

Seward, Z. M. (2013, April 3). The first mobile phone call was made 40 years ago today. *The Atlantic.* Retrieved from http://theatln.tc/2mf2ZHX.

Shan, X., Wang, Z., & Prabu, D. (2016). Media multitasking and well-being of university students. *Computers in Human Behavior, 55*, 242–250.

Sigman, A. (2012). The impact of screen media on children: A Eurovision for parliament. *Improving the quality of childhood in Europe 2012*, 88–121.

Skinner, C. H., Robinson, D. H., Robinson, S. L., Sterling, H. E., & Goodman, M. A. (1999). Effects of advertisement speech rates on feature recognition, and product and speaker ratings. *International Journal of Listening, 13*, 97–110.

Smith, A. (2003). The concept of noise sensitivity: Implications for noise control. *Noise & Health, 5*, 57–59.

Smith, A., & Stansfeld, S. A. (1986). Aircraft noise exposure, noise sensitivity and everyday errors. *Environment and Behavior, 18*, 214–226.

Tugend, A. (2008, October 29). Multitasking can make you lose… um… focus. New York Times on the Web Learning Network. Retrieved from www.nytimes.com/learning/teachers/featured_articles/20081029wednesday.html.

Turkle, S. (2011). *Alone together.* New York: Basic Books.

Turkle, S. (2015). *Reclaiming conversation.* New York: Penguin.

Weinstein, N. D. (1978). Individual differences in reactions to noise: A longitudinal study in a college dormitory. *Journal of Applied Psychology, 63*, 458–466.

Wise, A. F., Hausknecht, S., N., & Zhao, Y. (2014). Attending to others' posts in asynchronous discussions: Learners' online "listening" and its relationship to speaking. *International Journal of Computer-Supported Collaborative Learning, 9*, 185–209.

Worthington, D. L. (2017). Noise sensitivity (WNSS-21). In D. L. Worthington & G. D. Bodie (Eds.), *The sourcebook of listening research: Methodology and measures* (pp. 475–481). Malden, MA: Wiley.

Yeung, N., & Monsell, S. (2003). Switching between tasks of unequal familiarity: The role of stimulus-attribute and response-set selection. *Journal of Experimental Psychology-Human Perception and Performance, 29*, 455–469.

Zimmer, K., & Ellermeier, W. (1999). Psychometric properties of four measures of noise sensitivity: A comparison. *Journal of Environmental Psychology, 19*, 295–302.

Zurbriggen, E. L., &Morgan, E. M. (2006). Who wants to marry a millionaire? Reality dating television programs, attitudes toward sex and sexual behaviors. *Sex Roles, 54*, 1–17.

Part II

Listening as a Social Function

6   Listening in the Conversational Context

Case Study 6.1 Stressed Out

Hey Namii, did you get the message I sent you? Will you be able to go with me to interview Dr. Wood, the family therapist?

Oh, hi Tamarah, I was just about to text you back. What type of information are we trying to get? We have so many things going on right now, that I'm having problems keeping some of it straight.

You seem to be a little stressed. Want to grab a cup of coffee and talk a bit? It'll make you feel better and we can coordinate our part of the group project. I think I'll try a caramel macchiato…

Thanks, I think I could use both the caffeine and the shoulder. Of course getting at least one project organized won't hurt any, either.

For most of us, engaging in a conversation is something we do frequently. Seldom, unless the topic or situation is emotionally charged, do we think a great deal about the communication process that is going on. And, we rarely, if ever, stop to think about the impact of listening on the conversation. However, conversations are important to our general wellbeing.[1] We tend to be happier engaging in social activities and interactions, no matter if they are with friends, family or acquaintances. Enjoyable conversations lead to positive feelings. Notably, research examining actual conversations (using the mobile app, My Social Ties) found that our enjoyment increases when we talk less (and presumably, listen more).[2]

In this chapter we look at listening as a critical element of conversations in general. Then we will look at two types of conversational situations that we regularly face – giving and receiving social support and handling conflict.

Conversations and Interaction

Traditionally, listeners have been considered part of the background of a conversation, meaning that a listener was simply considered a speaker in waiting.[3] As one communication scholar puts it, when looking at a conversation, many researchers focus on the source or the effect not at the process which includes listening.[4] Laura Janusik, a listening scholar, says that such a perspective ignores the true nature of conversations, where all parties are both a sender and a receiver, creating a transactional process where the listener both receives and responds.[5]

David Bohm, a world-renowned physicist and modern day Renaissance man, suggests that human relationships are essentially collaborative activities and a process of creation.[6] He also believes that in many listening instances, we are "blocked" from fully understanding the other. Our need to protect ourselves, and the meanings we create, often get in the way of our ability to truly understand one another. Bohm argues that ideally, when we communicate with others, we should engage in a collaborative dialogue. Such a dialogue is based on the co-creation of meaning. It necessarily entails an ability to truly listen to others: without bias, without trying to influence them, and, with a willingness to move beyond our own beliefs. To do this, Bohm essentially argues that we embrace and acknowledge our "blockages," while at the same time fully give our attention to what our conversational partner is saying. It is at this point, Bohm would say, we are truly communicating with one another.

In our case study at the beginning of the chapter, our characters leave us with the idea that they are going to have a real conversation. Tamarah recognizes and acknowledges Namii's mood, and understands how it could have an impact on what they are going to talk about as well as how they interact. Had Tamarah been more focused on her own message rather than recognizing how stressed Namii felt, chances are a misunderstanding would have occurred.

Professors Bavelas, Coates and Johnson from the University of Victoria in British Columbia, Canada offer one explanation for why scholars have largely ignored the importance of the listener to a conversation. They believe the problem may be traced back to the Shannon–Weaver model of communication.[7] Chances are you learned about this model in a basic speech course. As you may recall, this model is based on a linear view of communication (see Figure 6.1). In this type of model, the receiver (listener) takes the back seat to the sender. As one scholar points out, the sender (speaker) has the front channel and the receiver (listener) takes the back channel.[8] From

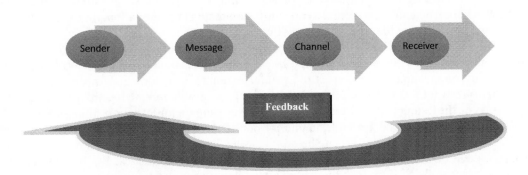

Figure 6.1 Shannon–Weaver Model of Communication

this perspective, the role of the listener is to respond minimally and in a non-interruptive manner until it is his or her turn to be the sender.

Clearly, conversation is much more involved than the model indicates. Good listening is a critical part of any successful conversation. To support this assertion, we have only to look at research examining what happens when a listener fails to participate fully in a conversation. This research has shown consistently that when appropriate listening behavior is removed, reduced, or eliminated, the performance of the sender as well as the quality of the communication suffers.[9] The findings of this body of research are quite interesting. For example, when listener feedback is reduced or absent, speakers tend to use more words.[10] However, more words do not necessarily make for greater understanding. Other research finds that listeners better understand a speaker's message when they are allowed to provide feedback. What's more, speakers are so sensitive to listener nonverbal behavior that they will restart a phrase if the listener looks away and then looks back.[11] These research results support claims that a conversation is a cooperative interaction between speakers and listeners.

Grice's Maxims

To help us understand this cooperative interaction, we can look at expectations we have for conversations. Noted researcher, Herbert Paul Grice proposed four conversational maxims based on the key principle that we engage in an interaction to get the maximum amount of information possible and that we expect the other party to cooperate in this effort. This expectation is called the **principle of cooperation**.[12] In order to get the information, we must focus on both the actual words of the message as well as any information implied in the comment. That is, as we listen to a conversational partner, we draw inferences based on what is said. These inferences help us complete the picture of what the speaker intends to convey.

In essence, Grice's maxims lay out a logic for what we expect from the cooperating partner when we participate in a conversation. As listeners, if we embrace these expectations, they will shape both what we listen for and the types of inferences we make. The first maxim is **quality.** This maxim suggests that we expect the other person to tell us the truth or at least what they believe to be the truth. The second is the **maxim of quantity,** which leads us to expect the speaker to give us useful information that we don't already know, without overwhelming us with too much information. This maxim allows us to rely on our own storehouse of knowledge to interpret the speaker's comments. For example, if one of your friends tells you that studying for a test really paid off, he doesn't have to tell you he passed the test, you will assume that from his statement. If, on the other hand, you know someone who seems to constantly dominate the conversation, then she or he may be violating or breaking this unwritten rule of conversation.

The next two maxims address the interaction itself. The **maxim of relation** leads us to believe the information we get is going to be relevant to the purpose of the interaction and contribute to the flow of the conversation. So, we expect to get information that we don't already obviously know and that is relevant to the conversation. When this expectation is violated, it frequently leads to confusion or the feeling that we were being misled. It is common for television situational comedies to use this technique. For example, in one episode of the Big Bang Theory, Penny has jammed the lock in her apartment door. When Sheldon sees what happens, he doesn't ask how he can help. He provides a physics-based discussion on why the key is stuck in the lock. We may not know a brilliant scientist like Sheldon, but think about what happens when you are in a conversation and the other person inserts a statement that seems to be totally random. Doesn't it cause you to wonder if you (or they) "zoned out" and missed something critical?

The final maxim, the **maxim of manner**, leads us to expect the speaker to be brief, orderly and unambiguous. Unfortunately, this maxim assumes that we share the same level of ability and knowledge about the language we use to converse. If this assumption isn't correct, that is, we are talking with someone who isn't as well versed in our language, we tend to rely on tactfulness and politeness to help us cope with this turn of events.[13] For example, when you talk with a young child, you adjust your expectations of her ability to use the language in a sophisticated manner. Likewise, when you visit another country, you don't expect the residents to have the same ability in your language as you do. And, you hope they, in turn, don't expect you to have a perfect ability in their language.

> ***Think on it:*** Chances are you have met international students on your campus. How do your expectations and conversational behaviors differ when you talk with a non-native speaker of your language?

Defining Conversation

So after all of this discussion, what is a conversation? We define **conversation** as "an orderly joint managed sequence of utterances produced by at least two participants who may or may not share similar goals in the interaction."[14] This definition stresses the importance of all parties in the interaction *jointly managing* the sequencing of the speakers' utterances. Doing so requires appropriate responding on the part of the listener(s), or receiver(s). That is, the listener must remain engaged in the interaction and respond either verbally or nonverbally in a manner that is appropriate for what was said. This definition excludes situations where people happen to be in the same space talking past each other.

On visits to an assisted living facility, Professor Fitch-Hauser saw one resident in the recreation room. Anytime he saw someone new enter the room, he would smile and start talking. Often, the people entering the room didn't know the gentleman was talking to them and would walk on to where they were going. Regardless, the man would continue to talk for a few minutes. He wasn't conversing; he was just talking. Chances are you are feeling some sympathy for the man and you may even think the scenario just applies to old people. Unfortunately, similar scenarios play out daily in such places as airports, restaurants and student unions. Have you ever been involved in or seen an exchange like the one in Case Study 6.2?

Case Study 6.2 Conversational Bypassing

Carter and Ben are sitting at a table studying.

> Carter: *I don't know how I'm going to get everything done! I have a Chem test on Monday, a draft of my Polymer Sciences paper due on Tuesday plus Professor Merritt wants to meet with our group. On top of all that, Dad is taking me to a Bulls game on Saturday, so I have to go to Chicago for the weekend.*
>
> Ben: *Sounds nice. I wish I were going to a Bulls game. My cousin's son is having a Bar Mitzvah on Sunday and I have to go. I've only met him one time. I don't know why my parents insist I go.*
>
> Carter: *Maybe we could ask Professor Merritt to postpone the meeting. What do you think?*
>
> Ben: *What's there to think about, my dad insists that I go.*
>
> Carter: *Ben, what you talking about?*

Notice that our definition of conversation *does not* specify face-to-face interactions. Thanks to modern communication technology many of our conversations take the form of emails, instant messages, or text messages. Regardless of whether the conversation is in person or electronically mediated, as conversational listeners, we engage in a conversation specifically to interact with another party for some purpose. The ultimate result of a conversation is a product of the interaction itself.

Conversations as Co-creations

While conversations are one of the most ordinary of our communication events, they are also one of the most important. In fact, many scholars see conversations as fundamentally important to language, to communication, to being human.[15] It is through our conversations that we learn about our families, our friends, our co-workers. We solve problems and make both ordinary and significant decisions. It is what makes us "social" beings.

As noted in the previous section, many of us focus on the speaker when we think about a conversation. Consider a recent conversation you participated in. What do you remember? Chances are that you remember what you said and at least part of what the other person said, but likely don't remember much (if anything) about your or the other person's listening behavior. Isn't it funny that we don't really think about the role of listening in conversation?

Well known communication scholars, Stephen Littlejohn and Kathy Domenici address this point by saying: "We normally think of conversation as an event in which people take turns talking. How would conversations change if we thought of them as taking turns at listening?"[16] They note that while it is important to let conversational participants speak their minds, we need to think of conversations as dialogues or exchanges. When we take this perspective, listening, not talking, becomes the centerpiece of any conversation.

To illustrate more fully how important listening is to the flow and development of a conversation, we go back to Professors Bavelas, Coates and Johnson and their research examining listeners as co-narrators of an interaction.[17] While many studies have addressed this topic, the work by Bavelas and her colleagues differs because they examined actual conversations (instead of written descriptions) and their line of investigation raises a number of important points for us to consider.

First, they point out something that all of us know, not all listening responses are verbal or actual words. The researchers identify two kinds of listener responses. The first of these is **generic responses**. Generic responses include nonverbal actions like nodding and vocalizations such as "mhm," or "uh-huh." Another term that has been used to describe this type of response is **back channel**. Generic or back channel responses aren't specifically connected to what the speaker is saying. Instead, they serve as markers that we are cognitively engaged in what the speaker is saying. So, we might nod to indicate we are listening to the speaker, regardless of what the topic or emotional load of the narration is. If we give generic responses when we *aren't* cognitively engaged, we are merely making **listening noises** and essentially deceiving the speaker.

The second type of listener response identified by Bavelas, Coates and Johnson is **specific responses**. As you can guess, these are responses that are directly tied to what the speaker is saying. One obvious direct response is eye gaze. Our eye contact, commonly called **gaze behaviors**, is used to signal attention as well as to coordinate turn-taking behavior in social interactions. Several early studies suggest that speakers look at the other party(ies) more often while speaking. It is believed they do so to help monitor understanding. In contrast, listeners tend to gaze for longer.[18] Notably, speakers often use observable behaviors, such as head movement and eye direction, as transactional cues to signal to their conversational partners that it is their turn to direct the interaction.[19] Recent research has found that speakers tend to signal the end of their turn by directly looking at the listener, while listeners tends to begin their turn by briefly looking away or averting their gaze.[20] If a speaker pauses or hesitates and they *are not* ready to turn over their speaking turn to the listener, they will actually avert their gaze as a signal that they want to continue speaking.[21] However, conversations are dynamic and interactive. Speakers don't always control who speaks and when. Listeners provide transitional cues as well. They may increase their gestures and increase head and gaze shifting as essentially a nonverbal means of requesting a turn.[22] Gazing behaviors remain an important means of coordinating social interactions even in joint activities (e.g., walking and talking).[23]

Of course, our behaviors and responses should be appropriate for the content and emotional load of the speaker's narration. So, a sad facial expression is appropriate feedback when we listen to a sad story and so forth. Interestingly, some of these specific responses can even get incorporated into the speaker's narration. The conversation in Case Study 6.3 illustrates how this can happen.

Case Study 6.3 Co-creating Conversation

Tamarah: *I went with my mom on one of her visits to a homeless shelter. You know she's a social worker.*

Ben: *Was it depressing?*

Tamarah: *Well, it wasn't as bad as I expected. The place was pretty clean, airy, and not nearly as loud as I thought it would be. And, the kitchen was efficiently run. The cots were …*

Ben: *(interrupting) probably crowded and not very comfortable.*

Tamarah: *all in a row and pretty crowded. I sure wouldn't have found it comfortable. Anyway, I left there feeling very thankful.*

Notice that Tamarah incorporates Ben's thoughts into her narration. She may or may not have intended to talk about the crowding or comfort. Later, when she tells the same story to another friend, she may again incorporate Ben's description of the sleeping area of the shelter into her story. Consequently, the story will include both her experience and Ben's assumptions.

Think on it: Can you think of an example where your story about one of your experiences has incorporated someone else's thoughts or observations? If you can, what is it about the information that makes you remember the source? If you can't, does it make you wonder how your stories might have changed over time?

It is also important to remember that listeners don't always respond verbally and interrupt the speaker as Ben does in our example. Many of our responses are nonverbal. Research has shown that speakers are particularly sensitive to facial expressions and eye gaze.[24] If listeners engage in appropriate responses, whether verbal or nonverbal, conversations flow smoothly. In order for this to happen, both individuals must track the conversation closely.

When listeners are distracted, they tend to make fewer responses of any kind, particularly specific responses. In turn, when speakers notice how disengaged or distracted the listener is, their narration suffers and they begin to use coping strategies. They may abruptly end the message, they may become less articulate, or they may feel the need to justify elements of the story.[25] Regardless of their coping strategy, their role as speaker is adversely affected as is the overall interaction. Good conversations are clearly dependent on both the speaking and listening roles of the participants. In fact, listening in good conversations illustrates all of the primary elements of the Listening MATERRS Model: the interactants must be motivated to stay engaged, they must attend to each other, they must interpret the message, and they must provide appropriate responses.

Conversational Variables

The best conversations require a willingness to truly express our opinions, feelings, or ideas, and a willingness to listen to the same from others. Susan Scott, author of the book *Fierce Conversations*, talks about the importance of "fierce" conversations; conversations that thrive on openness and debate, not anger and hostility. She believes that our successes and failures are built "one conversation at a time," and stresses that "the conversation *is* the relationship"[26] She argues that when our conversations slow or stop, our relationships are weakened. Conversations are proof that we are responsive to the others in our lives. However, in order to be responsive, in order to engage in fierce conversations, we have to be open to change.

You'll notice that we haven't said anything about being able to come to an agreement as being important. Sometimes we have to agree to disagree, but in these types of conversations, our goal is to understand the point of view of others and for them to understand ours. When we assess conversational listening, our assessments should include who the speaker is, what is said and how it is said, as well as the reasons underlying why it was said. When we assess these elements, we get into the importance of considering the differences in the individuals participating in the conversation.

Individual Differences

As you recall, in Chapter 4 of this text we talked about how individual differences affect how we listen. Not surprisingly, individual differences can also impact our conversations with others. In this section we will briefly discuss how several individual differences affect conversational listening.

As discussed in Chapter 4, one way we differ is in terms of our **cognitive complexity**, or the number of personal constructs we use when evaluating messages or our conversational partners. The potential impact on conversational listening can be seen in the findings of early research. This research established that those who are cognitively complex tend to be more accurate when processing information about others, are better able to imagine themselves in the other person's place, and tend to withhold judgment when forming impressions of others.[27] In contrast, people who are less complex are more likely to form initial impressions quickly and find it more difficult to change that impression. Thus, when they receive contradictory information (e.g., Ella's evil stepmother does something nice for Ella), they may choose to minimize or ignore it. From this research we can see how cognitive complexity can make us more flexible as listeners in social situations. Those who are cognitively complex should be more capable of keeping an open mind and responding in ways that are appropriate for the specific conversation. However, a good listener, regardless of how cognitively complex, must continue to work on being a good listener. Being cognitively complex doesn't mean that we are always open minded. After all, all of us, even the cognitively complex, are human.

> ***Think on it***: What might happen in conversations where Carter is highly cognitively complex and his friend, Joe is not? What differences would occur in their conversations, especially those related to listening?

Linked to cognitive complexity is another individual trait, **Individual Receiver Apprehension**. Individual Receiver Apprehension is more specialized than the general Communication Apprehension we discussed in Chapter 4. This is a type of anxiety that impairs our ability to manage information. Those who are high in this type of apprehension tend to experience anxiety and anger or antipathy when facing an interaction. These heightened emotions, in turn, have a negative impact on their willingness to receive or interpret incoming messages.[28] In other words, people who are highly receiver apprehensive don't want to listen. One reason they may not want to listen is that they also tend to be intellectually inflexible and fear having to comprehend complex or abstract information.[29]

Just as individuals who are highly complex are quite adaptable in social situations, so are high self-monitors. **Self-monitoring** occurs when we attempt to manage the impressions we leave with others. All of us do this to varying degrees. However, *low self-monitors* tend to be more consistent in the "face" they present to others. What this means is that they act about the same regardless of who is in the conversation, or what the context may be. According to scholar Mark Snyder, low self-monitors are more likely to look at a situation and ask, "Who am I and how can I be me," while the *high self-monitor* will ask, "Who does this situation want me to be and how can I be that person."[30] In their effort to adapt, they are more likely to use ambiguous language, particularly in situations where they may not agree, but don't believe the situation or context really allows for disagreement (e.g., dinner party, casual coffee with friends). Thus, high self-monitors will listen and respond in a more nuanced way than low self-monitors. In addition, to understanding the impact of individual differences on your conversations, other variables can also affect your conversational listening.

> ***Think on it:*** Looking back at Chapter 4, how might other individual differences affect our conversational interactions with others?

Accommodation

Closely related to self-monitoring is **accommodation** or how we adjust our communication behavior to the other party. While this theory was first developed to look at adjustments in speech behavior, more recent applications have wisely begun to look at receiving behavior as well. Accommodation allows us to respond to the needs of the other party whether it be for privacy or empathy. In the case study at the beginning of the chapter, Tamarah is very perceptive of NaMii's mood and shifts her focus from doing the interview to providing support for NaMii. Like Tamarah, when we use accommodating listening behavior, we take into account the other party's uniqueness and social identity. This accommodation will include making adjustments in your delivery style as well as your nonverbal behavior. For example, if you were to engage in a conversation with NaMii's grandparents, you would take into consideration that they are Korean. As an adroit listener, you would accommodate your responding behavior so that you showed respect for both their age and their culture. So, you would keep your voice fairly quiet and your eye contact indirect, rather than direct.

As listeners, when we accommodate our conversational partner, we attempt to fit our responding behavior to that person.[31] We would listen closely, put ourselves in the other person's perspective (be empathic), and respond in a way that is respectful of the other person. Unfortunately, we aren't always successful in our accommodation. Sometimes we will *under-accommodate* or fail to appreciate, pay sufficient attention to, or be simply unwilling to take into account, the needs of the other party. Think about talking with your grandparents and their friends. If you have a negative stereotype of older people, you may ignore their needs for you to talk more clearly, use terms they are unlikely to understand or would misinterpret (e.g., squad, salty, RT), or fail to appreciate their life's experiences. It is very easy to dismiss (or zone out from) what the other person is saying when we haven't directly experienced the same thing. Not surprisingly, intergenerational and intercultural communications seem particularly susceptible to under-accommodating because of this difference in experience.

On the other end of the spectrum is *over-accommodation.* Over-accommodating can best be characterized as talking down to or being condescending. Examples of this type of behavior include using diminutives (e.g. "sweetie," "my dear," or "little darling"), overly simplistic grammar, over enunciation, or excessively slow speech in combination with continual head nodding and excessive smiling and touching.[32] Unfortunately, we once again find that this type of accommodation behavior seems to be common in intergenerational and intercultural conversations as well as in inter-ability encounters. For instance, this type of behavior has been documented in health care settings when nurses talk in a patronizing way to patients.[33]

Once again, as listeners we need to be aware of any biases or stereotypes that might lead us to over-accommodate and be negative participants in an interaction. Another set of negative behaviors can be found in non-accommodating behaviors. *Non-accommodation* occurs when we engage in behavior that in some way either excludes the other party or makes them feel excluded.[34] Perhaps the easiest way to illustrate this type of conversational behavior is to review research examining language use in male-dominated workplaces.[35] One study found the dominant male group excessively used sports metaphors and sexual innuendos. Not surprisingly, women in this workplace felt excluded and sometimes offended. The resulting interactions between the two groups led to a cycle of behavior that was detrimental to the workplace (e.g., difficulty communicating, minimum communication, uncooperative group interactions). On a larger stage, we can see the failure to accommodate people who sound or look different from the group in the majority. You can see this in the news as you watch and listen to stories about ethnic strife around the globe. People with disabilities often experience this as well.

As a good conversational listener, you want to remember the importance of taking into account the background and needs of the other party so you can engage in a mutually beneficial interaction. Of course the setting and purpose of the interaction will also have an impact on how the conversation progresses.

Conversational Context

One of the elements of conversation that we need to explore is the setting, or context where a conversation takes place. For example, if a conversation is taking place in a noisy setting, the dynamics of the conversations will be different from when the conversation is taking place in a quiet place. As you would expect, conversations have difficulty succeeding in noisy settings.[36] As you remember from the discussion of our model, Listening MATERRS, we must first be able to attend to a stimulus in order to listen. In a noisy setting, picking up the conversation or the message can be either impossible or extremely challenging. Being noise sensitive will make it even more difficult. If the setting is too difficult, the listener loses motivation to remain engaged. In addition, it is very difficult to respond appropriately in ways that will sustain a conversation.

Think on it: Think of the last time you were sitting with a large group at a dinner party or restaurant. Who did you end up talking to? What were some of the topics of conversation? How do you think the context affected the conversation?

Research in this area shows that listeners tend to engage in certain coping behavior in a very noisy setting. One of the strategies is to withdraw from the conversation. With this strategy, the listener may physically remain in the location, but mentally seems to withdraw. More proactive approaches occur when listeners make comments about not being able to hear or attempt to change the topic. While telling the speaker that you can't hear is usually appropriate, changing the topic, on the other hand, may be perceived negatively. If nothing is done to help the listener hear better, that person will probably withdraw. No matter the approach that is used, if speakers are not responsive, listeners will ultimately tend to be non-responsive, or fail to take up the conversation. If they do respond, that response probably isn't going to be based on the speaker's comments.[37] Consequently, the relationship with the conversational partner may be negatively impacted – "You never listen to me!" "You have no idea how I feel!" "You didn't say anything when I mentioned it before!" Importantly, it is not always the physical location that provides a context for listening; other factors such as the state of the relationship between the interactants also contribute to the context in which the conversation occurs.

Self-verification

As seen above, conversations tend to occur in the context of some type of relationship. The next two chapters will focus on listening in specific relationships; however, it is important to look at some general impacts of the relationship on a conversation. First, we'll examine the importance of storytelling. Author and artistic consultant Henning Mankell wrote of an encounter while in Mozambique.[38] While sitting on a bench, he overheard two elderly African men. The first man described his last visit to a mutual friend who had just passed away. One of them said,

I was visiting him at his home. He started to tell me an amazing story about something that had happened to him when he was young. But it was a long story. Night came, and we decided that I should come back the next day to hear the rest. But when I arrived, he was dead.

The second man was quiet, finally responding, "That's not a good way to die – before you've told the end of your story." Mankell goes on to write,

It struck me as I listened to those two men that a truer nomination for our species than Homo sapiens might be Homo narrans, the storytelling person. What differentiates us from animals is the fact that we can listen to other people's dreams, fears, joys, sorrows, desires and defeats – and they in turn can listen to ours.

Mankell's observation is certainly very true.

> ***Think on it:*** Author Henning Mankell makes several observations about storytelling, particularly African storytelling: You can find his full article, "The Art of Listening" at the following link: http://bit.ly/the_art_of_listening.

Storytelling is an important part of our conversations with others. Chances are if Tamarah listens to NaMii's stories about living with her grandparents, she will learn a great deal about both NaMii and the Korean culture. In the exchange, Tamarah will experience something called self-verification.[39]

Self-verification refers to how we as individuals construct our own social worlds. The social world we construct is based upon perceptions of ourselves, including our self-concept and self-esteem. It helps us to support our beliefs about ourselves (e.g., smart, funny, witty). For example, if you view yourself as funny, you are more likely to tell personal stories that reflect the funny things that you did or that happened to you in the last week. If you value work over play, then you are more likely to tell tales related to the work or projects you completed (or did not complete). Tamarah takes pride in her ability to help others (remember she works in public safety and takes emergency calls) as well as her cultural sensitivity. As the daughter of the tribal leader of the Choctaw Nation, she knows first hand the challenges of living in two cultures. As she and NaMii talk and exchange stories, Tamarah will tell stories that reflect these beliefs about herself.

> ***Think on it:*** Have you been listening to a story and been shocked or surprised by what the person said? Did you tell them you disagreed with their opinion/interpretation or with what they chose to do? What affected your decision to openly disagree (or not)?

Storytelling and Identity

With our storytelling, we maintain and change our identity. A number of theorists in this area believe that personal storytelling is important to the development of self-identify – not just when we are children or young adults, but throughout our lives.[40] The previous example helps illustrate this. Like Tamarah, we seek personal confirmation of who we are through our stories.

How people respond to our stories is also important, because their response to our storytelling can actually affect the self-confirmation or verification process. Self-verification is possible when our family, friends, and other significant individuals agree with our personal views. As we have relayed throughout this text, listening is a dynamic process. The roles of speaker and listener are constantly changing during the ebb and flow of the conversation. As the roles change, listeners can agree or disagree with a story which in turn impacts the self-verification process. Thus, when you tell the story about someone being rude to you, your listener may disagree with your interpretation. Because we tend to tell stories that support our self-view, we tend to find it problematic when others don't agree with our interpretation. Thus, if our friends and family disagree outright with our story, we may feel we have been disconfirmed.

Worse than disagreeing, another means of disconfirming a story is inattentive listening. Attentiveness is central to social interactions. We can tell when others are paying attention to our stories by the verbal, "uh, huh's" or nonverbal eye contact and head nods. These attentional cues are also important for maintaining the flow of conversations, and provide the means by which we let others know we understand and support (or don't support) what they say. Distracted listeners are generally not very good at providing these cues or signals.

Attentiveness affects our storytelling in other ways. For example, when we feel someone is really listening to us, our stories tend to be longer and more detailed. We also tend to be more expressive and more eloquent.[41] Essentially then, distracted listeners affect both the quantity and quality of our storytelling.[42]

Interestingly, while we may be seeking a responsive, supportive listener to validate our identity, we can deal with an attentive, disagreeing listener better than we can an inattentive listener. Attentive listeners, whether they agree or disagree with us, confirm that the experience or event that we are recounting is both understandable and worthy of attention. Both types of listeners provide us with the opportunity to elaborate on the story. Distracted listeners, however, aren't keeping up their end of the listening "bargain." If you think about the previous discussion of Grice's maxims, you know that when we face a non-listening situation, we need to cut short our story or run the risk of violating these conversational norms.[43] Clearly, the so-called listener finds no importance in what we are saying. Importantly, when telling stories of personal verification, if we are faced with an inattentive listener, we are more likely to feel the person is disconfirming the part of our identity we seek to validate. Subsequently, the way others listen to us, and the way we listen to them, has important implications for how we think about ourselves and how much we are willing to reveal about ourselves.

Listening researchers often bemoan the negative effects of living in a *polymediated* world. As we pointed out in our discussion in Chapter 5, televisions, computers and mobile devices pose a particular challenge to our ability to attend to others. We can, however, use them to build and confirm relationships. Mobile phones, in particular, are one means of augmenting our social bonds via their ability to enhance our dialogue with others.[44] For instance, imagine you tell a friend that you're stressed about an upcoming class presentation. If your friend sends you a quick encouraging text on the day of the presentation, you will feel encouragement for the presentation, but that text also confirms feelings of being listened to. This said, we must note that research into the impact of mobile technology in social support is still in its infancy.

Social Support

Perhaps one of the most important functions of conversation is giving and receiving social support. When we receive sensitive social support, particularly emotional support, it tends to make us feel better and we can more effectively address our problem. It may even lead us to feel mentally and physically better.[45] Social support has been identified as one of the most desired and essential types of support we seek from our close relationship partners.[46] Individuals who personally value emotional support and are good at providing it tend to be more popular, have more satisfying relationships, and are less lonely, and less likely to be rejected by their peers.

As you can see, positive social support benefits both the sender and the receiver. The difficulty is often trying to determine how to provide such support. Research by Loretta Pecchioni and Kelby Halone shows that part of the answer depends on the type of relationship and the support that is required.[47] Other research suggests that the wording of the message also impacts how it will be received. **Highly person-centered messages** tend to be better received.[48] These messages encourage others to express their feelings, elaborate upon them (i.e., describe, clarify), and explore them as required by the nature of their emotions and the situation. In contrast, **low person-centered messages** tend to ignore the speaker's feelings or deny or criticize them.

In a conversation with NaMii about living in a household with multiple generations, if Tamarah asks NaMii how she is balancing the Korean expectations of her grandparents with the realities of being an American college student, she will send a highly person-centered message. If on the other hand, she says something like, "NaMii, you shouldn't care so much what her grandparents think," it would be low person-centered.

Directive and Non-directive Social Support

To better understand how to give positive social support we need to explore just what social support looks like. First, we can distinguish between two categories of support: directive and non-directive.[49] **Directive support** involves providing *unrequested* specific types of coping behaviors or solutions for the recipient of the support. If you tell someone to take three deep breaths to calm down, that is directive support. **Non-directive support** shifts the focus of control from the giver to the receiver. The recipient dictates the support provisions. If Radley were to ask your advice on how to handle a problem with a group member in his health communication class and you suggest he make an appointment to see his instructor, your suggestion is considered non-directive support because Radley specifically asked for the advice. Non-directive support tends to be more effective than directive support. The listening challenge is often in identifying when someone is asking for support. In Case Study 6.4, we look at an example that might sound familiar to you.

Case Study 6.4　Listening for Tone

Carter: *Hey Tamarah, how you doing?*

Tamarah: *Oh, hello Carter. I'm fine. How about you?*

Carter: *Hmmm, you don't sound like you're doing "fine." What's going on?*

Tamarah: *Oh, nothing – really, I'm **fine.***

Chances are you have been involved in an exchange similar to the one presented in the case study. An aware listener will know that the underlying paralanguage and nonverbal messages are as important, if not more important than the actual words. At the point where we stopped in the example, Carter has a couple of options. He can say, "okay," accepting the face value of the message and continue the social exchange, he can choose to leave, or he can drop the line of questioning. On the other hand, he can be sensitive to the entire message, notice that the emphasis on the last "fine" indicates just the opposite, and offer social support. He can engage in active-empathic listening and say something like, *"Are you sure? Did something happen at work last night that upset you? If you'd like to talk about it, I'm here to listen."* Saying this particular script might be a little uncomfortable for some. Another alternative would be for Carter to say and do something a bit less "touchy, feely." He could ask if he could join her and sit down at the table and ask her about how work is going. Essentially, Carter is trying to create a feeling of **psychological safety** for Tamarah. Either response will give Tamarah the choice of whether to share her frustration and seek social support. Listening that is "non-judgmental, non-evaluative, and non-threatening" is an important means of generating feelings of safety.[50]

Finally, the interactive nature of listening must be considered. In Chapter 4, we introduced the different listening styles and how individuals focus on particular listening goals when selecting a style (e.g., relational, analytical, critical, task-oriented). Recent research found that the style of listening by message receivers is important in supportive contexts. For example, if you are faced with an upsetting incident and are discussing it with a friend, your discussion will be affected by whether you believe the listener's using a relational style versus one of the other styles.[51] When listeners engage in a relational style in situations of social support, they provide the attention and responsiveness necessary to establish a trusting relationship. It is believed that relational listening goals encourage speakers to disclose more because speakers feel the listener is more accepting of and also less judgmental of the message. As a result, the speaker feels greater comfort from the encounter and may be willing to engage in similar interactions in the future.

Additional Attributes of Social Support

As we point out above, *effective social support tends to be non-directive as well as invisible.*[52] That is, the recipient isn't consciously aware that support is being given and consequently doesn't feel any negative consequences of being the recipient. Negative consequences include feeling obligated to the support giver, losing self-esteem, drawing more attention to the problem, and feelings of inequity.[53] One way we see negative social support is in the form of over-protectiveness. If you think about your family for instance, you likely remember times when your parents or older siblings were overly protective. Chances are you didn't appreciate their very visible support. However, in retrospect, you can probably also think of times when you received support but were unaware of that support because it just fit into the naturalness of the event or was in some other way very unobtrusive. Some possible examples would include your roommates going to the library or out with friends when you are planning on having a study group over the night before a big exam without you asking them to do so, or one partner taking care of everyday household chores when the other is ill.

> ***Think on it:*** Can you think of a time when you tried to be supportive or help someone and that person got angry or showed resentment? What elements of negative social support can you identify in that event? Using your "20/20 hindsight" what could you have done differently?

Effective Support is also Reciprocal.[54] Reciprocity is especially important in intimate relationships. Both people need to feel supported by the other. When one person feels he or she is doing the majority of the supporting in the relationship, resentment and conflict tends to build and undermine the relationship. Professor Burleson provides several suggestions for how we can respond as supportive conversational listeners.[55] These suggestions are listed below:

Positive Social Support Behaviors

- Express your understanding of the situation and their feelings (but avoid saying "I know exactly what you're going through"... every situation and every person is different).
- Convey your interest in listening.
- Use open-ended questions.
- Encourage the other to talk or explain the situation or their feelings, to "tell their story" (as much as the person desires or is willing to disclose).
- Clearly express your desire to help.
- Express positive regard or affection. (Remember, one reason people seek emotional support is that their self-esteem may have been threatened or invalidated.)
- Express concern and active interest in the situation.
- Show that you are available for the person.
- Express your support (I've got your back; I'm behind you all the way).

As you recall from previous discussions, social support is using supportive communication to help others make sense of what they are experiencing. Clearly, being supportive or receiving support is important for all of us. However, research shows that in order to be effective, *social support must be well timed*.[56] Up to this point, we have talked about the importance of effective social support. However, it is important to point out that not all of us want social support all of the time. There are times when we can be upset, but we don't seek social support. If, or when, we seek support is determined by several factors such as our perceptions of our relationship with the other person and their views of what has upset us. Other factors can include our personality (some people simply don't feel the need for lots of social support) and our views of the risks and benefits of seeking support (i.e., your friend may make fun of you).[57] Whether or not the timing is right seems to be dependent on how willing the partners are to engage in direct communication and listen to both the spoken message as well as the nonverbal message.

As an example, let's look at the following scenario between Nolvia and her mother in Case Study 6.5.

Case Study 6.5 A Long Day

Mrs. Guetierez: *What a day this has been. My feet hurt, my head hurts, and all of the new regulations affecting pharmacies on top of the impending merger are about to drive me nuts.*

Nolvia: *Oh ma, I'm so sorry you are feeling stressed. Is there anything I can do for you? Why don't I run a bubble bath. That always makes me feel better. And, don't worry about dinner – I have some time before my study meeting. I'll stir something up and make certain the kids and Papa are taken care of. Just go relax.*

Mrs. Guetierez: *Thank you, dear, but no. I have everything laid out to cook pollo con papas and you know how your dad loves that. Plus, I think the tamalitos are ready.*

At first glance, you probably think that Nolvia's considerate offer is just what Mrs. Guetierez needs in order to decompress from her very stressful day. However, a closer examination might show that Nolvia is actually adding to her mother's stress level. Remember, in order for social support to be effective good communication is necessary. One lesson that we can learn from the example is to listen to the entire message before jumping to conclusions. Notice that Nolvia quickly offers social support for her mother. However, she forgets to listen to the entire message. As a good listener, she should have used her inquiry or responding skills (remember Listening MATERRS) to get more information. Notice that her idea of social support is to offer solutions, not to listen more deeply. As a mother and a wife, Mrs. Guetierez may feel the need to provide care for her children and her husband. And, she certainly wouldn't want to interfere with Nolvia's study group.

Think on it: Review our discussion of red, yellow, and green listening in Chapter 2. What type of listening is Nolvia using in Case Study 6.5? What advice would you offer her the next time her mother has a long, stressful day.

Identifying Negative Social Support

The problem is that, even with the best of intentions, we often find ourselves engaging in behaviors that are not supportive of our friends and family. One scholar who spent a good portion of his career studying social support, empathy, and related social interaction skills is Brant Burleson. Professor Burleson identified several types of messages we should avoid.[58] Most of the following examples, if engaged in, will make someone feel that their feelings are unwelcomed. The list below illustrates ways people *don't* show social support. You'll notice that many of them reflect low person-centered messages.

Negative Social Support Behaviors

- Be wary of giving advice (it should be desired, it should… have the ability to actually solve the problem, with few significant disadvantages).
- Avoid platitudes, such as "it will all work out." Maybe it will, but when someone is in the middle of a crisis, they likely won't feel that way.
- Don't tell people they should stop crying, etc. Everyone releases emotions differently.
- Avoid telling people that what they are feeling (or saying) is wrong, embarrassing, etc.
- Don't minimize what people are feeling ("It's not such a big deal").
- Avoid making the support seeker "bad" or responsible for the problem ("Well, you didn't lock your car; no wonder your backpack was stolen").
- Don't tell others how they should be feeling, or that they should forget about the problem, or ignore their feelings.

As you can see, social support attempts that include advice giving and downplaying feelings expressed by others are often perceived as ineffective.[59] Drawing from Chapter 2, you know that these types of responses fall into the yellow category of listening. That is they acknowledge the speaker, but in some way downplay the person's concerns. Other times, our attempts to provide social support actually lead the other person to be more dependent.[60] For example, if we constantly jump to help others rather than giving them the option of helping themselves, we may empower a sense of helplessness, rather than actually helping the person. For example, many nursing home residents are wheelchair bound. If you have recently visited a nursing home you may have noticed residents rolling themselves around the facility. The caregivers in that facility likely encourage residents to do as much for themselves as possible, rather than doing everything for them. This allows residents to feel some sense of independence and pride in knowing they aren't helpless, which in turn contributes to their self-esteem. In addition, the response also keeps the focus off of their fragile physical condition and on the more positive aspect of being able to partially take care of themselves.

So how does this information translate into your world? Think about your various relationships. Do you have a friend who seems constantly to turn to you for solutions to problems? Notice the question doesn't ask if someone asks you for *advice*, instead it focuses on asking you for *solutions*. In this type of case, if you constantly provide solutions for the other person, it disempowers that person from taking responsibility for his or her actions.

Now, let's re-examine the interaction between Nolvia and Mrs. Guetierez in Case Study 6.5. In her attempts to be both a good daughter and a supportive family member, Nolvia isn't giving her mother the gift of listening. Instead, she is trying to "fix" the problem. Isn't it possible that Mrs. Guetierez just needs to let off a little steam to a willing ear? If Nolvia had used reflexive responding skills and said something like, "You sound like you've had a hard day. What can I do to help?" or "Today must have been pretty rough. Want to have a glass of tea and chat a while?" she would have invited her mother to accept support in the form of either action or being listened to.

Problem and Emotion-focused Support

Previously we talked about directive and non-directive social support. Two additional types of support are **problem-focused support** and **emotion-focused support**. Sometimes, we seek support in order to solve a problem (e.g., you flunked the last exam, your dog keeps jumping the fence), while other times we seek emotional support (e.g., your significant other just dumped you, your dog was hit by a car). According to Professor Burleson, emotional support "includes helping distressed others work through their upset by listening to, empathizing with, legitimizing, and actively exploring their feelings."[61] **Emotional support** is particularly important given that the stress and emotional pain often "stem from the invalidation of the self, either directly (e.g., rejection by a valued other), or indirectly (e.g., failing at something connected to one's self-concept)."[62]

In addition, emotional support for others is one of the primary means we use for showing others we care, are interested in and committed to them. Thus, it is a means of showing compassion and love. As a result, social support is a relationally significant behavior.[63] In fact, a number of researchers suggest that social support skills are fundamental to social competence at all ages (childhood through adulthood) and can affect our ability to have close personal relationships, such as friendships and dating relationships, marriage and quality parent–child relationships.[64]

One of the biggest problems we face as conversational listeners and support givers is that we often feel pressure to speak. Simply being quiet and allowing the other person to have his or her say is difficult. Thus, one of the most important conversational listening lessons we can learn is to refrain from speaking and simply listen. The fact is not everything we think needs to be said. This statement is especially true in the realm of social support. Whether providing emotional or problem-focused support, listening provides the key to giving the type and amount of support that is being sought.

Meeting Social Support Needs

How we feel about the social support we receive is affected by several things, including the type and amount of support. First, the support we receive should match the support we feel we need. In other words, if you are seeking emotional support, but the person you are talking to is giving you problem-focused support, you are likely going to be dissatisfied. In addition, we tend to want a certain level or amount of support – we don't want too much or too little.[65] For example, you may complain to your parents about a teacher at school, but would be mortified if they took it upon themselves to call him or her. As you can see, support-givers can be in a bit of a bind. How can we tell what type of support someone wants or how much support to give them? The problem can sometimes be made worse when those seeking support are indirect or ambiguous about their needs. When this occurs, we may not recognize that assistance is being sought.

Central to support giving of any type is listening. In an ideal world, we could immediately tell the type of support a person wanted, or they would tell us, "Hey, I need you to help me solve this problem," or "I just need someone to let me talk out my frustration." Unfortunately, people are seldom this direct.

Thus, as support givers we sometimes rely on those indirect and ambiguous cues mentioned earlier. We have to pay attention to both verbal and nonverbal behaviors that can help us determine who actually wants support and what type of support they are most likely seeking. Communication scholar April Trees studied these nonverbal and verbal behaviors. Focusing on conversations between young adults (aged 17 to 29) and their mothers, Trees found that emotional disclosures (e.g., "I'm really upset," "This is driving me crazy") at the beginning of a conversation were a sign that these adults were seeking social support – either emotional or problem-focused. When we hear emotional disclosures (that are more in depth or stronger than those normally given) it may be a cue that the person we are talking with is upset or stressed and in need of support. Trees' work also indicates that people may start off with emotional disclosures no matter the type of social support they ultimately are seeking. As listeners, it's important to be aware that emotional disclosures are not necessarily a sign that a person is just seeking emotional support. In terms of nonverbal behaviors, Trees reports that few of her study participants appear to use nonverbal cues strategically when seeking social support. However, mothers in her study tended to be good at determining when their children were seeking problem-focused support. A louder voice combined with less movement (e.g., kinesics and proxemics) apparently suggests to moms that their children were having problems that they needed advice or help with. Most of us believe that people have less control over their nonverbal behaviors, which may be one reason we cue into them as an indicator of stress.

Seeking and providing social support is one of the primary communication goals we engage in during our daily conversations. However, we also face times when misunderstandings and miscommunications can occur. Occasionally, these miscommunications can result in conflict.

Conflict

Conflict can be defined as "the interaction of interdependent people who perceive incompatible desires, goals, personal comforts or communication preferences, and the possibility of interference from others as a result of this incompatibility."[66] Conflict can occur at any time and any place and it will always present a challenge to us as listeners. It is important to note, however, that it is a normal part of every healthy relationship. Listening during conflict can be quite difficult, in part, because it is emotionally defined, addresses our identity, and affects our relationships.[67] At the same time, many of us lack the confidence to speak assertively (rather than confrontationally) when we are facing a difficult problem or situation.

We also know that conflict can cost – often a lot. On a personal level we lose sleep or can't eat. We don't speak to our brother for a week, missing the opportunity to say happy 21st birthday. We may dismiss what our teacher has to say, and so do more poorly on an exam or assignment. We break up with our significant other, losing a close confidant. In the workplace, employees leave and new ones must be trained.

In essence, where there are people there is the potential for conflict: at home, in computer chat rooms, at school, on freeways, or at the office. Regardless of the location and circumstances, there seems to be a number of **sources of conflict**.[68] For example, we differ in our:

- judgments of what constitutes good evidence (e.g., is global warming real or just a weather blip in the history of the world);
- personal interests (e.g., who gets the dog in the divorce);
- beliefs about how something should be done (e.g., flip a coin to decide the winner or have a playoff);
- role expectations (e.g., beliefs in what a role entails or power imbalances from the roles);
- communication (e.g., how something is said, how it is interpreted);
- values (e.g., what is most important to us – spending money on cancer research or reducing carbon emissions);
- views of relationships (e.g., lack of trust, respect, or honesty, don't feel listened to).

Any of these sources may lead to disagreements, and it's not uncommon for multiple sources to be involved. In addition, what you perceive to be the source of conflict may not fit the other person's perceptions at all. Thus, when addressing any conflict, we have to keep in mind our perceptions of the conflict as well as the actual underlying issues related to the dispute. We also need to keep in mind how the other person perceives the conflict and manages conflict. Getting stuck on who said what and taking ownership of particular ideas is simply counterproductive. So, how can you show others you are willing to engage in productive conflict resolution?

Handling Angry People

Good listening skills form the basis for being able to handle the angry person successfully. The **Bannon Four Stage Conflict Process** is one means of approaching this type of situation.[69] First, *you should inquire,* using your active listening skills to focus fully on the other person's concerns. For example, you might say, "You seem to be upset that you couldn't have Saturday off. Is there something going on we need to know about?" (It's important to let the other party do the talking once you begin exploring their concerns.) Second, you should empathize by connecting with the other person on his or her emotional level. This is particularly important in an emotionally charged situation such as when you are dealing with someone who is angry or experiencing other very strong emotions. As a part of his second stage, Bannon suggests *expressing empathy,* using a two-step model. Step one goes something like this: I _____ your _____. The blanks can be filled in with phrases such as "I understand your frustration," "I appreciate your concern" and other similar words. This type of statement helps the other know you are attempting to connect with them and better understand why they are upset. In the second step of this stage, Bannon suggests using phrases such as, "I, too _____." This blank will be filled in with words that let the other person know that you feel or have felt the same type of emotion (e.g., "I've also missed a family reunion because I couldn't get off from work"). In the third stage, Bannon suggests *asking for permission.* Ask if the other person wants more information, don't just assume that you should automatically give him/her further explanations. By asking, you give the other person some control over the interaction and it reduces the chance that you will engage in unwanted problem solving. For example, a question that you would use in a situation like this is "What information would be helpful?" Be sure to listen carefully to the answer so your response will be appropriate and allow you to move on to the last step. Finally, you should both *explain and offer choices.* If you get a yes in the third stage, you can continue the other person's positive involvement by explaining the situation and offering options from which the other party can select. While Bannon's suggestions won't resolve all your conflicts, they will help aid you in many of the common conflicts you face.

Hopefully, these tips will help you build greater confidence in your conflict-solving abilities. Attitude, as with most things, is important. When we see conflict as a problem to be solved mutually rather than an adversarial or combative interaction, we've taken an important first step in solving the conflict.

Conflict and Culture

Finally, a critical component in how we perceive and manage conflict seems to be cultural background. Research done in the US indicates people from diverse backgrounds will react to conflict differently.[70] Some examples of this include findings that when compared to Americans of European decent, African Americans seem to prefer a highly affect-laden conflict style, while Asian Americans seem to prefer avoiding conflict or turning to a trusted third party and seeking mediation.[71] Further research has indicated that Native Americans take a restrained approach to conflict and often turn to tribal elders to help settle the conflict.[72] From this description, you can see that Namii and Tamarah who come from Asian and Native American backgrounds, respectively, probably have some commonality in their approaches to managing conflict. As listeners, we need to be sensitive to these different approaches when we either find ourselves in a conflict situation with someone with a different cultural background or are called upon to mediate such a conflict.

In any context, one of the keys to managing conflict successfully is being a good listener. When you find yourself in a conflict remember to listen to the other parties' perspectives, use rational arguments, value contributions from all parties, and try to understand points of view other than your own.[73] Trying to do all of this may sound like a "tall order," and it is. Of course, it is impossible to understand other points of view if you aren't listening carefully. This suggests that you focus on what the speaker is saying and keep quiet until he or she is finished. It is also a good idea to paraphrase what you heard before you state your perspectives. This shows the other party that you have indeed remained attentive to what was said. Chances are you have experienced a conflict in which all of these suggestions have been ignored. How might the exchange have been different if you and the other party had followed these guidelines?

It is unrealistic for us to think all conflict is going to be resolved. However, with skill, care, and good listening, we can often arrive at solutions that will resolve at least part of the issues in dispute. If the unresolved issues are really important, you may want to go through the process again focusing on the unresolved issues. The feeling we are being heard is central to conflict resolution. At the same time, close listening to the other person will hopefully help us to better understand the underlying causes of the disagreement, another central element of resolving conflict.

Summary

This chapter began with an example of a conversation between two friends. In that case study we can find elements of conversation that we talked about in this chapter: sensitivity to the other person, appropriate responding, and interaction within the context of a relationship. Listening is an essential element of any conversation. Whether we are engaged in a conflict or a pleasant social exchange, without listening there is no conversation. Here is a summary of the main points covered in this chapter:

- Conversations are interactions. To have an interaction, there must be listening.
- Meanings in a conversation are co-created by the participants.
- Conversations are based on the principle of cooperation.
- Conversations thrive on openness.
- Sensitive conversationalists are aware of individual and cultural differences and make appropriate accommodations.
- Good conversationalists provide social support for their partners.
- Conversations take place within the context of a relationship.
- Conflict resolution calls for well developed conversational and listening skills.

One of the main points made in the chapter is that conversations take place in the context of a relationship. The next two chapters will focus on listening in key relationships of our lives – family, friends, and romantic partners.

Key Concepts

Grice's maxims
    Principle of Cooperation
    Quality
    Quantity
    Relation
    Manner
Co-creating Conversations
    Generic Responses
    Back Channel
    Listening Noises
    Specific Responses
    Gaze Behaviors
Individual Differences
    Cognitive Complexity
    Receiver Apprehension
    Self-monitoring
Accommodation
    Under-accommodation
    Over-accommodation
    Non-accommodation
Context
Self-verification

High and Low Person-Centered Messages
Directive and Non-directive Social Support
Psychological Safety
Positive and Negative Social Support Behaviors
Problem and Emotion-focused Support
Conflict
Sources of Conflict
Bannon's Four Stage Process
Conflict and Culture

Discussion Questions

1. Do you feel like you are guilty of regularly violating one or more of Grice's four maxims? How do you think the violations affect your interactions with others? Which one do you think you violate the most? Why? Describe two to three things you can do to better to meet this maxim? Which do you notice other people violating most frequently? Why do you think this maxim stands out for you?

2. Would you rather be high in cognitive complexity or be a high self-monitor? Why? What are communicative consequences of each?

3. Do you think the amount and type of social support given is influenced by gender? Why or why not? If so, in what ways do you think it varies?

Listening Activities

1. Audio or video record a short conversation. It may be between you and a friend, two friends talking over a cup of coffee, or even a short discussion in the classroom. As you listen to the conversation, how do you see/hear Grice's maxim's exemplified? How do they help contribute to the flow of the conversation? People often break rules when trying to make a point (e.g., sarcasm, irony). Were there any rules broken? If so, which ones? Did the other person realize a rule was being broken? How did a broken rule affect the conversation?

2. Using the same conversation from the exercise above or a short conversation from a movie or television show, explore how the conversation was "co-created." First, note everything, verbals and nonverbals, that the speaker did to get his/her point across better. Next, listen to the same conversation from the listener's perspective. What did the listener appear to do to assist the speaker? Were there any behaviors by the speaker or listener that may have negatively affected their conversation? Based on what you've read in this chapter, what could they do differently to improve their conversation experience?

3. How can you use Bannon's stages of conflict resolution? Try the following role playing exercise. First, write a brief description of a conflict you are dealing with. Get into a group of three. You can role play the other party while one of your classmates plays you. The third person will coach each of you in how to incorporate Bannon's strategies into your interaction. So, if the "coach" hears you making a judgmental statement, he or she will point out the behavior and coach you through the process of incorporating good conflict resolution behavior.

Notes

1 See for example, Fiori, Windsor, Pearson, & Crisp, 2013; Sandstrom & Dunn, 2014; Sandstrom et al., 2016
2 Sandstom et al., 2016
3 Bavelas, Coates, & Johnson, 2000
4 Rubin, 1990
5 Janusik, 2007
6 Bohm, 2006
7 Bavelas, et al., 2000
8 Yngve, 1970, 2004
9 See Bavelas, et al. (2000) for a good summary of research in this area.
10 Krauss & Wienheimer, 1966; Krauss, Garlock, Bricker, & McMahon, 1977; see also Manusov & Patterson, 2006
11 Goodwin, 1981; Kraut, Lewis, & Swezey, 1982; see also Manusov & Patterson, 2006
12 Grice, 1957
13 Brown & Levinson, 1987
14 Slugoski & Hilton, 2001, p. 194
15 Clark & Wilkes-Gibbs, 1986; Schegloff, 1995; Shotter, 1993; Shotter & Gergen, 1994; Stewart, 2012
16 Littlejohn & Domenici, 2001, p. 35
17 Bavelas, et al, 2000
18 Duncan & Fiske, 1977
19 Duncan, 1972
20 Ho, Foulsham, & Kingstone, 2015
21 Bavelas, et al., 2000
22 Harrigan, 1985.
23 Mayor & Bangerter, 2016
24 Bavelas & Chovil, 1997; Bavelas, et al., 2000; Goodwin, 1981
25 Bavelas, et al., 2000
26 Scott, 2004 (pp. 5–6) credits poet and author David Whyte with the original quote.
27 For a review, see Allen, 2002
28 Wheeless, Eddleman-Spears, Magness, & Preiss, 2005
29 Schrodt & Wheeless, 2001; Schrodt, Wheeless, & Ptacek, 2000; Wheeless & Schrodt, 2001
30 Snyder, 1974, 1979
31 Giles, 2008
32 Ryan et al., 1995
33 Williams, Kemper, & Hummert, 2003
34 Giles, 2008
35 Boggs & Giles, 1999
36 McKellin, Shahin, Hodgson, Jamieson, & Pichora-Fuller, 2007
37 McKellen, et al., 2007
38 Mankell, 2011
39 Pasupathi & Rich, 2005
40 McAdams, 1993; Pasupathi, 2001; Thorne, 2000
41 See, for example, Bavelas, et al, 2000; Dickinson & Givon, 1995; Tatar, 1998
42 Pasupathi & Rich, 2005, p. 1057
43 Bavelas et al., 2000; Grice, 1957
44 Gergen, 2003
45 For a brief review, see Burleson, 2003
46 Xu & Burleson, 2001
47 Pecchioni & Halone, 2001
48 High & Dillard, 2012

49 Fisher, 1997; Harber Schneider, Everard, & Fisher, 2005
50 Castro, Kluger, & Itzchakov, 2017
51 Keaton, Bodie, & Keteyian, 2015
52 Bolger & Amarel, 2007; Bolger, Zukerman, & Kessler, 2000; Rafaeli & Gleason, 2009
53 Rafaeli & Gleason, 2009
54 Rafaeli & Gleason, 2009.
55 Burleson, 2003, pp. 566–567
56 Rafaeli & Gleason, 2009
57 See for example, Collins & Feeney, 2000; Cutrona, Suhr, & MacFarlane, 1990; Goldsmith & Parks, 1990
58 Burleson, 2003, pp. 567–568
59 Rafaeli & Gleason, 2009
60 Bass, Tausig, & Noelker, 1988–1989
61 Burleson, 2003
62 Burleson, 2003
63 Burleson, 1990
64 Burleson, Kunkel, Samter, & Werking, 1996; Burleson, Kunkel, & Birch, 1994; Cunningham & Barbee, 2000; Stevenson, Maton, & Teti, 1999
65 Cutrona, Cohen, & Igram, 1990; Cutrona, 1996; Horowitz et al., 2001
66 Folger, Poole, & Stutman, 2008, p. 5
67 Bodtker & Jameson, 2001
68 Isenhart & Spangle, 2000
69 Bannon, 2003
70 Bresnahan, Donohue, Shearman, & Guan, 2009
71 Hecht, Jackson, & Ribeau, 2003; Ting-Toomey & Chung, 2005
72 Ting-Toomey & Chung, 2005
73 Simonsen & Klispch, 2001

Additional Readings

Fine, D. (2005). *The fine art of small talk*. New York: Hyperion.
Molder, H., & Potter, J. (Eds.). (2005). *Conversation and cognition*. New York: Cambridge University Press.
Oetzel, J. G., & Ting-Toomey, S. (Eds.). (2006). *The SAGE handbook of conflict communication: Integrating theory, research, and practice*. Thousand Oaks, CA: Sage.
Tannen, D. (2005). *Conversational style: Analyzing talk among friends*. New York: Oxford University Press.

References

Allen, M. (2002). A synthesis and extension of constructivist comforting research. In M. Allen, R. W. Preiss, B. M. Gayle, & Nancy Burrell (Eds.), *Interpersonal communication research: Advances through meta-analysis* (pp. 227–246). Mahwah, NJ: Lawrence Erlbaum.
Bannon, J. (2003, Oct.). Anger at work: Whether it's others' or your own, here's how to deal with it. *Talent Development, 57*(10), 64+.
Bass, D. M., Tausig, M. B., & Noelker, L. S. (1988–1989). Elder impairment, social support and caregiver strain: A framework for understanding support's effects. *Journal of Applied Social Sciences, 13*, 80–115.
Bavelas, J. B., Coates, L., & Johnson, T. (2000). Listeners as co-narrators. *Journal of Personality and Social Psychology, 79*, 941–952.
Bavelas, J. B., & Chovil, N. (1997). Faces in dialogue. In J. A. Russell & J. M. Fernandez-Dols (Eds.), *The psychology of facial expression* (pp. 334–348). Cambridge: Cambridge University Press.
Bodtker, A. M., & Jameson, J. K. (2001). Emotion in conflict formation and its transformation: Application to organizational conflict management. *International Journal of Conflict Management, 12*, 259–275.

Bohm, D. (2006). *On dialogue.* London: Routledge.

Boggs, C., & Giles, H. (1999). "The canary in the cage": The nonaccomodation cycle in the gendered workplace. *International Journal of Applied Linguistics, 22*, 223–245.

Bolger, N., & Amarel, D. (2007). Effects of social support visibility on adjustment to stress: Experimental evidence. *Journal of Personality and Social Psychology, 92*, 458–475.

Bolger, N., Zuckerman, A., & Kessler, R. C. (2000). Invisible support and adjustment to stress. *Journal of Personality and Social Psychology, 79*, 953–961.

Bresnahan, M. J., Donohue, W. A., Shearman, S. M., & Guan, X. (2009). Research note: Two measures of conflict orientation. *Conflict Resolution Quarterly, 26*, 365–379.

Brown, P., & Levinson, S. C. (1987). *Politeness: Some universals in language usage.* Cambridge, UK: Cambridge University Press.

Burleson, B. R. (1990). Comforting as everyday social support: Relational consequences of supportive behaviors. In S. Duck (Ed.), *Personal relationships and social support* (pp. 63–104). Beverly Hills, CA: Sage.

Burleson, B. R. (2003). The experience and effects of emotional support: What the study of cultural and gender differences can tell us about close relationships, emotion, and interpersonal communication. *Personal Relationships, 10*, 1–23.

Burleson, B. R., Kunkel, A. W., & Birch, J. D. (1994). Thoughts about talk in romantic relationships: Similarity makes for attraction (and happiness, too). *Communication Quarterly, 42*, 259–273.

Burleson, B. R., Kunkel, A. W., Samter, W., & Werking, K. J. (1996). Men's and women's evaluations of communication skills in personal relationships: When sex differences make a difference – and when they don't. *Journal of Social and Personal Relationships, 13*, 201–224.

Castro, D. R., Kluger, A. N., & Itzchakov, G. (2017). Does avoidance-attachment style attenuate the benefits of being listened to? *European Journal of Social Psychology, 46*, 762–775.

Clark, H. H., & Wilkes-Gibbs, D. (1986). Referring as a collaborative process. *Cognition, 22*, 1–39.

Collins, N. L., & Feeney, B. C. (2000). A safe haven: Support-seeking and caregiving processes in intimate relationships. *Journal of Personality and Social Psychology, 78*, 1053–1073.

Cunningham, M. R., & Barbee, A. P. (2000). Social support. In C. Hendrick & S. S. Hendrick (Eds.), *Close relationships: A sourcebook* (pp. 272–285). Thousand Oaks, CA: Sage.

Cutrona, C. E. (1996). *Social support in couples; Marriage as a resource in times of stress.* Thousand Oaks, CA: Sage.

Cutrona, C. E., Cohen, B. B., & Igram, S. (1990). Contextual determinants of perceived social support. *Journal of Personal and Social Relationships, 7*, 553–562.

Cutrona, C. E., Suhr, J. A., & MacFarlane, R. (1990). Interpersonal transactions and the psychological sense of support. In S. Duck & R. Silver (Eds.), *Personal relationships and social support* (pp. 30–45). London: Sage.

Dickinson, C., & Givon, T. (1995). Memory and conversation: Toward an experimental paradigm. In T. Givon (Ed.), *Conversation: Cognitive, communicative, and social perspectives* (pp. 91–132). Amsterdam: John Benjamin.

Duncan, S. (1972). Some signals and rules for taking speaking turns in conversations. *Journal of Personality and Social Psychology, 23*, 283–92.

Duncan, S., & Fiske, D. W. (1977). *Face-to-face interaction: Research, methods, and theory.* New Jersey: LEA.

Fiori, K. L., Windsor, T. D., Pearson, E. L., & Crisp, D. A. (2013). Can positive social exchanges buffer the detrimental effects of negative social exchanges? Age and gender differences. *Gerontology, 59*, 40–52.

Fisher, E. B., Jr. (1997). Two approaches to social support in smoking cessation: Commodity model and nondirective support. *Addictive Behaviors, 22*, 818–833.

Folger, J. P., Poole, M. S., & Stutman, R. K. (2008). *Working through conflict: Strategies for relationships, groups, and organizations* (6th ed). Boston: Allyn & Bacon.

Gergen, K. (2003). Self and community and the new floating worlds. In K. Nyíri (Ed.), *Mobile democracy: Essays on society, self and politics* (pp. 61–69). Vienna, Austria: Passagen Verlag.

Giles, H. (2008). Accommodating translational research. *Journal of Applied Communication Research, 36*, 121–127.

Goldsmith, D., & Parks, M. (1990). Communication strategies for managing the risks of seeking social support. In S. Duck (Ed., with R. Silver), *Personal relationships and social support* (pp. 104–121). London: Sage.

Goodwin, C. (1981). *Conversational organization: Interactions between speakers and hearers.* New York: Academic.

Grice, H. P. (1957). Meaning. *Philosophical Review, 66*, 377–388.

Harber, K. D., Schneider, J. K., Everard, K., & Fisher, E. (2005). Nondirective support, directive support, and morale. *Journal of Social and Clinical Psychology, 24*, 691–722.

Harrigan, J. A. (1985). Listeners' body movements and speaking turns. *Communication Research, 12*, 233–260.

Hecht, M. L., Jackson, R. L., & Ribeau, S. (2003). *African American communication: Exploring identity and culture* (2nd ed.). Mahwah, NJ: LEA.

High, A. C., & Dillard, J. P. (2012). A review and meta-analysis of person-centered messages and social support outcomes. *Communication Studies, 63*, 99–118.

Ho, S., Foulsham, T., & Kingstone, A. (2015). Speaking and listening with the eyes: Gaze signaling during dyadic interactions. *PLoS ONE, 10*, e0136905.

Horowitz, L. M., Krasnoperova, E. N., Tatar, D. G., Hansen, M. B., Person, E. A., Galvin, K. L., & Nelson, K. L. (2001). The way to console may depend on the goal: Experimental studies of social support. *Journal of Experimental Social Psychology, 37*, 49–61.

Isenhart, M. W., & Spangle, M. (2000). *Collaborative approaches to resolving conflict.* Thousand Oaks, CA: Sage.

Janusik, L. A. (2007). Building listening theory: The validation of the conversational listening span. *Communication Studies, 58*, 139–156.

Keaton, S. A., Bodie, G. D., & Keteyian, R. V. (2015). Relational listening goals influence how people report talking about problems. *Communication Quarterly, 63*, 480–494.

Krauss, R., Garlock, C., Bricker, P., & McMahon, L. (1977). The role of audible and visible back-channel responses in interpersonal communication. *Journal of Personality and Social Psychology, 35*, 523–529.

Krauss, R. M., & Wienheimer, S. (1966). Concurrent feedback, confirmation, and the encoding of references in verbal communication. *Journal of Personality and Social Psychology, 4*, 343–346.

Kraut, R., Lewis, S., & Swezey, L. W. (1982). Listener responsiveness and the coordination of conversation. *Journal of Personality and Social Psychology, 43*, 718–731.

Littlejohn, S. W., & Domenici, K. (2001). *Engaging communication in conflict.* Thousand Oaks, CA: Sage.

Mankell, H. (2011, December 10). The art of listening. *The New York Times.* Retrieved from www.nytimes.com/2011/12/11/opinion/sunday/in-africa-the-art-of-listening.html.

Manusov, V., & Patterson, M. L. (2006). *The Sage handbook of nonverbal communication.* Thousand Oaks, CA: Sage.

Mayor, E., & Bangerter, A. (2016). Flexible coordination of stationary and mobile conversations with gaze: Resource allocation among multiple join activities. *Frontiers in Psychology, 7*, article 1582.

McAdams, D. P. (1993). *The stories we live by: Personal myths and the making of the self.* New York: Guilford.

McKellin, W. H., Shahin, K., Hodgson M., Jamieson, J., & Pichora-Fuller, K. (2007). Pragmatics of conversation and communication in noisy settings. *Journal of Pragmatics, 39*, 2159–2184.

Pasupathi, M. (2001). The social construction of the personal past and its implications for adult development. *Psychological Bulletin, 127*, 651–672.

Pasupathi, M., & Rich, B. (2005). Inattentive listening undermines self-verification in personal storytelling. *Journal of Personality, 73*, 1051–1085.

Pecchioni, L. L., & Halone, K. K. (2001). Relational listening: A grounded theoretical model. *Communication Research Reports, 14*, 59–71.

Rafaeli, E., & Gleason, M. E. J. (2009). Skilled support within intimate relationships. *Journal of Family Theory & Review, 1*, 20–37.

Rubin, R. B. (1990). Communication competence. In G. Phillips & J. T. Wood (Eds.), *Speech communication: Essays to commemorate the 75th anniversary of the Speech Communication Association* (pp. 94–129). Carbondale, IL: Southern Illinois University Press.

Ryan, E. B., Hummert, M. L., & Boich, L. (1995). Communication predicaments of aging: Patronizing behavior toward older adults. *Journal of Language and Social Psychology, 13*, 144–166.

Sandstrom, G. M., & Dunn, E. W. (2014). Social interactions and well-being: The surprising power of weak ties. *Personality Social Psychology Bulletin, 40*, 910–922.

Sandstrom, G. M., Tseng, V. W.-S., Costa, J., Okeke, F., Choudhury, T., & Dunn, E. W. (2016). Talking less during social interactions predicts enjoyment: A mobile sensing pilot study. *PLoS ONE, 11*(7), e0158834.

Schegloff, E. A. (1995). Discourse as an international achievement III: The omnirelevance of action. *Research on Language and Social Interaction, 28*, 185–211.

Scott, S. (2004). *Fierce conversations.* New York: Berkley.

Schrodt, P., & Wheeless, L. R. (2001). Aggressive communication and informational reception apprehension: The influence of listening anxiety and intellectual inflexibility on trait argumentativeness and verbal aggressiveness. *Communication Quarterly, 49*, 53–69.

Schrodt, P., Wheeless, L. R., & Ptacek, K. M. (2000). Informational reception apprehension, educational motivation, and achievement. *Communication Quarterly, 48*, 60–73.

Shotter, J. (1993). *Conversational realities: Constructing life through language.* Beverly Hills, CA: Sage.

Shotter, J., & Gergen, K. (1994). Social construction: Knowledge, self, others, and continuing the conversation. In S. Deetz (Ed.), *Communication yearbook 17* (pp. 3–33). Thousand Oaks, CA: Sage.

Simonsen, A., & Klispch, K. (2001, December). Conflict with class. *Parks & Recreation*, 77–79.

Slugoski, B. R., & Hilton, D. J. (2001) Conversation. In W. P. Robinson & H. Giles (Eds.), *The new handbook of language and social psychology* (pp. 193–219). New York: Wiley.

Snyder, M. (1974). Self-monitoring of expressive behavior. *Journal of Personality and Social Psychology, 30*, 526–537.

Snyder, M. (1979). Self-monitoring process. In L. Berkowitz (Ed.), *Advances in experimental social psychology* (Vol. 12, pp. 85–128). New York: Academic.

Stewart, J. (2012). Communication and interpersonal communicating. In J. Stewart (Ed.), *Bridges not walls.* (11th ed). New York: McGraw-Hill.

Stevenson, W., Maton, K. I., & Teti, D. M. (1999). Social support, relationship quality, and well-being among pregnant adolescents. *Journal of Adolescence, 22*, 109–121.

Tatar, D. (1998). *Social and personal consequences of a preoccupied listener.* Unpublished dissertation. Stanford University, Stanford, CA.

Thorne, A. (2000). Personal memory telling and personality development. *Personality and Social Psychology Review, 4*, 45–56.

Ting-Toomey, S., & Chung, L. C. (2005). *Understanding intercultural communication.* Los Angeles, CA: Roxbury.

Wheeless, L. R., Eddleman-Spears, L., Magness, L. D., & Preiss, R. W. (2005). Informational reception apprehension and information from technology aversion: Development of a new construct. *Communication Quarterly, 53*, 143–158.

Wheeless, L. R., & Schrodt, P. (2001). An examination of cognitive foundations of informational reception apprehension: Political identification, religious affiliation, and family environment. *Communication Research Reports, 18*, 1–10.

Williams, K., Kemper, S., & Hummert, M. L. (2003). Improving nursing home communication: An intervention to reduce elderspeak. *The Gerontologist, 43*, 242–247.

Xu, Y., & Burleson, B. R. (2001). Effects of sex, culture, and support type on perceptions of spousal social support: An assessment of the "support gap" hypothesis in early marriage. *Human Communication Research, 27*, 535–566.

Yngve, V. H. (1970). On getting a word in edgewise. *Papers from the Sixth Regional Meeting, Chicago Linguistic Society* (pp. 567–578). Chicago, IL: Chicago Linguistic Society.

Yngve, V. H. (2004). The conduct of hard-science research. In V. H. Yngve & Z. Wasik (Eds.), *Hard-science linguistics* (pp. 342–367). London: Continuum International.

7 Listening and Relationship Building

The Family Context

Case Study 7.1 All in the Family

Carter, you are so lucky that your sisters are older and have moved away. My sisters are driving me crazy. They call me all the time and complain about our parents. Personally, I don't see how my mom and dad deal with having two teenage girls in the house. They seem to either be talking and giggling or whining. And, when I give them advice about whatever they're complaining about, they ignore me. Man, I hope my little brother doesn't get that way when he gets a little older.

Wow Radley, you sound pretty frustrated. I always thought you were lucky to be the oldest and have siblings at home. I kind of felt like an only child when I was growing up since my youngest sister is 15 years older than me. You and your family always seem to be so close.

Well I guess we really are. Even though both Mom and Dad are really busy, they have always stressed the importance of having family time to talk and listen to one another. Even the "brats" seem to set aside their adolescent nonsense and listen – you know, I even kind of like them then.

Radley, you'd better not let one of them hear you call them brats…

Listening in Relationships

Listening is a critical element in successful relationships. We feel this so strongly that we devote two chapters to the subject. The first chapter focuses on family relationships, while the second examines our relationships with friends and romantic partners. Certainly, there are similarities in listening needs in any type of relationship. However, as you will see, some of the listening demands placed on you will vary as you interact with others on different relational levels. For instance, think about how you listen to your best friend, your boyfriend or girlfriend (or spouse), your teacher or advisor, your parents, or your cousin. Don't you listen to all of them just a little bit differently? Don't you expect them to listen to you in different ways?

All humans depend on relationships. In fact, one of the most fundamental of human needs is the need to connect with others, to establish and maintain human relationships.[1] As infants, our parents and other family members were our first introduction to relationships. The attitudes expressed by our families and the experiences we share with them profoundly influence us – our self-concept and self-esteem, how we listen and express ourselves, and ultimately, how we view and build our own relationships. Relationship history develops over time and over our life course. The first and most important relationships we have begin with our family. We define family as a "social group of two or more persons characterized by ongoing interdependence with long-term commitments that stem from blood, law, or affection."[2]

One of the most challenging aspects of looking at listening in the family context is the very shape of families today. Many of us grew up with a mental picture of a family that we picked up from television. That mental picture, whether it be like the Cleavers of the 1950s television comedy, *Leave It to Beaver*, or the Simpsons from the show by that same name, probably includes a married, heterosexual couple, with both biological parents present. Chances are, however, fewer than 50% of you come from that type of family.[3] More current shows are portraying a different picture of a family. For example, the television show, *Modern Family*, features two characters, Mitchell and Cameron as a long-term stable couple, raising their adopted Vietnamese-born daughter, Lily. Many children today are being raised by a single-parent, same-sex parents, are in shared-custody arrangements, are part of blended families, or are being raised by grandparents or other relatives. Today, Dads are choosing to stay home and take on primary parenting roles.

> ***Think on it***: Think about your own family. How many members does it have? How old are you? Your parents? Siblings? Grandparents? What about your ethnic background and culture? How do you think your family make-up affects the relationships and communication within it?

The age factor in families can vary significantly and can have a major impact on how family members interact with one another. In many countries, the average age of first time mothers has increased significantly. For example, from 2000 to 2014, the average age of a first time mother in the US increased from 24.9 to 26.3, while the proportion of first time mothers under the age of 20 dropped 42% during this time period.[4] In 2010, the US Census Bureau reported that the median age of a first time grandmother and grandfather in the United States was 50 and 54, respectively.[5] However, as mothers wait to have children (and this trend is expected to continue), the age of first time grandparents will continue to rise. Needless to say, the abilities and contributions of parents, grandparents and other relatives to family life can be affected by their age.[6]

Cultural and ethnic background also affect family functions and communication. Who does what, who has power (or doesn't), and nonverbal expressiveness are just a few things that are affected by the culture, society, and family we are born in to. For example, the characters featured in the cases at the beginning of each chapter come from different backgrounds. Consequently, their family communication is likely to be different. Nolvia is Honduran and her grandparents play a very important part in her family. NaMii is Korean and since her father is the oldest son, his parents live with them. Tamarah is Native American, Ben is Jewish, and so forth. Much like the "characters" who are part of your lives, each of them faces slightly different family concerns. However, regardless of the family make-up or background, it is safe for us to say that the family in which we grow up as well as other adults who are important to us, have a profound impact on our listening behavior.

Finally, smartphones and similar devices have opened new channels of communication for family members. Rising global migration and family separation (e.g., divorce, work transfers, extended family members living in other areas of the country) provide family members the opportunity to sustain relationships.[7] The theory of **polymedia** helps explain how we use media in personal communication. We make strategic media choices, selecting a medium based on its ability to express emotions and manage mediated relationships based on the context and goal of the interaction.[8] And, as we will see later in the chapter, we also select a medium based on its ability to manage our privacy concerns. However, before we can address these topics, we need to understand the factors that can affect listening skills and communication behaviors in the family context.

Why Study Listening in Families?

The primary means by which children develop their social competencies is through observing family communication and social processes. Our observations affect our interactions as well as our goals, strategies, and behavior both inside and outside our family.[9] Of the many communication behaviors advocated by family communication experts, listening is the most common.[10] One of the problems, however, is that most of our parents were not taught good listening skills. If we're lucky, we end up in a family that values and teaches good listening like Radley's in the case study at the beginning of this chapter. If we aren't so lucky, we have to spend a lot more time learning the basics on our own, often through our mistakes.

> ***Think on it:*** How was communication handled in your family? Did you feel free to express your concerns? Do you feel family members listened to you? Did you listen to family members?

The importance of the communication in our families on us can't be overemphasized. A family's communication patterns can influence information processing in children (e.g., political views, media use), behaviors (e.g., conflict styles and behaviors, self-disclosure), and psychosocial tendencies (e.g., anxiety, self-concept, relational satisfaction, communication apprehension).[11] To illustrate the importance of the impact of family communication patterns, think of your family as your first "communication classroom."[12] A number of family-related variables affect how we develop and use social and communication skills with our friends and peers. How we learn to talk and listen to one another, how we discuss and argue, and how we give and receive affection are all profoundly influenced by our family relationships. Importantly, the communication skills we practice as children with family and peers enable us to successfully adjust later in life.[13]

People who are skilled communicators tend to enjoy a number of positive psychosocial outcomes. For example, they tend to be less lonely, be more accepted by their peers, have better relationships, and are generally more sociable. Other positive social behaviors include being friendly, having greater impulse control, being more person-centered when communicating and having a greater tendency to be more helpful, share more, and comfort others. In addition, communication and social competence appear to be linked.[14] Socially skilled children are better able to regulate their own and to "read" others' emotions and nonverbals, are better able to strategically choose the best communicative means of reaching personal and social goals (e.g., persuasion, compromising, etc.), and are better able to balance personal goals while maintaining positive relationships with others.[15]

To gain a better understanding of the role listening plays in family communication and how it is related to these positive outcomes, we first look at several general family communication factors. Next, we study the impact of family stories and family conflict on our attitudes and behaviors toward listening. We wrap up the chapter with a look at an examination of the communication between parents and children, and factors affecting our communication with older adults.

Family Communication Features

In order for us to understand the role and impact of listening in family relationships, we need to establish a background about family communication in general. Just as we established in the last chapter, listening is a critical component of any context in which a conversation occurs. First, however, we need to explore the impact of the family itself on the conversations that occur in that context. Regardless of how a family is structured and the roles parents play, how a family functions has a huge impact on the quality of family life. Good communication often sets successful families apart from the rest. According to many scholars, the family is one of the most important contexts for learning key social skills.[16] Some even suggest that we learn how to structure and interpret messages from the communication patterns we learn at home.[17]

Family Orientation Schemas

To illustrate just how family can impact your future listening and communication behavior, we need to examine factors that affect our schemas and look at how schema theory applies to family communication. In Chapter 3 you learned about the impact of schemas on how you take in, perceive, process, and store information. The schema that you learn from the communication patterns in your family influences whether you value listening and are willing to listen in a relationship. **Family communication** schemas have been defined as "knowledge structures that represent the external world of the family and provide a basis for interpreting what other family members say and do."[18] These schemas may well influence our interactions in all our future relationships.[19] Researchers Ascan Koerner and Mary Ann Fitzpatrick feel that these schemas are originally shaped by how parents communicate with each other and their children. They also feel that these schemas are reflected in the communication behaviors of family members as they interact with each other.

Koerner and Fitzpatrick propose that families have one of two orientations to or schemas about communication – conversation orientation and conformity orientation.[20] The choice is important as the orientation significantly affects the family's communication climate. **Conversation orientation** is the degree to which a family encourages its members to participate in unrestricted discussions about a wide variety of subjects. If a family has *low conversation orientation*, members don't feel free to share their thoughts or opinions with each other and discussions of feelings are rarely reciprocated. Over time, children in these families learn to keep their feelings to themselves. One study found that children who receive negative reactions when trying to share their feelings with their mothers eventually learn to control how they express their emotions.[21] The problem is that this type of response can negatively affect a child's emotional development. In contrast, families with a *high conversation orientation* have members who interact frequently and embrace open and direct conversations regardless of how controversial the topic may have been. Children from these families are better able to recognize, understand, and manage their emotions across a variety of situations. For example, children from high conversation-oriented families are better able to handle test anxiety.[22] In contrast, children growing up in a family with a low conversation orientation often have lower emotional intelligence, which can result in higher levels of reticence.[23]

The second orientation that Koerner and Fitzpatrick propose is **conformity orientation.** Conformity orientation is the extent to which a family stresses the importance of having homogenous attitudes, values and beliefs. Families with a *high conformity orientation* typically stress the importance of hierarchy and clear rules. Parents enforce the rules and don't tolerate deviation from family norms and expectations. This type of family tends to avoid conflict. *Low conformity orientation* families encourage the diversity of thought and opinion. They also encourage children to ask questions and challenge family rules. That is, they tend to encourage healthy conflict management as well as freedom to negotiate house rules.[24]

Conformity and conversation orientation are reflected in family communication patterns, which then affects how families function in areas such as family rituals, conflict and cohesiveness.[25] As you think about the family orientations we just covered, you can begin to see how family communication patterns can have great impact on your development as a communicator and listener. Families that encourage open interaction on a variety of topics tend to create an environment that encourages active listening and critical thinking, while those from high conformity families tend to have more listening anxiety and greater intellectual inflexibility.[26]

While our family backgrounds set the stage for our listening behavior, we have the choice of whether we want to perpetuate the pattern and follow the same communication scripts. In the following sections we will talk about three aspects of family communication we feel influence what type of communication orientation a family has: talk, confirmation, and self-disclosure.

> ***Think on it:*** What type of conversation orientation and conformity orientation did your family exhibit when you were growing up? How does it differ from that of some of your friends? How do you think it has impacted your interactions with others?

Family Talks

Talking goes beyond saying, "I love you," to include direct conversations about our family relationships. As we noted in the last chapter, conversations are part of what makes us social animals. The sharing of daily events, addressing problems that arise, and comparing perceptions are important for developing a relationship. It is through talk that people are connected. Think about the case study at the beginning of the chapter. Radley feels connected to his siblings because they talk regularly. Carter, whose sisters are much older and left home while he was a child, feels less connected with them. The true difference is that Carter and his sisters had less opportunity to talk than do Radley and his sisters. However, talk is at best only half of the equation. Feeling loved and accepted are two goals that are closely tied to family conversations. Notice that Radley, even in his frustration with his adolescent sisters, recognized the power of listening to the talk in his family. He clearly feels love and acceptance. When family members listen, they establish high conversation orientation or an atmosphere that encourages family talk time. This in turn, as you read in the previous section, establishes listening as an important and valued skill.

Research validates this conclusion. One dimension of family communication is family strength.[27] **Strong families** are characterized by:

- Commitment to the family and wellbeing of its members
- Appreciation and affection
- Positive communication and the ability to engage in constructive conflict management
- Regular expression and confirmation of affection among family members
- Enjoyment of quality time together
- Shared values
- A feeling of spiritual wellbeing
- Ability to manage stress and crisis situations effectively.

As you read the list, you can see that listening is critical to several of these characteristics. For example, in order to have positive communication and expression and confirmation of affection both speaking and listening must occur. A review of studies from almost 40 countries finds that that families around the world share remarkably similar views of family strength.[28]

Other research into strong families illustrates the relationship between family talk and family schema. For instance, strong stepfamilies engage in more everyday talk, openness, and family problem solving than do families struggling to blend.[29] Families who value expressiveness are more likely to be cohesive and adaptable, while those who hold a schema of structural traditionalism and conflict avoidance tend to be less cohesive and flexible.[30] Overall, research supports the conclusion that families' attitudes toward talk, or expressiveness, is an important aspect of the family schema. Of course, when a family supports talk, we assume that the positive attitude toward expressiveness includes the supportive element of listening. Listening is an important means of providing confirmation to others.

Confirmation

Confirming messages are one of the primary ways in which the identities we seek to construct are maintained. These messages imply an acceptance of and by others. However, messages are not always verbal. We can engage in confirmation nonverbally as when we include others in our conversations. Ignoring people, talking about them as if they were not there, or excluding them from conversations (verbally or nonverbally) are just a few of the ways we can send disconfirming messages. When we get disconfirming messages, we assume we aren't being listened to, and when we send non-confirming messages, we are sending messages that indicate we aren't willing to listen.

Think on it: Who do you look toward for confirmation? Who looks toward you for confirmation? Can you identify any patterns in confirmation behavior in your family?

Whether we are prone to sending confirming or disconfirming messages appears to be part of the family communication schema. For example, spouses use many of the same nonverbal behaviors when they convey negative emotions toward something their partner is saying.[31] This commonality for the type of back-channel messages (nonverbal messages) being sent would indicate that the family (or at least the parents) have developed a schema for how to react in such situations.

Further support for the inclusion of confirmation in our family schema is seen in the behaviors associated with family communication patterns. In families with high conformity orientation,

"If you want me to look at you when you talk to me, why don't you just FaceTime me?"

parents often set the pattern of withdrawing confirmation and affection when the child failed to conform to the expected family standards.[32] In contrast, families low in conformity and high in conversation tend to be much more forthcoming with positive confirmation.

Many messages we rely upon for confirmation are responses to various levels of intimacy. For example, if you are very close to someone, you will probably use a pleasant voice when talking with him or her as well as have a more pleasant facial expression. In addition, you will probably also confirm the relationship and your feelings for the person by using personal nicknames and increasing the level of verbal intimacy.[33] On the other hand, when the level of intimacy is less, as when you are talking with someone you don't know well or are in the midst of a conflict, you may compensate by leaning forward and increasing attention, almost as if you are trying to establish a connection with the other person. The level of intimacy will be determined by the levels of affection, trust, involvement, similarity and familiarity you feel toward the other person.[34] For many of us, our most intimate relationships are with family members. When those we care for and depend upon, our family, sends us confirming messages, we tend to feel more confident and listened to. We also tend to be more comfortable with self-disclosure.

Self-disclosure

By now, you have an understanding of the importance of self-disclosure in our lives. However, self-disclosure takes on an even greater importance in families. It is in families that we first come to trust others and to open up to them to tell them something personal or private. As young children we may not have fully realized that we were engaging in self-disclosure. However, as we grow older, we come to realize the implications of disclosing to family (and friends).

Keeping in mind that families construct the social reality of children, it's easy to see how the pattern for self-disclosure practice by your family impacts your willingness to share your thoughts, background, and feelings with others.[35] Families high in conversation orientation encourage open discussion, including self-disclosure.

Interestingly, self-disclosure in parent–child relationships suggests that the amount and nature of disclosure differs between family members. Not surprisingly, the parent who is seen as the most nurturing and supportive tends to receive greater disclosure. In addition, parents are often very good at reading their children's nonverbals. They can tell when children are pretending to be upset or scared, and when they actually are. In such cases, nonverbals may lead to a parent inviting self-disclosure from a child. Higher levels of disclosure tend to occur more often in dyads.[36] It can be difficult for families with multiple children to have alone time with one child. It may be even less likely to happen in blended families. Trust (and liking) leads to self-disclosure, and the time we spend together is necessary to building trust and developing liking. Research in family communication suggests it can take blended families (e.g., stepfamilies) as long as five years or more to develop a solid foundation of positive social relationships.[37] As seen in our interview in this chapter with foster parent Jeremy Walden, foster families face even greater challenges in building trust.

Marriage and family therapist Glenn Boyd, believes that "listening changes the relationship."[38] The truth of this statement is most evident when we look at the impact of how family members react to disclosure. When our family listens to us, we are more likely to engage in self-disclosure. Feeling listened to provides us with a sense of being rewarded for our openness. So, families that show that they are interested in each other's feelings and emotions, and who want to know what's going on in each other's lives, are more likely to disclose. Once again we can see the positive impact of a high conversation/low conformity family.

Think on it: Looking at your own family members, do you disclose some information to your mom and other information to a sibling? Or, a grandparent? How and why does your disclosure differ?

Similar patterns of disclosure are seen across all types of families – stepfamilies, single-parent, or two-parent biological families.[39] How we disclose is more often related to the family structure or system. Does your family sit down together at meals? Without the television on? Do you take family vacations together? Is there an expectation that you share what went on in your day? One family we know tends to take an evening walk together almost every day. During that time, with few interruptions, they are able to catch up on each others' day and stay connected with one another. The walk is family listening time.

Of course, the value of self-disclosure occurs only when we attempt to be honest and accurate in our disclosures. Such disclosure brings people together. However, not everyone is so honest. Some individuals may attempt to manipulate or control us by engaging in pseudo self-disclosure. At other times, individuals may not self-disclose because they believe it might hurt the other's feelings. For example, if your little brother takes up the tuba and is really awful at it, you may be rather circumspect in your comments so that you don't discourage him. As a perceptive family listener, you will know when to be direct and when to be kind. As seen here, disclosure is quite important in family life. If fact, many of the topics we discuss in this and other chapters are closely related to the concept of self-disclosure.

Foster Parenting: Listening Lessons

Jeremy Walden
Foster Parent

When my wife and I are notified of a child needing foster care, we are given a brief synopsis of why the child is being removed from his or her current situation. This snapshot is limited at best. That's where listening comes in. As foster parents, we try to piece together the child's past so we can best know how to meet his needs. It definitely means listening empathically to the child. But, being a foster parent ushers in a new set of important conversations with biological parents, relatives, social workers, lawyers, judges, teachers, physicians, etc. Every conversation adds to the puzzle we are trying to piece together. Yet, we have also had to become critical listeners because some of these conversations are full of exaggerations, half-truths, and hidden agendas. We became foster parents because we love children. We've discovered that sometimes listening is the most loving thing we can do.

The Role of Family Stories

Another important element of family communication is family stories. As family communication scholar Jody Koenig Kellas writes,

Stories and storytelling are one of the primary ways that families and family members make sense of everyday, as well as difficult, events, create a sense of individual and group identity, remember, connect generations, and establish guidelines for family behavior. With so many important functions, storytelling is a significant but still understudied communicative process for the family.[40]

Family stories are also one of the ways that we become family. Listen closely to your own family stories. As listeners, we are often unaware of the influence that stories may have on us and our family life. Our understanding of what family is (and isn't) and what family members do (and don't do) are embedded in the stories we hear. Thus, stories are one of the many contexts where listening is central to family life. Hearing about your grandmother's wedding day catastrophe, your Aunt's lottery win, the cousin who was told she would never have children but did, implicitly and explicitly, inform our views of what it means to be a family.

Establishing Family Schemas and Scripts

Family stories are one means of establishing and/or reinforcing family scripts or schemas. As you learned in Chapter 3, **scripts** (i.e., expectations, beliefs, norms) help us assign meaning to an interaction and act as a guide to behavior. When scripts are "broken" or violated by one family member, other family members may see that break as a threat to family stability and attempt to bring that family member back into line.[41] Just as with other schemas, family communication schemas provide a basis for interpreting the communication and actions of other family members. They also tend to establish how members of a family communicate, as you learned earlier in this chapter. When family members have a common family communication schema they are more likely to agree on other dimensions of family life.[42] For example, family members may be more likely to agree on the dimension of **expressiveness,** the level to which family members (including children) are encouraged to express viewpoints, ideas, and emotions. The family communication schema will also have an impact on the types of stories that are told. Since stories reflect the family values and norms, the family schema will necessarily reflect what is emphasized in the stories.

Another aspect of family schema is **structural traditionalism**, which is how much family members embrace conventional notions of marriage and family life (i.e., parents have the ability/authority to get children to conform to family life). While the structure of the family itself doesn't affect listening, the rigidity of the value may reflect how willing family members are to listen to points of view that challenge their beliefs. For example, if someone feels that a family is only two heterosexual people legally connected to each other (i.e., a marriage license), they may not be open to considering other perspectives on family. They may also feel that children should be strictly subservient to parental control, and therefore not encourage children to express themselves.

Yet another aspect of family schema is **avoidance**. Avoidance addresses how much family members will avoid conflict (e.g., avoid engaging in an unapproved behavior; avoid certain topics of conversation). Researcher Paul Schrodt suggests that families that are more expressive and willing to address issues of contention (e.g., willing to engage in some conflict, address uncomfortable topics) tend to have stronger emotional family bonds.[43] More importantly from a listening perspective, this indicates such families encourage listening to dissenting voices.

Think on it: What commonalities can you find between structural traditionalism and avoidance, and conversation and conformity orientation?

Regardless of the schema, you will hear the related values reflected in the stories that a family tells, particularly those that are told repeatedly. As a member of a family, you learn a great deal about who you are, what is expected of you, and how you should behave from these stories.

Professors Sunwolf and Frey, who have written extensively about the role of storytelling in our lives, agree with Professor Kellas' comment on the relationship between storytelling and personal identity. They argue that "storytelling is a tool for the construction of shared identities and communities."[44] As we grow up listening to the tales told by our families our lives are influenced in many ways: our self-concept is shaped, our notion of individual choice (both ability and range) is developed, our perception of our individual power is formed, and our view of community (and our place in it) is molded. This is one reason why Sunwolf and Frey believe that we are socialized via the stories we hear (by our family, friends, teachers, religious leaders, etc.).

It is also through narratives that our culture makes itself known. The attributes that are important to your family (and your culture) are often expressed in the stories you hear. For example, many of the stories told by the Landreth side of Professor Worthington's family stress individual sacrifice for the family. Her great grandmother's family moved from downtown to outside the big city of Atlanta (at the turn of the last century) because the doctor said her brother (one of 16 siblings) needed fresh country air to cure him of "consumption." Stories told by the Owens side of her family stress hard work, frugalness, and religious conviction. Professor Fitch-Hauser's stories are quite different. Being both Korean and adopted, her family's stories emphasize family as residing in the heart and not based on biological ties. They also emphasize the importance of making one's own mark in the world, independent of family history. Other stories emphasize the character building aspect of the struggle to fit in and the importance of accepting others, regardless of their ethnic background, physical abilities, or appearance.

> ***Think on it***: What type of stories have you heard in your family? What do they tell you about yourself? Your family? Your culture? Their beliefs, attitudes, and values? What is valued? (And, just as importantly, what is not?)

As we noted earlier, family stories are one of the primary ways that we communicate family identity. Previous research has found family storytelling to be related to overall family satisfaction and family functioning.[45] It is through family stories we learn the norms, values, and goals of our family, and subsequently, stories then help establish the standards for family relationships. Other research has found that families differ in their level of storytelling engagement, turn-taking, perspective-taking, and coherence.[46] **Engagement** refers to both the overall responsiveness and liveliness of other family members (verbal and nonverbal) during the telling of the story, as well as the level of warmth embedded within the story. **Turn-taking** is discussed more in depth elsewhere in the text, but here it not only refers to turns of talk, but also how dynamic and/or polite family members are when they listen. **Perspective-taking** refers to family members' ability to confirm the perspectives of other family members, and to take those perspectives and experiences into account while telling a story. Finally, **coherence,** is related to family members' ability to work together during the joint telling of a story to be able to integrate it into a larger whole.

> ***Think on it***: Engage your family in a storytelling session. (If possible, audio tape it.) Analyze the session in terms of engagement, turn-taking, perspective, and coherence. How does your family work together to tell stories?

Some families engage in storytelling more than others. If you want to learn more about your family, try the following:

- Generally, ask open-ended questions (e.g., where were you born, what was your favorite birthday celebration, what was your favorite class, teacher, or friend, in school).
- Of course, listen. Interest is often the key to getting a person to feel more at ease and willing to share their stories with you.
- Try getting a storytelling session going around a holiday or other family event. You may have relatives there who are not part of your everyday life.
- Record family stories and provide copies for relatives living away from home. They may be able to add additional details.

Today, family stories are shared through any number of mediums. Oral and visual mediums include face to face, via webcam (e.g., Skype, FaceTime), and by mobile phone. Written stories are shared via e-mail, blogging, and text messaging. What we don't often realize is that the medium we use when sharing family stories both enable and constrain narrative content and process.[47]

Our personal propensity for storytelling, the family schemas we hold, and the family orientations we share are all learned behaviors. While we interact with many family members, our parents (or those holding parental roles) tend to be among the most influential. The next section examines the influence of parents on our communication and listening attitudes and skills.

Parents as Communication Teachers

Learning Conversational Rules

In the previous chapter, we discussed the relationship between Grice's conversational maxims and listening. Parent/guardian–child conversations are where most children learn these rules. For example, children as young as two years can follow some aspects of the cooperative principle, and kindergarteners are amazingly good at identifying utterances that violate Grice's maxims (i.e., quantity, quality, manner, and relation).[48] When small children do violate a maxim, they often do not respond (quantity) or don't understand the communication well enough to respond appropriately (relation).[49] Interestingly, some research suggests mothers and fathers respond differently to these rule violations.[50] For example, fathers were more likely to point out violations by using repetition to encourage an appropriate response, or by modeling correct responses. Both moms and dads seem to use clarification to notify children of rule violations (i.e., often by making a statement or asking a question). However, mothers were more likely to not respond to a violation, most likely because of a greater concern for maintaining the conversation. For example, if a child responded off topic, mothers were more likely than fathers to change topics to match the child's.

Since family interaction is our first communication learning laboratory, we learn about the rules of conversations from observing and interacting with our parents and other family members. As children, we learn much more than the semantics and syntax of the language spoken in the home. We also learn the most basic rules for how to carry on a conversation usually by the age of four.[51] As we learn the rules of conversation, we also learn the importance of listening and being listened to. These lessons come directly from what our parents say and the behavior they model. An acquaintance told us a story about her young daughter who asked her to listen to something. Our friend, who was busy at the time, told her daughter to go ahead and tell her the story because "mommy is listening." Her daughter responded by going over to her mother, placing her hands on either side of her mother's face, turning it toward her, and saying "now you're listening." Clearly, the mother had previously taught her daughter that she had to stop what she was doing and look at her mother in order to listen.

Learning Social Support

As we noted above, our observations of our family interactions help us to develop our own interpersonal communication competencies. Research suggests that family communication patterns (i.e., conversation and conformity orientations) lead us to develop individual communication preferences and behaviors that we may use to guide our interpersonal interactions, particularly if distressed.[52] Research by Professors Andrew High and Kristina Scharp support this claim. Their study found that individuals who grow up in a family with a strong conversation orientation were more likely to engage in intentional, goal-directed support seeking.[53] Thus, families that regularly encourage open communication tend to produce children who are more adaptable communicators, and who are more skilled at and more motivated to seek direct social support (and to avoid indirect support). As we noted earlier in the chapter, highly conversation-oriented families provide their children with numerous opportunities to practice talking and listening to one another regarding both positive and negative events in their lives. They aren't discouraged from seeking help, and when they do seek help, their requests are met with support.[54]

Parents can encourage their children to become more comfortable with seeking direct social support in several ways.[55] For example, parents can:

- Identify times to discuss the day (e.g., meal times, drive home from school, etc.), encouraging their children to seek help when needed. Feelings of being listened to and accepted encourage sharing.
- Model effective social support behaviors (e.g., being responsive to positive and negative situations, engaging in direct support seeking). Again, we learn through observation.
- Coach children in open communication practices (e.g., listening, withholding judgment). Observation is not always enough. Providing feedback can help children further refine their communication skills and behavior.

Doing the above (as well as additional behaviors we introduce below), will increase a child's motivation to seek direct support and increase their skills. High and Scharp emphasize the role of social learning and illustrate how family listening and communication behaviors can affect our support-seeking strategies. Of course, additional factors such as the relationship we have with someone, the context of the conversation, the communication medium (e.g., face to face, text), and other individual characteristics (e.g., communication apprehension, willingness to listen, etc.) may influence our support seeking style.

Learning Problem Solving

In addition to learning how to listen and communicate, family communication also sets the tone for how children learn to address problems and other life challenges. Recent research at Vanderbilt University indicates that children seem to learn more when their mothers listen.[56] Child psychologists Bethany Rittle-Johns, Megan Saylor, and Kathryn Swygerty, found that children who have to explain the solution to a problem to their mothers have a much improved ability to solve similar problems later on. In their study, they asked the moms to listen, without providing assistance. Of the various methods they tested (e.g., having the child restate the answer, having the child explain the solution to themselves, or having the child explain the solution to their moms), the act of their mother's listening to the explanation was the one most effective in aiding the children's learning process. Explaining the reasoning behind the problem's solution to a parent (or someone else they know), not only appears to help children better understand the problem, but also helps them apply what they learned to other situations.

Learning to Manage Emotions

Parents also influence how children learn to express and manage emotions. For example, through their parents, preschoolers learn about "the appropriate expression of emotions, possible reactions to others' positive and negative emotions, the nature of emotional expression, and the types of situations that are likely to elicit emotions."[57] Think about how you react to emotional situations. Chances are if you come from an emotionally expressive family, you, too, are expressive. Likewise, if your family is more restrained, you probably are too. If you learn to perceive emotional expressiveness as normal, you will probably be more comfortable listening to emotionally expressive messages.[58] On the other hand, if you come from a restrained family, you may be very uncomfortable listening to those expressive messages. Through our parents we learn what emotions can be expressed (or not) within the family and in specific contexts.[59] Think back to your early years, or to conversations your parents had with a younger sibling. Did they verbally discuss an emotion and how it related to an event? If so, they may have been acting as an **emotion coach**. Parents who engage in this type of coaching actively discuss their children's emotions, helping them to distinguish between differing emotions, and assisting them with their emotional skill building (i.e., identification, experiencing, and regulating them).

Expressiveness (the ability and willingness to express emotions) is particularly important for parent–child relationships. Individual parental expressiveness appears to affect a variety of factors such as a child's emotional expressiveness, social popularity and prosocial behaviors (e.g., helpfulness, empathy).[60] Importantly, children often carry these modeled behaviors of expressiveness into their relationships with friends and romantic partners. While children who are exposed to and learn about expressiveness may not necessarily be more emotionally expressive themselves, they are oftentimes considered more socially competent by their peers.[61] We can assume that this perceived competence is due to the ability to listen for emotional content and impact. These expressiveness styles are often reflected in their dating relationships.

Not all parents are comfortable with emotion coaching. These parents are sometimes called **dismissing parents** because in their efforts to be helpful and make their child feel better, they often ignore the child's emotions. In other more negative cases, parents may be dismissive by actually punishing the child for either showing or asking about emotions. Whatever the situation, dismissing parents deprive their children of the opportunity to reflect upon themselves and their feelings. Unfortunately, it also teaches a child that listening to emotions is unimportant. Conversations provide important coaching moments in which to address feelings and emotions and how to manage them. For example, moms who both talk about and spend time discussing emotions, tend to have young children who are more "emotionally competent." While coaching and dismissing are often associated with handling a child's negative or "upset" emotions, learning to express affection is also very important.[62] It is one of the ways to gain positive attention from a parent. Children want and need positive interactions with their parents, as well as attention to distress or pain. Greater understanding of emotions becomes important as children learn and develop an understanding of empathy and empathic behaviors. Children from low conformity families seem better able to develop the flexibility and spontaneity necessary to cope with relational maintenance messages. They learn early that listening to and accepting different feelings is important.[63]

If you reflect back to Case Study 7.1, you can see from Radley's comments that his family is low conformity. From the research we have discussed, we can expect their norm of having family listening time will help the children be more socially successful.

Ultimately, emotional communication is embedded in our interpersonal and social relationships and transactions.[64] Family interactions form the foundation for how we express emotions and cope with emotional issues.[65] In a sense, our emotional views are socially constructed and based on personal experiences and events, as well as the stories that family members tell. Family stories often emphasize what behaviors (emotional and otherwise) are acceptable and which are not. These family interactions become a primary conduit by which we learn our "emotion scripts" and interpretive schemas.[66] Of course, you know by now that schemas "color our world" biasing how we approach relationships, interact with others, and interpret both our own and others' emotions. In addition, our emotional schemas may predispose us to experience some emotions over others.[67] These schemas may also affect our world view. For example, if we grow up in an emotionally expressive family, we may view the world, and those in it, as empathic and demonstrative. Finally, our schemas can affect the meaning we attach to an emotional event, which in turn may affect our emotion-related behavior.[68] If your anger schema frames anger as something that is always negative, then you may become anxious when someone around you gets angry, instead of viewing it more objectively and exploring the causes.

Think on it: Consider the adults in your life. Who makes you feel the most listened to? Why?

Molding Children's Listening Behaviors

Of course, active listening is one of the most frequently suggested techniques for improving parent–child interactions (by both parents and children). Another suggestion focuses on *responsive style.* As we pointed out in our discussion of emotions, how parents respond to their children and teenagers helps them to name feelings, shows that it's okay to have those feelings, and provides a means of addressing them constructively. It is clear then that it is especially important for parents to be non-judgmental in how they respond to their children, especially when emotions are involved. When parents are able to achieve these things, they become a resource person for their children.

Ideally, parents will teach and model good listening behavior.[69] Whether you are a parent, a cousin, a brother, or an aunt, a review of advice on how best to raise good listeners tends also to emphasize positive modeling of good listening behaviors. We offer **six suggestions to improve your listening with young children:**

- *Avoid distractions.* Children don't listen (nor do adults) when distracted. Turn off the TV and put away toys or videogames. Some experts argue that cutting down on the electronic "noise" in children's lives makes it easier for them to listen, that they shouldn't even be allowed to "plug in" until the weekend. While most people won't go to this extreme, we do agree that removing distractions during important conversations should be done.
- *Be a good role model*. Asking a child to attend to what you have to say when you then turn around and tune them out, doesn't encourage them to be good listeners. "Do as I say" and actually "Do it" when it comes to teaching and practicing good listening habits (like the daughter we described in the previous example who made her mom look at her in the eyes). Allow

them to finish their thoughts, listening closely and without criticism. Avoid giving too much advice, denying feelings, jumping to conclusions, interrupting (except when needed for clarification), or brushing children off, all of which send the message that they and their concerns aren't important to you. One means of achieving this end is to try sitting and having a pleasant conversation. These conversations help kids to experience positive outcomes to listening.

- *Be direct.* Avoid making statements in the form of a question. "Wouldn't you like to go study now?" It sounds like an option or choice is being offered when in reality it is not.
- *Ask children to paraphrase* (or write it down). Whether orally or written, good listening requires the ability to analyze and summarize information. Practice will help them learn this important listening skill. One tip, avoid yelling across the room, down the hall, or out the door. Tell them you need their attention for a specified amount of time (e.g., 5 minutes). Clearly make eye contact (even if you have to sit down or kneel to make this happen), tell them what you need, then ask for the all-important paraphrase.
- *Allow children to look away.* Yes, we just said you should make eye contact when *telling* something to a child, but be aware that *gaze aversion* is often a sign that the child is taking time to formulate a response.[70] Giving children some time to answer a question (i.e., don't interrupt their thinking) can be beneficial if you want to improve the accuracy of their responses. The human face is "stimulating" to small children, which increases their cognitive load and leads to longer response times.
- *Reward good behavior.* Children (and adults) like praise. So, letting them know they've done a good job of listening is an important means of encouraging future good listening habits.

Unfortunately, there will be times when a child has to face the music. If a child repeatedly doesn't listen, then he or she shouldn't depend on you constantly repeating yourself. If you say you're leaving the house at 1 p.m., with or without him or her, then do it. Leave (assuming there's an adult around). Next time, we bet he or she will be ready.

Why Parents "Don't Listen"

Listening is the foundation of authentic communication, representing a basic human need. In fact, listening has long been identified as a key component in parent–teen relationships. Given its importance, it's not surprising that one of the most common adolescent and teenage complaints is that their parents don't listen to them. (Isn't it interesting that the same complaint is expressed by parents about their teens?) As we have noted throughout this text, listening is one of the primary ways that we show others that we believe them to be a valued, worthwhile person. It shows respect for their opinions (even if we don't agree), that we care about them as individuals, and that we respect them as individuals. Thus, a supportive family listening environment is important. When parents listen respectfully to their children, they are more likely to have children who will return the favor. Of course, there are a number of reasons why quality listening can be problematic in parent–child relationships. Here are just a few, along with suggestions for improvement:[71]

Think on it: Identify an adult that you really made a connection with while growing up. It may be a parent, the parent of a friend, a teacher, coach, etc. What made for such a strong connection? Perhaps you felt they really understood you… that they really listened to you?

Role Definition. Parents can sometimes think that to be successful parents their children must espouse the same views and values that they have. When they don't, it can become difficult for parents to listen fully. In addition, parents often see the parent–child relationships as asymmetrical (one up/one down). However, the best listening occurs when we treat the other person as an equal partner in the listening process. This common sense conclusion is supported by research that indicates that open communication behavior on the part of mothers promotes reciprocal communication from their children. This same research also suggests that the quality of discussion during a conflict may be important to a child's mental health and ability to internalize problems.[72]

Confusion Over Acceptance. The best listening occurs when we accept a person just the way they are, and accept their views (this doesn't mean we have to agree). Sometimes parents think that if they truly listen, they will necessarily have to accept their child's views. This is not the case. It does mean that parents have to understand both the content and the underlying emotions involved. So, parents can empathize with the need to maintain solid friendships, but still disagree with having a friend stay overnight during the school week. Ideally, parents will fully listen to their children even when they know in the first few minutes what the child is requesting is an unfeasible idea (e.g., it costs too much, child isn't old enough). Such moments provide opportunities for understanding what's important to, and what's going on in, their child's or their teenager's life.

Inability to Accept Criticism. Some parents see disagreements as attacks on their parenting skills. They can become defensive when their teenagers offer even constructive criticism. Parents who are aware they are not perfect, especially those with a good sense of humor, are usually accepting of their children's comments and criticisms. In fact, such comments from teenagers are often a test – one that tests their ability to point out parenting (or personal) flaws and still be loved and accepted by their parents.

Lack of Time. It's a busy world for both parents and teens. Finding opportunities to interact and engage one another can be difficult. Unfortunately, watching television or simply eating together are activities that most researchers agree *do not* constitute "quality" time.[73] An important strategy, however, is to acknowledge when we are too busy to listen. Impatience and distraction are often evidenced in our nonverbals, leading the speaker to feel devalued and less likely to want to enter into future conversations. Set a time when each person can listen closely – and keep that promise. Turning off the mobile phone and TV and laying down the tablet clearly signal that we respect and are willing to listening to the other person. For example, one parent we know who works from home physically turns her back to her computer whenever one of her children comes in to speak with her. This simple gesture is a clear signal to her children that she is truly focused on them. Some family communication specialists suggest that weekly family meetings are one way to build in quality listening time. At these meetings, accomplishments as well as concerns are addressed. Other "spontaneous" moments can be utilized more effectively as listening moments (e.g., cleaning the kitchen, running errands together). Finally, when possible, it's great for parents and children to set regular one-on-one appointments with each other. Saturday lunch with Mom, Wednesday night dinner with Dad, etc. As young adults, you can take the initiative, and offer to take mom or dad to lunch – even a fast food place, at an off time (to reduce noise and distractions), is fine. The point is to make opportunities to share your lives with each other.

Willingness to Listen. This is an attitudinal issue. Sometimes it seems that parents and children work at cross purposes. When one is ready to listen, the other isn't ready to talk. Recognizing and taking the opportunities to actively engage each other is crucial for quality family listening. Adolescents who come from families that encourage expressing both negative and positive feelings are more likely to maintain close relationships with their parents.[74] Like all of us, adolescents and teens want and need to share their joys, problems and concerns. However, how they ultimately share that information is often dependent on the relationships they have with both their parents and their peers. If they feel that their parents aren't willing to listen, they are more likely to begin excluding them in favor of friends. In fact, during their prime teenage years, peers will trump parents in most cases.

Perspective and Parent–Teen Interactions. Of particular interest is how parents and children, particularly teenagers, view the lines of communication between them.[75] Chances are that you and your parents had slightly different perspectives about just how freely you could communicate while you were going through your adolescent years. Pioneer listening scholars Caroline Coakley and Andy Wolvin found that parents tend to see the lines of communication as open or very open, while teens see them as open or somewhat open.[76]

This finding supports our conclusion that there are perceptual differences between each group's views of this aspect of their relationship. Interestingly, parents and teenagers tended to agree about their assessment of their parents' listening skills. Parents tended to rate themselves as "good" listeners, and their teens tended to also view them as good listeners. In contrast, parents were more likely to rate their teens as excellent listeners, while teens generally rated themselves as average listeners. Of note, the majority of topics of discussion between parents and their teens focused on the teen (e.g., college, social activities, grades, career plans). What doesn't get discussed? Sex. Both parents and teenagers listed sex-related topics as the ones causing them the greatest discomfort. We're pretty certain this finding doesn't surprise any of you. However, recent research indicates that the willingness of families to talk about sensitive subjects as well as how they go about this sensitive communication is based on the communication climate in the family.[77] For example, parents who have an open style of communication with their adolescents and are able to express their own values, beliefs and expectations are more likely to delay the onset of sexual activity as well as risky behavior on the part of their child.[78] This finding also suggests that in addition to being an open listener, a parent can present information in ways that will make it more listenable. By tailoring information to the individual adolescent's physical, emotional, and psychological level of development as well as taking into account the social environment (i.e., peer pressure), parents can present sensitive information to fit the specific needs of the child.[79]

Managing Privacy. Of course, as we grow older, personal privacy becomes more important. **Communication Privacy Management Theory,** developed by Professor Sandra Petronio, focuses on the consequences of revealing private information.[80] Disclosing information has implications for all the parties concerned – you, a friend, a parent or significant other. Petronio suggests that we use communication to negotiate and coordinate *privacy boundaries* – what we reveal and what we conceal – between ourselves and others. There are five basic assumptions to the theory:

- We believe we own our private information.
- We believe we have the right to control what information is shared with others.
- We establish *privacy rules* that guide the permeability of our privacy boundaries (i.e., how and when to open a boundary and share private information).

- Once information is shared, the other person essentially becomes a co-owner of the information and further acts of sharing become a collective act requiring the development of additional privacy rules.
- *Boundary turbulence* arises when privacy rules are disrupted or confidentiality is violated. Turbulence can result in mistrust, anger, and reluctance to share additional information.

Communication privacy management theory is particularly appropriate for applying to central family dyads such as that between a parent–child, between siblings, and spouses. It may also include other members of one's social network who are information shareholders or co-owners.[81] An important consideration when revealing private information is the response we receive from others. Our expectation of acceptance even trumps the relationship between those involved (e.g., parents, siblings, peers).[82] Privacy considerations have also gained renewed study with the advent of social media and wireless technology, whether Facebook Friend requests, texts, or traditional phone calls. For example, recent research has found that mobile phone users manage privacy concerns by strategically choosing their method of communication (e.g., instant messaging, SMS, voice). Each method comes with its own set of privacy concerns, with some mediums conveying perceptions of greater ownership and having thicker privacy boundaries than others.[83] For instance, texts or SMS messages are assigned greater privacy, and are seen as more confidential, than voice calls. At the same time, mobile phones and related technologies have increased collaborative ownership of private information, but has also made it (and its users) much more vulnerable to becoming public.

Not surprisingly, adolescents and teens tend to have fewer interactions with their parents and more with friends and peers, in part because of privacy concerns. While peers eventually take the place of parents as the primary receiver of self-disclosure (and listening), it is important that parents continue to be available to listen. There are real consequences if they don't. For example, teenage girls who believed their parents or guardians were unavailable or unwilling to listen to them, tended to score higher on eating disordered measurements (e.g., drive for thinness, bulimia, interpersonal distrust). Thus, family interaction patterns appear to contribute to the psychological and behavioral traits associated with eating disorders.[84] Unfortunately, not all communication between parent and child is happy. As with all relationships, this one too is subject to conflict.

Parent–Child Conflict

We touched on important aspects of conflict and conversation in the last chapter. Here, we explore attributes specific to family life. Not surprisingly, an important aspect of family communication is how the family unit handles conflict. It is no surprise that most of us first come into contact with conflict (and conflict management) within our own families. We observe how others in the family engage in conflict, including conflict strategies. Of course, family conflict has both tangible and intangible elements.[85] **Tangible conflict** elements focus on specifics of the conflict, such as what time curfew should be. **Intangible conflict** elements address issues such as what makes your family unique (to yourself and to others) and what binds you together (besides blood, marriage, or choice). It can include your level of inclusion or exclusion in the family (e.g., the golden child versus the black sheep). Thus, an issue of curfew may be one of autonomy and authority. Family disputes can affect individual personal and social identity (i.e., both in and out of the family).

As we discussed earlier in the chapter, family communication climate will have an impact on how you handle conflict. For example, adolescents from families with higher levels of positive family expressiveness tend to have better family relationships (i.e., less conflict, better communication, less trouble addressing family problems).[86] Our family communication orientation patterns also provide insight into family conflict interactions. If your family has a high conformity orientation, chances are that conflict is discouraged, whereas if your family is conversation oriented, you are encouraged to express yourself and view conflict as an opportunity to both express and learn.[87] This difference between positive and negative expressiveness is important for understanding family conflict.

Families can be classified into one of four types – pluralistic, consensual, laissez-faire or protective – depending on how low or high they are on each of the orientations:[88]

- Members of *pluralistic families* tend to be high in conversation and low in conformity. They are more willing to embrace conflict and appear to be able to productively handle conflict and the negative emotions that may accompany it.
- *Consensual* families are high in conversation and high in conformity. Conflict is seen as a threat to family harmony. The high conversational orientation leads parents in these families to take the time to explain their positions and involve their children in family discussions. When conflict arises, these families readily vent their negative feelings. At the same time, however, their desire for positive closure to the conflict leads them to seek support and agreement from family members.
- *Laissez-faire* families are low in both conversation and conformity orientation. In these families, the children essentially act as they wish; other family members avoid being involved in the conflicts that arise or the ensuing decisions. Subsequently, laissez-faire families tend to practice conflict avoidance.
- *Protective* families are low in conversation, but are high in conformity. Family members are pressured to agree as a means of getting along with others. As a result, conflict is suppressed. The unfortunate result is that family members gain less experience at handling conflict, expressing negative emotions, and sharing feelings and concerns.

Ultimately, your family orientation and how your family handles conflict tends to predict how you will handle conflict in your personal and romantic relationships.[89] For good or ill, we typically model our conflict behaviors after those we witness being used by the adults in our life (mostly your parental figures). Inter-parental conflict particularly affects conflict schema formation for children and adolescents.[90] Children often blame themselves for the conflict, and subsequently experience a great deal of emotional distress.[91] Much of this distress can be allayed by parents talking with the child, listening to his or her concerns, and providing reassurance that the child is blameless in the conflict.[92]

Given the high saliency, emotional arousal, and personal relevancy, it's no wonder that children (even very young children) quickly form schemas for parental arguments. Children exposed to constructive conflict generally feel less threatened and have fewer negative emotions, and will believe that the conflict will be effectively resolved. They also tend to feel that the conflict won't negatively affect them or their family. Family conflict schemas are also affected by consistency. The more consistent parents are in how they express and resolve conflict, the stronger a schema will likely become. Children of these parents often develop strong expectations for how conflict "plays itself out." If parents, however, rarely argue or have inconsistent patterns of conflict behavior, then their children's conflict schemas tend to be less developed, often leading these children to focus greater attention on conflict events.

Once developed, these schemas are often activated when we enter intimate relationships. Children who witness hostile, negative conflict may respond to peers and dating partners with fear and avoidance, or may be aggressive or coercive so as to get "the upper hand" first.[93] These latter behaviors are more likely to occur if children believe they are successful means of goal attainment.

Good listening habits aren't going to stop the inevitable arguments that parents and children experience. However, family therapist Michael Nichols suggests that responsive listening is one means of handling parent–child conflicts.[94] His technique is designed to provide children with greater opportunity to express themselves, while at the same time reducing the odds of a major meltdown. His method relies on mutual respect, cooperation, and empathy. He believes that when parents begin to "argue back" with their kids, they are being drawn down to their children's level, in many cases unnecessarily. He feels that good listening skills can end many disagreements before they actually get started. Some of his primary suggestions for handling parent–child conflict are outlined below.

First, he suggests that parents *get the right attitude.* Parents need to understand that **conversations are about listening,** not arguing or establishing who's right or in authority. They have to be committed to not only encouraging their children to speak their mind, but to making sure they understand what their children actually *mean.* Oftentimes, parents don't recognize that they don't "get it," resulting in additional misunderstandings and conflict. He also notes that *parents are in charge.* Nichols believes that taking on the role of listening is a purposive, active event, one that puts parents in charge. He argues that as long as parents keep this in mind, when their child starts yelling, "I hate you," they can respond more actively (and more calmly) (e.g., "You really didn't like what I said, did you?"). Such responses place ownership of the statements. The child's outburst remains his or her own, but at the same time, the parent acknowledges the reaction to what triggered the outburst.

Third, he notes that it's okay to *postpone decision-making.* It's important for parents to make a considered decision. This gives children the feeling that they are being listened to, while at the same time giving parents the opportunity to actually consider all sides of the issue. An immediate "no" is very likely to trigger an immediate argument. Of course, this assumes that a parent will be open-minded enough to actually see the issue or problem from their child's point of view. Careful, thoughtful decisions often lead to compromises.

Nichols also believes it's important to *keep it simple.* Parents don't always need to provide long reasoned out justifications for their actions. Long justifications can invite debate. If crossing the street against the light is unsafe, a child does not need a long explanation about traffic patterns. A simple, "No, it's not safe," should suffice. Finally, he reminds parents that *children grow up,* and their listening needs change as they grow and mature. As you know, small children accept parental authority more readily than adolescents and teenagers. Nichols believes that paying a lot of attention to the needs and wants of adolescents and teenagers is an important means of staying connected. As noted earlier, children who feel their parents are willing to listen are more likely to talk to them. Again, parents can reject a child's point of view, but parents have to listen in order to hear that viewpoint.

Think on it: Identify a parent/child relationship that you can observe (perhaps you have nieces and nephews). Think about the interactions you viewed. Did you see any of Dr. Nichol's suggestions at work? If so, what was the impact on the conversation? If not, how did the participants in the interaction ultimately react? What recommendations would you make based on what your observations?

Sibling Relationships

An important family group that we have ignored up to now is siblings. While it has been described as "the most enduring and egalitarian connection of all family relationships," it has received much less attention in the communication literature than parent–child relationships. The odds are that most of you reading this book have at least one brother or sister. Even if you are an only child, understanding sibling relationships will help you to understand your friends better and, perhaps, future romantic partners. For those of you with brothers and sisters, you understand how sibling relationships pervade your life. As children, the impact of these relationships may not have been as apparent. In your early years, you probably didn't view your brothers and sisters as providing much more than companionship and emotional support (when you weren't fighting with each other). You may have been a babysitter for a younger sibling, occasionally worked together to manage your parents, and helped each other out in specific situations (e.g., ride to a party, loaning money, etc.), but you probably didn't view them as an important source of social support. In fact, you still may not view them as an important source of social support. However, research in this area suggests that as we age, particularly in late adolescence and early adulthood, our relationships with our siblings change, leading us to grow emotionally closer.[95]

The emotional closeness you feel with your siblings is based on "shared experiences, trust, concern, and enjoyment of the relationship."[96] Emotional closeness may be expressed in affectionate communication and communication-based emotional support, both of which have been related to concepts such as relational satisfaction, relational closeness, and self-disclosure. In addition, individuals who are highly affectionate communicators tend to be more outgoing and have higher self-esteem.[97] In general, if you and your sibling(s) are affectionate and emotionally supportive of each other, the odds are that your commitment to each other will remain stable throughout your life.[98] This commitment is related, in part, to the loyalty that you feel toward one another, and loyalty is related to your feelings of family obligation. Thus, even if you really dislike your sister's spouse, you'll still get together for major holidays and other family events. You won't allow your dislike to overcome your loyalty to your sister. Similarly, even if you disapprove of some of the things your sister does (e.g., quitting that perfectly good job in order to start her own business), if you're committed to each other, you will still be loyal and likely supportive (even as you may voice your disapproval and disbelief).

Sibling commitment is also related to sibling intimacy. Close sibling relationships are based as much on friendship, as on blood or marriage ties. Self-disclosure or confiding help build sibling relationships. And, as we have discussed a number of times already, listening is an important part of the foundation that makes us feel comfortable disclosing. We have some young (tween) friends, who are also siblings. In age, they are about a year apart. It has been very interesting to watch them grow up and develop a close brother/sister relationship. The most noteworthy aspect of their bond is that they seem to be each other's best friend. They are supportive of each other and confer with one another when making important decisions. Their family encourages open communication, so we suspect this close relationship will last through the challenges of adolescence and into adulthood.

Sibling relationships can become even more significant as we age. For example, approximately 80% of older adults living today have living siblings.[99] In addition, while we may experience ups and downs in our sibling relationships, most of us will maintain some level of contact with our brothers and sisters. Our sibling relationships provide a means of maintaining and sharing our common background, the uniqueness of our family life. In addition, sibling relationships tend to be the longest relationship of our life. Reminiscing about family roots help us to remember and reinforce those things that make families unique. They also provide a network for personal support and ears to listen.

Communicating with Older Adults

As children age, so do parents. In later stages of life, adult children (and their parents) face changing roles. Listening is central to these changed relationships as well.[100] Good listening becomes important to identifying, recognizing, and enacting the social support that older family members need. If parents don't feel their children listen to them, then they are less likely to approach them in times of real need. Older parents need our time, just as much as we needed theirs when we were young. Taking the time to truly listen to aging parents can open up avenues of kinship and love that can surprise us and gratify us. However, just as when we are young, our parents need to feel that they are more important to us than our business or other social relationships.

As adults age, they also face specific listening needs based upon changes in physiology. The one immediately related to listening is a **loss of hearing acuity.** Even small hearing losses result in increased difficulties in understanding speech in our daily lives.[101] These difficulties are multiplied in situations where there are multiple talkers, or sudden topic changes. The question for researchers is how much of this common problem can be attributed to hearing problems and how much should be attributed to cognitive declines. Understanding the source has profound implications on how hearing-related problems can be or should be addressed. Recent research in audiology suggests two important things.[102] First, when listening is viewed as information processing, then hearing loss can profoundly affect our normal flow of information. Second, with some limitations, we appear to have the ability to "tune" our hearing. This tuning function can occur when expectations for a particular noise (i.e., frequency) have been triggered. So, if someone tells us the cat has a particularly low rumble of a purr, we'll tune into that frequency to hear it better. This ability also can be triggered by context. In particularly noisy environments (or when age-related hearing loss occurs), we tune our entire hearing system (perception, memory, etc.) to help us to "fill in" the information that is being lost (via noise or poor hearing). Such cases also affect our processing resources, another issue that can affect our ability to listen. Not surprisingly, if we have difficulty in hearing, we are less likely to contribute to an interaction.

Related to hearing, another common belief is that our memory worsens as we age. Research into age-related changes in memory has helped pinpoint some of the attributes that lead to this common belief (and experience).[103] Important to listening is that, as we get older, we tend to have more problems with our working memory. In general, there is a reduced capacity in our processing speed. As you recall, working memory involves both storage and processing of information. It seems that as we grow older, our processing resources become more limited.[104] One of the reasons for this is that it appears that older adults have more difficulty in "clearing" their working memory of irrelevant information. However, an important question we should ask is how much memory is adequate. Just because memory studies of older adults (usually over age 50) show age-related deficits (when usually compared to 20 year olds) does not mean their memory is "broken" or that they are working at a memory "deficit." It does, however, suggest that young adults may have memories that work at a much higher capacity than really needed for everyday functioning. Thus, downward changes in adult memory are more aggravating than anything else.

Many older adults, and even younger adults, don't want to acknowledge to themselves or to others that they are experiencing hearing problems. While this is often done to protect their self-image, recent research in communication suggests that hiding a hearing loss or disability may actually have the opposite effect.[105] In fact, older adults, and especially younger individuals, with a hearing problem, who acknowledged the problem, tended to be viewed more favorably, despite hearing-related communication difficulties.

Finally, there are many methods of connecting with older family members (with or without hearing problems). If hearing loss makes it difficult to speak with a family elder, online communication may be a good alternative. As we noted in Chapter 5, technology provides us with many choices of communicating with others. While face-to-face communication is consistently identified as the preferred means of communicating in close relationships, email, texting, FaceTime, and other means of communication allow us to maintain ties with family members.[106]

Summary

As we have suggested throughout this chapter, families need quality communication to enhance and maintain healthy family function.[107] Quality communication means that true conversations occur when the involved family members take turns talking and listening. Effective communication enables families to balance cohesiveness and adaptability. Clear and open communication among family members brings families closer together, enhances member personal identity and wellbeing, and leads to better social and coping skills.[108] As we have seen in this chapter, quality listening is an important element of quality family communication, helping to bring families closer together, contributing personal family member personal identity and wellbeing, and enhancing social and individual coping skills.[109]

Perhaps as important as any other contribution that family communication makes to the development of the children are the foundations it establishes for future interaction. The communication lessons we learn from our families help us develop schemas about interpersonal communication in general and how to engage in relational maintenance behavior with our friends.[110] In the next chapter, we turn to friendships and romantic relationships.

Key Concepts

Polymedia
Family Orientation Schemas
    Conversation orientation
    Conformity orientation
Family strength
Confirming messages
Back-channel
Family Schema and Scripts
    Structural traditionalism
    Avoidance
Family Stories
    Engagement
    Perspective-taking
    Coherence
Managing Emotions
    Emotion coaching
    Dismissing parents
Parental Responsive Style

Discussion Questions

1. How are structural traditionalism and avoidance related to conversation and conformity orientation?
2. Think of the stories frequently told by your family members. What do those stories tell others about your family? How it handles conflict, views about family structure, etc.?
3. Therapist Michael Nichols offers a number of suggestions for parents. Of his suggestions, which do you think is the most important? Why?
4. Have you noticed changes in how your parents listen to you over time? If so, how has their listening changed? What do you think led to this change?
5. Looking at the discussion of the importance of storytelling to family life and culture, how do you believe it can contribute to sibling relationships?

Listening Activities

1. The next time you visit with your family, keep a diary of your interactions. Identify positive and negative listening behaviors that we've discussed in this chapter. Of the behaviors you've identified, do you personally tend to engage in them, or not? If you engage in negative behaviors, choose one and develop a plan for substituting a positive listening behavior in its place. Next, set your plan in motion. Track your success over a five day period. Do you think you are improving? Why or why not? If not, what do you think can be done to help you further improve your listening?
2. There is an old African proverb that states, "when an old man dies a library burns." When we lose someone, the knowledge, wisdom, and stories of a lifetime are lost. This activity encourages family communication and storytelling. Identify a grandparent or other family member that you know relatively little about (e.g., an uncle who passed away at a young age, a grandparent who lives far away). Contact two to five family members and ask them to tell you a story about her or him. What do the stories have in common? [Alternatively, you could choose a well-known event (e.g., recent immigration, birth of quadruplets) and gather stories about it.]
3. Each family has its own unique family communication pattern. Looking back on your interactions with your family members, identify conversation and conformity behaviors. What type of family (pluralistic, consensual, laissez-faire or protective) best reflects the communication patterns of your family?

Notes

1 Baumeister & Leary, 1995
2 Baxter & Braithwaite, 2006, p. 3

 3 US Census Bureau, 2010
 4 Mathews & Hamilton, 2016
 5 MetLife, 2011
 6 For a comprehensive review, see Johnson, Bengtson, Coleman, & Kirkwood, 2005
 7 See for example Madianou, 2014
 8 Madianou & Miller, 2013
 9 Bridge & Schrodt, 2013; Koerner & Fitzpatrick, 2006
10 Coakley & Wolvin, 1997
11 Schrodt, Witt, & Messersmith, 2008
12 Wilkinson, 2003
13 Rubin, Bukowski, & Parker, 2006
14 Odom & McConnell, 1992
15 Burleson, Delia, & Applegate, 1995; Mills & Rubin, 1993; Rubin & Rose-Krasnor, 1992
16 Braithwaite & Baxter, 2005; Koerner & Fitzpatrick, 2002; Ledbetter & Schrodt, 2008
17 Ledbetter & Schrodt, 2008
18 Fitzpatrick & Ritchie, 1994, p. 276
19 Ledbetter, 2009
20 Koerner & Fitzpatrick, 2002
21 Jones, Abbey & Cumberland, 1998
22 Akbari et al., 2014
23 Keaton & Kelly, 2008
24 Ledbetter & Schrodt, 2008
25 Dumlao & Botta, 2000; Keaton & Kelly, 2008; Koerner & Fitzpatrick, 2002; Schrodt, 2005
26 Ledbetter & Schrodt, 2008
27 DeFrain & Assay, 2007; DeFrain & Stinnett, 2002
28 Assay, DeFrain, Metzger & Moyer, 2014
29 Golish, 2003
30 Schrodt, 2005, 2009
31 Doohan, 2007
32 See Schrodt, et al., 2008, for a meta- analysis of family communication pattern research
33 Guerrero, Jones, & Burgoon, 2000
34 Mikkelson & Hesse, 2009
35 Schrodt, et al., 2008
36 Galvin, Bylund, & Brommel, 2004
37 Galvin & Cooper, 1990, as cited in Galvin et al., 2004
38 Boyd, 2003 p. 354
39 Caughlin, 2003
40 Kellas, 2008
41 Byng-Hall, 1988
42 Fitzpatrick & Ritchie, 1994
43 Schrodt, 2005
44 Sunwolf & Frey, 2001, p. 122
45 Kellas, 2005
46 Kellas & Trees, 2005
47 Kellas & Horstman, 2015
48 Ackerman, 1981; Eskritt, Whalen, & Lee, 2008; Shatz, 1983
49 Pellegrini, Brody, & Stoneman, 1987
50 Pellegrini, et al., 1987
51 Eskritt, et al., 2008
52 High & Scharp, 2015; Jones, Bodie & Koerner, 2017
53 High & Scharp, 2015

54 Koerner & Fitzpatrick, 2002
55 High & Scharp, 2015; Cupach & Olson, 2006
56 Rittle-Johnson, Saylor, & Swygert, 2008
57 Denham & Kochanoff, 2002; see also, Eisenberg, Fabes, Carlo, & Karbon, 1992
58 Gentzler, Contreras-Grau, Kerns, & Weimer, 2005
59 See Denham & Kochanoff, 2002, for a review of literature related to parental emotional coaching.
60 Gottman, Katz, & Hoover, 1996; Halberstadt, Crisp, & Eaton, 1999
61 Gottman et al., 1996; Orrego & Rodriguez, 2001
62 Dunn, Brown, & Beardsal, 1991
63 Ledbetter, 2009
64 Saarni & Buckley, 2002
65 Saarni & Buckley, 2002, p. 235; see also, Gentzler, et al., 2005
66 Saarni, 1999; Saarni & Buckley, 2002
67 Malatesta, 1990
68 Saarni & Buckley, 2002, p. 235
69 Miller, 2001
70 Phelps, Doherty-Sneddon, & Warnock, 2006
71 See Coakley & Wolvin, 1997, for a review of parent–teen listening/communication and additional suggestions.
72 Brown, Fitzgerald, Shipman, & Schneider, 2007
73 Brecher & Brecher, 1987, as cited in Coakley & Wolvin, 1997
74 Gentzler, et al., 2005
75 Coakley & Wolvin, 1997
76 Coakley & Wolvin, 1997
77 Eisenberg, Sieving, Bearinger, Swain, & Resnick, 2006
78 Eisenberg, et al., 2006
79 Eisenberg, et al., 2006
80 Petronio, 2002, 2009, 2013
81 Petronio & Caughlin, 2005
82 Aldeis & Afifi, 2013
83 Child & Westermann, 2013; Häkkilä &Chatfield, 2005; Worthington, Valikoski, Fitch-Hauser, Imhof, & Kim, 2012
84 Larson, 1991
85 Taylor, 2002
86 Capaldi, Forgatch, & Crosby, 1994; Flannery, Montemayor, & Eberly, 1994
87 Barbato, Graham, Perse, 2003
88 Koerner & Fitzpatrick, 1997
89 Reese-Weber & Marchand, 2002
90 Grych & Cardoza-Fernandes, 2001
91 See Brown, et al., 2007 for a discussion.
92 Brown, et al., 2007
93 Grych & Cardoza-Fernandes, 2001, p. 172
94 Nichols, 2005
95 Fowler, 2009; Goetting, 1986; also see Conger, Bryant, & Brennon, 2004
96 Lee, Mancini, & Maxwell, 1990, p. 433
97 Floyd, 2002
98 Rittenour, Myers, & Brann, 2007
99 McKay & Caverly, 2004
100 Ross & Glenn, 1996
101 Schneider, Daneman, & Pichora-Fuller, 2002
102 Schneider, et al., 2002

103 See Maylor, 2005, for a short, in-depth review on age-related changes in memory.
104 Verhaeghen, Marcoen, & Goossens, 1993
105 Ryan, Anas, & Vuckovich, 2007
106 For reviews, see Green & Clark, 2015; and Kraut & Burke, 2015
107 Coakley & Wolvin, 1997, p. 95; Olson & Gorall, 2003
108 Galvin & Brommel, 2000; Nelson & Lott, 1990
109 Noller & Callan, 1991; Riesch & Forsyth, 2007
110 Ledbettter, 2009

Additional Readings

Braithwaite, D. O., & Baxter, L. A. (Eds.). (2006). *Engaging theories in family communication: Multiple perspectives* (pp. 35–49). Thousand Oaks, CA: Sage.
Flora, J., & Segrin, C. (2015). Family conflict and communication. In L. H. Turner & R. West (Eds.), *The SAGE handbook of family communication* (pp. 91–106). Thousand Oaks, CA: Sage.
Tuner, L. H., & West., R. (2006). *Perspectives on family communication* (3rd ed.). New York: McGraw-Hill.
Vangelisti, A. L. (Ed.). (2009). *Feeling hurt in close relationships.* New York: Cambridge University Press.

References

Ackerman, B. (1981). When is a question not answered? The understanding of young children utterances violating or conforming to the rules of conversational sequencing. *Journal of Experimental Child Psychology, 31*, 487–507.
Akbari, A., Khormaiee, F., Keshtkar, A., Mehboodi, K., & Amrai, M. (2014). The prediction of test anxiety based on family communication pattern dimensions: The mediating role of academic resilience among first year high school students. *International Journal of School Health, 1*, 322–363.
Aldeis, D., & Afifi, T. D. (2013) College students' willingness to reveal risky behaviors: The influence of relationship type, message type, and self-esteem. *Journal of Family Communication, 13*, 92–113.
Assay, S. M., DeFrain, J., Metzger, M., & Moyer, B. (Eds.). (2014). *Family violence from a global perspective: A strengths-based approach.* Los Angles, CA: Sage.
Barbato, C. A., Graham, E. E., & Perse, E. M. (2003). Communicating in the family: An examination of the relationship of family communication climate and interpersonal communication motives. *The Journal of Family Communication, 3*, 123–148.
Baumeister, R. F., & Leary, M. R. (1995). The need to belong: Desire for interpersonal attachments as fundamental human motivation. *Psychological Bulletin, 117*, 497–529.
Baxter, L. A., & Braithwaite, D. O. (Eds.). (2006). *Engaging theories in family communication: Multiple perspectives.* Thousand Oaks, CA: Sage.
Boyd, G. E. (2003). Pastoral conversation: Relational listening and open-ended questions. *Pastoral Psychology, 51*, 345–360.
Braithwaite, D. O., & Baxter, L. A. (Eds.) (2005). *Family communication: Multiple perspectives.* Thousand Oaks, CA: Sage.
Bridge, M. C., & Schrodt, P. (2013). Privacy orientations as a function of family communication patterns. *Communication Reports, 26*, 1–12.
Brown, A. M., Fitzgerald, M. M., Shipman, K., & Schneider, R. (2007). Children's expectations of parent-child communication following interparental conflict: Do parents talk to children about conflict? *Journal of Family Violence, 22,* 407–412.
Burleson, B. R., Delia, J. G., & Applegate, J. L. (1995). The socialization of person-centered communication: Parents contributions to their children's social-cognitive and communication skills. In M. A. Fitzpatrick & A. Vangelisti (Eds.), *Explaining family interactions* (pp. 34–76). Thousand Oaks, CA: Sage.
Byng-Hall, J. (1988). Scripts and legends in families and family therapy. *Family Processes, 27*, 167–179.

Capaldi, D. M., Forgatch, M. S., & Crosby, L. (1994). Affective expression in family problem-solving discussions with adolescent boys: The association with family structure and function. *Journal of Adolescent Research, 9,* 28–49.

Caughlin, J. P. (2003). Family communication standards: What counts as excellent family communication and how are such standards associated with family satisfaction? *Human Communication Research, 29,* 5–40.

Child, J. T., & Westermann, D. A. (2013). Let's be Facebook friends: Exploring parental Facebook friend requests from a communication privacy management (CPM) perspective. *Journal of Family Communication, 13,* 46–59.

Coakley, C. G., & Wolvin, A. D. (1997). Listening in the parent-teen relationship. *International Journal of Listening, 1,* 88–126.

Conger, K. J., Bryant, C. M., & Brennon, J. M. (2004). The changing nature of adolescent sibling relationships: A theoretical framework for evaluating the role of relationship quality. In R. D. Conger, F. O. Lorenz, & K. A. S. Wickrama (Eds.), *Continuity and change in family relations: Theory, methods, and empirical findings* (pp. 319–344). Mahwah, NJ: LEA.

Cupach, W. R., & Olson, L. N. (2006). Emotion regulation theory: A lens for viewing family conflict and violence. In D. O. Braithwaite & L. A. Baxter (Eds.), *Engaging theories in family communication* (pp. 213–228). Thousand Oaks, CA: Sage.

DeFrain, J., & Assay, S. (Eds.). (2007). *Strong families around the world: The family strengths perspective.* New York: Haworth.

DeFrain, J., & Stinnett, N. (2002). Family strengths. In J. J. Ponzetti, Jr. (Ed.), *International encyclopedia of marriage and family* (2nd ed., pp. 637–642). New York: Macmillan Reference Group.

Denham, S., & Kochanoff, A. T. (2002). Parental contributions to preschoolers' understanding of emotion. *Marriage and the Family Review, 34,* 311–343.

Doohan, E. (2007). Listening behaviors of married couples: An exploration of nonverbal presentation to a relational outsider. *International Journal of Listening, 21,* 24–41.

Dumlao, R., & Botta, R. A. (2000). Family communications patterns and the conflict styles young adults use with their fathers. *Communication Quarterly, 48,* 174–189.

Dunn, J., Brown, J., & Beardsal, L. (1991). Family talk about feeling states and children's later understanding of others' emotions. *Developmental Psychology, 27,* 448–455.

Eisenberg, M. E., Sieving, R. E., Bearinger, L. H., Swain, C., & Resnick, M. D. (2006). Parents' communication with adolescents about sexual behavior: A missed opportunity for prevention? *Journal of Youth & Adolescence, 35,* 893–902.

Eisenberg, N., Fabes, R. A., Carlo, G., & Karbon, M. (1992). Emotional responsivity to others: Behavioral correlates and socialization antecedents. *New Directions for Child Development, 55,* 57–73.

Eskritt, M., Whalen, J., & Lee, K. (2008). Preschoolers can recognize violations of the Gricean maxims. *British Journal of Developmental Psychology, 26,* 435–443.

Fitzpatrick, M. A., & Ritchie, L. D. (1994). Communication schemata within the family: Multiple perspectives on family interaction. *Human Communication Research, 20,* 275–301.

Flannery, D. J., Montemayor, R., & Eberly, M. B. (1994). The influence of parent negative emotional expression on adolescents' perceptions of their relationships with their parents. *Personal Relationships, 1,* 259–274.

Floyd, K. (2002). Human affection exchange: V. Attributes of the highly affectionate. *Communication Quarterly, 50,* 135–152.

Fowler, C. (2009). Motives for sibling communication across the lifespan. *Communication Quarterly, 57,* 51–66.

Galvin, K. M., Bylund, C. L., & Brommel, B. J. (2004). *Family communication: Cohesion and change* (6th. ed.). Boston: Allyn & Bacon.

Gentzler, A. L., Contreras-Grau, J. M., Kerns, K. A., & Weimer, B. L. (2005). Parent–child emotional communication and children's coping in middle childhood. *Social Development, 14,* 591–612.

Goetting, A. (1986). The developmental tasks of siblingship over the life cycle. *Journal of Marriage and the Family, 48*, 703–714.

Golish, T. D. (2003). Stepfamily communication strengths: Understanding the ties that bind. *Human Communication Research, 29*, 41–80.

Gottman, J. M., Katz, L. F., & Hooven, C. (1996). Parental meta-emotion philosophy and the emotional life of families: Theoretical models and preliminary data. *Journal of Family Psychology, 10*, 243–268.

Green, M. C., & Clark, J. L. (2015). Real or ersatz? Determinants of benefits and costs of online social interactions. In S. S. Sundar (Ed.), *The handbook of the psychology of communication technology* (pp. 247–269). New York: Wiley.

Grych, J. H., & Cardoza-Fernandes, S. (2001). Understanding the impact of interparental conflict on children. In J. H. Grych & F. D Fincham (Eds.), *Interparental conflict and child development,* (pp. 157–187). New York: Cambridge University Press.

Guerrero, L. K., Jones, S. M., & Burgoon, J. K. (2000). Responses to nonverbal intimacy change on romantic dyads: Effects of behavioral valence and expectancy violation. *Communication Monographs, 67*, 325–346.

Häkkilä, J. & Chatfield, C. (2005). "It's like if you opened someone else's letter": User perceived privacy and social practices with SMS communication. In M. Tscheligi, R. Bernhaupt, & K. Mihalic (Eds.), *Proceedings of the 7th International Conference on Human Computer Interaction with Mobile Devices & Services* (pp. 219–222). New York: ACM.

Halberstadt, A. G., Crisp, V. W., & Eaton, K. L. (1999). Family expressiveness: A retrospective and new directions for research. In P. Philippot & R. S. Feldman (Eds.), *The social context of nonverbal behavior: Studies in emotion and social interaction* (pp. 109–155). New York: Cambridge University Press.

High, A. C., & Scharp, K. M. (2015). Examining family communication patterns and seeking social support direct and indirect effects through ability and motivation. *Human Communication Research, 41*, 459–479.

Johnson, M. L., Bengtson, V. L., Coleman, P. G., & Kirkwood, T. B. (Eds.). (2005). *The Cambridge handbook of age and ageing.* New York: Cambridge University Press.

Jones, D. C., Abbey, B. B., & Cumberland, A. (1998). The development of display rule knowledge: Linkages with family expressiveness and social competence. *Child Development, 69*, 1209–1222.

Jones, S. M., Bodie, G. D., Koerner, A. F. (2017). Connections between family communication patterns, person-centered message evaluations, and emotion regulation. *Human Communication Research.* Advance online publication. doi: 10.1111/hcre.12103.

Keaton, J., & Kelly, L. (2008). Emotional intelligence as a mediator of family communication patterns and reticence. *Communication Reports, 21*, 104–116.

Kellas, J. K. (2005). Family ties: Communicating identity through jointly told family stories. *Communication Monographs, 72*, 265–389.

Kellas, J. K. (2008, July 22). Call for Papers: Special Issue of the Journal of Family Communication on Narrative and Storytelling in the Family. Posted on the Communication Research and Theory Network (CRTNT). [Electronic mailing list message]. CRTNET: Conferences & Calls #10473. Retrieved from www.natcom.org/CRTNET.

Kellas, J. K., & Horstman, H. K. (2015). Communicated narrative sense-making: Understanding family narratives, storytelling, and the construction of meaning through a communicative lens.In *The SAGE handbook of family communication* (pp. 76–90). Thousand Oaks, CA: Sage.

Kellas, J. K., & Trees, A. R. (2005). Interactional sense-making in joint storytelling. In V. Manusov (Ed.), *The sourcebook of nonverbal measures: Going beyond words* (pp. 281–294). Mahwah, NJ: LEA.

Koerner, A. F., & Fitzpatrick, M. A. (1997). Family type and conflict: The impact of conversation orientation and conformity orientation on conflict in the family. *Communication Studies, 48*, 59–78.

Koerner, A. F., & Fitzpatrick, M. A. (2002). Toward a theory of family communication. *Communication Theory, 12*, 70–91.

Koerner, A. F., & Fitzpatrick, M. A. (2006). Understanding family communication patterns and family functioning: The roles of conversation orientation and conformity orientation. *Communication Yearbook, 26,* 37–68.

Kraut, R., & Burke, M. (2015). Internet use and psychological well-being: Effects of activity and audience. *Communications of the ACM, 58,* 94–100.

Larson, B. J. (1991). Relationship of family communication patterns to eating disorders: Inventory scores in adolescent girls. *Journal of the American Dietetic Association, 91,* 1065–1067.

Ledbetter, A. M. (2009). Family communication patterns and relational maintenance behavior: Direct and mediated association with friendship closeness. *Human Communication Research, 35,* 130–147.

Ledbetter, A. M., & Schrodt, P. (2008). Family communication patterns and cognitive processing: Conversation and conformity orientations as predictors of informational reception apprehension. *Communication Studies, 59,* 388–401.

Lee, T. R., Mancini, J. A., & Maxwell, J. W. (1990). Sibling relationships in adulthood: Contact patterns and motivations. *Journal of Marriage and Family, 52,* 431–440.

Madianou, M., & Miller, D. (2013). Polymedia: Towards a new theory of digital media in interpersonal communication. *International Journal of Cultural Studies, 16,* 169–187.

Madianou, M. (2014). Smartphones as polymedia. *Journal of Computer-mediated Communication, 19,* 667–680.

Malatesta, C. (1990). The role of emotions in the development and organization of personality. In R. Thompson (Ed.), *Socioemotional development: Nebraska Symposium on Motivation* (Vol. 36, pp. 1–56). Lincoln, NE: University of Nebraska Press.

Mathews, T. J., & Hamilton, B. E. (2016, Jan.). Mean age of mothers is on the rise: United States, 2000–2014. *NCHS Data Brief, No. 232.* US Department of Health and Human Services. Retrieved from www.cdc.gov/nchs/data/databriefs/db232.pdf.

Maylor, E. A. (2005). Age-related changes in memory. In M. L. Johnson, V. L. Bengtson, P. G. Coleman, & T. B. L. Kirkwood (Eds.), *The Cambridge handbook of age and ageing* (pp. 200–208). Cambridge, UK: Cambridge University Press.

McKay, V. C., & Caverly, R. S. (2004). The nature of family relationships between and within generations: Relations between grandparents, grandchildren, and siblings in later life. In J. F. Nussbaum & J. Coupland (Eds.), *Handbook of communication and aging research* (2nd ed., pp. 251–271). Mahwah, NJ: LEA.

MetLife. (2011, July). *MetLife report on American grandparents.* New York: MetLife Mature Market Institute. Retrieved from www.metlife.com/assets/cao/mmi/.../studies/.../mmi-american-grandparents.pdf.

Mikkelson, A. C., & Hesse, C. (2009). Discussions of religion and relational messages: Differences between comfortable and uncomfortable interactions. *Southern Communication Journal, 74,* 40–56.

Miller, S. A. (2001). Listen to this! *Early Childhood Today, 16,* 32–33.

Mills, R. S. L., & Rubin, K. H. (1993). Parental ideas as influences on children's social competence. In S. Duck (Ed.), *Learning about relationships* (pp. 98–117). Newbury Park, CA: Sage.

Nelson, J. & Lott, L. (1990). *I'm on your side.* Rocklin, CA: Prima.

Nichols, M. P. (2005). *Stop arguing with your kids.* New York: Guilford.

Noller, P., & Callan, V. (1991) *The adolescent in the family.* New York: Routledge.

Odom, S. L., & McConnell, S. R. (1992). Improving social competence: An applied behavior analysis perspective. *Journal of Applied Behavior Analysis, 25,* 239–244.

Olson, D. H., & Gorall, D. M. (2003). Circumplex model of marital and family systems. In F. Walsh (Ed.), *Normal family processes* (3rd ed., pp. 514–547). New York: Guilford.

Orrego, V. O., & Rodriguez, J. (2001). Family communication patterns and college adjustment: The effects of communication and conflictual independence on college students. *Journal of Family and Communication, 1,* 175–189.

Pellegrini, A. D., Brody, G. H., & Stoneman, Z. (1987). Children's conversation competence with their parents. *Discourse processes, 10,* 93–106.

Petronio, S. (2002). *Boundaries of privacy: Dialectics of disclosure*. Albany, NY: SUNY Press.

Petronio, S. (2009). Privacy management theory. In S. Littlejohn, & K. Foss (Eds.), *Encyclopedia of communication theory* (pp. 797–799). Thousand Oaks, CA: Sage.

Petronio, S. (2013). Brief status report on communication privacy management theory. *Journal of Family Communication, 13*, 6–14.

Petronio, S., & Caughlin, J. P. (2005). Communication privacy management theory: Understanding families. In D. Braithwaite & L. Baxter (Eds.), *Engaging theories in family communication: Multiple perspectives* (pp. 35–49). Thousand Oaks. CA: Sage.

Phelps, F. G., Doherty-Sneddon, G., & Warnock, H. (2006). Helping children think: Gaze aversion and teaching. *British Journal of Developmental Psychology, 24*, 577–588.

Reese-Weber, M., & Marchand, J. F. (2002). Family and individual predictors of late adolescents' romantic relationships. *Journal of Youth and Adolescence, 31*, 197–206.

Riesch, S. K., & Forsyth, D. M. (2007). Preparing to parent the adolescent. *Journal of Child and Adolescent Psychiatric Nursing, 5*, 32–40.

Rittenour, C. E., Myers, S. A., & Brann, M. (2007). Commitment and emotional closeness in sibling relationship. *Southern Communication Journal, 72*, 169–183.

Rittle-Johnson, B., Saylor, M. & Swygert, K. (2008). Learning from explaining: Does it matter if mom is listening? *Journal of Experimental Child Psychology, 100*, 215–224.

Ross, C., & Glenn, E. E. (1996). Listening between grown children and their parents. *International Listening Journal, 10*, 49–64.

Rubin, K. H., Bukowski, W. M., & Parker, J. G. (2006). Peer interactions, relationships, and groups. In N. Eisenberg, W. Damon, & R. M. Lerner (Eds.), *Handbook of child psychology: Vol. 3, Social, emotional, and personality development* (6th ed., pp. 571–645). New York: Wiley

Rubin, K. H., & Rose-Krasnor, L. (1992). Interpersonal problem solving and social competence in children. In V. B. Van Hasselt & M. Hersen (Eds.), *Handbook of social development: A lifespan perspective* (pp. 283–323). New York: Plenum.

Ryan E. B., Anas A. P., &Vuckovitch M. (2007). The effects of age, hearing loss, and communication difficulty on first impressions. *Communication Research Reports, 24*, 13–19.

Saarni, C. (1999). *The development of emotional competence*. New York: Guilford.

Saarni, C., & Buckley M. (2002). Children's understanding of emotion communication in families. *Marriage & Family Review, 34*, 213–242.

Schneider, B. A., Daneman, M., & Pichora-Fuller, M. K. (2002). Listening in aging adults: From discourse comprehension to psychoacoustics. *Canadian Journal of Experimental Psychology, 56*, 139–152.

Schrodt, P. (2005). Family communication schemata and the circumplex model of family functioning. *Western Journal of Communication, 69*, 359–376.

Schrodt, P. (2009). Family strength and satisfaction as functions of family communication environments. *Communication Quarterly, 57*, 171–186.

Schrodt, P., Witt, P. L., & Messersmith, A. S. (2008). A meta-analytical review of family communication patterns and their associations with information processing, behavior, and psychosocial outcomes. *Communication Monographs, 75*, 248–269.

Shatz, M. (1983). Communion. In J. H. Flavell & E. Markman (Eds.), *Handbook of child psychology* (Vol. 3, pp. 841–890). New York: Wiley.

Sunwolf, & Frey, L. R. (2001). Storytelling: The power of narrative communication and interpretation. In W. P. Robinson & H. Giles (Eds.), *The new handbook of language and social psychology* (pp. 119–135). Sussex: Wiley.

Taylor, A. (2002). *The handbook of family dispute resolution*. San Francisco: Jossey-Bass.

US Census Bureau. (2010). *Families and living arrangements*. Retrieved from www.census.gov/population/www/socdemo/hh-fam.html.

Verhaeghen, P., Marcoen, A., & Goossens, L. (1993). Facts and fiction about memory aging: A quantitative integration of research findings. *Journals of Gerontology: Psychological Sciences, 48*, 157–171.

Wilkinson, C. A. (2003). Expressing affection. In K. M. Galvin & P. J. Cooper (Eds.), *Making connections: Readings in relational communication* (3rd ed., pp. 183–190). Los Angeles, CA: Roxbury.

Worthington, D. L, Valikoski, T., Fitch-Hauser, M., Imhof, M., & Kim, S. (2012). Listening and privacy management in cell phone conversations among young adults: A cross cultural comparison of Finnish, German, Korean, & US American Students *Empedocles: European Journal for the Philosophy of Communication, 3*, 43–60.

8   Listening and Relationship Building

Friends and Romance

Case Study 8.1 What Makes a Relationship?

We find the group gathered around a table at the coffee shop in the student union. Carter and Nolvia are concentrating on her laptop screen.

Carter, I'm so glad everyone likes my idea of conducting a survey about what students are looking for in a relationship. It will help me in my survey research class and give us some original research that we can incorporate into our listening project. I've put in some standard demographic questions, but what specific relationship and listening questions should we ask?

Well, I was thinking we could do a list of attributes and ask people to indicate the importance of them. You know, things like being honest, open, responsive – stuff like that.

Great, I'll start on those questions. Should we list the attributes and ask respondents to check the ones that they feel are important? I guess we'd better specify what type of relationship, too.

In the previous two chapters, we explored a number of factors associated with relationship building. In this chapter, we expand on this discussion, focusing on two additional significant relationships – friendships and romantic partners. More specifically, we will explore how the joys and pressures of being a friend (however casual or romantic that friendship might be) affect listening. We will also discuss ways you can be a better listening friend or partner.

Making and Becoming Friends

Chances are when the students in the case study at the beginning of this chapter tabulate their survey results, they will find people most desire trust and respect, warmth and kindness, expressiveness and openness, and a sense of humor in their relationships no matter the type (e.g., intimate or casual, or same and opposite-sex friends). If so, their research will reflect the findings of academic researchers who report that we value intrinsic attributes more than traditional *external* qualities (such as good looks, money, or social status).[1] These characteristics reflect both the motivation and the ability on the part of our friends and lovers to provide us with social and emotional support. Interestingly, we seem to value these traits even more in our romantic partners than our friends. In fact, these attributes are fundamental to establishing and maintaining *all* interpersonal relationships.

Before we specifically address listening, we need to first briefly look at what we know about friends and the role they play in our lives. This background will lay the groundwork for seeing how and why we use different types and levels of listening as relationships progress.

Friendships are based on perceptions that each person is an equal and that the feelings of friendship are *reciprocated*. That is, you both feel close to one another, you don't feel the relationship is forced (i.e., your friendship is your choice, not because your moms are best friends).[2] Perhaps most importantly, friendships are founded on the interpersonal skills of the individuals involved.[3] In general, we are more fully engaged when interacting with our friends than when interacting with peers or strangers. Even as children, we tend to show greater prosocial behaviors (sharing snacks, toys, etc.) and engage in more positive communication behaviors (eye contact, smiling, talking, laughing, etc.) with our friends than with acquaintances.[4] In fact, Dr. Kathryn Wentz argues that prosocial behavior (i.e., sharing, helping, and cooperating) is a "hallmark of social competence throughout childhood."[5] Some researchers suggest these are friendship behaviors. For example, our problem-solving and memory skills are enhanced when working on tasks with friends rather than an acquaintance.[6] All of this begs the question, "How do we develop friendships?"

Early Friendships: Early and Middle Childhood

As early as age four, we begin to use the word **friend**. At this age, however, we often mean "friend" in terms of the level of familiarity we have with a peer.[7] The more time a four-year-old spends with someone, the more likely the word friend will be used to identify that child (of course, this label is often reinforced by family). Friendships are important across our life-span. Children and adults with few or no friends are more likely to have adjustment problems (e.g., dropping out of school, drug and alcohol abuse, thoughts of suicide, depression, and anxiety).[8] Thus, friendship is positively associated with increased health and both mental and physical wellness.

Friendships generally possess several fundamental characteristics, including voluntariness, equality and reciprocity. In other words, we *voluntarily* enter into a friendship, with someone we see and treat (and expect them to see and treat us) as an *equal*, where we expect the relationship to be returned or *reciprocated*.[9] However, as we age, our expectations of what it means to be a friend, and the functions our friendships serve, change.[10] As we grow out of early childhood, our friends are no longer defined by proximity or who is available to play.

Unlike very young children, older children (five to eight years) begin to develop a broader, and narrower, view of friendship. Friendship becomes more closely associated with supportive or helping behaviors (i.e., social support). For example, friends *help* with homework, doing tasks, or serve as sounding boards for ideas and complaints, as well as play. Children also become more skilled at entering into ongoing games or activities, sharing, and generally don't insult or behave aggressively. As you would expect from this discussion, friendship listening skills begin to develop more fully at this time. For example, assume that Carter's sister, Sylvia, is a socially competent nine-year-old. Chances are she will listen and attend to the activities of a group that is already engaged in play prior to joining it. By doing so, she can determine what is the best means of "inserting" herself into the game in a smooth and ideally non-disruptive manner.

We will also notice if we observe Sylvia that she is beginning to develop same-sex friendships. It is at this same time, we see sex-related differences beginning to emerge. For example, girls tend to play in smaller groups or dyads, while boys often prefer larger groups. This finding has, in part, led researchers to describe girls' friendships as "exclusive and dyadic," and boys' friendships as "inclusive and group-oriented."[11] Similar differences in play also begin to appear at this age. Girls focus greater attention on collaborative conversation making than do boys. Girls will also be more likely to "express agreement, acknowledge what a previous speaker has said, show concern for turn taking, and refrain from interruptions."[12] If you think back to the Listening MATERRS Model, you will see that girls seem to be actively developing good responding listening skills during this period of their lives.

In contrast, boys express greater competitiveness than girls of this age. So as a youngster, Carter probably focused his conversations and behaviors on establishing a social hierarchy with those with whom he interacted.[13] This tendency for boys to have "fewer close friendships and to experience lower levels of intimacy within these relationships" is likely related to peer group culture.[14] It is important to note, however, that while different, boys also develop close, same-sex friends as sources of social support. The understanding, acceptance, trust, and respect boys (and later, young men) gain from these close relationships help build confidence, self-esteem, and help buffer them against outside peer pressure.[15]

Think on it: Researchers don't explicitly address how these differences in development may affect listening behaviors. How might the differences in how girls and boys play together affect how they learn to listen to one another? Do you believe listening behaviors will differ? If so, how?

In several chapters in this book, we talk about the importance of emotional intelligence (EI). EI seems to develop in middle childhood (eight to 12 years) as children develop an understanding of emotional communication. Specifically, they seem to develop competence in accurately understanding and labeling emotions as well as regulating or managing their emotions (i.e., how well a child manages intensely felt emotions).[16] At this stage, in order to be viewed socially competent by their peers, children must learn how to express emotion, but do so in a somewhat regulated way (i.e., avoiding temper tantrums, uncontrolled crying, hitting, and so forth). These important skills are often distinguishing characteristics of "popular" children. Thus, popular children are better at recognizing what is expected in a certain situation as well as when the emotional reaction is out of proportion to the situation.[17] A more emotionally mature child (and probably a more popular child) recognizes that expressing sadness over a broken toy is acceptable but throwing a temper tantrum about the loss isn't. Another way of looking at this is to recognize that the child is beginning to develop skills in sorting through the nuances of a social situation.

The example in Case Study 8.2 illustrates the intersection of biological sex differences, emotional intelligence and reading a social situation.

Case Study 8.2 Ben's Story

I remember once when my family went to a neighborhood party at the local park for a picnic. My older sister, who was about eight, wanted the two of us to go down the slide together. While she tried to figure out a way for that to happen, I pushed her out of the way and climbed up the steps to the top of the slide. I just wanted to go down the slide and didn't really care whether she went or not. Funny thing was that she didn't get mad; she just got sad about us not doing something together. Some of the other children invited her to join them in some game they were playing. They didn't ask me – I don't think it was because I was too young, I think it was because I was being a brat. In retrospect, the difference may have been that I was acting like a typical, competitive boy and she was more emotionally mature.

Not surprisingly, many communication skills develop during childhood. As seen in this case study, we learn what it means to be a friend as well as the communication and listening skills needed to sustain such a relationship. In addition to developing communication-related skills, most of us also mature emotionally. These skills are important to later friendships, romances, and commitments to others.

Adolescent Friendships

With friendships come obligations. For adolescents, friendship obligations typically include loyalty, trust, and emotional support.[18] However, as noted earlier, friendships are dynamic and as you go from early to late adolescence, your relational orientations and friendship dynamics undergo a number of changes.[19] First, you begin to appreciate the differences between yourselves and your friends. For example, as young children you may tease a less skilled friend, but you understand and are more accepting of varying skill levels in late adolescence. For example, NaMii tells the group that she played soccer from the time she was five until she was 13. Unfortunately she wasn't very good as a small child and some of the other children teased her for being a "klutz." By the time she entered her teens, the teasing had become less hurtful.

By late adolescence you also become more attuned to the importance of effectively handling conflict to maintaining and sustaining our friendships. While having similar values and interests is still important, you become more cognizant of the values and beliefs you share (or don't share). Of course, listening to others is the primary way adolescents learn about the similarities and differences they share with others. As we have noted throughout the text, a willingness to listen to others' self-disclosure is fundamental to supporting and maintaining all relationships. Adolescence is the time period where you truly begin to see, and hopefully understand, the importance of listening to maintaining relationships. It is also at this time that you mature to the point where you realize that you have a responsibility as a listener in a relationship.

Early research by listening scholars Andy Wolvin, Carolyn Coakley, and Kelby Halone found that prior to adolescence, children failed to express any responsibility for listening, essentially leaving it up to the speaker. However, most adolescents acknowledge that they have a role in listening.[20]

Importantly, your level of self-esteem can "color your friendship world." One recent study suggests that high self-esteem adolescents are better able to address conflict with their friends and move on. However, those with low self-esteem tend to engage in avoidance, while remaining mentally fixated on the problem.[21] Remaining fixated on a problem can result in a number of negative listening behaviors. For example, you keep thinking of what you "should have said," thus missing what is currently being discussed. You may also find that your unresolved feelings interfere with how you perceive, interpret or translate later communication. Thus, when your friend asks about how your date went, you interpret the statement as sarcasm indicating that you really didn't have a date or as an attempt to make fun of the person with whom you went out.

Adult Friendships

Friendships play a number of important roles as we become adults. Our friends help us make career decisions, assess our romantic relationships, and negotiate changing self-perceptions.[22] One of the primary ways we maintain our friendships is through "everyday" talk.[23] While women tend to focus on personal topics more than men, the conversation itself strengthens and reinforces our relationships with our friends. Such conversations are evidence of both the existence and the importance of the friendship.[24] As we established in Chapter 6, we must have listening in order to have a good conversation.

People also use several **explicit strategies to maintain relationships**. However, the strategy varies depending on the nature and stage of the relationship.[25] Among the many strategies we can use are *openness* (as evidenced by self-disclosure), *assurance* (as exemplified by supportiveness), *joint activities* (i.e., spending time together), *positivity* (working to keep exchanges pleasant), and *avoidance* (avoiding discussing specific issues or avoiding the person). Of these strategies, openness, assurance and joint activities tend most closely to apply to friendships, while positivity and avoidance are used more frequently in romantic and family relationships. Self-disclosure, as it occurs in everyday conversations, is a primary implicit relationship maintenance strategy for friends. Supportiveness is also generally viewed as a "given" in friendships. Friendships provide us with social support, comfort, assistance in solving problems, etc., as well as more instrumental support as reflected in providing a ride, etc. Perhaps one of the more important means of maintaining friendships is simply doing things together. Engaging in joint activities with your friends means that you are immediately available to engage in self-disclosure and to provide support, ultimately helping to sustain that relationship.

As you can see from the discussion above, listening is fundamental to the strategies we use to maintain relationships. Talking with friends can also be good for your relationships. Previous research indicates that spending time with common friends also helps maintain our romantic relationships, especially marriages. How does this work? Our friendships provide an outlet for expressing feelings toward and about our romantic partners.[26] Friendships appear to be particularly important for married women. Through their friendships, married women have an avenue for expressing anger, frustration, or other similar emotions. Expressing these emotions helps diffuse them, with the side effect of increasing marital stability and commitment.[27]

Friendships and Mediated Communication

We're sure you find it no surprise that mobile and computer-mediated communication have become major means by which friendships (and romance, discussed below) are developed and maintained. Tweets reveal your feelings about your values, beliefs, or views of your favorite sports team. You post to Facebook, Instagram or similar sites sharing both the highs and the lows of the day or making simple observations. You use FaceTime, Skype and other video software to visit with friends and family both far and near. As we noted in Chapter 7, individuals differ in their need for privacy. What medium you use affects what, when and how you disclose. Also, you may choose a particular medium because of the nature of the information you wish to disclose. Thus, you will strategically choose to disclose some information face to face, while other information may be disclosed via instant messaging, video chat, or a social networking site. Social networking sites are typically described as a **non-directed medium** of disclosure, as the disclosure is not addressed to a particular individual or group. In contrast, when self-disclosure has a more specific target it is more likely to be delivered via a **directed medium** (e.g., you text your uncle, email your teacher, call your best friend). Directed mediums have been more closely identified with interpersonal communication.[28] In many ways, the research is still out on how mediated communication affects our self-disclosure. Some researchers feel that we will disclose more when using computer-mediated communication, while others feel that face-to-face communication still wins the day.[29]

Mobile and social media also provide you with important ways to maintain relationships. You may keep up with high school friends at other universities or chat with friends who are working or doing internships across the country or even around the world. The sharing of information, essentially being a part of each others' lives, is a primary way that we maintain our friendships and other relationships. However, the medium we choose is influenced by the nature of the relationship. We tend to call or text those who are closest to us.[30] Phone calls are a *rich* medium because they are better at relaying immediacy and other social cues (e.g., tone of voice, emotional overtones, affection sharing). *Leaner* mediums, such as instant messaging, allow for interactions where voice calls are not allowed or impractical. Of course, there are alternative mediums such as FaceTime and Skype; however, practicality and cost often restrict their use.[31]

> ***Think on it:*** Think of your high school classmates. How many of them do you keep in touch with? Are there any differences in how you interact with those you considered friends versus just classmates?

Building Friendships

As we get older, it can become more difficult to develop new friendships. Our lives are busy, we have less leisure time and more family and work-related duties. However, as seen above, the social support that comes from our friends help us physically, psychologically, and emotionally. Anna Miller, in an article published in the *Monitor on Psychology*, outlines several research-based suggestions for how we can build new friendships:[32]

- **Be a familiar face.** Psychologist Harry Reid found that whether we interact online or in person, the more we interact, the greater the level of liking. This can be done in a number of ways when we use consistency and routines strategically. For example, you may have five coffee stores to choose from, but going to the same one provides greater opportunities to see (and ultimately meet) others. Have a new job? Ditch working through lunch and join others going out or in the corporate break room. Join a yoga or spin class and go to it regularly. You'll see and be seen and you'll have something in common with everyone else in the room.
- **Share yourself. Reveal a secret.** We discuss the importance of self-disclosure throughout the text. When we divulge a secret, we signal that we trust the person we are disclosing to. Keep in mind that disclosures typically deepen over time. Thus, telling an acquaintance or newly acquired friend your deepest secrets will likely scare them off. Research in friendship building suggests we should begin with more neutral questions (What's your favorite dessert; What was your favorite vacation and why?) and build to more intimate questions (How did you feel when your mother died?).
- **Focus on others.** If you are lonely, you may become so preoccupied with your own feelings that you don't realize that you are neglecting the feelings of those you are hoping to befriend. When we focus on the welfare of others, we will appear warmer, more friendly, and more socially competent. A good way to do this is to share positive moments from our day with others (i.e., that you hit every green light on the way to work, lucked into a great parking space behind your building, or that your first quiche was a success).

- **Use social media, but do so with caution.** Social media appears to work best with people who are already well connected. An overreliance on virtual relationships (i.e., online groups, Facebook, etc.) can actually make you feel more isolated. However, using social media to build on established relationships can be beneficial.
- **Go slow.** Trying to force a friendship is a good way to make sure it doesn't happen. Also, how many friends a person needs varies with each individual. Some people will say they have 10–15 "close" friends, while others are satisfied with two or three. Some are very close to their friends; others are satisfied with acquaintances. In addition, those who are less socially active may be less interested in adding to their social network. If you are interested in expanding your own network, follow the advice we give you here and it should grow naturally over time.
- **Be yourself. Be authentic.** We delve more deeply into the idea of authenticity later in the chapter. For now, keep in mind that you shouldn't try to change yourself for others. Good friendships can last a lifetime. Do you really want to base that friendship on a false foundation?

Above we've discussed techniques we can use to develop new friendships. We develop many new friendships over the course of our lives. Some of these friendships will deepen into more intimate relationships, the topic of our next section.

Listening in Intimate Relationships

You may be surprised to learn that our romantic relationships can actually have a negative impact on friendships. Interpersonal communication scholar Chris Segrin notes that when we enter into committed relationships, particularly marriage, we often "cut back" on our social network of friends.[33] However, if our partner dies or we get divorced, we'll need close friends to help us weather the ensuing life changes. Thus, making new friends and maintaining old friendships can be good for our mental health – we'll have someone to listen to us in both good times and bad.

As often happens, some friendships take on an added dimension – romance. In this section, we address the role of listening in developing serious intimate relationships. We begin with dating, or initiating romantic relationships, then move to developing and maintaining relationships, followed by listening in committed relationships.

Dating/Initiating Romantic Relationships

One of the first sites for listening in dating is in the context of an opening line.[34] Opening lines offer, and are interpreted by the listener as an invitation to get to know one another more fully. Interestingly, several listener characteristics can affect how opening lines are received and interpreted. For example, men and women appear to evaluate opening lines differently. Men tend to respond to opening lines more positively than women do. In fact, it is not unusual for women to feel threatened when listening to opening lines. In other words, women can feel threatened when men attempt to initiate relational contact via an opening line (whether it was a good one or a bad one). In fact, women are more likely to report trying to avoid or withdraw from the interaction.[35] Male listeners, in contrast, generally do not feel as threatened by opening lines. Many men indicate they are happy to be receiving any type of opening line, whether it is a good quality one or even an obnoxious one. The fact that they receive an opening line at all appears to positively dispose men towards relating with the sender (i.e., they're flattered). This response can be mediated by a person's willingness to listen.

Think on it: What's the best and worst opening line you've received? Compare your examples to others in your class. What distinguishes good openings from bad openings? How did you (and your classmates) react when receiving a good opening versus a bad one? What was the impact on your listening?

Importantly, however, is that individuals who are higher in "readiness to listen" appear to be less threatened by opening lines, particularly if it was a good quality opening line. For example, men who scored as highly ready to listen were more likely to positively respond to a good quality opening line than men who scored low or moderate in readiness to listen. While women in general appear somewhat leery of opening lines, it appears that those higher in readiness to listen found them less threatening than women low in readiness to listen. So, if you're looking for advice on opening lines, research suggests avoiding many of the opening line clichés (e.g., "Do you come here often?") and, instead, be direct (e.g., "I'd like to meet you"). This technique appears to be preferred by both men and women.[36]

While many of us may think that getting the first date is the hard part of dating, previous research suggests that communication is the most common dating problem.[37] Just as in our other relationships, we use scripts to guide us – whether asking someone out on a first date or guiding our behaviors and expectations while on a date. It's no surprise that a lot of listening goes on during a date. However, there is a lot of speaking as well. Our attempts at conversation, as we search for common interests, are considered part of the script for dating.[38]

Underlying these "get to know you" dating moments is Grice's concept of reciprocity. As you may remember from the conversation chapter, a conversation only occurs if there is an exchange of information or a real interaction. We also have an expectation that if we reveal something personal to someone else, that person will, at some time, share something equally personal. However, if one conversational partner feels that he or she has to "carry" the communication load during a date, or if one person discloses too much personal information too fast, there may not be a second date.

Just as in other parts of our lives, we tend to have well-developed scripts for key events in our dating lives (e.g., being asked out, first dates, relationship development and termination).[39] Interestingly, these scripts appear to be commonly held by most members of mainstream North American culture. Of course, just because our dating scripts have much in common does not mean that every person carries exactly the same dating script around in their head.

Recent research suggests that when the expectations set up by our scripts do not match with that of our relationship partner, we may view the relationship less positively. The more similar the scripts, the easier it becomes for individuals who are dating to predict each other's future behavior.[40] So, if you like someone, but your interactions seem to be unusually awkward, it may be that you're operating from different dating scripts. At such times, direct communication about your expectations is the best route for maintaining and further developing the relationship.[41]

Think on it: What was the most awkward dating experience you ever had? Were there long pauses in the conversation? Can you think of things that you could have done as a communicator and listener that could have made the situation less awkward? Using the information presented in this section, diagnose the communication elements of that experience.

In today's world, we must also consider communication technologies and their impact on relationship development.[42] **Communication affordance** refers to what goal we can reach with a particular communication medium. For example, what does using email allow us to do (or not do)? We can take time to carefully compose a message, our agitated gestures and tone of voice are not processed by the receiver. The message also allows the receiver time to process the message before responding. Thus, the timing (synchronous versus asynchronous), message (level of self-disclosure), personal motivations (self-protection), and reduced imposition affect the choice of communication medium. Early in a relationship, when we have greater concerns about self-presentation, saving face, and fear of rejection, we may choose a medium that allows us to protect ourselves and provides greater control over the interaction (e.g., instant messaging versus FaceTime). These features allow us to maximize the positive experiences in our interactions. This is particularly important at the beginning of a relationships because we don't know the other person that well and can easily say or do something that they may dislike or find offensive. At the same time, the greater control we feel with asynchronous mediums (e.g., email, texting) may actually increase the amount and depth of self-disclosure in comparison to face-to-face interactions in the initial stages of a relationship.

Developing and Maintaining Romantic Relationships

Assuming that all goes well, the odds are that you will eventually find one of these initial dates developing into a more serious relationship. Once it is fully developed, you then have to engage in relational maintenance. What does **relational maintenance** mean? Well, it depends on who you ask. Researchers who study this area of relationships variously define it as keeping a relationship in existence, keeping it at its current level of development, maintaining relational satisfaction, and/or keeping a relationship in repair (i.e., addressing problematic issues).[43] We tend to take a broad view of relational maintenance, believing that in order to have relational satisfaction, partners must work to keep the relationship at a mutually satisfactory level. This necessitates relationship repair, including handling conflict (discussed in Chapter 6 and again later in the chapter).

While some individuals are quite direct in their approach to growing a relationship (e.g., "I'd like to date you," "Let's go steady," "Want to move in together?" "Will you marry me?" etc.), many individuals prefer a more indirect route.[44] The indirect route includes a variety of techniques and strategies, including increasing the amount and time spent communicating or in contact with the other person, and verbal and nonverbal expressions of affection (e.g., expressing interest in your values and goals, expressing love, compliments, doing favors, giving gifts, making compliments, revealing more personal information, seeking or giving support). Needless to say, careful listening to these and similar cues lets us know that the other person wishes to escalate (i.e., make more serious) the relationship – giving you the opportunity to respond in a way you wish (i.e., welcoming or distancing). If you are the one hoping to make the relationship more serious, then listening becomes the means by which you can more accurately assess both the state of the relationship, and the other's view of it. Many of the same techniques used to escalate a relationship can and are used to test or assess the current state of the relationship. Thus, the rest of this section focuses on "involved daters."[45]

Involved daters are "emotionally involved in a reciprocal love relationship with one person."[46] In contrast, **casual daters** are dating any number of individuals. Research suggests that communication issues become more salient as we become more "involved" in the relationship. For example, nonverbal communication becomes more important and receives greater attention by both partners in more serious dating relationships. As a result, there appear to be fewer *"cross-cues"* (verbal and nonverbal messages that don't match) between involved relationship partners, likely leading to reports of increased relational satisfaction. Thus, as individuals become more vested in a relationship it appears that they work harder on their communication messages, especially making sure that verbal and nonverbal modes of communication are congruent. Why is congruency

"You're the first guy I've met who really listens and blah, blah, blah..."

important? It can help us listen more effectively and efficiently. Incongruences between channels make it more difficult to decode and process information. As a result, we may miss part of the message or misinterpret it, which can lead to misunderstandings and conflict.

Relationship scholars Kathryn Dindia and Lindsay Timmerman note that "relationships do not maintain themselves."[47] Communicative interactions are the foundation of our relationships. Dindia and Timmerman argue that that there are several **relationship functions** that help maintain our relationships, among them are *maintaining interaction, maintaining liking* and *maintaining intimacy, conflict resolution* and *emotional support*. These functions are most frequently expressed through the time we spend together, and the activities we share together.[48] However, relationship partners can't be together 24/7. "Talk," whether general conversations or catching up with one another at the end of the day is one of the most important relationship maintenance strategies we engage in. In fact those "end of the day" or "while we were separated" conversations appear to be one of the important ways that relational partners define their "togetherness." The same research has found these catching-up conversations to be positively related to relational satisfaction.[49]

These conversations become a means of addressing relational discontinuity (i.e., time apart). These moments are important sharing times, and often include moments of empathy, self-disclosure, and social support – all of which require excellent listening skills and all of which are fundamental to maintaining satisfying relationships. They are also likely related to another important aspect of relationships maintenance – liking.

At its simplest level, it makes sense that we should like the person we are in a relationship with. It is important, however, that expressions of liking (affection) are verbally and nonverbally expressed by both parties. **Verbal assurances** stress our commitment to the other, show our love for them, and demonstrate our faithfulness to them.[50] Some research suggests that the longer (and more serious) our relationships become, the more frequently we engage in assurances. Importantly, relational satisfaction, commitment and liking appear to be related to relational assurances.[51] In other words, we like to hear them. We also appreciate partners who are positive, cheerful, and overall engage in prosocial communication (i.e., avoid criticism, engage in conflict avoidance).[52] In fact, these types of conversations are often the foundation of the next type of relationship we discuss – committed couples.

However, before we move on, we want to address how couples use communication technology at this stage of their relationship. We again touch on the Communication Affordance Utilization Model proposed by Professor Erin Ruppel.[53] As we noted above, at the beginning of a relationship, people often choose communication technologies that provide them with greater control over the interaction. These concerns remain important in moderately developed relationships. However, as we become more familiar with our partner, we typically become less focused on self-presentation and thus feel less of a need to control our interactions through our strategic communication technology choices. We may choose the medium that is most convenient, in part, because we worry less about self-presentation and are more willing to reveal ourselves to others as their relationships develop. As a result, the original advantages afforded by some communication technologies become less salient and subsequently comprise a smaller proportion of our communication interactions. In particular, as a relationship progresses it appears that asynchronous methods such as texting decrease and the use of synchronous mediums increases (e.g., mobile phones, FaceTime). One reason for this is that we listen and learn more about one another over time. We can be more confident that our suggestions and plans will be acceptable to our partner. This trend continues as we continue to disclose to one another beyond the superficial depths when we first meet someone. However, at this level of a relationship there are still face threat concerns and we may still be cautious and superficial in our interactions on some subjects. In such cases, we may revert back to asynchronous communication mediums that allow us to learn more about one another, while still reducing possible embarrassment or awkwardness.

At high levels of relationship development, Ruppel notes that partners are much less concerned with self-presentation and face threats. They also have a better understanding of how to compose effective messages with their partner, which topics are "touchy" and should be avoided or at least approached with caution, and better at predicting how their partner will respond to a message. Because of their greater knowledge and past experiences, they are less fearful that a single negative transaction could end or harm the relationship. This experience lends greater stability to more developed relationships. Subsequently, there is less focus on the benefits of a particular communication technology. By this time, calling someone is seen as a superior medium to email, partners desire synchronous communications which include vocal and verbal cues, particularly as a topic becomes more personal or intimate.

An important aspect of romantic relationship development and maintenance is **interpersonal trust.** At its core is the expectancy that the people in our lives can be relied upon and that they will keep their word, their promise, etc. Interpersonal trust can be applied to all our interpersonal relationships, but in romantic relationships it refers to our belief that our partner will look out for our interests, even in situations where their own interests are at question.[54] Interpersonal trust has been associated with listening anxiety and verbal aggressiveness.[55] Generally speaking, the greater the interpersonal trust we have with our romantic partner, the less likely we are to experience listening anxiety and the less verbally aggressive we tend to be with our partner. In other words, we find it easier to talk with and receive information from those romantically close to us. Of course, the reverse is also true, as trust decreases, our listening anxiety increases. In the worst scenario, we can end up with a *negative sentiment override*, where negativity begets more negativity. We begin viewing most all of the messages we receive negatively. This downward spiral may lead to a negative message cycle that ultimately damages the interpersonal trust in the relationship and leads us to engage in self-protective behaviors, one of which is verbal aggressiveness. No relationship is perfect. An awareness of the association between interpersonal trust, listening anxiety, and verbal aggressiveness is important in times of relationship trouble. Knowing that reduced trust can lead to a negative spiral – where we interpret partner behaviors and statements negatively and subsequently say and do things that further damage a relationship – can help us to try to break the spiral. When we acknowledge that we are angry, that our trust has been shaken, we can then make the conscious effort to re-evaluate our initial perceptions of our partner's message or behavior. Researchers in personality and social psychology have found that we can successfully intervene in this biased-perception conflict spiral when we listen openly to others and avoid listening in a critical, counter arguing way.[56] This is easy for us to say, and we acknowledge that it is hard to do. However, it may be one of the most important gifts you can give to your partner – the benefit of the doubt.

Committed Couples

In their early work, *Marriage and the Social Construction of Reality*, Peter Berger and Hansfried Kellner write, "The reality of the world is sustained through conversation with significant others."[57] Whether a spouse or committed partner, individuals in close relationships are important sources of feedback in our interactions with the social world. We discuss committed couples, rather than married couples for a reason. Across the globe, the number of couples who marry has declined significantly. In 1960, approximately 72% of US adults were married, while only 51% had rings on their fingers in 2012.[58]

No matter our sexual orientation, it is through marriage and marriage-like relationships (e.g., sustained, long-term, co-habitation, etc.) that we experience our most intimate adult relationship – one that serves as our primary source of affection and support.[59] Central to this type of close relationship is intimacy – a sense of being close to and connected to the other person.[60] This feeling of closeness develops through our communication with our partner.[61] The process of intimacy is based on self-disclosure and partner responsiveness. *Responsiveness* occurs as you respond to your partner's disclosure in a way that validates the other person and shows caring and understanding. Intimacy develops through reciprocal responsive communication. As you know, listening is fundamental to responsiveness. A key aspect of developing feelings of closeness is our perception of our partner's responsiveness. When we perceive our partner to be responsive, we feel more valued by the listener. Responsiveness also encourages additional disclosure, helping further to establish a close, intimate relationship. This listening process is "dynamic and fluid, with each person taking on the role of speaker and listener."[62] Thus, feelings of intimacy are moderated by our perceptions and evaluations of how the other responds to our disclosures. This appears to apply particularly to disclosures of emotions.[63]

Relatively few studies have examined the relationships between communication and relational intimacy, especially sexual intimacy.[64] However, research in this area does suggest that self-disclosure and personalized communication (e.g., "we" language, pet names, etc.) is related to maintaining liking and maintaining intimacy. Scholars Deborah Borisoff and Dan Hahn suggest that intimate relationships are founded on self-disclosure, interdependence, trust, reciprocated commitment, and quality communication.

Borisoff and Hahn were particularly interested in listening differences of men and women. They believed that men and women differ in what they listen to as well as how they express their listening behavior, and suggest that these differences can be a source of relational problems. For example, they suggest that when women share their problems and experiences, that the process of the conversation itself is viewed as a means of expressing empathic communication. Men, in contrast, are often more utilitarian in their approach to a conversation. They see the conversation as the opportunity to solve a problem. Thus, a woman may be seeking understanding, while the man in her life sets out to provide (sometimes unwanted) advice.[65] Both individuals may end up feeling hurt or exasperated wondering "Why doesn't s/he listen?"

Think on it: Do you agree with Borisoff and Hahn? Do you believe that men and women listen differently? What experiences lead you to draw this conclusion?

Professors Borisoff and Hahn have two primary suggestions for improving listening in close relationships. First, you have to ***accept and validate your partner's contributions*** to the relationship. They write that "accepting others and encouraging their self-expression reflects a true gift of love."[66] This is most possible when we are able to look at the world through our partner's eyes – see the world from their perspective. Second, you need to ***understand how your partner listens.*** Professors Borishoff and Hahn also believe that while men and women may hear the same message, how it is interpreted, how they listen to it, can be quite different. Awareness of this difference may help you better understand your partner's response to a listening moment.

Self-disclosure (by both individuals) and partner responsiveness are strongly related to feelings of intimacy by both husbands and wives. However, they seem to be particularly important to women. In other words, wives' ratings of relationship closeness and intimacy seem to focus on "feeling understood, validated, accepted, and cared for" by their spouse. Reflecting the importance of responsiveness, women tend to be more communicatively responsive than men. Men, in contrast, experience greater relationship intimacy with increased self-disclosure. As you can see, men and women emphasize different parts of the communication process affecting what and how they listen to one another.

However, both men and women value the feeling of ***mutual commitment.*** According to some researchers, mutuality of commitment is a key element we look for in our close relationships.[67] We want partners who feel the same way about the relationship and have the same expectations. A recent study examined how romantic partners communicate their commitment to each other.[68] The study generated 928 communication behaviors which they collapsed into the ten commitment indicators listed below:[69]

- providing affection
- providing support
- maintaining integrity
- sharing companionship
- making effort to communicate regularly
- showing respect
- creating a relational future
- creating a positive relational atmosphere
- working on relationship problems together
- reassuring one's commitment.

Typically, the greater the level of mutuality of commitment, the more committed partners use the ten commitment indicators.[70]

Marital Satisfaction

In addition to mutuality of commitment, self-disclosure is also important to the success of marital (or marriage-like) relationships. (We describe relationships in this section as marriages because much of the research has focused on married couples, but it is applicable to other marriage-like relationships.) Early research by Fitzpatrick found self-disclosure to be correlated to marital satisfaction. Related to self-disclosure are debriefing conversations.[71] As we discussed earlier, debriefing conversations are also important to building a sense of intimacy. Discussing daily routines, how one's day went, etc., can then lead to topics that are more important and perhaps touch their lives more deeply.

For these conversations to enhance the relationship, the partners must listen to each other and show they are listening. Marriage therapist John Gottman claims that he can predict within five minutes whether a couple will remain together. Interestingly, *one* of the behaviors he looks at is the way the couple listens. If one or both of them stonewalls, or continually avoids listening to the other one, particularly to unpleasant messages, chances are the relationship will fail.[72] However, when partners are responsive to each other, verbally and nonverbally signaling they are listening, the chances of relationship survival are much greater.

Thus, husbands and wives who regularly self-disclose and listen to one another appear to be happier, with some limitations. For example, if one partner has a high amount of negative feelings, and regularly discloses those feelings, it may lead to lower marital satisfaction. Like many things in life, too much of a good thing can be detrimental. Essentially, people can only listen to a certain amount of negativities before becoming overloaded, as seen in the following example: In a recent conversation, one of our students asked his mother why she and his father had divorced. His mother told him that his father had gone through a period where he was really dissatisfied with his job. He would come home every day and spend much of his time (sometimes hours) talking about how the job was driving him crazy and how much he disliked it. His mother said that it got to the point where she was making excuses to work late because she could not take listening to it day in and day out any more. With his wife's encouragement, the father eventually sought counseling. The counselor understood the need to vent. However, he also understood the negative impact it could have on others. The counselor recommended that the father only complain about his job for 30 minutes when he first got home. Eventually, the job situation improved, but the continual negative talk and disclosures put the marriage on shaky ground, setting it on a downward spiral, from which they never recovered.

As seen in this example, self-disclosure follows rules similar to that of Grice's maxim of quantity. However, there are times when we also need to evaluate the content and the quantity of our self-disclosure. Sharing some information can actually hurt a relationship. Does one spouse tell another about an affair, or simply vow to never let it happen again? What would the knowledge do to the relationship? While this is certainly an ethical question and responses will vary based on personal backgrounds and beliefs, the fact is that such a self-disclosure will have profound implications for the relationship of those involved. Thus, one of the things we have to consider when self-disclosing is boundary management. ***Boundary management*** is an element of Privacy Management Theory (introduced in Chapter 7). It refers to the decisions we make about what information and feelings we will share with others, and our awareness of the potential cost of sharing that information. Our boundary management decisions are generally tied to other relationship rules (e.g., family background, family status, gender, traditions). Previous research in this area suggests that we are most satisfied with our relationships when moderate amounts of self-disclosure are provided. If there is too little disclosure, we may feel the other person doesn't trust or love us, but when there is too much, we may be overwhelmed or feel manipulated.

> ***Think on it:*** Have you had a time when you felt that someone was manipulating you in a relationship? What happened? Do you feel that your listening was affected? If so, how?

Self-disclosure is also related to **authenticity** (i.e., genuineness) in relationships.[73] Authenticity is based on a number of factors, including *awareness, unbiased processing, behavior, and relational orientation.*[74] When we possess greater amounts of these characteristics within a relationship, we can say that it is more authentic. It reflects a willingness to allow others to see both the good and the bad about ourselves, to express ourselves openly and honestly. While we introduce it in the context of romantic relationships, it applies to all of our relationships. Thus, self-disclosure is a key element of revealing who we are and forms the foundation of building mutual intimacy and establishing trust. If you think about your own relationships, you can likely tell when you are being authentic and when you are not. We guess that you are more authentic in close, emotionally significant relationships, such as with family, close friends, and romantic partners.[75] We build authenticity within relationships, in part, based on close, supportive listening. When we provide an open, supportive environment for sharing information, we have the opportunity to learn more about our relationship partners.

Authors Harold Bloomfield and Robert Cooper believe that "one of the reasons that love wanes is neglect, and one of the principal kinds of neglect is the inability to listen well."[76] As you can see from our discussion in this section, listening increases validation and makes your partner feel appreciated. Through listening you gain greater empathy and understanding of your partner, which can make him or her feel more valued and loved.

Previous research indicates that positive and responsive listening tends to be "more characteristic of happily married than of unhappily married couples."[77] It is also associated with greater marital satisfaction. Positive and responsive listening is characterized by emotionally positive facial expressions, frequent eye contact, back-channel vocalizations (e.g., umm, hmm). To the extent such behaviors are missing, we will judge listening to be more neutral or negative (with negative nonverbal expressions).[78]

Couples in Conflict

All relationships face their ups and downs, conflicts and conciliations. The fact is that it can be difficult for us to respond in a positive, prosocial way to someone when we are in conflict. In many cases, the responses we provide are more constructive than those that we initially thought of or those we really wanted to say.[79] While much of the early research in marital functioning focused on studying and solving marriage problems, today there is a growing focus on identifying the positive communication and interactions necessary to maintain marriages (and other committed permanent bondings). How couples maintain positive regard and intimate connections is just as important, if not more so, as understanding how couples handle conflict.[80] Linda Roberts and Danielle Greenberg, researchers in family studies, believe that relational harmony may depend on how well each partner engages in positive behaviors and communication during their interactions together. They suggest that when relational partners regularly engage in behaviors that encourage relational closeness those behaviors help to establish and maintain "the climate of security, trust, and acceptance that characterize well-functioning relationships," and argue that when relational partners ignore or neglect this important aspect of their relationship, greater hostility and more negative conflicts may result.[81] Essentially, positive emotional expressions are reassuring for the other partner, even when in the middle of an argument, while negatively expressed behaviors create greater problems.[82]

> ***Think on it:*** Looking at a current or previous relationship, what are things that you did to help your partner "save" face? Why did you do them? How did it affect the relationship? Was your partner aware you were trying to help them save face? What impact do you think it had on your relationship?

Related research suggests that decreases in expressions of affection and partner responsiveness distinguish couples who eventually divorce from those who remain married.[83] Certainly, one important way we provide responsiveness is through listening. This research suggests that active listening is one of the means we can provide this type of relational support and emotional responsiveness.

Relational research has also found that when we or our partners engage in intimacy avoidance it can increase marital dissatisfaction. **Intimacy avoidance** occurs when our partner avoids or withdraws from us when we try to confide in them. In other words, they don't want us to self-disclose to them; they are avoiding having to listen to us. If you remember in our discussion of self-disclosure and conversation, reciprocity is an important component of both. If we try to avoid receiving disclosures, we don't have to provide them, and it lessens the closeness and understanding we have with our partner. This can be quite important, given that previous research suggests that greater levels of self-disclosure occurs between married spouses than in our relationship with our closest friend.[84]

Professors Roberts and Greenberg explored a number of behaviors that are associated with emotional supportiveness and care giving.[85] These behaviors include direct expressions of caring or indirect vulnerable disclosures. For example, **direct expressions of caring** (either verbal or non-verbal) may be expressions of love, affection and concern. **Validation** occurs when we engage in behaviors that enhance our partner's self-esteem and show we accept and have confidence in them. *Active understanding* is evidenced by behaviors such as paraphrasing, which show we are available, empathic, and understanding of the other person's feelings. Other intimacy processes such as *open questions* encourage our partner to provide greater disclosure, while *general sharing* refers more to the factual sharing and disclosing of information. If these behaviors sound familiar, it's because they reflect good responding and empathy building behaviors discussed earlier in this book. **Indirect vulnerable disclosures** are often expressions that signal the need for emotional support and understanding. For example, the wife of one couple participating in a study by Roberts and Greenberg expressed concern for her weight. An appropriate response from the husband would directly (e.g., "You sound like you want to start a diet"; "Why do you think you've gained weight," etc.) or indirectly (e.g., confirming nod of the head, squeeze her hand, etc.) address her concern. Such responses signal active listening, care giving, and emotional validation. Silence, as actually occurred in this case, was inappropriate. In fact, the wife eventually became angry with her husband because he was not providing the expected emotional support.

Think on it: Looking at a current or previous relationship, what are things that you did to help your partner feel validated? Why did you do them? How did it affect the relationship? Was your partner aware you were trying to help them feel validated? What impact do you think it had on your relationship?

Related to listening processes, couples in distressed (unhappy) marriages and relationships tend to have problems decoding nonverbal communication of their spouses. Interestingly, this **decoding deficit** appears to be specific to that relationship. The couples don't appear to have the same problem decoding the nonverbals of other individuals. Notably, strangers observing a conflict between individuals in an unhappy relationship tend to be better at decoding the nonverbals than the individuals actually in the distressed relationship.[86] Needless to say, an important aspect of listening is being able to decode and interpret a message. Couples who are having marital problems apparently get a "double whammy." Not only are they having problems, but their problems make it more difficult for them to communicate with each other. This communication difficulty is further compounded by the fact that couples are generally quite confident in their interpretation of the spouse's message.[87] Researchers believe that one reason for this overconfidence lies within the nature of the relationships itself – the partners know each other so well (or think they do).[88]

Distressed couples also exhibit other related communication problems. For example, they interrupt more, tend to criticize and complain more, and are more likely to provide negative solutions (e.g., "It's hopeless"; "Just forget it").[89] They are also less likely to self-disclose, to offer acceptance or empathy, and to make eye contact or smile at their partner.[90] In fact, nonverbal behaviors appear truly to set happy couples apart from unhappy couples.[91] Previous research indicates that the ratio of positive to negative behavior (30:1) distinguishes happy couples from unhappy couples (4:1).[92] Distressed couples are also less able to engage in problem description, have poorer active listening skills, and have difficulty in creating constructive solutions to problems.

The overall state of the marriage can be quite important to how messages and behavior are interpreted. Individuals in distressed marriages are more likely to assign negative connotations to ambiguous communication and behavior, while people in happy marriages will use a more positive lens for interpreting those same behaviors and communications.[93] The focus on the positive likely has a better chance of successfully resolving conflict. Unfortunately, distressed couples also are more likely to respond negatively, thus reciprocity occurs; however, it is a negative spiral, often resulting in an escalation of the conflict.[94] Not surprisingly, this pattern of behavior not only reduces marital satisfaction, but has also been associated with increased rates of divorce.[95] One of the contributors to these conflicts is social perception.

Social perception addresses "what one attends to or the impressions one forms of another."[96] Distressed couples often have significant differences in how they describe relationship events, reflecting the effect of cognitive schemas and personal biases. For example, a distressed spouse is more likely to attribute a marital problem to something inherently related to the other (e.g., personality attributes such as laziness) rather than to extrinsic causes (stressed out from work). In contrast, happily married couples tend to view their partner more positively, even than their partner viewed themselves! In addition, they are more likely to give their partner the benefit of the doubt. Giving another the benefit of the doubt when assessing events increases the likelihood that we'll focus on behaviors that confirm our perceptions of our spouse, and makes it much easier for us to respond positively when in conflict.[97]

Listening Responses to Conflict

Relational dissatisfaction and conflict are givens in close relationships. How we respond to these moments is most important to relational repair. If we are to engage in constructive conflict, we need to *avoid* a variety of negative behaviors including "defensiveness, criticism, contempt, avoiding the issue, mindreading [and] making negative attributions toward the partner."[98] Avoiding blame, ensuring we understand the other's perspective (via paraphrasing), and avoiding personal attacks (by focusing on the annoying behavior) generally will increase our overall satisfaction with our relationship.[99] Relationship scholar Tara Emmers-Sommer summarizes the research in this area: "Overall, the prescription [is] simple: Be nice to your partner to maintain your relationship, if you transgress, engage in prosocial, communicative behaviors to repair the relationship."[100]

The relationship between speaking and listening is particularly apparent in marital conflict. How the listening partner responds to the speaking partner can impact whether a conflict increases or decreases in intensity. For example, when observing other relationships, you may have noticed that when one partner feels ignored, he or she may talk more loudly or continue to pick on the same minor point over and over. Thus, a speaker who feels he or she isn't receiving the appropriate quantity or quality of listening response may escalate the argument in order to get some type of response from the listener (even negative). The fact is withholding listening responses or "freezing someone out" may be a worse response to conflict.

In addition, as we mentioned earlier, the ratio of positive to negative behaviors is related to overall marital satisfaction and marital stability.[101] In general, marital stability can be maintained when there are five positive behaviors to each negative behavior. Thus, the balance between positive and negative marital behaviors becomes important for maintaining a marriage. As outlined below, poor communication, including poor listening, are related to increased negativity and greater marital instability.

Communication Patterns

Research in conflict suggests that there are distinct differences in the communication and conflict patterns of distressed and non-distressed couples.[102] Table 8.1 presents types of conflict communication based on hostile speaking behavior and withdrawn listening behavior. In the table, **regulation** and **non-regulation** refers to the ratio of positive to negative behaviors that a couple exhibits over time.[103] Thus, a non-regulated couple would have a higher ratio of negative to positive behaviors, while a regulated couple would exhibit more positive behaviors than negative behaviors. Examples of negative speaking behaviors include verbally attacking each other, including belittling, blaming or contemptuousness.[104] **Conflict withdrawal** is often characterized by negative listening behaviors such as physically turning away from the other person, changing the topic, and avoiding back-channel behaviors (e.g., head nods and verbal encouragements to continue speaking).[105]

Table 8.1 Typology of Marital Conflict Styles

	Regulated Listening	*Non-regulated Listening*
Regulated speaking	Conflict engagers	Avoiders
Non-regulated speaking	Hostile	Hostile detached

Couples that engage in non-regulated behaviors tend to be unhappy with their relationship. They express more negative and less positive emotions, are more stubborn, withdraw more, and are more defensive.[106]

Thus, couples who are *conflict engagers* are more likely to express regard for their significant other by directly addressing potentially contentious issues, listening closely, and responding appropriately. As a consequence, they actually will express more negative emotions than avoiders. However, conflict engagers also express more positive behavior as well. *Avoiders*, in contrast, are more likely to withdraw from listening, likely because the act of really listening carries with it the expectation of a response.

Hostile and hostile-detached couples also differ from one another. *Hostile* couples engage in less negative and more positive behaviors than hostile-detached couples. Some research suggests that hostile and hostile-detached couples tend to be the most unstable and prone to divorce.[107] *Hostile-detached* couples are the most likely to experience problems when attempting to co-parent a child. Their disengagement with and hostility towards one another appears to spill over in their relationships with their children and can ultimately influence their children's own interpersonal interactions. Withdrawal, in the face of hostility, exemplifies a type of emotional disregulation – behavior which can negatively affect children's interactions with peers and other individuals, if they model their parents' conflict behaviors.

It is important to note that the above discussion holds true for both same-sex and cross-sex couples.[108] However, some research suggests that same-sex couples have several advantages when it comes to engaging in conflict.[109] First, the divorce rate for gay and lesbian couples is half that of their straight counterparts. One explanation for this lower rate is that gay and lesbian partners tend to be more accepting of criticism and are less defensive when addressing relationship problems. In addition, they tend to use more humor and affection in their interactions. They also tend to be less physiologically aroused (e.g., increased blood pressure, etc.) when they do fight. Why these differences? There is some speculation that the experiences with discrimination and criticism that same-sex couples face outside their relationships teach them how to address the conflict that may arise within it more effectively.

Culture and Commitment

Intercultural relationships can face a number of additional difficulties as related to the expectations of each romantic partner. Thus, interracial and interethnic couples have to work hard at understanding and recognizing how cultural differences can affect their relational maintenance beliefs and behaviors, especially those related to communication and listening.[110] For example, while Americans often focus on fairness and equity in each partner's contributions to the relationships, Koreans do not. Because equity is much less important to them, Koreans are more likely to take for granted that their marriage partner will remain in the relationship. As a result, they do not track the types of commitments or obligations that an American couple would. In addition, Koreans may feel less need to express and/or acknowledge displays of affection and commitment.

Cultural differences in self-disclosure can also occur. While we have stressed the importance of self-disclosure to listening and relationships, our examples often reflect our individualistic cultural orientation. Self-disclosure in individualistic cultures often will emphasize individual accomplishments, abilities, and characteristics. In collectivistic cultures, a more interdependent view of self-disclosure emerges such that restraint and harmony are emphasized, and likely lead to differences in both the quantity and the quality of individual self-disclosure.[111]

Summary

One of the most important elements of our lives is the relationships that we use to define who and what we are. As we have seen in this chapter, our listening skills grow as we age and mature. With effective communication and listening skills, we are better able to establish friendships and enter into long-term, committed relationships. We are also better able both to elicit and provide the social support needed to validate your own and others' self views. Over the last two chapters we have examined the influence of listening and listening processes on the most important relationships we will form over the course of our lives. However, as we have discussed earlier in the text, listening occurs in context. The next section of the book explores four common listening contexts – organizations, education, health and the law.

Key Concepts

Friend
Friendship Characteristics
Strategies to Maintain Relationships
Directed versus Non-directed Medium
Techniques to Build Friendships
Relational Maintenance
Involved versus Casual Daters
Relationship Functions
Verbal Assurances
Interpersonal Trust
Conflict Resolution
Emotional Support
Cross-cues
Mutual Commitment
Boundary Management
Authenticity
Intimacy Avoidance
Direct Expressions of Caring
Validation
    Active understanding
    Open questions
    General sharing
Indirect Vulnerable Disclosures
Decoding Deficit
Social Perception
Marital Conflict Styles
    Regulation/Non-regulation
    Conflict Withdrawal

Discussion Questions

1. Make a list of the many qualities you like about your best friend or friends. Compare your list to those sitting around you. How is the importance of listening seen in your list? How many

things on your list would be considered an intrinsic quality? An extrinsic quality? What does your list tell you about what you and others value in your friendships?

2. Some people find it easy to make friends, while others find it more difficult. What qualities lead someone to be described as "friendly." How are those qualities related to listening? What advice or tips would you give to someone who may find it more difficult to make friends?

3. Earlier in the chapter we discussed the ethical dilemmas committed couples often face. Do you believe that if one member of a couple has an affair that they should tell their partner? Do you know someone who has received news like this? How did it affect their relationship? If the couples remained committed, how do you think it affected their relationship? Their conflict communication patterns? Their listening?

Listening Activities

1. As a communication consultant, you've been asked to develop a survey to help individuals identify their "best" friend. Develop ten items. What type of questions did you put on the questionnaire? Why? Compare your survey to others in your class. What similarities and differences do you observe? Would you use the same questions if you were trying to identify a romantic partner?

2. Soap operas seem to thrive on conflict. Over the course of a week, pick a soap opera and observe the interactions of a primary couple on the show. What are some of the qualities of committed couples do you observe? Do their interactions reflect real life? What you've learned in this chapter? In other areas of the text? What impact might soap operas have on the schemas and scripts children or adolescences develop about dating relationships? How couples communicate and listen to one another?

3. Interview a committed couple in your life. It may be your parents, grandparents, an aunt and uncle, or good friends. How did they meet? What drew them together? What qualities did they admire about each other when they first met? Who "escalated" the relationship and how? How does what you learned reflect the discussion of communication and relationship development presented in this chapter?

4. In a group of three to four people, imagine that you have been asked to develop a Conflict Management Workshop for committed couples. What tips would you offer and why? As a class, compare your tips. Are they similar or different? What would the class top five or six tips be? Each group should develop a two to three minute role play to present to the class illustrating one of the tips.

Notes

1 Sprecher & Regan, 2002; Larson, Whitton, Hauser, & Allen, 2007; du Plessis & Corney, 2011
2 Hartup & Abecassis, 2002
3 Asher et al., 1996; Guerrero, 1997
4 Fehr, 1996; Halpern, 1997; Newman & Newman, 2015
5 Wentz, 2015
6 Andersson & Ronnberg, 1997; Newcomb & Brady, 1982
7 Hartup, 1993
8 For reviews see, see Fehr, 1996, and Ladd, 1999.
9 Samter, 2003; Collins & Steinberg, 2006

10 Samter, 2003
11 Samter, 2003, p. 642
12 Samter, 2003, p. 642
13 Berndt, 1981a, 1981b; Thorne, 1986
14 Chu, 2005, p. 7
15 Chu, 2005; du Plessis & Corney, 2011
16 Gertner, et al. 1994
17 Iannotti, 1985
18 Azmitia, Ittel, & Radmacher, 2005
19 Azmitia et al., 2005
20 Wolvin, Coakley, & Halone, 1995
21 Azmitia et al., 2005
22 Rawlins, 1992
23 Duck, 1994
24 Fehr, 2000
25 Canary & Stafford, 1994
26 Bell et al., 1987; Dindia & Baxter, 1987; Stafford & Canary, 1991
27 Oliker, 1989
28 Nguyen, Bin, & Campbell, 2012
29 See Ruppel, et al., 2017, meta-analysis for a review; also, see Amichai-Hamburger, Kingsbury, & Schneider, 2013) for commentary.
30 Liu & Yang, 2016
31 Liu & Yang, 2016
32 Miller, 2014, summarizes the work of a number of studies.
33 Segrin, 2006
34 Cline & Clark, 1994
35 Cline & Clark, 1994
36 Kleinke, 1981; Senko & Fyffe, 2010.
37 McGinty, Knox, & Zusman, 2003
38 Berger & Bell, 1988; Miell & Duck, 1986; Pryor & Merluzzi, 1985
39 See Hormberg & MacKenzie (2002) for a review.
40 These claims are based on early research by Hormberg & MacKenzie, 2002
41 Hormberg & MacKenzie, 2002
42 Ruppel, 2015 provides an extensive review and proposes an affordance utilization model to explain the effect of communication technology on user conversations and relationships.
43 See Dindia & Canary, 1993 for a review
44 Dindia & Timmerman, 2003
45 McGinty, Knox, & Zusman, 2003
46 McGinty, et al., 2003, p. 68
47 Dindia & Tommerman, 2003, p. 705
48 See Dindia and Timmerman, 2003 for a review.
49 Vangelisti & Banski, 1993
50 Dindia & Timmerman, 2003, p. 707
51 Stafford, 2003; Stafford & Canary, 1991
52 Canary & Stafford, 1994; Dindia & Baxter, 1987
53 Ruppel, 2015
54 Gottman, 2011
55 Hoskins, Woszidlo, & Kunkel, 2016
56 Kennedy & Pronin, 2010
57 As quoted in Neff & Karney, 2002, p. 32
58 Livingston & Caumont, 2017

59   Laurenceau, Feldman, & Rovine, 2005; Levinger & Huston, 1990; Miller, 2013; Kurkek, 2005
60   Laurenceau, et al., 2005
61   Perlman & Fehr, 1987
62   Laurenceau, et al., 2005
63   Laurenceau, Feldman, & Pietromonaco, 1998
64   See Dindia & Timmerman, 2003, p. 708, for a brief review; cf., Borisoff & Hann, 1992
65   Tannen, 1990
66   Borisoff & Hahn, 1992, p. 35
67   Knobloch & Solomon, 1999; Weigel, 2008
68   Weigel & Ballard-Reisch, 2002
69   As reported by Weigel, 2008, p. 26
70   Weigel, 2008
71   Fitzpatrick, 1987
72   Gottman, and Silver, 1999
73   Petty, Pazda, & Knee, 2010
74   Kernis, 2003
75   Lopez & Rice, 2006
76   Bloomfield & Cooper, 1995, p. 93
77   Pasupathi, Carstensen, Levenson, & Gottman, 1999
78   Gottman, 1989, as cited in Pasupathi et al., 1999
79   Yovetich & Rusbult, 1994
80   Roberts & Greenberg, 2002
81   Roberts & Greenberg, 2002, p. 121
82   Pasupathi et al., 1999
83   Huston, Caughlin, Houts, Smith, & George, 2001
84   Tschann, 1988; Kito, 2005
85   Roberts & Greenberg, 2002
86   Gottman & Porterfield, 1981; Noller, 1981
87   Noller & Venardos, 1986
88   Sillar & Scott, 1983
89   See Kelly, Fincham, & Beach, 2003 for a review of the literature.
90   See Kelly et al., 2003 for a review of the literature.
91   Gottman, et al., 1977; Smith, Vivian, & O'Leary, 1990
92   Birchler, Weiss, & Vincent, 1975; Fincham, Bradbury, Arias, Byrne, & Karney, 1997
93   Noller & Fitzpatrick, 1993
94   Gottman, 1994
95   Gottman, 1994
96   Kelly et al., 2003
97   See Kelly et al., 2003 for a review.
98   Gottman, 1994, as described by Emmers-Sommer, 2003
99   Gottman, 1994
100 Emmers-Sommer, 2003, p. 199
101 Gottman & Levenson, 1992
102 See for example, Christensen & Heavey, 1990; Fitzpatrick & Indvik, 1982; Gottman, 1993, 1994;
     Kurdek, 1995
103 Gottman & Levenson, 1992
104 Brown & Smith, 1992, Gottman, 1993
105 Christensen & Heavey, 1990; Gottman, 1993
106 Gottman & Levenson, 1992
107 Gottman, 1993, 1994
108 Holley, Sturm, & Levenson, 2010; Miller, 2013

109   Miller, 2013
110   Yum & Canary 2003
111   Markus & Kitayama, 1991

Additional Readings

Duck, S. W., & McMahan, D. T. (2009). *The basics of communication: A relational perspective.* Thousand Oaks, CA: Sage.

Flora, C. (2013). *Friendfluence: the surprising ways friends make us who we are.* New York: Doubleday.

Galvin, K. M. (2010). *Making connections: Readings in relational communication* (5th ed.). New York: Oxford University Press.

Guerrero, L. K., Andersen, P. A., & Afifi, W. A. (2007). *Close encounters: Communication in relationships* (2nd ed.). Thousand Oaks, CA: Sage.

References

Amichai-Hamburger, Y., Kingsbury, M., & Schneider, B. H. (2013). Friendship: An old concept with a new meaning? *Computers in Human Behavior, 29,* 33–39.

Andersson, J., & Rönnberg, J. (1997). Cued memory collaboration: Effects of friendship and type of retrieval cue. *European Journal of Cognitive Psychology, 9,* 273–287.

Azmitia, M., Ittel, A., & Radmacher, K. (2005). Narratives of friendship and self in adolescence. In N. Way, & J. V. Hamm (Eds.), *New directions for child and adolescent development* (No. 107, pp. 23–39). San Francisco: Jossey-Bass.

Asher, S. R., Parker, J. G., & Walker, D. L. (1996). Distinguishing friendship from acceptance: Implications for intervention and assessment. In W. M. Bukowski, A. F. Newcomb, & W. W. Hartup (Eds.), *The company they keep: Friendship in childhood and adolescence* (pp. 366–405). New York: Cambridge University Press.

Bell, R. A., Daly, J. A., & Gonzalez, C. (1987). Affinity-maintenance in marriage and its relationship to women's marital satisfaction. *Journal of Marriage and the Family, 49,* 445–454.

Berger, C. R., & Bell, R. A. (1988). Plans and the initiation of social relationship. *Human Communication Research, 14,* 217–235.

Berndt, T. J. (1981a). Age changes and changes over time in prosocial intentions and behavior between friends. *Developmental Psychology, 17,* 408–416.

Berndt, T. J. (1981b). Effects of friendship on prosocial intentions and behavior. *Child Development, 52,* 636–643.

Birchler, G. R., Weiss, R. L., & Vincent, J. P. (1975). Multimethod analysis of social reinforcement exchange between martially distressed and nondistressed spouse and stranger dyads. *Journal of Personality and Social Psychology, 31,* 349–360.

Bloomfield, H. H., & Cooper, R. K. (1995, July). Take 5 to make love last. *Prevention, 47,* 90–97.

Borisoff, D., & Hahn, D. F. (1992). Dimensions of intimacy: The interrelationships between gender and listening. *Journal of the International Listening Association, 6,* 23–41.

Brown, P. C., & Smith, T. W. (1992). Social influence, marriage, and the heart: Cardiovascular consequences of interpersonal control in husbands and wives. *Health Psychology, 11,* 88–96.

Canary, D. J., & Stafford, L. (1994). Maintaining relationships through strategic and routine interaction. In D. J. Canary & L. Stafford (Eds.), *Communication and relational maintenance* (pp. 3–22). San Diego, CA: Academic Press.

Christensen, A., & Heavey, C. L. (1990). Gender and social structure in the demand/withdraw pattern of marital conflict. *Journal of Personality and Social Psychology, 59,* 73–81.

Chu, J. Y. (2005). Adolescent boys' friendships and peer group culture. In N. Way & J. V. Hamm (Eds.), *New directions for child and adolescent development* (No. 107, pp. 7–22). San Francisco: Jossey-Bass.

Cline, R. J. W., & Clark, A. J. (1994). "I've fallen for you like a blind roofer": Some effects of listener characteristics on interpreting opening lines. *International Journal of Listening, 8*, 80–97.

Collins, W. A., & Steinberg, L. (2006). Adolescent development in interpersonal context. In N. Eisenberg (Ed.), *Handbook of child psychology* (6th ed., vol. 3, pp. 1003–1067). Hoboken, NJ: Wiley.

Dindia, K., & Baxter, L. (1987). Strategies for maintaining and repairing marital relationships. *Journal of Social and Personal Relationships, 4*, 143–158.

Dindia, K., & Canary, D. J. (1993). Definitions and theoretical perspectives on maintaining relationships. *Journal of Social and Personal Relationships, 10*, 163–173.

Dindia, K., & Timmerman, L. (2003). Accomplishing romantic relationships. In J. O. Greene & B. R. Burleson (Eds.), *Handbook of communication and social interaction skills* (pp. 685–721). Mahwah, NJ: LEA.

Doohan, E. (2007). Listening behaviors of married couples: An exploration of nonverbal presentation to a relational outsider. *International Journal of Listening, 21*, 24–41.

Duck, S. (1994). Steady as (s)he goes: Relational maintenance as a shared meaning system. In D. J. Canary & L. Stafford (Eds.), *Communication and relational maintenance* (pp. 45–60). San Diego, CA: Academic Press.

du Plessis, K., & Corney, T. (2011). Trust, respect and friendship: The key attributes of significant others in the lives of young working men. *Youth Studies Australia, 30*, 17–26.

Emmers-Sommer, T. M. (2003). When partners falter: Repair after a transgression. In D. J. Canary & M Dainton (Eds.), *Maintaining relationships through communication* (pp. 185–205). Mahwah, NJ: LEA.

Fehr, B. (2000). The life cycle of friendship. In C. Hendrick & S. Hendrick (Eds.), *Close relationships: A sourcebook* (pp. 71–82). Thousand Oaks: Sage.

Fehr, B. (1996). *Friendship processes.* Thousand Oaks, CA: Sage.

Fincham, F. D., Bradbury, T. N., Arias, I., Byrne, C. A., & Karney, B. R. (1997). Marital violence, marital distress, and attributions. *Journal of Family Violence, 11*, 367–372.

Fitzpatrick, M. A., & Indvik, J. (1982). The instrumental and expressive domains of marital communication. *Human Communication Research, 8*, 195–213.

Fitzpatrick, M. A. (1987). Marriage and verbal intimacy. In V. J. Derlega & J. H. Berg (Eds.), *Self-disclosure: Theory, research and therapy* (pp. 131–154). New York: Plenum.

Gertner, B. L., Rice, M. L., & Hadley, P. A. (1994). Influence of communicative competence on peer preferences in a preschool classroom. *Journal of Speech and Hearing Research, 37*, 913–923.

Goffman, E. (1967). *Interaction ritual: Essays on face-to-face behavior.* New York: Pantheon.

Gottman, J. M., Markman, H., & Notarius, C. (1977). The topography of marital conflict: A sequential analysis of verbal and nonverbal behavior. *Journal of Marriage and the Family, 39,* 461–477.

Gottman, J. M. (1993). The roles of conflict engagement, escalation, and avoidance in marital interaction: A longitudinal view of five types of couples. *Journal of Consulting and Clinical Psychology, 67*, 6–15.

Gottman, J. M. (1994). *What predicts divorce.* Hillsdale, NJ: LEA.

Gottman, J. M., & Levenson, R. W. (1992). Marital processes predictive of later dissolution: Behavior, physiology, and health. *Journal of Personality and Social Psychology, 63*, 221–233.

Gottman, J. M., & Porterfield, A. L. (1981). Communicative competence in the nonverbal behavior of married couples. *Journal of Marriage and the Family, 43*, 187–198.

Gottman, J. M., & Silver, N. (1999). *The seven principles for making marriage work.* New York: Crown Publishers.

Gottman, J. M. (2011). *The science of trust: Emotional attunement for couples.* New York: W.W. Norton.

Guerrero, L. K. (1997). Nonverbal involvement across interactions with same-sex friends, opposite-sex friends, and romantic partners: Consistency or change? *Journal of Social and Personal Relationships, 14*, 31–58.

Halpern, J. J. (1997). Elements of a script for friendship in transactions. *Journal of Conflict Resolution, 41*, 835–868.

Hartup, W. W. (1993). Adolescents and their friends. In B. Laursen (Ed.), *Close friendships in adolescence* (pp. 3–21). (New Directions for Child Development, No. 60). San Francisco: Jossey-Bass.

Hartup, W. W., & Abecassis, M. (2002). Friends and enemies. In P. K. Smith & C. H. Hart (Eds.), *Handbook of childhood social development* (pp. 286–306). Maiden, MA: Blackwell.

Holley, S. R., Sturm, V. E., & Levenson, J. W. (2010). Exploring the basis for gender differences in the demand–withdraw pattern. *Journal of Homosexuality, 57*, 666–684.

Hormberg, D., & MacKenzie, S. (2002). So far, so good: Scripts for romantic relationship development as predictors of relational well-being. *Journal of Social and Personal Relationships, 19*, 777–796.

Hoskins, N. S., Woszidlo, A., & Kunkel, A. (2016). Words can hurt the ones you love: Interpersonal trust as it relates to listening anxiety and verbal aggression. *Iowa Journal of Communication, 48*, 96–112.

Huston, T. L., Caughlin, J. P., Houts, R. M., Smith, S. E., & George, L. J. (2001). The connubial crucible: Newlywed years as predictors of marital delight, distress and divorce. *Journal of Personality and Social Psychology, 80*, 237–252.

Iannotti, R. J. (1985). Assessments of prosocial behavior in preschool children. *Developmental Psychology, 21*, 46–55.

Kelly, A. B., Fincham, F. D., & Beach, S. R. H. (2003). Communication skills in couples: A review and discussion of emerging perspectives. In J. O. Greene & B. R. Burleson (Eds.), *Handbook of communication and social interaction skills* (pp. 723–751). Mahwah, NJ: LEA.

Kennedy, K. A., & Pronin, E. (2010). *The way we listen matters: Non-counterarguing listening as an intervention in the bias-perception conflict spiral.* Paper presented at the Society for Personality and Social Psychology annual meeting; Las Vegas, Nevada.

Kernis, M. H. (2003). Toward a conceptualization of optimal self-esteem. *Psychological Inquiry, 14*, 1–26.

Kito, M. (2005). Self-disclosure in romantic relationships and friendships among American and Japanese college students. *The Journal of Social Psychology, 145*, 127–140.

Kleinke, C. L. (1981). How not to pick up a woman. *Psychology Today, 15*, 18–19.

Knobloch, L. K., & Solomon, D. H. (1999). Measuring the sources and content of relational uncertainty. *Communication Studies, 50*, 261–278.

Kurdek, L. A. (1995). Predicting change in marital satisfaction from husbands' and wives' conflict resolution styles. *Journal of Marriage and the Family, 57*, 153–164.

Kurkek, L. A. (2005). What do we know about gay and lesbian couples? *Current Directions in Psychological Science, 14*, 251–254.

Ladd, G. W. (1999). Peer relationships and social competence during early and middle childhood. *Annual Review of Psychology, 50*, 333–359.

Larson, J. J., Whitton, S. W., Hauser, S. T., & Allen, J.P. (2007). Being close and being social: Peer ratings of distinct aspects of young adult social competence. *Journal of Personality Assessment, 89*, 136–48.

Laurenceau, J-P., Feldman, B. L., Pietromonaco P. R. (1998). Intimacy as an interpersonal process: The importance of self-disclosure, and perceived partner responsiveness in interpersonal exchanges. *Journal of Personality and Social Psychology, 74*, 1238–1251.

Laurenceau, J-P., Feldman, B. L., & Rovine, M. J. (2005). The interpersonal process model of intimacy in marriage: A daily-diary and multilevel modeling approach. *Journal of Family Psychology, 19*, 314–323.

Levinger, G., & Huston, T. L. (1990). The social psychology of marriage. In T. Bradbury & F. Fincham (Eds.), *The psychology of marriage* (pp. 19–58). New York: Guilford.

Liu, D., & Yang, C. (2016). Media niche of electronic communication channels in friendship: A meta-analysis. *Journal of Computer-Mediated Communication, 21*, 451–466.

Livingston, G., & Caumont, A. (2017, February 13). 5 facts on love and marriage in America. *FactTank: News in the numbers.* Pew Research Center. Retrieved from www.pewresearch.org/fact-tank/2017/02/13/5-facts-about-love-and-marriage.

Lopez, F. G., & Rice, K. (2006) Preliminary development and validation of a measure of relationship authenticity. *Journal of Counseling Psychology, 53*, 362–371.

Markus, H. R., & Kitayama, S. (1991). Culture and the self: Implications for cognition, emotion, and motivation. *Psychological Review, 98*, 224–253.

McGinty, K., Knox, D., & Zusman, M. E. (2003). Nonverbal and verbal communication in "involved" and "casual" relationships among college students. *College Student Journal, 37*, 68–71.

Miell, D. E., & Duck, S. (1986). Strategies in developing friendships. In V. J. Derlega & B. A. Winstead (Eds.), *Friends and social interaction* (pp. 129–143). New York: Springer-Verlag.

Miller, A. (2014, January). Friends wanted. *Monitor on Psychology, 44*, 54.

Miller, A. (2013, April). Same-sex couples: A model for straight pairs? *Monitor on Psychology, 44*, 45.

Neff, L. A., & Karney, B. R. (2002). Self-evaluation motives in close relationships: A model of global enhancement and specific verification. In P. Noller and J. A. Feeney (Eds.), *Understanding marriage* (pp. 32–58). Cambridge, UK: Cambridge University Press.

Newcomb, A. F., & Brady, J. E. (1982). Mutuality in boys' friendship relations. *Child Development, 53*, 392–395.

Newman, B. M. & Newman, P.R. (2015). *Development through life: A psychosocial approach.* Stanford, CT: Cengage Learning.

Nguyen, M., Bin, Y. S., & Campbell, A. J. (2012). Comparing online and offline self-disclosure: A systematic review. *Cyberpsychology, Behavior and Social Networking, 15*, 103–111.

Noller, P. (1981). Gender and marital adjustment level differences in decoding messages from spouses and strangers. *Journal of Personality and Social Psychology, 41*, 272–278.

Noller, P., & Fitzpatrick, M. A. (1993). *Communication in family telationships.* Englewood Cliffs, NJ: Prentice Hall.

Noller, P., & Venardos, C. (1986). Communication awareness in married couples. *Journal of Social and Personal Relationships, 3*, 31–42.

Oliker, S. J. (1989). *Best friends and marriage: Exchange among women.* Berkeley, CA: University of California Press.

Pasupathi, M., Carstensen, L. L., Levenson, R. W., & Gottman, J. M. (1999). Responsive listening in long-married couples: A psycholinguistic perspective. *Journal of Nonverbal Behavior, 23*, 173–193.

Petty, K. N., Pazda, A., & Knee, C. R. (2010). *A situational manipulation of relationship authenticity.* Paper presented at the Society for Personality and Social Psychology annual meeting; Las Vegas, Nevada.

Perlman, D., & Fehr, B. (1987). The development of intimate relationships. In D. Perlman & S. W. Duck (Eds.), *Intimate relationships: Development, dynamics, and deterioration* (pp. 13–42). Beverly Hills, CA: Sage.

Pryor, J. B., & Merluzzi, T. V. (1985). The role of expertise in processing social interaction scripts. *Journal of Experimental Social Psychology, 21*, 362–379.

Rawlins, W. K. (1992). Young adult friendships. In W. K. Rawlins, *Friendship matters: Communication, dialectics, and the life course* (pp. 103–123). New York: Aldine de Gruyter.

Roberts, L. J., & Greenberg, D. R. (2002). Observational "window" to intimacy processes in marriage. In P. Noller and J. A. Feeney (Eds.), *Understanding marriage* (pp. 118–149). Cambridge, UK: Cambridge University Press.

Ruppel, E. K. (2015). The affordance utilization model: Communication technology use as relationships develop. *Marriage & Family Review, 51*, 669–686.

Ruppel, E. K., Gross, C., Stoll, A., Peck, B., Allen, M. R., & Kim, S. (2017). Reflecting on connecting: Meta-analysis of differences between mediated and face-to-face self-disclosure. *Journal of Computer-Mediated Communication, 22*, 18–34.

Samter, W. (2003). Friendship interaction skills across the life span. In J. O. Greene & B. R. Burleson (Eds.), *Handbook of communication social interaction* (pp. 637–684). Mahwah, NJ: LEA.

Segrin, C. (2006, April 24). Loneliness takes its toll. *USA Today,* 8D.

Senko, C., & Fyffe, V. (2010). An evolutionary perspective on effective vs. ineffective pick-up lines. *The Journal of Social Psychology, 150*, 648–667.

Sillars, A. L., & Scott, M. D. (1983). Interpersonal perception between intimates: An integrative review. *Human Communication Research, 10*, 153–176.

Smith, D. A., Vivian, D., & O'Leary, K. D. (1990). Longitudinal prediction of marital discord from premarital expressions of affect. *Journal of Consulting and Clinical Psychology, 58*, 790–798.

Sprecher, S., & Regan, P. C. (2002). Liking some things (in some people) more than others: Partner preferences in romantic relationships and friendships. *Journal of Social and Personal Relationships, 19*, 463–481.

Stafford, L. (2003). Maintaining romantic relationships: A summary and analysis of one research program. In D. J. Canary & M. Dainton (Eds.), *Maintaining relationships through communication* (pp. 51–77). Mahwah, NJ: LEA.

Stafford, L., & Canary, D. J. (1991). Maintenance strategies and romantic relationship type, gender and relational characteristics. *Journal of Social and Personal Relationships, 8,* 217–242.

Tannen, D. (1990). You just don't understand: Women and men in conversation. New York: HarperCollins.

Thorne, B. (1986). Girls and boys together... but mostly apart: Gender arrangements in elementary school. In W. W. Hartup & Z. Rubin (Eds.), *Relationships and development* (pp. 167–184). Hillsdale, NJ: Erlbaum.

Tschann, J. M. (1988). Self-disclosure in adult friendship: Gender and marital status differences. *Journal of Social and Personal Relationships, 5,* 65–81.

Vangelisti, A. L., & Banski, M. A. (1993). Couples' debriefing conversations. *Family Relations, 42,* 149–157.

Weigel, D. J. (2008). The concept of family: An analysis of laypeople's views of family. *Journal of Family Issues, 29,* 1426–1447.

Weigel, D. J., & Ballard-Reisch, D. S. (2002). Investigating the behavioral indicators of relational commitment. *Journal of Social & Personal Relationships, 19,* 403–424.

Wentz, K. (2015). Prosocial behaviour and schooling. *Encyclopedia on Early Childhood Development.* Centre of Excellence for Early Childhood Development (CEECD) and the Strategic Knowledge Cluster on Early Child Development (SKC-ECD). Retrieved from www.child-encyclopedia.com/prosocial-behaviour/according-experts/prosocial-behaviour-and-schooling.

Wolvin, A., Coakley, C., & Halone, K. (1995). A preliminary look at listening development across the lifespan. *International Journal of Listening, 9,* 62–83.

Yovetich, N. A., & Rusbult, C. E. (1994). Accommodative behavior in close relationships: Exploring transformation of motivation. *Journal of Experimental Social Psychology, 30,* 138–164.

Yum, Y., & Canary, D. J. (2003). Maintaining relationships in Korea and the United States: Features of Korean culture that affect relational maintenance beliefs and behaviors. In D. J. Canary & M. Dainton (Eds.), *Maintaining relationships through communication* (pp. 277–296). Mahwah, NJ: LEA.

Part III

Listening as a Critical Professional Competency

9 Listening in Context

Education

Case Study 9.1 Classroom Listening

Tamarah, I'm glad to see you could make our meeting. We didn't know if you would be able to get off work and we really need your input.

Hey, Carter. Fortunately I was able to get a little time off. Good thing, too. I have so much going on in the listening class and my other classes. Have you been working on your part of our project?

Well, not as much as I should have. But you know, all of that information Professor Merritt talked about the other day about the amount of time we spend listening has gotten me thinking. Remember that study by Imhof? She said that students listen about 60% of instructional time? Of course she didn't include college students, but I started thinking that we should look more closely at classroom communication and show what happens when students don't listen.

Well, it will at least give us a starting point. Remember we also talked about some other research that shows how college students spend their time. Maybe we could track a typical student's day rather than just the classroom. Oh, look here comes Nolvia. Over here, Nolvia... wow you look excited.

I just came from my literature class. We've been struggling through Beowulf for a week and I think I'm finally beginning to understand it. I've really had problems with the old English sounds, you know, it's just like a foreign language. Anyway, today we watched a movie version. I could actually understand what the actors were saying. I wonder if we can put something in our project about listening difficulty and other languages?

Introduction

As college and university students, you have reached a point in your life where you are assuming greater personal accountability in all aspects of your life, including academic listening. You are expected to be independent learners, who take responsibility for your learning. For good or ill, you may choose to begin writing a paper two weeks in advance, or the night before. You can decide whether you want to review assigned material the night before going to class or spend the evening out with your friends. Bottom line, all of your choices about how you approach school will have an impact on how you listen. As we cover the material in this chapter, remember you ultimately bear at least half of the responsibility for your communication with your instructor and in spite of whether you like or dislike the way the instructor teaches, you bear the full responsibility for your learning.

Throughout this text you have read about the importance of listening in achieving a successful personal life. As children, teens, and young adults, school is one of the places where you spend significant portions of your time. As you know, speaking and listening are the primary methods by which you acquire knowledge. However, the educational aspects of listening begin long before you start school. Think, for example, about how you acquired language. Your parents and other family members encouraged you to talk to them. As they coaxed you to say certain words and names, you listened to the sounds until the day you were able to actually form it. Listening, then, is the first of the communication skill that a child develops. It is fundamental to speaking, reading, and writing.[1] Thus, we learn to listen then speak, speak then read, and read then write.

In spite of the fact you learned to listen very early in your life, teachers often complain that students never seem to listen. To put the impact of that statement into perspective, you spend just under seven hours communicating at school and approximately 35% of that time or 1.75 hours is spent listening in the classroom.[2] However, few, if any of you, have received any listening training.[3] Sadly, despite the importance of listening to learning, few schools have stand-alone courses that teach students listening skills, and few classes (including communication classes) incorporate units on listening into their course schedules.[4]

> **Think on it:** Looking back at your previous classes, what listening "lessons" have you received? Sometimes, you may not recognize it as training that can help you listen. Did you practice how to recognize main points during a speech? Did you take any courses that provided note-taking training?

Moreover, how well you listen can affect your overall success in college. Previous studies suggest that listening skill has a greater impact on college success and student retention than reading skills or academic aptitude.[5] In addition, students who are trained listeners often make higher grades.[6]

In the U.S., at both the national and state levels, listening is increasingly being recognized as an important aspect of education. For example, the proposed Common Core standards explicitly address the role of listening:

> Students must learn to work together, express and listen carefully to ideas, integrate information from oral, visual, quantitative, and media sources, evaluate what they hear, use media and visual displays strategically to help achieve communicative purposes, and adapt speech to context and task.[7]

Individual states have incorporated similar statements as part of their own K-12 learning standards. If you are enrolled in a listening class, it is a sign that your institution and instructor believe listening is important. The class you are taking provides you with the opportunity to hone your listening skills in the classroom and a variety of other contexts.

> **Think on it:** Before you read the next section on academic listening, make a list of the ways you believe conversational listening and academic listening differ. Then read the section and see how your list compares to ours.

Teaching: Listening Lessons

Margarete Imhof
Professor
Johannes Gutenberg Universität Mainz, Germany

As a teacher, I view listening as the twin sister of learning. Teaching and learning takes place, when individuals talk to each other, discuss, exchange views, explain, argue, ask questions, state hypotheses, collect, present, and weigh evidence. All the talking involved in these activities falls silent if it is not complemented by listening. Listening takes effort – to monitor attention, to store and organize information, to activate and use prior knowledge and thinking skills, and to regulate thoughts, emotions, and behavior.

Therefore, teaching material, such as texts, tasks, projects, should be reviewed for two criteria: first, what are the listening skills which learners can use and develop through this material and, second, what can I do to tailor the material in a way which stimulates learners to invest their listening skills?

Consequently, it is helpful to evaluate instructional settings along these lines: How does the learning environment help learners to ask questions, to focus attention on the relevant information? How does the material encourage learners, to look for logic and coherence? Does the material challenge learners to access prior knowledge and connect new and old information in an intelligent way? And, finally, how and when did learners acquire these skills and what would be my contribution to strengthen and increase their listening skills?

Academic Listening

Most students take the listening skills used with daily conversations and simply apply them to the academic context. However, as you will see, listening in the educational context differs substantially from our normal everyday listening. You can be a great listener, but lack fundamental skills and so do poorly in a class. On the other hand, you may be a poor listener in the classroom, but able to compensate by reading the text and following written directions. Academic listening is related to and affected by a number of factors including motivation, learning style, and teaching method. Academic listening impacts how you and your teachers communicate and how you communicate with your classmates.

Margarete Imhof, a noted listening scholar, suggests that effective academic listeners should be able to integrate information from numerous sources, manage their attitudes and motivation, focus attention, activate and modify cognitive schemas, and use metacognitive strategies to encode and retain information.[8] In her interview in this chapter, she also outlines instructor responsibilities. While you may do all of these things to some extent in everyday listening, they are critical to being good academic listeners.

John Flowerdew, a senior lecturer at City University of Hong Kong, has researched academic listening extensively. Compare your responses to the previous *Think on it* box with the differences in academic and conversational listening Flowerdew identified and which are presented in Table 9.1.

Table 9.1 Comparing Elements of Conversational and Academic Listening

	Conversational Listening	**Academic Listening**
Determining Relevancy	*Somewhat important* Individuals jump from topic to topic	*Very important* Important to note-taking, main purpose of lecture, etc.
Background Knowledge	*General* Not expected to be specialist in all areas/topics under discussion	*More specialized* Expected to prepare for class or have background in subject matter
Turn-taking	*Essential*	*Only when required or allowed.*
Level of implied meaning	*High* Necessary for complete understanding	*Low* Focus is on information transfer
Concentration	*Varies* Depends on context or situation	*High* Necessary to comprehend large amounts/long periods of talk
Note-taking	*Unusual*	*Usual or Expected* Requires decoding, comprehending, identifying main points, determining when/what to record, writing quickly and clearly.[a]
Information Integration	*Not necessary*	*Necessary* Integrate information from a variety of media (handouts, power point, readings, video clips, etc.).

[a] James, 1977

As you can see, academic listening is constrained in a number of ways. We will be discussing several of these differences (as well as others) as we continue this chapter.

Individual Differences in the Learning Experience

The first area of difference we will examine is individual differences or how your own traits and responses to the learning situation affect your listening. These areas include relevancy, learning styles, emotional intelligence and apprehension.

Relevancy

When you feel or understand the importance of a topic to your personal life or needs, the topic has **personal relevancy**. Think back over classes you've taken. Wasn't it easier to listen to the instructor when you were interested in the topic? On the other hand, wasn't it more difficult to listen in classes you expected to be boring? And, what about those classes that violated your expectations and were more interesting than you thought they would be? In this situation, chances are the instructor was able to peak your interest and make the topic relevant to you. Whether inspired by the instructor or the topic, creating links between what you are learning and personal interest is an excellent way to enhance your academic listening – the more meaningful the lesson, the more likely you will listen and retain the information in your long-term memory.[9]

Related to relevancy is **motivation**. You are the only person who can assess your motivation. In a listening situation, particularly an academic one, ask yourself, *"Why am I here?"* Few people seek to be bored or confused, and it is very easy to blame the instructor when we are. However, a motivated listener will be proactive by prepping for class and identifying reasons to listen. Reasons (or motivators) can range from intrinsic, "This will help me in my career," to extrinsic, "It's going to be on the next exam." Interestingly, it is not unusual for students to report that they find it easier to listen in their major-related courses, and more difficult in other classes. So, if your world isn't rocked by information about the Paleolithic period, find a reason to motivate yourself to listen to that lecture. Reasons can range from wanting to maintain a high grade point average (GPA) to using the information to "wow" your friends or critique the next dinosaur movie you see.

Learning Style

Just as motivation affects our listening in the classroom, so can other individual differences. One in particular is your learning style. Eugene Sadler-Smith, a professor of management development and organizational behavior, defined **learning style** as "an individual's propensity to choose or express a liking for a particular instructional technique or combination of techniques."[10] The three main learning styles identified in much research are auditory, visual, and kinesthetic.[11] Each of these styles represents ways of taking in and storing information. So, an *auditory learner* prefers spoken information, while a *visual learner* wants to see, observe and write down information. The *kinesthetic learner*, on the other hand, better absorbs information through demonstration or physical involvement with that information. Research into learning style suggests that we not only find learning easier when we receive information in a manner that matches our learning preference, but we also tend to have better comprehension and retention of the material.[12] Thus, fundamental to our learning style is how we take in information, process it, remember it, and apply it. As you can see, learning style and listening both address information processing. We will look more closely at one perspective on learning styles to better illustrate the relationship between listening and learning preferences.

The **Kolb's Experiential Learning Model** is likely the best known of the learning style models.[13] David Kolb views learning as a *four stage process* or cycle. He suggests we begin with our actual, concrete experiences, observe and reflect on these experiences, and then integrate them into related schemas. The resulting cognitions are then used to process future experiences. The Kolb model is based on two primary dimensions. The first dimension includes **concrete experience** (sensing/feeling) and **abstract conceptualization** (thinking), while the second addresses our preference for **active experimentation** (doing) and **reflective observation** (watching). *Concrete experience* addresses our preference for relying on concrete facts. *Abstract conceptualization* or thinking focuses on our preference for relying on and using more abstract ways of processing information. *Active experimentation* identifies our need for "hands-on" learning (doing) versus a preference for learning via *reflective observation* (watching). As seen in Figure 9.1, these dimensions result in four learning styles – diverging, assimilating, converging and accommodating.[14]

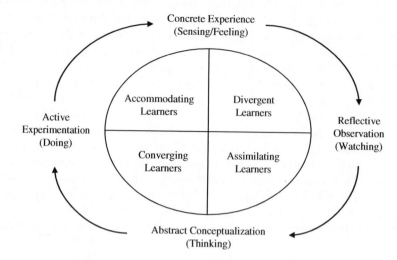

Figure 9.1 Kolb's Learning Process and Style Types

Converging Learners. As you can see in the model, converging learners have doing and thinking as their dominant learning abilities. If this is your learning style, you tend to focus on practical applications for the ideas you learn, prefer dealing with technical problems rather than interpersonal issues, and enjoy experimenting with new information in the way of simulations or role play. It's probably no surprise that one of your strengths is problem solving. If you are a converging learner, be mindful of your tendency as a listener to tune out when you fail to see the applicability of the information or when you think something is too "touchy feely" or interpersonally based. Relating back to individual differences introduced in Chapter 4, if you are a MBTI thinker, then you may prefer this learning style. When listening, thinkers enjoy direct, clear messages. When instructors get off topic, you may sit in class wondering when they are going to get to the point.

Diverging Learners. As you can see in Figure 9.1, diverging learners prefer sensing/feeling and reflective observation. These learners tend to be imaginative and emotional and prefer working in groups. If this is your learning style, you appreciate situations that call for brainstorming or coming up with ideas from different perspectives, you are probably skilled at deconstructing events to better understand how the parts affect the whole, and you're likely good at seeing all sides of an issue. Being "people-oriented," you likely enjoy learning about other people and cultures. Because it is particularly important for you to work at making personal connections to what is being taught, you learn best when personal relevancy is high. Otherwise, you may tune out.

One of your listening strengths is that you tend to keep an open mind while listening to different perspectives. This suggests that you would probably be open to receiving personalized feedback. However, you may have a tendency to tune out feedback that is presented in an impersonal manner.[15]

Learn more: If you'd like to learn more about your own learning style, try visiting the following website: http://bit.ly/Learning_Style_Inventory. It provides you with an idea of whether you are a tactile, visual or auditory learner.

Accommodating Learners. If you are an accommodating learner, your learning strengths combine sensing/feeling with doing. You would fall in the kinesthetic learning category that we introduced earlier. That is, you prefer to learn primarily via doing and experimentation. For example, when you get a new smartphone you probably start playing with it rather than reading the accompanying manual. If your attempt to take and post a selfie online fails, you have learned what not to do in the future. More importantly, you also tend to apply what you learn from your mistakes to other situations you face. You enjoy new challenges, embrace change, like flexibility, and welcome risk taking. Chances are you also like to develop a plan and then carry it out. Accommodating learners have a tendency to act on their "gut" feelings rather than logic. Consequently, as a listener, you may face several challenges. For example, when answering a teacher's question, you may be less able to provide a logical reason for how you arrived at your answer. In addition, your desire for change and challenges may result in you becoming bored in the classroom. You will need to focus on personal motivation and topic relevancy to stimulate your listening. For example, you could concentrate on future assignments and consider how the topic or material can help you complete them.

Assimilating Learners. Assimilating learners are particularly good at synthesizing material because their strengths as learners are thinking abstractly and reflecting on observations. If you are an assimilating learner, you like a wide range of information but want it in a concise, logical form. You may impress your instructors with your ability to pull in material from previous classes or readings and integrate it into the topic under discussion. Not surprisingly, you enjoy learning abstract information such as theories and related processes. You will probably relate best to analytical listening, you want information presented in a logically organized manner with well-supported examples. As a result, you are likely an excellent listener in traditional, lecture-format types of classes. However, in classes where there are a lot of group activities, your search for theory and continuity may cause you to feel frustrated. You may also feel frustrated if you feel the lecture or discussion is getting off topic or if you are not given sufficient time to reflect on the information before taking action.

Think on it: In Chapter 4, we introduced individual listening style preferences – relational, analytic, task-oriented, and critical. We have noted several ways they may be related to learning styles. In what other ways may they be related? What about other individual differences we've introduced?

Emotional Intelligence

Another individual difference that can impact your academic listening is emotional intelligence. As you recall from Chapter 4, emotional intelligence is "the ability to perceive and express emotions, to understand and use them, and to manage them to foster personal growth."[16] How you handle your emotions can influence how you approach assignments and how you work with your peers.[17] For example, one longitudinal study found that preschoolers who were better at delaying immediate gratification (waiting for a marshmallow) later tended to have higher SAT scores and be more interpersonally liked by teachers and peers.[18] Delaying gratification shows that you can deal with one important emotion – frustration. If you can manage frustration, you can likely manage other emotions as well. Being able to *recognize* your own feelings and the feelings of others, being able to *manage* your emotions, *motivate* yourself, and *handle relationships* all positively affect academic success.[19] For example, you will likely be able to recognize and cope with the frustration you feel when you don't understand an assignment, receive a poor grade, or deal with group members who aren't pulling their weight. Frustration can generate internal noise, which as you know can negatively impact listening ability.

Communication and Individual Receiver Apprehension

Another individual difference introduced in Chapter 4 was **communication apprehension** – the generalized fear we may experience when put into a particular communication situation. Students who experience communication apprehension may respond in several ways.[20] First, they may try to physically or psychologically withdraw from the situation. For example, they may write the bulk of a group paper in order to reduce or eliminate their presentation speaking time. When asked a question by their instructor, they may say, "I don't know." Although rare, some students will respond by overcommunicating. These are the students who seemingly dominate a group or class discussion, when in actuality they are apprehensive and essentially talking their way through their anxiety.

High communication apprehension can result in a variety of negative academic outcomes, including lower grades, negative attitudes toward school, and a greater likelihood of dropping out of school. In addition, these students often have fewer classroom friends and have difficulty asking their teachers for help.[21] Finally, it is not unusual for someone suffering from high communication apprehension to be apprehensive in several communication areas.[22] Consequently, they may be apprehensive when working both interpersonally and in groups – two contexts used extensively in the classroom. Not surprisingly, the greater one's level of apprehension in an area (e.g., public speaking, groups, dyads, etc.), the more difficult it is to listen. People who suffer from apprehension concentrate so much on what they are going to say and their feelings of incompetency that it becomes difficult for them to focus on what others' have to say.

One category of communication apprehension closely related to listening is **receiver apprehension**, or feeling anxiety about being on the receiving end of the communication process. This fear is particularly problematic for listeners in the classroom. As you learned at the beginning of the chapter, the educational setting requires great amounts of academic listening. In the classroom, receiver apprehension is more likely to occur when you are anxious about the course content (e.g., math frightens you), or by the teacher's behavior (e.g., you find him or her to be intimidating). Research indicates that receiver apprehension negatively effects listening and information processing and is associated with several negative outcomes, including:

- lower test scores,
- negative attitudes toward the course and the instructor,
- less motivation to learn, and
- lower perceptions of one's ability to learn.[23]

The good news for you if you do experience communication apprehension is that it doesn't have to be a barrier to listening. Those of you who are motivated can turn your listening anxiety into an opportunity.

Teachers can have a great effect on how well students listen and can be particularly helpful for those who suffer from apprehension. You may know someone who is highly motivated but feels intimidated by the subject matter in a class. Usually these students feel stressed or anxious about learning the class material and may end up experiencing high levels of apprehension. Imagine that Nolvia told her group about her attempts to learn German. As the conversation progressed, she noted that the more she tried to hear and learn the language (e.g., studying daily, doing all the homework, and even working with a tutor), the more anxious she became about the class. Fortunately, having the right kind of teacher can help you if you are like Nolvia. Specifically, *teacher clarity* and *teacher immediacy* may help highly apprehensive students.[24] Teacher clarity results from clear, understandable presentations that incorporate personally relevant examples. Such presentations are easier to absorb and process, in part, because they make the material easier to incorporate into our schema about the subject matter. In contrast, teachers who speak too quickly or use unfamiliar terms are difficult to listen to. The reduced understanding can increase our levels of apprehension.[25]

Part of the reason anxiety has a negative impact on listening is that it makes you feel disempowered or not in control of learning. Teacher immediacy behaviors (e.g., smiling, using humor, engaging in dynamic movement, utilizing appropriate eye contact) have been associated with increased positive feelings about the teacher and the class, as well as increased perceptions of control over one's learning. Researchers argue that teacher clarity and teacher immediacy work together to decrease receiver apprehension in the classroom. Less apprehension leads to less anxiety, which makes it easier for you to pay attention to both instructors and peers. (We discuss immediacy in more detail below.)

How can you address your own apprehension? First, try to **build motivation.** Carefully choosing classes that you are interested in or classes taught by instructors who are known for motivating their students can help you develop a positive outlook toward the class. Second, ***be prepared.*** Coming properly prepared for class is a major element of reducing anxiety. You can link what you're hearing to what you've learned out of class. You'll also know what areas may be confusing you and can ask for further clarification when it is covered during class. The more you can prepare for a particular interaction, the greater your personal feeling of control. So, thoroughly reading class materials, seeking out the instructor or classmates in the class to clarify concepts, searching out helpful websites, or hiring a tutor when necessary are just a few of the things you can do to enhance feelings of control. You may also find it helpful to choose an instructor that uses a teaching method that you prefer. We discuss various teaching methods in the following section.

In the Classroom: Listening Lessons

Joanna B. Boyd
First Grade Teacher
Dean Road Elementary School
Auburn, Alabama

As an educator I believe that listening skills play a vital part in student performance. If the student is not engaged in the learning process completely, they cannot fully grasp all of the concepts the teacher is trying to present. At the very beginning of the school year when we begin setting our classroom rules, the students always put "Being a Great Listener" at the top of the list. We also spend time discussing *The 7 Habits of Happy Kids* by Sean Covey, and one of those key habits is "Seek first to understand than to be understood." As a class we discuss ways to be a good listener, and how to make it a habit.

Creating an atmosphere where students understand the importance of being a great listener is also essential to the learning process. I believe that in order to keep students engaged you must provide hands-on activities for them to participate in throughout the day, and offer opportunities for the students to share their own ideas. Students are very interested in what their peers think, and they can gain new ideas and broaden their vocabulary just by listening.

Technology is also an important tool that students use on a regular basis. I integrate technology daily by providing a listening center for students to use. This center allows students the opportunity to improve their listening skills through read aloud stories and activities. I feel that great listening skills create a strong foundation in every area of life, especially in the classroom.

Teaching Goals and Methods

You know from your own experience that instructional methods are as varied as teachers and students. The type of listening required varies with the teaching method. Some instructors will choose methods that they personally prefer, in keeping with their own learning preferences. Other teachers recognize and attempt to accommodate a variety of learning styles. Of course, the subject matter can sometimes dictate the method that is chosen. Kenneth Moore, in the book *Effective Instructional Strategies*, groups teaching methods into three main areas – direct, indirect, and integrated.[26] Each type has distinct differences and affect classroom listening in unique ways. **Direct methods** often are teacher centered with the instructor acting as the primary information source, and often involve lecturing, using class workbooks, etc. It's likely that many of your college introductory classes utilize this method, especially if they are large classes. The goal of such classes is to provide a large amount of information in an efficient method. Not surprisingly, these classes largely focus on comprehensive listening. In contrast, **indirect methods** tend to focus on "showing." If your professor uses this method, he or she tends to act as a facilitator of learning. Classes that use case studies or other readings as spring boards to developing knowledge and building skills likely use this method. The teacher will essentially jumpstart the discussion, making sure that the class or group understands the nature and purpose of the discussion, keeping the discussion on track, and ensuring everyone has the opportunity to participate. Many instructors integrate a variety of teaching methods. If your instructor uses this method, he or she likely expects a greater emphasis on critical listening.

Instructors who use **integrated methods** not only "tell" their students, they show them, and give them access to learning on their own. While comprehensive listening may be used at times, critical listening is the primary focus of this type of teaching. This method emphasizes self-directed learning. Of the three methods we discuss, this approach gives you the greatest control over your own learning.[27] It works best with students who are internally motivated and who accept that they are responsible for much of their own learning. For example, each year our university hosts a robotics championship where groups of students are given buckets of parts and asked to solve a problem (e.g., a machine that could facilitate a repair to the Hubble Telescope, a robot that could collect particular molecules). Even though all of the groups were given the same parts, no two groups develop the same robot, or solve the problem in exactly the same way. Students take their technical know-how, do additional research (i.e., access to learning), and develop a number of fun, funky, and truly incredible robots.

> ***Think on it:*** Class discussion methods can take two forms – whole-class discussion and small-class discussion (e.g., small groups of four to six students discussing a topic, brainstorming ideas, or completing an assigned task). Does active listening differ between large and small group discussion? If so, how? Does one type have distinctive advantages? Disadvantages? What have been your experiences with classroom discussion? How does the classroom environment affect class discussion?

Whatever the method, developing critical thinking skills is generally one of the main goals of teaching. In fact, it is one of the primary goals of education today, and not just in the United States. Professors at the University of Putur Malaysia also stress the importance of listening to developing critical thinking skills for college students.[28] They note that it is through communication skills (including listening) that students grow personally and academically. They argue that critical listening and critical thinking share a number of attributes, including: assessing main ideas, differentiating between facts and opinions, and recognizing language problems (e.g., loaded language and logical fallacies).

As you can see, integrated methods tend to emphasize collaboration. This type of collaboration is increasingly moving beyond the classroom. The best online or hybrid classes will provide students with the means to collaborate actively. Educators who take a social constructionist view of learning believe that learning is essentially a social activity rather than an individualistic one.[29] In other words, we learn through our conversations with others and through shared problem-solving. Importantly, collaborative learning has been associated with increased understanding of a subject as well as higher motivation and improved communication. Listening to others is a key component of collaborative learning both in and out of the classroom. Students using FaceTime and other online educational collaborative tools must listen carefully to one another in order to learn effectively and successfully complete group and/or project goals. Of course, as we noted

"You're listening to what you hear. I like that in a teacher."

in Chapter 5, research indicates that students distinguish between tasks that are appropriate for online and those which should be done face to face. Generally, the more complex the project or activity, the more the surveyed students wanted to work together in person.[30]

Listening and the Educational "Audience"

There are a number of educational audiences – teachers, administrators, students, parents, alumni, and other community members. Addressing all of these audiences is beyond the scope of this text. In the pages that follow, we focus on your interactions with your instructors – in and out of the classroom. Lev Vygotsky, an early learning theorist, suggests that our relationship with our teachers is fundamental to our learning.[31] As we discuss the importance of listening in your interpersonal and classroom interactions with your instructors, consider how they reflect Vygotsky's perspective.

Communicating Interpersonally: Teachers and Students

Emerson once said, "The secret of education lies in respecting the pupil." We would add that an additional secret is respect for the teacher. As you learned earlier in this text, respect for one another is one of the foundations of good listening. We have also stressed remaining open minded as essential to good listening. Teachers and students who can establish such a foundation have the beginning of a strong learning relationship. There are several things you can do to be a better academic listener regardless of your personality, listening style, or the teaching method of your professor:

- Respect your instructor's role as a content specialist
- Recognize and respect that you each have your own "style"
- Prepare for any interaction with your instructors
- Think before you speak
- Be aware of your academic attributions

Respect your Instructor's Role as a Content Specialist. Showing respect tends to lessen any defensiveness and tends to motivate both parties to listen more closely. We also find it's much easier to listen to others empathically, when we feel they also respect us as individuals.

Recognize and Respect that you each have your own "Style." However, don't use that style as an excuse to be a poor listener. While you have your own learning and listening styles and your teachers use a variety of different teaching methods, you must accept responsibility for your own learning and adjust to the listening demands of the situation. By doing so, you will find it easier to motivate yourself to listen to those subjects that less very interesting to you.

Prepare for any Interaction with your Instructors. If you schedule meetings with your instructors, plan out what needs to be discussed in advance by making note of your questions and concerns. This will keep your meeting on track, ensure you don't forget something important, and show that you understand how busy your professor is. All listeners appreciate clear, concise presentations of concerns on a busy day.

Think Before you Speak. If a situation arises where you disagree with an instructor, lab assistant, or other school personnel, keep in mind that your choices about how you react may have long-term impact on future interactions with that person. Our biggest piece of advice – be respectful! While you often don't have control over what happens to you, you can choose how you react. If you view disagreements as a problem to be solved rather than a personal attack, it will be easier for you to focus on listening to the other party. How can you do this? Basically, you should take time to assess the situation objectively. Did you study the wrong material? Misunderstand the wording on the exam question? You certainly have the right to discuss your concerns with your professors, and you should. However, you need to be in a frame of mind where you are truly willing to listen, and you want to create an atmosphere where your professor will be open to your comments and concerns.

Be aware of your "Academic Attributions." Attributions refer to our belief in underlying causes of an event or situation. When you talk to instructors about classes, they tend to assess your explanations of your academic success and failure. Your explanation can lead them to draw conclusions about your future performance in the class. Students tend to attribute performance to one of the following: effort, ability, luck, and task difficult.[32] *Effort* ("I didn't study enough") and *ability* ("I'm not an economics person") are related to **internal attributions**, while *luck* ("I guessed right") and *task difficulty* ("This project is unreasonable") are related to **external attributions**. If you are attributing a grade to internal causes, then you are taking responsibility for the grade, while attributing it to external causes indicates you are avoiding responsibility. For most of us, these attributions can change from class to class. When they do so, they are called an *unstable attribution.* Thus, you may claim to be "deaf" to foreign languages, but really "get it" in your chemistry class. Some students, however, develop a pattern response based on one of these attribution areas to explain their success or failure in every class (Figure 9.2). As a listener, if you have a *stable internal attribution*, you take responsibility for your listening behavior in all of your classes, not just the ones you like.

Academic attributions are important because they affect your expectations of success, your view of your own ability, your emotional reactions (pride in your achievement, helplessness, or hopelessness) to classroom situations, and your willingness to apply and self-regulate your academic efforts.[33] Good teachers generally will encourage you to take "ownership" of your successes by focusing on your personal effort and ability. You can demonstrate that ownership by engaging in good academic listening.

Communicating in the Classroom

Listening is an important component of a positive classroom learning environment; it contributes to your motivation to meet high expectations and contributes to your academic success. The connection between students and teachers is the foundation of a positive **classroom climate.** Instructors who listen well are better able to understand their students' needs and preferences. By listening carefully and critically, teachers create a classroom climate that encourages student involvement.[34] For example, one colleague, after learning her students had an interest in gender issues and social movements, responded by introducing her class to material on the Women's March on Washington.

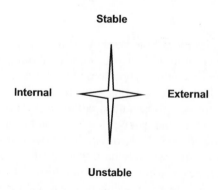

Figure 9.2 Attribution Dimensions

The foundation of a positive classroom climate is skilled listening – from both the teacher and the students. Students should feel comfortable expressing ideas, asking for clarification, and disagreeing with each other and their instructor. Mary Renck Jalongo, a professor at Indiana University of Pennsylvania, notes that "listening, in the full sense of the word, is both interactive and constructive. It is *interactive* because good listeners are involved with the message; it is *constructive* because listeners build meaning from what they hear."[35] A supportive classroom climate allows teachers and students to achieve academic listening that is interactive and constructive. These instructors motivate students by providing a clear purpose for listening, they model good listening and speaking behaviors (and expect their students to do the same), they reduce listening distractions, and promote (and expect) active listening in the classroom. As can be seen, you have much to contribute to a supportive classroom climate. When you no longer are part of a "listen and learn" classroom (i.e., straight lecture), your responsibilities for listening and enhancing the learning experience are expanded. Importantly, you have increased opportunity to practice your listening skills (e.g., informational/discriminative listening, clarification of concepts, elaboration on ideas, critical analyses via discussions). We discuss four of the elements related to a positive classroom climate: teacher self-disclosure, teacher immediacy, student engagement, and classroom management.

Teacher Self-disclosure. Previous research suggests that award-winning instructors engaged in moderate self-disclosure in their classes.[36] It is important that the self-disclosure be honest, relevant to course content, and/or be used to clarify concepts under discussion. Thus, in his public relations class, Professor Kim may discuss his experience working at Wilde Corporation as a public relations specialist. Such self-disclosure may lead students to feel more comfortable discussing their own work or group experiences. We also often find self-disclosure interesting or "motivating." Subsequently, we may listen more closely in class and may develop a more positive attitude toward both the teacher and the course.

Teacher Immediacy. Generally speaking, verbal and nonverbal immediacy behaviors tend to reduce the psychological distance between teachers and their students. As noted above, a number of behaviors contribute to teacher immediacy including eye contact, movement and gestures, and vocal variety. Highly immediate teachers address students by name, are comfortable using humor, and employ relevant personal examples during class. As a result, students will feel a more personal connection with their teachers.

> *Think on it:* As seen here, teacher self-disclosure, humor and personal examples have been associated with teacher immediacy. Are there times when these findings may not hold true? When could self-disclosure, humor or personal examples actually decrease student perceptions of teacher immediacy?

Student Engagement. One result of high teacher immediacy is student engagement. Student engagement is affected by a number of factors including personal interest in the topic. However, teacher interest can be just as important. Teachers who are enthusiastic and interested in the topic they teach, and who are willing to share that enthusiasm and interest with their students tend to be more effective in energizing the classroom.[37] When teachers can generate an atmosphere that connects and focuses student attention, they increase the chances that their students are actively listening in the classroom. How material is delivered or presented can also affect engagement. With the advent of PowerPoint, many classroom presentations became systematically, and semantically organized (e.g., bullet points using parallel language).[38] However, prior to this time, narrative formats, which are more episodic presentations, were the norm. Research by communication scholars has found that we actually retain more information when our teachers utilize narrative presentations.[39] Further, it is believed that the use of stories may also encourage a deeper processing of lecture content.

High immediacy similarly provides students with the sense that their teacher enjoys teaching and cares for them. It is this feeling that helps reduce communication apprehension. Another outcome is that students who feel valued by their teachers may put more effort into their own learning. One leading scholar on immediacy, Virginia Richmond, argues that teacher immediacy positively affects students by leading them "to listen more, learn more, and have a more positive attitude about school."[40]

Classroom Management. Have any of you ever been in a class where the students seemed to be more in control of the class than the instructor? If so, you have a real understanding of the effect of classroom management on creating a positive classroom and learning environment. The good news is that classroom management issues are usually not a problem in the university classroom. Some of the primary issues in today's college classes are associated with mobile phones ringing, students talking, and in computer labs, surfing the net. You understand the implicit rules of the college classroom (e.g., be on time, listen/pay attention, take notes, discuss/participate, and do not study or work on other class materials). Of course, there are the explicit rules (what you can and cannot do), basic class procedures (how to contact your instructor and so forth), and stated standards (what it takes to make an A). All of these elements contribute directly to classroom management and classroom climate. Established rules, procedures and standards guide not only our behaviors, but our expectations about the class.

> ***Think on it:*** How is the classroom climate affected by disruptive student behavior? Do different teacher management techniques affect classroom listening and learning differently? Do some management techniques contribute to a positive classroom climate more than others?

Listening and Taking Notes

While note taking is a writing activity, to do it well takes effective listening skills. In this section we will address how you can use your listening skills to become a better note-taker.

Mary O'Hair and colleagues found that over 75% of the students they polled felt their notes were essentially useless when it came time to actually study,[41] while a more recent study found students record less than 40% of what they hear.[42] Needless to say, incomplete and useless notes aren't very helpful when it comes to enhancing exam and other class grades. One reason notes may be "worthless" is that students are not fully attending to or processing the information they receive. For example, students may have difficulty discriminating between what is important and what is not. Listening and good note taking are strongly connected. As O'Hair and friends note, "meaningful notes result from carefully planned listening for structure and from fighting distractions."[43] They also found a number of barriers to good note taking.[44] These barriers include lectures that are boring because the pace is too slow or frustrating because the pace of delivery is too fast. In either case, it is difficult to stay attentive and listen.

Think on it: When Dr. Alan Shields, a former professor of sociology at Auburn University, introduced students to his class, he gave the following piece of advice, "If you write down everything that I'm saying, you're not listening to me."

What do you think Dr. Shields meant? Think about how you take notes. Do you write down key words or phrases or do you attempt to write down everything the professor or instructor says? What does this statement tell us about listening and note-taking? What of other aspects of classroom communication?

Another set of barriers is internal and external distractions. As we discussed in Chapter 3, *internal noise* are your own thoughts and emotions which may pop up in your mind during the lecture. *External interference*, of course, comes from the environment like noise in the halls. Your emotional or evaluative reactions can also derail your listening and subsequent note taking. When you focus on judging either the speaker or the topic, it is difficult to take notes. Other times, your listening and note taking might be hurt by relying too much on only the oral presentation. Or, you may rely on the PowerPoint slides provided by the instructor and so may not fully attend to the presentation. Let's face it, some topics are easier to understand when we can see a good picture or diagram. Can you imagine a math, computer programming, or physiology class without some illustrations? However, we typically need to listen to the lecture that goes along with the visual to get the "full" picture. In fact, one recent study suggests that when students overly rely on PowerPoint slides, taking fewer notes, their exam grades may actually go down.[45] However, if you remember from Chapter 5, students who took handwritten notes outperformed those who typed their notes while listening to a class lecture.

Think on it: What teaching techniques help or hinder your note-taking? Are they related to classroom climate? Motivation?

Building Your Note-taking Skill. So what's a student to do? Like any skill, you can improve your note-taking listening ability with a bit of practice. Table 9.2 identifies some things you can do to improve your note-taking.

As you can see, many of the ideas we have talked about in this book can be applied to helping you be a better note-taker. In assessing your attitudes, remember **motivation** is a key to good listening. It helps to develop a positive attitude and find a personal reason to focus your attention in class. Of course motivation is closely related to awareness of both your attitudes and biases. You will be a better listener when you don't prejudge others, including the teacher, by focusing on content and keeping an open mind.

Another interesting strategy in Table 9.2 is to use the "predict then confirm strategy." This approach requires you to prepare in advance (e.g., read the text, previous notes), then make predictions of what is likely to be covered by generating questions over the lecture content. We think this is a great suggestion for two reasons. First, you will obviously come prepared to class. Second, your reading will likely be reinforced by what you hear. You can also ask for clarification as needed. One of our students, who is very much a visual learner, added to these suggestions, noting that diagramming or outlining the reading helps her not only make predictions, but enabled her to make connections to what was covered in class and lecture. Her outlines also helped her to quickly identify differences between what is covered in the reading, but *was not* covered in class.

Table 9.2 Tips for Improving Classroom Listening and Note-taking[a]

Behavioral	Mental/Cognitive	Psychological
Intentionally focus attention	Activate appropriate schemas	Check attitudes and bias toward topic
Block out internal and external distractions	Identify prior knowledge about topic	Get emotionally ready to listen
Control energetic arousal	Use mental organizers to revise schema based on the incoming information.	Monitor nonverbal input from speaker
Get physically ready to listen and take notes	Mentally summarize the key points of the lecture	Monitor your own listening
Ask questions to gain information needed to understand the topic	Use predict and confirm strategy	
Physically revise and complete notes after the lecture	Listen for organizing cues	
Practice note-taking for accuracy and discrimination ability		

[a] Drawn from Imhof (1998) and O'Hair, et al. (1988).

These types of questions also help place the information into her long-term memory, where hopefully she could draw upon it during the next exam.

A key to taking good notes is to listen for **organizational lecture cues** such as *verbal signals* used to help clarify the relationships between ideas ("The three main things to remember are…" "This concept can be divided into two broad themes"), *transitional statements* that signal the conversation is moving from one topic to another ("Now, that we understand what an attitude is, let's look at how it differs from beliefs"), and *summary statements* which remind listeners of topics that have just been covered ("So, now that we've covered attitudes, beliefs, and behaviors, let's move on to…").[46] Research demonstrates that **organizational clarity** also contributes to student learning.[47] So, listen for the pattern. The organizational pattern will help you process the information by providing natural breaks, which allows you to "chunk" the information and store it more easily in your short-term memory. It also facilitates schema development, which assists you with long-term memory. Of course, better organized lectures help you to determine what is important and streamline the note-taking process. As a result, your notes may be better in terms of quality and quantity. In other words, they may be better organized, and you may actually be able to record more material. Recording more class material (obviously quality notes are important) may increase your success on exams by increasing your overall recall of information.[48]

Culture and Diversity

No look at academic listening would be complete without a discussion about the impact of culture, diversity, and socialization in the classroom. This is particularly true when we consider those students who are listening in a language other than their native one. We will take a brief look at selected socialization-related factors and then examine second language factors.

Gender

All of us are socialized in gender roles. As you were growing up, you learned what girls and boys were "supposed" to do (i.e., established gender schemas). While the way you have been socialized is probably a bit different from the way we were because of generational differences, each of you is still taught certain beliefs about the way you are supposed to interact with the world. As we have noted elsewhere, your gender socialization can affect how you listen. It can also affect how you act and react in school. For example, previous research supports claims that, as early as the first grade, boys and girls are treated quite differently in educational settings. These differences usually advantage boys and men, over girls and women.[49] Specifically, boys tend to get more attention (both positive and negative) than girls, get more detailed instructions than girls, and get more praise for intellectual content than girls. Girls, on the other hand, usually have to wait longer for attention, which tends to be neutral or negative (especially if the girl is a minority student), and they are more often recognized for neatness and form. Another interesting difference can be found in where teachers place the locus of control (or cause) for poor performance. With boys, teachers tend to stress internal attributions such as lack of effort, while external causes for failure or poor performances are emphasized for girls (e.g., that problem was particularly difficult, it's hard to concentrate in a hot room).

While the above paragraph presents only a small sample of the differences in how boys and girls are treated in the classroom, you can see the beginnings of a pattern. Essentially, the research indicates that male students become empowered in the educational setting while female students are encouraged to be passive listeners. In addition, the emphasis on an external locus of control suggests that female students may feel less responsibility for listening in the classroom. Boys and men, in contrast, expect more from their teachers and are not afraid to ask for it (e.g., clarification of an instruction, expanding on a topic).

The research also indicates that the interpersonal interaction with the teacher will influence how students feel about a subject as well as their interest in studying it.[50] As you know by now, motivation is an important element of listening and learning. Thus, male students, who are often shown preference in their communications with their instructors, may be more motivated to listen. The way they are treated may also help them to develop attitudes favoring accountability and ownership – features associated with academic success.[51]

Communication scholar Deborah Tannen suggests that men listen confrontatively, while women listen collaboratively.[52] Thus, boys and men will be more comfortable challenging the teacher's comments, engaging in classroom discussions, and verbally critiquing class readings. They will gravitate towards debate-type activities. These activities encourage, if not require, students to engage in critical listening. Girls and women, in contrast, will be more comfortable responding while working in small groups where they can provide the nonverbal feedback (smiles, head nods, etc.) they prefer, and where they are better able to utilize clarification and other encouraging verbal cues. Thus, female students often prefer classroom activities that emphasize relational listening. They also place greater importance on having the right answer, which suggests that they may emphasize comprehensive listening more than their male classmates.

Socioeconomic Differences

Another area of socialization is socioeconomic background. In the classroom, a disproportionate number of underachievers are from lower socioeconomic groups. Unfortunately, these students, who are likely experiencing a number of economic and learning disadvantages, often get less support from their teachers than they need. Research suggests that instructors allow underachieving students less time to respond to questions, give them less attention, provide them with fewer non-verbal supportive behaviors (smiles, etc.), and generally interact with them less.[53] As a result, teachers essentially listen less to these students. No surprise then that underachievers often feel their teachers simply don't care about them. Earlier in the text, you learned the importance of feeling valued in a relationship to both listening and relationship development. It is unlikely then that these students have the motivation to listen in the classroom. It is important to remember that not all underachievers come from disadvantaged families, just as not all disadvantaged students will end up being underachievers. In fact, just the opposite may occur. It is true, however, that students who feel excluded and undervalued by their teachers are more likely to become turned off by school, stop listening, start acting out, or engage in other negative behaviors.

Culture and Ethnicity

Another factor that impacts how you interact with your teacher is culture. Classroom communication experts, Robert Powell and Dana Caseau write,

> Culture influences what people know, how they came by that knowledge, what roles they play and how they should play them, what they value, and how they put their values in action... culture plays a significant role in the education process.[54]

For example, teachers in the United States often cultivate an informal relationship with their students, encouraging students critically to evaluate and challenge material presented in class. This approach reflects the Western view that speakers are responsible for the clarity and understandability of their speech. Japanese students have a very different experience. In contrast, the classroom socialization process for Japanese students encourages them to become skilled at attentive listening.[55] In the Japanese classroom, the teacher both supports and facilitates listening by creating opportunities for students to listen actively to their peers, and setting an expectation of active listening. It is not unusual for instructors to withhold their own evaluation of student presentations and comments in order to encourage reaction turns (i.e., peer commentary and response). Thus, students have more self-autonomy in Japanese classrooms. In fact, teachers who are more directive, who do not foster student spontaneity, or who force their personal opinion onto students, are viewed as ineffective and unsuccessful.

The differences above also reflect the differences that exist between high-context and low-context cultures. Most US classrooms reflect the fact that the US is a low-context culture. **Low-context cultures** focus more attention on verbal expression and pay less attention to nonverbal cues. As a result, US students listen for linearly organized presentations (e.g., topically, chronologically, cause–effect) and clear and explicit directions. Likewise, teachers listen for answers to questions that are understandable, direct and precise. Teachers and students from **high-context cultures** are challenged in US classrooms because their communication and listening expectations are not dependent upon direct or explicit messages – much of the communication is embedded in the situation and is thus implied. As a result, they focus more on communicative elements such as nonverbal communication, physical context, environment, or even a speaker's mood.

Often academic listening is hampered by ingrained stereotypes or expectations of what is considered to be appropriate behavior. For example, Asian students are often viewed as polite, motivated, obedient, and modest.[56] As a listener, if you aren't Asian, you should be aware that smiles and laughter may reflect confusion or embarrassment, not excitement or happiness. Also, don't be surprised if your Asian friend engages in longer periods of silence than you are used to; silence has greater communicative importance in Asian cultures than in most Western cultures. In addition, emotional restraint, formality, and politeness are important guides to Asian social behavior. As a result, students from traditional Asian homes may view their primary role in the classroom as one in which they principally absorb information from their instructor. Challenging a teacher is generally viewed as inappropriate classroom behavior.[57] Thus, students from other cultures, particularly Asian cultures, may think US American students are disrespectful of their teachers.

> ***Think on it:*** Is there a relationship between cultural background and preferred teaching method? Will individuals from some cultures likely prefer the direct method? Indirect? Or some integrated approach?

As the above example illustrates, nonverbal behaviors differ between cultures and can affect our interpretations and perceptions as listeners. For example, Native American and Hispanic children are taught that it is disrespectful to look at parents and other authority figures directly. However, as Americans we value and expect direct eye contact. As a culturally sensitive listener, you will want to check how much of your interpretation of the nonverbal messages sent by the other party is based on your biases and expectations rather than your knowledge (or lack of knowledge) of the other culture.

Special Challenges for Non-native Speakers

Classes that primarily utilize a lecture format can be particularly challenging to non-native-speaking students. Unfortunately for many of these students, they do not receive adequate listening training prior to entering the foreign language classroom. For example, students are seldom exposed to a spontaneously delivered lecture. Instead, they often listen to scripted lectures delivered at a slow speaking rate rather than a conversational one. As a result, they experience listening-related problems associated with the features of spoken language, instructor interpersonal strategies, how discourse is structured, media usage, and even where they sit in the classroom.[58]

> ***Think on it:*** How have cultural differences affected your experiences? With other students? With your instructors?

Spontaneous spoken language can be problematic largely because of the nonverbal elements. For example, non-native speakers may have trouble classroom reading a professor's kinesics (i.e., body language) since the amount and type of body language varies between cultures. Head nods, eye contact, the "quizzical" eyebrow lift, can alter the meaning of what a professor is saying, indicate agreement, or signal displeasure. Another major language feature that non-native speakers may have difficulty addressing occurs at the "***micro-structure***" level of a lecture. This type of structuring is quite different from the conversational speaking and listening required in many foreign language classes. Micro-structuring refers to the unfilled pauses and verbal fillers (e.g., "um," "ah," "okay," "so") that are a natural part of the spontaneous lecture. This type of structure is also marked by numerous incomplete clauses, the use of contractions, and other forms of "incomplete" thoughts that make up a lecture. Finally, micro-structure includes our use of false starts, redundancy, and repetition. It is not unusual for us to begin a thought, change our mind in "midstream," and begin our thought again. Good teachers will include some redundancy and repetition in their lectures to allow students to catch material they initially missed or give them the opportunity to think on a question that's been asked. However, it can be confusing for the non-native speaker.

Of course, the examples here primarily apply to non-native speakers entering an American classroom. If you are considering becoming an exchange student, you will want to research the types and effects of language differences as they occur in the classes you will be attending.

Summary

Whether at home or in the classroom, we all appreciate the feeling that we are listened to. This chapter has primarily focused on the role of listening in classroom and teacher–student interactions. It does not address the overall lack of listening training that students receive during their K-12 years of school nor the increasing importance of listening in a hyperconnected world. Madelyn Burley-Allen, author of *Listening: The Forgotten Skill*, reports that students are provided 12 years of writing instruction, average seven years of reading instruction, approximately two years of speech instruction, but average less than half a year of listening instruction.[59] Richmond Bowman, Professor Emeritus at Winona State University, argues that tomorrow's classrooms should focus on developing listening skills in order to create a safe listening environment, to build interpersonal trust, and to foster a democratic society.[60] He believes that students must "practice listening to understand by probing, paraphrasing, and supporting others in telling their own truth, even when another's truth may be uncomfortable for both the sender and the listener."

As we noted in Chapter 1, listening well is a skill that requires instruction and practice – whatever the context. Unfortunately, educators often do not model this important skill, nor is it explicitly valued by the educational system. However, every year of school places greater demands on your listening skills, skills that are generally underdeveloped. You're lucky. You are attending a school that values and understands the importance of listening. You have an instructor who is guiding you in skill-building activities. Hopefully, you have the motivation not only to learn the material in this text, but to apply it to your daily life.

Key Concepts

Relevancy
    Personal relevancy
    Motivation
Learning Styles
    Auditory
    Visual
    Kinesthetic
Kolb's Learning Model
    Converging
    Assimilating
    Accommodating
    Divergent
Emotional Intelligence
Apprehension
    Communication Apprehension

Receiver Apprehension
Teaching Methods
    Direct
    Indirect
    Integrated
Interpersonal Tips
Academic Attributions
    Effort
    Ability
    Luck
    Difficulty
Internal and external attributions
Stable and unstable attributions
Classroom Climate
    Teacher self-disclosure
    Teacher immediacy
    Student engagement
    Classroom management
Organizational Lecture Cues and Tips
Organizational Clarity
Culture and Diversity
    Gender
    Socioeconomic differences
    High versus Low Context Cultures
    Micro-structures

Discussion Questions

1. What differentiates the boring lecture from the interesting one? Are differences related to class size? Topic? Personal interest? How have your teachers gotten you interested and involved? What have you observed about your listening behavior?

2. There is one questioning technique that your instructors probably use quite frequently. It is not a question per se, but is often attached to the questions they ask. This technique emphasizes the importance of silence. It is called *wait-time*. Wait-time occurs when a teacher asks a questions and then pauses for a response. The silence prior to someone answering the question is wait-time. Given enough time, someone in the class will try to answer the question – the silence becomes too much for him or her! Looking back at classes you've had over the last week, did you have an instructor engage in extended wait-time with you? Under what circumstances did it occur? How have previous instructors used wait-time in their classes? Was it tied to the topic? Student interest? Student confusion?

3. Going back to our discussion of teaching methods (e.g., direct, indirect, and integrated), how does teaching method affect classroom interactions (e.g., student preparation for class, turn-taking, note-taking, type of listening)?

4. Many professors use PowerPoint when teaching. What is their potential impact on classroom listening and discussion? When do you find PowerPoint slides to be most useful? Least useful? What types of problems can they cause when you're trying to listen to a lecture?

Listening Activities

1. Following a short class lecture, compare notes with others in your class (one person or a small group of three to four students). What similarities and differences exist? What does this suggest about how you listen? What explanations do you have for the differences in your note-taking? For explaining the similarities?

2. Practice note-taking. Go to a play and outline the plot, or watch a television program such as *Nova* and note main ideas and sub-points of its content. Both suggestions have their own advantages. Choose a play that is well known enough that you can get a written copy to assess your listening skills or you can record the television program and review it again while you compare. Focus on identifying main points, primary sub-points, and enough examples or explanations to reflect your understanding of the plot.

3. In groups of four to five people, develop PowerPoint slides for this chapter. What do you include as main points? Sub-points? What type of background would you use? Font? How many words would you put on the page? Why should you consider these things when developing PowerPoint slides? If possible, each group should display two to three slides for the class. Which slides are received the most favorably? What makes them stand out or work for others in the class?

4. During class, chart the micro-structures the instructor engages in. Do you normally pay attention to these structures? What impact do you think they might have on the listening for non-native speakers?

5. Interview one to two non-native speakers. Do they have problems listening in class? What type of problems do they have? Do they prefer a particular teaching method? Which one and why?

Notes

1 O'Hair, O'Hair, & Wooden, 1988; Wolvin, Coakley & Disburg, 1992
2 Janusik & Wolvin, 2009; Emanuel, et al., 2008
3 Gilbert, 1988; Imhof, 1998
4 Wolvin, et al., 1992; Worthington, 2005
5 Conaway, 1982
6 Newton (1985) reported that first year college students who took a listening class had significantly higher GPAs than those who did not take the class.
7 Common Core State Standards Initiative, 2016
8 Imhof, 1998
9 Kyle & Rogien, 2004
10 Sadler-Smith, 1997, p. 51
11 Beall, Gill-Rosier, Tate, & Matten, 2008
12 Beall, et al., 2008
13 Kolb & Kolb, 2005; Kolb, Boyatzis, & Mainemelis, 2002
14 Diagram adapted from Loo, 2002a, 2002b and McCarthy, 1990
15 Kolb & Kolb, 2005
16 Salovey, Mayer, Caruso, & Lopes, 2003, p. 251
17 Powell & Caseau, 2004
18 Healy, 1998; as described in Goleman, 2005
19 Powell & Caseau, 2004
20 McCroskey & McCrosky, 2002
21 McCroskey & McCrosky, 2002; McCroskey & Andersen, 1976; McCroskey, Booth-Butterfield, & Payne, 1989
22 Chesebro et al., 1992
23 Preiss, Wheeless, & Allen, 1990; Scott & Wheeless, 1977

24 Chesebro & McCroskey, 2001
25 Wheeless, Preiss, & Galye, 1997
26 Moore, 2011
27 Moore, 2011
28 Habibah & Pihie, 2003
29 Steffe & Gale, 1995
30 An & Frick, 2006
31 Van der Veer, 2007
32 Alderman, 1990
33 McNary, Glasgow, & Hicks, 2005
34 Coty, 1994
35 Jalongo, 1991, p. 7
36 Downs, Javidi, & Nussbaum, 1988
37 Long & Hoy, 2006
38 Glonek & King, 2014
39 Glonek & King, 2014
40 Richmond, 2002, p. 70
41 O'Hair, et al., 1988
42 Titsworth, 2004
43 O'Hair, et al. 1988, p. 114
44 O'Hair, et al., 1988, p. 116
45 Worthington & Levasseur, 2015
46 Titsworth, 2001
47 Cowan, 1995; Titsworth, 2001
48 Kiewra, 1983; Titsworth & Kiewra, 1998
49 Powell & Caseau, 2004; Wood, 2001
50 Powell & Caseau, 2004
51 Rawlins, 2000
52 Tannen, 1994
53 Gollnick & Chin, 1994; Good & Brophy, 1997
54 Powell & Caseau, 2004
55 Cook, 1999
56 Powell & Caseau, 2004
57 Powell & Caseau, 2004
58 Flowerdew & Miller, 1997; Hurtig, Sörqvist, Llung, Hygge, & Rönnberg, 2016
59 Burley-Allen, 1995, as cited in Sandall, Schramm, & Seibert, 2003
60 Bowman, 2015

Additional Readings

Flowerdew, J. (Ed.). (1994). *Academic listening.* New York: Cambridge University Press.

Fassett, D. L., & Warren, J. T. (Eds.). (2010). *The SAGE handbook of communication and instruction.* Thousand Oaks, CA: Sage.

Glonek, K. L., & King, P. E. (2014). Listening to narratives: An experimental examination of storytelling in the classroom. *International Journal of Listening, 28,* 32–46.

Kraft, M. A., & Dougherty, S. M. (2013). The effect of teacher-family communication on student engagement: Evidence from a randomized field experiment. *Journal of Research on Educational Effectiveness, 6,* 199–222.

Mazer, J. P., & Stowe, S. A. (2016). Can teacher immediacy reduce the impact of verbal aggressiveness? Examining effects on student outcomes and perceptions of teacher credibility. *Western Journal of Communication, 30,* 21–37.

References

Alderman, M. K. (1990, September). Motivation for at-risk students. *Educational Leadership, 48,* 27–30.

An, Y.-J., & Frick, T. (2006). Student perceptions of asynchronous computer-mediated communication in face-to-face courses. *Journal of Computer-Mediated Communication, 11,* 485–499.

Beall, M., Gill-Rosier, J., Tate, J., & Matten, A. (2008). State of the context: Listening in Education. *International Journal of Listening, 22,* 123–132.

Bowman, R. F. (2015). Learning in tomorrow's classrooms. *The Clearing House, 88,* 29–44.

Chesebro, J. L., & McCroskey, J. C. (2001). The relationship of teacher clarity and immediacy with student state receiver apprehension, affect, and cognitive learning. *Communication Education, 50,* 59–68.

Chesebro, J. L., McCroskey, J. C., Atwater, D., Bahrenfuss, R., Cawelti, G., Gaudino, J., & Hodges, H. (1992). Communication apprehension and self-perceived communication competence of at-risk students. *Communication Education, 37,* 270–277.

Common Core State Standards Initiative. (2016). *Preparing America's students for success.* Retrieved from www.corestandards.org.

Conaway, M. S. (1982). Listening: Learning tool and retention agent. In A. S. Algier & K. W. Algier (Eds.), *Improving reading and study skills* (pp. 51–63). San Francisco, CA: Jossey-Bass.

Cook, H. M. (1999). Language socialization in Japanese elementary schools: Attentive listening and reaction turns. *Journal of Pragmatics, 31,* 1443–1465.

Coty, S. (1994). "Sometimes I wish I'd never did it." Removing communication road blocks from at-risk students. *Voices in the Middles, 1,* 19–25.

Cowan, N. (1995). *Attention and memory: An integrated framework.* New York: Oxford University Press.

Downs, V. C., Javidi, M., & Nussbaum, J. (1988). An analysis of teachers' verbal communication within the college classroom: Use of humor, self-disclosure, and narratives. *Communication Education, 37,* 127–141.

Emanuel, R., Adams, J. Baker, K., Daufin, E. K., Ellington, C., Fitts, E., Himsel, J., Holladay, L., & Okeowo, D. (2008). How college students spend their time communicating. *International Journal of Listening, 22,* 13–28.

Flowerdew, J., & Miller, L. (1997). The teaching of academic listening comprehension and the question of authenticity. *English for Specific Purposes, 16,* 27–46.

Gilbert, M. B. (1988). Listening in school: I know you can hear me – but are you listening? *International Journal of Listening, 2,* 121–132.

Glonek, K. L., & King, P. E. (2014). Listening to narratives: An experimental examination of storytelling in the classroom. *International Journal of Listening, 28,* 32–46.

Goleman, D. (2005). *Emotional intelligence.* New York: Bantam.

Gollnick, D. M., & Chin, P. C. (1994). *Multicultural education in a pluralistic society* (4th ed.). New York: Macmillan.

Good, T., & Brophy, J. E. (1997). *Looking in classrooms* (7th ed.). New York: Longman.

Habibah, E., & Pihie, Z. A. L. (2003). *Listening competence among University students.* Retrieved from https://eric.ed.gov/?id=ED478119.

Hurtig, A., Sörqvist, P., Ljung, R., Hygge, S., & Rönnberg, J. (2016). Student's second-language grade may depend on classroom listening position. *Plos ONE, 11*(6), 1–8.

Imhof, M. (1998). What makes a good listener? Listening behavior in instructional settings. *International Journal of Listening, 12,* 81–105.

Jalongo, M. R. (1991). *Strategies for developing children's listening skills.* (PDK Fastback Series Title 314). Bloomington, IN: Phi Delta Educational.

Janusik, L. A., & Wolvin, A. D. (2009). 24 hours in a day: A listening update to the times studies. *The International Journal of Listening, 23,* 104–120.

James, K. (1977). Note-taking in lectures: Problems and strategies. In A. P. Cowie & J. B. Heaton (Eds.), *English for academic purposes* (pp. 99–107). London: BAAL/SELMOUS.

Kiewra, K. A. (1983). The relationship between notetaking over an extended period and actual course-related achievement. *College Student Journal, 17,* 381–385.

Kyle, P. B., & Rogien, L. R. (2004). *Classroom management.* New York: Pearson.

Kolb, D. A., Boyatzis, R. E., & Mainemelis, C. (2002). Experiential learning theory: Previous research and new directions. In R. J. Sternberg & L. F. Zhang (Eds.), *Perspectives on cognitive, learning, and thinking styles* (pp. 227–248). Mahwah, NJ: LEA.

Kolb, A. Y., & Kolb, D. A. (2005). Learning styles and learning spaces: Enhancing experiential learning in higher education. *Academy of Management Learning and Education, 4*, 193–212.

Long, J. F., & Hoy, A. W. (2006). Interested instructors: A composite portrait of individual differences and effectiveness. *Teaching and Teacher Education, 22*, 303–314.

Loo, R. (2002a). A meta-analytic examination of Kolb's learning style preferences among business majors. *Journal of Education for Business, 77*, 25–50.

Loo, R. (2002b). The distribution of learning styles and types for hard and soft business majors. *Educational Psychology, 22*, 349–360.

McCarthy, B. (1990, October). Using the 4MAT system to bring learning styles to schools. *Educational Leadership, 48*, 31–37.

McCroskey, J. C., & Andersen, J. (1976). The relationship between communication apprehension and academic achievement among college students. *Communication Research, 3*, 73–81.

McCroskey, J. C., Booth-Butterfield, S., & Payne, S. (1989). The impact of apprehension on college student retention and success. *Communication Quarterly, 37*, 100–107.

McCroskey, J. C., & McCroskey, L. L. (2002). Willingness to communicate and communication apprehension in the classroom. In J. L. Chesebro & J. C. McCroskey (Eds.), *Communication for teachers* (pp. 19–34). Boston: Allyn & Bacon.

McNary, S. J., Glasgow, N. A., & Hicks, C. D. (2005). *What successful teachers do in inclusive classrooms.* Thousand Oaks, CA: Corwin Press.

Moore, K. (2011). *Effective instructional strategies* (2nd ed.). Thousand Oaks, CA: Sage.

Newton, T. (1985). *Description of the St. Edwards University directed listening skills project.* Paper presented at the International Listening Association Summer Conference, St. Paul, MI.

O'Hair, M., O'Hair, D., & Wooden, S. L. (1988). Enhancement of listening skills as a prerequisite to improved study skills. *International Journal of Listening, 2*, 113–120.

Powell, R. G., & Caseau, D. (2004). *Classroom communication and diversity: Enhancing instructional practice.* Mahwah, NJ: LEA.

Preiss, R. W., Wheeless, L. R., & Allen, M. (1990). Potential cognitive processes and consequences of receiver apprehensions: A meta-analytic review. In M. Booth-Butterfield (Ed.), *Communication, cognition, and anxiety.* (Special Issue), *Journal of Social Behavior and Personality, 5*, 155–172.

Rawlins, W. K. (2000). Teaching as a mode of friendship. *Communication Theory, 10*, 5–26.

Richmond, V. P. (2002). Teacher nonverbal immediacy: Use and outcomes. In J. L. Chesebro & J. C. McCroskey (Eds.), *Communication for teachers* (pp. 65–82). Boston: Allyn & Bacon.

Sadler-Smith, E. (1997). Learning style: frameworks and instruments. *Educational Psychology, 17*, 51–64

Salovey, P., Mayer, J. D., Caruso, D., & Lopes, P. N. (2003). Measuring emotional intelligence as a set of abilities with the Mayer-Salovey-Caruso emotional intelligence test. In S. J. Lopez & C. R. Snyder (Eds.), *Positive psychological assessment: A handbook of models and measures.* Washington, D.C.: American Psychological Association.

Sandall, N., Schramm, K., & Seibert, A. (2003, May). *Improving listening skills through the use of children's literature.* Master of Arts Action Research project. Saint Xavier University & SkyLight Professional Development, Chicago, IL. Retrieved from https://archive.org/stream/ERIC_ED482002#page/n0/mode/2up

Scott, M. D., & Wheeless, L. R. (1977). The relationship of three types of communication apprehension to classroom achievement. *The Southern Speech Communication Journal, 42*, 246–255.

Steffe, L. P., & Gale, J. (Eds.). (1995). *Constructivism in education.* Hillsdale, NJ: Erlbaum.

Tannen, D. (1994). *Gender discourse.* New York: Oxford University Press.

Titsworth, B. S. (2004). Students' note taking: The effects of teacher immediacy and clarity. *Communication Education, 53*, 305–320.

Titsworth, B. S. (2001). The effects of teacher immediacy, use of organizational lecture cues, and students' note taking on cognitive learning. *Communication Education, 50*, 283–297.

Titsworth, B. S., & Kiewra, K. (1998, April). *By the numbers: The effect of organizational lecture cues on note taking and achievement.* Paper presented at the American Educational Research Association Convention, San Diego, CA.

Van der Veer, R. (2007). *Lev Vygotsky: Continuum Library of Educational Thought.* London: Continuum.

Wheeless, L. R., Preiss, R. W., & Galye, B. M. (1997). Receiver apprehension, informational receptivity, and cognitive processing. In J. A. Daly, J. C. McCroskey, J. Ayres, T. Hopf, & D. M. Ayers (Eds.), *Avoiding communication: Shyness, reticence, and communication apprehension* (pp. 151–187). Cresskill, NJ: Hampton.

Wolvin, A. D., Coakley, C. G., & Disburg, J. E. (1992). Listening instruction in selected colleges and universities. *International Journal of Listening, 6,* 59–65.

Wood, J. T. (2001). *Gendered lives: Communication, gender and culture* (4th ed.). Belmont, CA: Wadsworth.

Worthington, D. L. (2005). *Listening Education: A Review of Current Listening Syllabi.* Paper presented to the Communication and Social Cognition Division at the annual meeting of the National Communication Association, Boston, MA.

Worthington, D. L., & Levasseur, D. (2015). To provide or not to provide course PowerPoint slides? The impact of instructor-provided slides upon student attendance and performance. *Computers & Education, 85,* 14–22.

10 Listening in Context

Organizations

Case Study 10.1 Cultural Differences and Organizational Listening

On his way home from work, Mr. Kim, a CPA with an auto parts manufacturing plant, is thinking about the executive meeting that occurred earlier in the day. The executive team reflects the international nature of the company. Mr. Kim is worried about whether some of the divisions are listening to the needs of their employees and setting the example necessary to have good morale. He really likes working for S&K, a Korean owned company. He feels culturally connected with the values and work expectations of the organization, but worries about his friend, Steve Goleman. Mr. Goleman is the Vice President of Human Resources and has expressed concerns about possible differences in the expectations of the employees and the values of the company. Mr. Goleman isn't sure that the company is really tuned into the needs of the predominately US born workers.

This past Sunday, the two families had gone on a picnic and their children, Ben and NaMii, had talked about listening as an important part of an organization's culture, a topic that had come up in their listening class. "There just might be something to this," Mr. Kim thinks as he navigates the traffic.

In the context of our model, Listening MATERRS, we can see that the situation in which an interaction takes place can profoundly impact the process of listening. As the case study above illustrates, our concern with listening extends beyond ourselves as individuals to the many situations we find ourselves in. Therefore, we need to focus on how listening is used and the impact of listening (good or bad) on different contexts. This chapter will explore listening in an organization. Since most of you will work within organizations, the information we discuss will be helpful to you as you research and interview with potential employers.

In this chapter we will look at the organization as a listening entity as well as areas of listening that are essential to the success of organizations. However, before we can talk about organizations as a listening context, we need to understand what an organization is. An **organization** is a dynamic system in which individuals engage in collective efforts for goal accomplishment.[1]

Just as individual listening skills are important for a person's success, the willingness of an organization to value listening in its relationship with employees, customers and any other important groups is a critical aspect of successful organizations. Effective organizational listening leads to improved morale, happier customers and a healthier bottom line.

To understand organizations as listening contexts, we first need to understand several important organizational concepts – purpose, mission, culture and climate. Once we have defined these concepts, we will look at organizations in general, how organizations exhibit listening, and how listening as an organizational value can affect communication, conflict, and the day-to-day operations of a business.

Understanding Organizations

The degree to which an organization listens will be determined by a several factors. Among them are purpose, mission, culture and climate. Additional factors include workplace social support and leadership. Even though we think of an organization as a collection of individuals, its unifying purpose, mission, and culture make it a listening entity. As a listening entity, organizations are subject to experiencing communication successes and failures, particularly with two of their main publics, customers and employees. Over the next few pages, we look at these factors and how they affect listening inside and outside the organization. Towards the end of the chapter, we discuss how these factors come together to create the listening organization.

Purpose and Mission

When we talk about the purpose of an organization, we are referring to what the organization exists to do, whether it is manufacturing something, raising funds, or providing services to the public. In our case study at the beginning of this chapter, Mr. Kim and Mr. Goleman, the fathers of Namii and Ben, work for S&K, a company whose purpose is to provide specific auto parts to other auto manufacturers. Of course, other companies focus on services such as home health, investment advice, or clothing sales.

An organization's **mission statement** is a declaration of its purpose. Organization expert, John Bryson, feels that mission statements should answer six questions: who are we, what are the basic needs or problems for which we exist, how do we respond to these needs, how should we respond to key stakeholders, what are our core values, and what makes us unique.[2] Patrick Hull, an entrepreneur and contributor to *Forbes* magazine, says that mission statements provide people in an organization with its framework and purpose.[3]

Sometimes companies will make separate values statements or ethics statements that highlight the values and principles upon which the organization is built and run. These statements are an extension and refinement of what appears in the organization's mission statement. For example, Ford Motor Company publishes a standards of corporate conduct that is given to all employees and is accessible on their website.[4] In a letter to employees regarding these standards, former executive chairman of the company, William Clay Ford Jr. stated:

> Henry Ford once said, "There is a most intimate connection between decency and good business." He believed that the main purpose of a corporation should be to serve customers, employees, and communities. By staying true to those values, he was able to build the greatest business enterprise of the 20th century.

> Today, the values of a company are even more critical to its success. As we move into the 21st century, expectations are higher and processes are more transparent. Now, more than ever, companies must not just proclaim the highest standards, they must live them every day.[5]

Mr. Ford's statement clearly establishes the organizational values that guide Ford Motor Company's daily operations. His statement also lets readers know that these values reflect the long and proud history of the company.

Table 10.1 Selected Mission Statements

WalMart	**Coca-Cola**
We save people money so they can live better.	Our Roadmap starts with our mission, which is enduring. It declares our purpose as a company and serves as the standard against which we weigh our actions and decisions.
	To refresh the world…
	To inspire moments of optimism and happiness…
	To create value and make a difference.
Ritz-Carlton	**American Cancer Society**
The Ritz-Carlton Hotel is a place where the genuine care and comfort of our guests is our highest mission. We pledge to provide the finest personal service and facilities for our guests who will always enjoy a warm, relaxed, yet refined ambience.	The American Cancer Society's mission is to save lives, celebrate lives, and lead the fight for a world without cancer.
The Ritz-Carlton experience enlivens the senses, instills well-being, and fulfills even the unexpressed wishes and needs of our guests.	

WalMart (2017); The Coca-Cola Company (2017); The Ritz-Carlton Hotel Company, LLC (2017); American Cancer Society (2017).

Most organizations, whether for profit or not, have mission statements – statements that vary tremendously. Imagine the differences between mission statements for a retailer, Walmart, a multi-national company like Coca-Cola, a high-end hotel chain like Ritz-Carlton and a not-for-profit organization like the American Cancer Society. Table 10.1 contrasts the mission statement of each of these organizations.

The uniqueness or persona of an organization is not just in its purpose and mission but also in the internal aspects of culture and climate.

> ***Think on it:*** Look at the mission statements presented in Table 10.1. Do they meet the guidelines established by John Bryson? What did you learn about the organizations based on their mission statements? Which mission statement suggests the organization values listening?

Organizational Culture

Organizational culture is the study of "an organization's way of life" – one created by the history of the organization, its leaders, and employees.[6] Edgar Schein, a noted scholar in the area of organizations, defined culture as

> a pattern of shared basic assumptions that was learned by a group as it solved its problems of external adaptation and internal integration, that has worked well enough to be considered valid, and therefore, taught to new members, as the correct way to see, think and feel in relation to those problems.[7]

Schein believes that cultural assumptions apply to how an organization sets strategies and establishes goals, selects methods of achieving those goals, and how it measures progress and controls its output. For instance, whether or not S&K establishes its annual production goals by consulting with the various departments in the organization or by board decree will reflect the S&K culture. Organizational culture also addresses how an organization deals with behavior that is "out of line" with either its goals or its accepted norms of behavior. As you know from your experiences in the classroom, such behavior can potentially lead to a conflict situation (e.g., a reprimand from the instructor to the "offending" student or a public dressing down by one of your classmates).

Organizational culture helps shape the context in which all interactions within an organization, even interpersonal exchanges, take place. As such it provides the context in which listening occurs as illustrated in our Listening MATERRS Model. The culture even influences the way people in the organization think and operate. Scholars, Eisenberg and Goodall call this tendency **organizational cognition**, meaning that members of the organization have shared meanings, values and rules.[8] Thus, Ben and Jerry's encourage their employees to have fun and be a bit goofy, especially when it comes to developing new names and flavors of ice cream. Ford Motors, on the other hand, is much more conservative in its day-to-day operations (refer back to the ethics statement above). Importantly, shared cognitions allow groups to share the meaning of symbols, metaphors and stories. A good example of this can be found in your school. Members of the student body know what the school motto means as well as the use of certain "insider" sayings. At Auburn University, the term "War Eagle" is often substituted for "hello" and "goodbye." Current and former AU students (and likely their parents) know these usages, but few people outside of the "Auburn Family" do. Chances are you can identify similar examples at your school. These shared cognitions serve to make people feel they are part of the organizational community.

> ***Think on it:*** Go online and look up the mission statement of three of your favorite companies or organizations. What do they have in common? How do they differ? What company values are reflected in their statements? How might those values affect listening both inside and outside of the company?

By looking at the definitions and characteristics of organizational culture, we can see that culture is a created "social reality" of how the organization operates, what it considers important, how it treats its employees and other publics. Underlying this "reality" are the values of the organization, or the underlying principles upon which it operates. These principles can include listening to employees and other important groups, and working toward mutually beneficial outcomes. Unfortunately, they can also do the opposite and reflect an organization interested only in the year-end financial reports. The importance of values is very evident whether they are formally stated or simply displayed in the day-to-day operation of the organization.

Culture Gaps. When an organization fails to live by the stated values it exhibits **culture gaps**. Culture gaps are differences in what an organization says it values and what it actually does in its day-to-day operations. These types of organizations are perceived to focus more on their own interests and often devalue listening by their actions. If these perceptions are indeed true, the organization often ends in failure. The business news is full of examples of organizations that illustrate what happens when they don't listen and don't live up to their stated values. Two recent examples are Wells Fargo Bank and Mylan Pharmaceuticals. Dominating business news at the time, both companies became visible examples of corporate failure to live by stated values and to "listen" to the needs of their customers.

Wells Fargo became front-page news when it was discovered that employees had opened millions of accounts in customers' names that the customers hadn't authorized.[9] The bank collected millions of dollars in fees from these accounts. News reports on the company say employees in several states were pressured to cross-sell products to existing customers even if the customer didn't want or understand the product.[10] Contrast this action with the company's stated values:

> We want our customers to trust us as their financial resource – whether it's giving them sound guidance, helping them reach their financial goals, completing transactions accurately and promptly, or providing them with products and services to meet their needs.

> We want our customers to trust all of us to act as risk managers – to ask the right questions, protect their assets, and help them reach their goals. We have to earn that trust every day by behaving ethically; rewarding open, honest, two-way communication; and holding ourselves accountable for the decisions we make and the actions we take. That's more important now than ever.

> We value what's right for our customers in everything we do.[11]

Obviously the actions of some bank employees did not match the values that Wells Fargo stated. The fallout from this scandal, as can be expected, resulted in the CEO resigning and a drop in business as well as customer loyalty. *Business Insider* reported that the customer loyalty score fell from 61.4% in November 2015, to 53.6% a year later, a drop of 13% in 12 months. New consumer checking accounts fell 41% during the same time period.[12]

Another example of a culture gap can be found in Mylan, one of the world's largest pharmaceutical companies. Among their values they list:

> *Integrity*
> Doing what's right is sacred to us. We behave responsibly, even when nobody's looking.

> *Service*
> We understand that "it's not about us" – it's about helping others – and we believe there's no situation we can't handle. We would do whatever it takes, work 'round the clock, cross any river and spare no effort – all to meet someone's need.

Mylan made widespread news when the CEO of the company, Heather Bresch, was called before Congress for a hearing about one of their products, the EpiPen, an epinephrine injector. As those of you who suffer from allergies know, epinephrine is a remedy for anaphylactic shock, a severe allergic reaction. Mylan developed the "injector pen" delivery system for the drug. The price of the EpiPen went from $100 for a two-pack in 2009 to $608 in 2016 (a 548% increase).[13] Ms. Bresch was unable to provide the Congressional Committee with an adequate explanation for the price increase. Subsequently, some members of the House committee and many in the public believed Mylan used its monopoly for the drug delivery system to take advantage of its customers. These events suggest that Mylan has a culture gap – one where company profits come at the expense of a patient's need for this life-saving drug.

Unfortunately, this situation is not uncommon. Similar situations seem to occur regularly, when institutions betray their customers' and investors' trust.

Organizational Climate

Closely related to culture, **organizational climate** is the perception, usually on the part of employees or organizational members, of how things are in an organization.[14] More specifically, climate is defined as an individual's perception of the important aspects of the work environment.[15] An individual's perceptions are based on his or her judgment of the beliefs, values, behaviors, and skills needed to be effective in the organization.[16] Essentially, climate is a response to the culture of an organization. Although we think of climate as an individual reaction, these reactions tend to be shared by members of a group. For example, if you feel that your school is a warm, supportive place, then that feeling is probably shared by the majority of other students at the school, particularly those students that you hang out with.

As the employees and other people associated with the organization act on their perceptions, they create the climate. Once the climate is created, it influences the way people work and interact. A survey by the Six Seconds Institute for Organizational Performance found a clear relationship between how people feel and how they perform.[17] This survey found that 43% of retention of employees is predicted by leadership, alignment, and collaboration. **Alignment** indicates the organization is listening to the needs and values of employees and working with those needs. This idea is evidenced in our introductory case study where Mr. Goleman is concerned about possible differences between company and employee expectations. **Collaboration** indicates employees work together in a selfless manner. When these conditions exist in an organization, it has a listening environment or climate, and retention of employees is higher. (We discuss leadership below.)

On the other hand, if employees are constantly fearful of losing their jobs or being reprimanded by supervisors, the climate is one of fear and dislike. Recently, one of our students told us about the unhappy environment at the public relations company she interned with. While she valued the hands-on experience and felt that she had learned a tremendous amount, she did not like how the supervisor talked to others in the group. She specifically said that she felt it was inappropriate for employees to be reprimanded in front of her. Basically, this student did not like the organizational climate of the firm.

Of course, most companies have more favorable climates. If people can feel relaxed and playful, the atmosphere is fun and employees tend to be very loyal to the company. It is important to note that a relaxed playful climate doesn't mean the business isn't serious. Ben & Jerry's is serious about the ice cream business even while encouraging their employees to be creative and have fun at work.

Climate can have a profound impact on the individuals in the workplace. Marketing professors Bernadett Koles and Balakrishnan Kondath identify several things that organizational climate affects. These areas are increased organizational success, lower employee turnover, and enhanced employee performance.[18] Their study of organizations in four countries found that the culture of the country in which the organization is located has a profound impact on the organization's climate. A study conducted in New Zealand discovered that people who feel a great deal of pressure on the job are more prone to suffer from burnout than those who feel less pressure.[19] Likewise, employees who feel their organization's climate is supportive, cohesive, and involved low pressure, are more likely to enjoy their work. When such a climate exists, it is said to be high in social support.

Organizational Social Support

As you learned earlier in the text, **social support** is based on the social relationships or networks that we develop. In our earlier discussions, we focused on family and friends as primary social support systems. However, good social support in the workplace has a number of positive implications for companies and other organizations. **Organizational social support** focuses on "the informational functions of supportive communication and the role that co-workers play in assisting one another in defining and making sense of their work environment."[20] Social support also helps members of an organization to "manage uncertainty."[21] In other words, social support seems to help us maintain a sense of control over our everyday and work lives.

Social support takes a number of different forms but can be summarized in two categories: **action-facilitating support** and **nurturing support**. Action-facilitating support includes instrumental and informational support while nurturing support covers emotional, esteem, and social network support.[22]

Instrumental support focuses on doing tasks and favors, while **information support** addresses how corporations share and provide information. Clearly there are many ways you can provide this type of support in the workplace. You can conduct an internet search for a friend; you can contribute relevant information to a discussion, or run an errand for someone. As a listener, when you provide a listening ear as someone talks through a problem, you provide instrumental support. Organizations provide instrumental support by making sure employees have access to the resources they need to do their jobs. Co-workers also provide instrumental support for each other when they work cooperatively on a task. When an organization's culture encourages cooperation, this type of support is evident. Innolect, a true listening organization, fosters a climate of instrumental support. The associates, or members of the Innolect group, often share information so that others can be successful in a job or have a leg-up in their effort to work with a particular client.

Unfortunately, some organizations are built on a culture of extreme competition and discourage instrumental support between divisions. In cases such as this, there is very little sharing of information or cooperation between the groups. We have been told of one large wine producer who supposedly operated in this fashion. It pitted the sales and production departments against each other. So, production tried to produce more product than sales could sell, and sales tried to sell more than production could produce. While this strategy kept people motivated to produce, it created a very stressful work environment, led to significant conflict, and resulted in divisions that would not cooperate with one another.

Fortunately, many organizations have cultures that encourage positive supportive social relationships. That is, they encourage **nurturing support**. These organizations tend to be listening safe climates, or climates in which one is free to express his/her views and to be listened to in a non-judgmental way. Social support thus becomes an important part of employee relations. A quick look at *Fortune's* list of 100 best companies to work for in 2017 will identify organizations that listen.[23] Google tops the list and has held that spot eight of the past 11 years. Google's organizational climate has helped make it one of the most financially successful companies in the world.

Listening, Social Support, and Corporate Climate. Although it is the individuals in the network who provide the support, the climate and culture of the organization will either motivate or demotivate the existence of that support. When people feel comfortable at work and enjoy their jobs, productivity goes up. Listening is one of the key ingredients in this type of atmosphere. Research indicates that most distressed individuals don't want advice, they want to be heard. In order for someone to feel heard, we need to engage in supportive listening. Communication scholar Brent Burleson suggested that this type of listening involves the following:[24]

- Focusing attention on the other person, not personal feelings or experiences.
- Staying neutral, avoiding being judgmental, and labeling information as good or bad. It also includes encouraging the speaker to do the same thing and describing the situation without judgment.
- Focusing on the speaker's feelings rather than events. More than likely, it is the person's feelings that need exploring.
- Supporting the other person's feelings rather than trying to fix them or direct them. Expressing understanding of how the person feels, rather than telling him or her how she/ he should feel.

This type of listening will help your friends and co-workers express themselves and may even help them work through a problem. Your esteem and emotional support can provide a safe listening zone where people can be open about potentially distressing topics such as flunking out of school or being fired. Additionally, it prevents us from discounting what other people feel by our misguided efforts to cheer them up. You might recall from Chapter 2, we talked about yellow listening, where we acknowledge the other person but don't listen to their real needs. Unfortunately, we often engage in yellow listening unless actively concentrating on providing emotional support. For example, often when someone is talking to us about something unpleasant, we give a yellow response by saying things can't be that bad. Good emotionally supportive listening will allow us to be good green listeners who are supportive of what the other person is feeling, whether we, as listeners, are comfortable or not. Some organizations talk about listening to their employees, but they often either only go through the motions or ignore the employee messages altogether.

> *Think on it*: What type of organization would you like to work for? What specific actions or comments would motivate you to continue working for an organization or be willing to put in those extra hours that are necessary to complete a task?

Another type of support, **social network support**, involves maintaining ongoing relationships. As students, you probably think of this type of support as your network of friends and family. In an organization, this type of network can be co-workers or others at your company or colleagues in the business or industry. As an example, both authors of this book have extensive, professional social networks. Not only do we, as co-workers, provide support to each other for our teaching and research, we work with scholars and practitioners in other organizations. Doing so provides us with differing perspectives, which help us to be open to new ideas and approaches. This type of network is an important part of a vital organization.

Examples of organizations which provide social support and listen to their employees can be found on the list of the top 50 not-for-profit organizations to work for.[25] The National Communication Association is ranked number six. The CEO of number 45 on the list, Boston-based Year Up,

Gerald Chertavian, says that to maintain a supportive working environment "requires constant listening, attention and willingness to adapt." He goes on to say to maintain employee satisfaction, "you've got to build the best listening mechanisms and systems you can and have people feel comfortable speaking the truth."[26]

As we discussed in Chapter 5, modern communication adds special challenges to maintaining a social network. The ability to create virtual communities makes it very easy for us to form a network outside of our particular organization. Chances are you communicate regularly with students at schools other than the one you are attending. This ease of communicating outside of our own organization can also provide some interesting communication and listening challenges.

Research by Andy Wolvin and Laura Janusik indicates that we are now spending over 15% of our time with email and the internet.[27] While scholars haven't decided whether this type of interaction constitutes listening, we can agree that these mediums provide us with virtual networks. In business settings, these networks allow people to communicate about key issues, particularly when time is short and distances are great. At the same time, however, as a leaner medium, electronic networking can lead to misunderstandings, since receivers don't have access to all of the information, such as facial expressions and vocal tones, needed to truly interpret someone's remarks.

Several years ago, Professor Fitch-Hauser was hired by an organization because they were having trouble with miscommunication among employees. After observing the situation, she discovered that many of the employees communicated with each other solely by email. Employees seemed to think that it was a waste of time to actually go into someone's office and have a face-to-face discussion, even if the person was in the next office. So, while email can save time, misuse of it can lead to communication problems. Think about it, if your "context" is limited to your office or cubicle, you may feel there is no need to actually go down the hall to talk with someone. It makes sense that if your sense of place and belonging is defined by a communication medium – email – and your office, then it becomes easy to feel threatened. Your feelings are likely due to the fact that you lack non-text-based information (e.g., nonverbal information), or a social network to help define the message. This may well be why so many of you prefer Facebook, SnapChat, and other richer mediums over email, since they provide greater context.

The previous example of the overuse of email clearly illustrates the importance of social support to an organization. In the example, the networks were weakened by an over-reliance on email. The absence of face-to-face interaction created a context in which it was impossible to listen fully. Subsequently, both employee morale and productivity were negatively impacted.

Leadership

Climate and culture are profoundly impacted by an organization's leadership. Not only do leaders of an organization reflect its values, they also have a critical role in defining those values. As one would expect, listening organizations have listening leaders. As John Yokoyama, owner of Pike Place Fish Market in Seattle, says,

> If I am not listening actively to my crew, I fail to create an environment where they will listen to one another and to our customers. If I don't listen to the needs and concerns of my staff, I can't reasonably expect them to listen to those same needs of their team members and our customers. My behavior sets the tone for our company.[28]

Clearly, Mr. Yokoyama understands the impact of organizational context on listening.

Learn more: To see what the Pike Place Fish Market is up to now, go to www.pikesplacefish. com. Click on the Mission tab for more on its history and company philosophy.

Communication consultant Chris Witt addresses the idea of listening leaders. He suggests that in order for leaders to be successful in contemporary business, they have to be good listeners.[29] If they listen, they are able to identify problems before they get out of control, uncover causes of miscommunication and conflict, understand people, build rapport, gather and evaluate information and generate solutions. Witt also suggests that listening leaders build organizations that value collaboration. This perspective is supported by research that indicates that leaders spend up to 89% of their time communicating with subordinates.[30]

Sometimes leaders have to shift an organization's culture so that it begins to value listening. The giant Korean electronics company, Samsung, is an excellent example of how a leader can lead the charge to redefine organizational values and direction. In the early 1990s, Samsung was known for producing cheap, discounted goods, not innovative high quality well-designed electronics. Today, the organization is one of the fastest growing companies in the world, and the recipient of numerous design awards.[31] As we look at the internal moves behind this transformation, we can find listening leaders who have developed a listening organization. Kun-Hee Lee, then chairman of Samsung, knew that things at the company had to change. He wanted to help the company create a distinctive identity – one built on innovative design that could meet global demand, while at the same time reflecting the ancient culture of Korea. In essence, he shifted the focus to designing and balancing opposite forces, commonly known as "yin" and "yang." One of the major changes he introduced was the creation of a collaborative work environment where employees know enough about other employees' jobs and related concerns that they mutually and willingly seek to address them. For example, he required designers at Samsung to take a year of mechanical engineering so they would think about how the product works, not just what it looks like. Engineers had to familiarize themselves with design concerns so they would have a realistic idea of how their products would be packaged. Now, engineers and designers work together to produce products that are electronically innovative and have pleasing, distinctively functional designs – that is, they balance their opposing forces. This balance has led to success. According to *Forbes*, in 2016 Samsung Electronics had become the 18th largest technology company in the world and the 16th most profitable.[32]

Think on it: What kind of leaders do you want to follow? The next time your school holds student government elections, ask yourself if you are voting for a listening leader.

Organizations that value this type of collaboration are typically based upon cultures that value inquiry and listening. **Inquiry** is the art of asking questions. Asking questions becomes an art when the questions link values with actions and results by opening up thoughtful exploration of possibilities and actions. The type of listening that is needed requires being open to what is truly being said, what needs to be expressed, and what is not being said.[33] Then, not only will the organization provide a listening supportive context, it will be a listening organization.

Leadership: Listening Lessons

Merrie Jo Pitera
Chief Executive Officer
Litigation Insights
Overland Park, Kansas

As a CEO of a mid-size litigation consulting firm, listening and understanding our employees is key to better communication and a smooth working environment. Because we have a diversified office in terms of generation, gender and ethnicity, everyone in our office has a different listening style based on their culture, experiences and sensibilities. Therefore, to ensure effective communication, and thus leadership, I have to take these differences into consideration when assigning projects and providing general instructions.

As for our clients, it is important to be a good listener. Our clients often communicate their goals for their projects. If we do not adequately hear those goals, we could effectively lose a project because we were not being responsive to their concerns. Therefore, listening to a client's goals and ensuring you have adequately heard those goals are critical to the success of running our business.

The Listening Organization

If we look at organizations closely, we can see that organizations, like people, make choices about whether or not to listen. They may choose to listen to their employees, customers, competitors, or the community just like the listener in our model, Listening MATERRS. As an entity with definable groups of people with whom it wants to build a relationship, an organization can be considered a party in potential listening situations. In order for a listening situation to exist, the organization and the group it wants to communicate with must have some type of relationship in which the actions of either the organization or the public will have an impact on the wellbeing of the other.[34]

Organizational listening can be described as the responsiveness of an organization to the needs of its public. When organizations listen, they tend to have better reputations, more productive employees, better quality products, and a happier customer base. Australian scholar, Judy Burnside-Lawry, says stakeholders in an organization describe competent organizational listening using the same terms scholars typically use to describe competent interpersonal listening.[35] From her perspective, competent organizational listening occurs when an organization incorporates both values and actions that contribute to the goal of listening accurately. That is, stakeholders perceive that the organization has received and understood their messages accurately and supportively and that the relationship between the stakeholder and organization is enhanced by the exchange and listening.

> **Think on it:** Can you think of any organization that you consider to be a listening organization? Maybe your school? Church? Favorite coffee shop? Discuss the listening qualities the organization exhibits.

As we noted at the beginning of the chapter, an organization is a dynamic system in which individuals engage in collective efforts for goal accomplishment.[36] The 21st century organization has undergone, and continues to experience, technological changes affecting how it communicates with its employees and other publics. Today, virtual organizations are as viable as their more traditional bricks and mortar counterparts. The advent of virtual organizations, organizations in which the work and employees are connected by a network, rather than a physical plant or office building, requires us to re-examine how we define organizations. An employee may work out of her home in Hawkinsville, Georgia, be supervised by someone in Seattle, and have clients in Detroit, Atlanta, and New Delhi. Regardless of how we define organizations, it is the process of communication that keeps them current, competitive, relevant, and viable. And, of course, an important part of that process is how well organizations listen to important groups or publics.

> **Think on it:** Colleges and universities, like all organizations, reflect the changing boundaries of what defines the institution. For example, do you take any online courses? How do online classes differ from the ones that require your physical attendance? What type of relationship do you have with your teacher? To get the other side of the story, ask one of your teachers who teaches an online course about the differences in teaching the two types of classes. See if you can identify the listening challenges that are part of each context.

To get us focused on organizations as listeners, we need to examine a model of how organizations interact with their publics. Public relations scholars James Grunig and Todd Hunt proposed a model of public relations that can easily be applied to the listening organization.[37] This model, the **Two-Way Symmetrical Model of Public Relations**, reflects an organization that engages in two-way communication with its many publics. **Publics** in this setting is any group of people with which the organization has an interdependent relationship (e.g., employees, customers, community). As Ebony Simpson, senior publicist for in-home entertainment at Click Communications writes, "The aim of this model is dialogue not monologue. The feedback that the organization gathers is used to change organizational practices."[38]

The assumptions of this model underscore the strength of the interdependence of an organization with its various publics. These assumptions include *telling the truth, seeking joint understanding,* and *managing the perceptions of the various viewpoints* represented in an organization or business relationship. Notice how the two-way symmetrical model fits with Burnside-Lawry's conceptualization of a listening organization.

Applied to this context, a listening organization is one that fully engages in developing and maintaining two-way symmetrical interactions between it and the public. This type of interaction requires a great deal of listening so that the organization can develop a relationship with the particular public in question. Just as people have relationships, organizations have relationships with groups with which they are interdependent. For example, your school has an interdependent relationship with you, the faculty, alumni, and numerous other groups.

An interdependent relationship suggests that both parties, the organization and the public, make important contributions necessary for the organization to achieve its goals. However, it is unlikely that these goals can be achieved if the different publics themselves are unwilling to listen. A balanced perspective – one in which the needs of the public are balanced against the needs of the organization – is crucial. Listening is the means by which such a perspective can be achieved. Just as caring people engage in good listening behaviors in their relationships, organizations also engage in activities that reflect good relational listening. In essence, effective listening can cut across the boundaries that traditionally separate organizations and their publics (e.g., customers and employees; employees and upper management). Listening, then, allows organizations to remain in touch with, and responsive to, their employees, their customers or clients, and any other important public.

In our case study at the beginning of this chapter, Mr. Kim and Mr. Goleman are concerned about whether S&K is tuned into the needs of a crucial public, the employees. If S&K is a good listening organization, it will listen to its employees and work to find mutually satisfactory ways of operating.

If we take the perspective that listening is a characteristic that helps an organization be responsive, we need to look at how organizations "listen" as well as the impact that organizational listening can have on both company morale and company profits. An analysis of research exploring various aspects of organizations and their critical relationships reveals a clear connection between the quality of communication and the nature of the relationship an organization has with its publics.[39] Other research suggests that an organization's relationship with its important publics can be assessed by: *how dynamic* they are; *how open* they are; *how satisfied* both the organization and the public are; and *how well each side understands, agrees, or arrives at consensus* with each other.[40] Other important elements in these relationships are *trust* and *credibility*.[41]

A little later in this chapter we will look at some specific publics with whom organizations have relationships. Before we do that, however, we need to look at what determines whether or not an organization chooses to listen. Just as individuals are motivated to make choices to attend to a message, organizations also make these decisions. This type of decision is usually based upon the culture and climate that exists within the organization.

The Learning (Listening) Organization

We previously discussed several important aspects of organizations that can affect how organizations communicate and listen. They included the purpose, mission, culture and climate of an organization, as well as social support and leadership. Fundamental to all of these elements is learning. Much has been written about learning organizations.[42] However, a review of the literature highlights one fundamental issue – listening. In fact, as you will see in the pages below, we feel that a more accurate label for these learning organizations is **the listening organization**. As we noted earlier, an organization that strives to maintain two-way symmetrical relationships listens to its publics and operates as a listening entity. Just as a good listener is one who keeps an open mind to changes in the world around her/him, a listening organization does the same. Such organizations are open to creating and acquiring knowledge and converting it into organizational changes and new ways of "behaving." Listening organizations listen to the information and find ways to incorporate it into appropriate adaptations to meet the publics' needs. Think about why a school would offer online courses. First, they learn about the technology, about the changes in the population that has caused a demand for the courses, and the willingness of faculty to work in that platform. Then, based on the mission and values of the school, they will change how they deliver classes to meet the publics' need to take classes at times convenient to them, not the school.

A listening organization must possess a certain level of emotional intelligence (EI). As you remember from Chapter 4, emotional intelligence reflects our "ability to recognize and express emotion, and to regulate emotion in the self and others."[43] A listening organization, then, not only listens to information, it also has a good grasp of the changes in the business climate and the emotional ups and downs of its employees and other publics. As you can see, a lot of listening goes on in these organizations. Listening organizations are "learning" organizations.

According to *The Superintendent's Fieldbook*, there are several ways to recognize a learning (listening) organization:[44]

- People in the organization ask a lot of questions and *listen* to one another.
- Employees have access to pertinent, accurate, and timely information.
- Individuals can explain their thinking when they share ideas with others.
- Employees are aware of what's going on in all parts of the organization.
- People in the organization embrace the rituals of the organization's culture.
- Members of the organization use language and metaphors appropriate to that organization in their conversations.
- Organizational members at all levels take improvement seriously.
- Individuals tend to approach conflict in a constructive, straightforward manner.
- Finally, employees should be self-motivated and open to giving and receiving accurate and truthful feedback.

Think on it: Watch this interview with two Harvard Professors on learning organizations: https://youtu.be/lUP4WcfNyAA. What similarities can you identify between learning and listening organizations?

Organization Structure and Change

Organizations that exhibit the above characteristics of learning and listening find they are better able to adapt to the changes they encounter. One challenge facing all organizations is the shift in **organizational structure** that is occurring. Organizational structure refers to the alignment of personnel, or who reports to whom, who works with whom on what tasks, etc. As noted above, organizations are moving away from traditional structures aligned to a specific place, to networks that literally span the globe. Such changes have been spurred on by the exponential changes occurring in technology that make it possible for employees to work without being at the company's physical location or office. Telecommuting is on the rise. In 2014, 24% of the US workforce did all or some of their work from home; this number increased to 34% by 2015.[45] Worldwide, the number of telecommuters is estimated to be about 20%.[46] This shift in the shape and definition of the workplace has forced organizations to adapt their operating and communication methods to meet the changing needs of employees.[47] Importantly, it appears that different communication strategies are needed with employees, depending on whether they work on site or telecommute. For example, the concept of openness needs to be applied differently. People on site tend to want to know more information about the organization's objectives, policies, performance evaluations and other day-to-day operating information. This type of information seems to enhance employee morale. However, it appears to have the opposite effect on telecommuters.[48]

Think on it: Do you know a business in your area that would qualify as a listening organization? What qualities does it possess that leads you to think so?

A listening organization will recognize the possible impact of the changing structure of the workplace and make changes necessary to keep the morale of employees high. They will also recognize that workplace needs are changing and make organizational changes to support those needs. For example, if a company has a large number of employees who telecommute, they might adjust the location of their training. Instead of holding training sessions at the home office in Des Moines, or at a set facility in Dallas all of the time, they can choose to do regional meetings, so that employees across the country have an easier time getting to the meeting. Alternatively, the company could use webcasts or other similar technology to provide necessary training. Professor Fitch-Hauser experiences something similar to this when she works directly with an organization's employee at the employee's home rather than at the organization's home office, which is located in another state. This arrangement saves the employee time and the company money.

Another characteristic of a listening organization is that it is better able to make other changes as well, including **systemic changes.** One type of systemic change is how an organization handles large-scale organizational conflict. PECO Energy, Pennsylvania's largest utility faced such a challenge in the mid-1990s.[49] The International Brotherhood of Electrical Workers campaigned to unionize the employees. Even though the attempt failed, and PECO retained its non-union status, the company listened to their employees and instituted changes in how it handled employee conflict. The union was successful in its campaign to unionize the organization in 2004.[50] Today, PECO states proudly that they value openness to ideas and forward thinking.[51] These values indicate they are a listening organization.

Listening and Organizational Conflict

As we can see in the PECO example, another hallmark of a listening organization is being able to manage conflict when it occurs. Just as all interpersonal relationships will encounter conflict, all organizations will encounter conflict. Anytime you have interdependent parties (or departments) you have a situation that is ripe for conflict. Listening organizations realize that conflicts can be managed and they foster open communication, trust, and acceptance. In effect, these companies establish **listening safe zones.** To understand better how conflict can be managed, we need to take a good look at listening in this context. Case study 10.2 below addresses this topic.

Case Study 10.2　When Corporate Cultures Collide

Steve Goleman gets home from a difficult day and finds his son, Ben, studying at the kitchen table.

Hey dad, you look beat. Have a rough day at work?

Well, I am a bit frazzled. I'm working with the new managers from the Ulsan, South Korea plant and I'm having some problems getting them to listen to me about the labor issues we are facing.

Well, have you tried talking with them?

Of course I have, but they keep wasting my time by talking about their experience and background and asking questions about mine. I don't understand why they are stalling and aren't willing to face the issues. I know they have been successful in dealing with labor problems in Ulsan.

Oh dad, you're good in situations like this. I'm sure you'll come up with a solution. How about a snack while we wait on dinner?

Is there an organizational listening problem? If so, what is it?

What type of listening behavior is Mr. Goleman exhibiting toward the Korean management team?

What type of listening is Ben exhibiting toward his father? What are some possible responses Ben could have given that would have modeled good listening behavior for his father?

Hint: Remember the discussion of red, yellow, and green listening in Chapter 2.

In order to manage conflict, an organization must use the type of listening that creates an atmosphere in which information can be exchanged freely and solutions emerge. Workplace dispute expert, Erik Van Slyke, suggests that we should define this type of listening as:

> the process of becoming aware of all the cues that another party emits. It is a process of allowing another person to communicate the conscious and subconscious, both what the other person knows and what she or he may not yet understand. It is the act of attending to what another person is saying and what he or she is not saying. Listening demands work, but is the key to constructive conflict resolution.[52]

Listening plays two critical roles in conflict resolutions. First, it is the channel we use to *get the information* we need to resolve a conflict. If an organization or its representatives don't take the time to gather the necessary information, they won't have a clear understanding of what the root of the conflict is, or what the other party really wants. Listening organizations care enough to want to resolve a conflict so that all parties' needs are met. This doesn't mean they cave in to all demands, but that they listen to discover what the real underlying issues are and work to find mutually beneficial solutions.

The second critical role of listening is to *reduce the personal issues* of conflict. Every conflict, even organizational ones, has objective issues and personal issues.[53] **Objective issues** deal with facts, data, and information. Consequently they are easier to resolve. **Personal issues**, on the other hand, are just that – personal – and are typically based on emotions. When an organization or an individual takes the time to listen, it tends to calm the emotional mind, according to Van Slyke. He contends that active listening that is voluntary and "involves recognizing, understanding and accurately interpreting the messages received" gives the emotions in a conflict situation time to slow down and let the rational mind catch up.[54] Parties who feel they are being listened to feel more trust and willingness to work toward a solution.

© Mike Baldwin/Cornered

"What's important is that we found some common ground. Let's try not to get bogged down over who found it first."

While all organizations will face conflict, a listening organization will resolve conflict in a manner that manages the situation. These organizations are sensitive to the multitude of factors that affect conflicts such as cultural sensitivity and personality types. Case study 10.1 presents a situation that calls for cultural sensitivity. Once Mr. Goleman recognizes that part of the conflict he thinks he perceives is based on cultural differences, he will be better able to resolve it in a manner that will be satisfactory to all parties. And, once Ben completes his listening class, he will recognize his father's need for an empathic, green response rather than the yellow one he gave.

Employee Relations

Many of the examples used in the previous section emphasize the importance of listening to employees. Employees are also an important "public" in any organization. To be economically viable, companies have to focus on reducing employee turnover (it's expensive to continually train new ones), maintaining employee morale (related to increased productivity), and keeping its employees long term (encouraging outstanding employees to stay). In order to do this, companies must not only listen to their workers, regardless of whether they are happy or angry, but they must also engage in appropriate follow-through. For example, after receiving complaints about rudeness on the part of certain employees, one city implemented a range of customer service training for all city employees. When asked what happens when an employee received praise, the response from city management was that the letter goes into a file and is used during the employee's annual review. When another organization was asked the same question, the response was one of surprise; the thought of catching employees doing something right had never entered its organizational mind.

Listening to an employee or coworker who is angry is a special challenge. Good listening skills are the base of being able to handle the angry person successfully. Chapter 6 outlined steps suggested by Jeff Bannon to handle conflict.[55] We briefly touch on them again. First, *inquire,* letting your coworker talk, while you actively listen. Second, *empathize.* People like to feel that you can connect to them emotionally, particularly when they are feeling strong emotions such as anger. Third, *ask permission*, don't assume that a coworker wants or needs additional information or explanation. Asking implies control, something that people who are angry or upset may feel they lack. By listening carefully, you can help ensure that you *respond appropriately* (e.g., "what would help you make a decision"), and that you are positioned to move toward the final step suggested by Bannon, *explaining and offering choices* (assuming they are desired). See Chapter 6 if you need a further refresher of these concepts.

Customer Satisfaction

Recently, a student told us that he called a local pizza company to place an order. After repeatedly explaining his order to the person on the other end of the phone, he became exasperated, and asked to speak to the manager. He wanted to tell the manager about the employee's rude behavior. The manager cut him off and asked for his order. Our student explained that he would never order pizza from that company again and hung up. So, because the manager would not take a few minutes to listen, they have lost a long time, loyal customer.

This example emphasizes another critical target public that an organization must listen to – its customers. Listening organizations focus on developing customer relations. These relationships are critical today because consumers have easier access to more choices than ever before. So, companies must really listen to their customers and respond quickly in order to remain competitive.

The survey by the Institute for Organizational Performance we mentioned earlier found that 47% of the difference in low and high scores on customer service was predicted largely by trust. In order for an organization to generate trust in its customers, the organization must listen. Listening is essential in customer service because it is the only way for an organization to identify what the needs and wants of the customers are.[56] The researcher emphasized the importance of clearly focusing on how customers describe their specific complaints. Only by listening carefully to customers can the organization address tough customer-focused problems and challenges, such as dissatisfaction. The goal of good listening is to have satisfied customers.

In his classic business book, businessman Mark McCormick suggested that business people should listen aggressively to get insight about people in general.[57] He felt that businesses that could find a responsive chord and then respond to it are more successful in business. McCormick's ideas were echoed a decade later when authors Robert Kriegel and David Brandt suggested that companies should try to give customers something they didn't expect.[58] To do so, they felt that companies had to listen to the customers, be truly willing to receive information, and then use that information to build empathic relationships with their customers.

Let's look at a very traditional business, banking, to see how important listening to customers can be. Back in the early 2000s, Biff Motley, then senior vice president retail banking and marketing with Whitney Bank in New Orleans looked through many customer comments and found that customers who were satisfied with their banks reported feeling that bank employees cared about them, listened to their needs, and went beyond just the job description.[59] Consequently, he became an advocate of "listening banks." This example is a far cry from the example of Wells Fargo discussed earlier.

Another excellent example of the importance of listening to customers can be seen in the Pikes Fish Market mentioned earlier in this chapter. John Yokoyama makes the following statement about the importance of listening to customers:

> To make a difference, a salesperson has to listen to the customer. And genuinely want to help that person. The salesperson needs to take an interest in the customer, not as a means to an end but as an end in itself…
>
> If you are going to listen powerfully to your customers, you can't do it in order to make more money. If you do listen for that reason, it is just a form of manipulation. You are going to listen through the filter of "Come on, say yes." Or "Come on! You can spend more than that." When you truly listen to someone, you hold that person in high regard. You see him or her as naturally valuable with something significant to contribute.[60]

As the above quotation indicates, listening is critical in building trust with customers. Research by Rosemary Ramsey and Ravipreet Sohifound and others finds that perceptions of a sales person's listening behavior influence customer satisfaction with the sales person and whether or not they would do future business with that individual.[61] *Business Week* columnist, Michelle Nichols, feels that good sales people engage in "round-trip communication where both parties interact and connect – that is both parties listen and talk."[62] She recommends that business people, particularly sales staff, use "whole-body listening" that goes beyond hearing the words and includes tuning in to the nonverbal signals the customer is sending. Using this skill helps the sales person "hear" the tone of voice and other things the customer isn't saying. For example, a good whole-body listener will notice whether a customer's face lights up or looks confused. This type of information is critical to the sales person in knowing what to do next. Sales people who listen have customers who buy. Top sales people are simply better at asking questions and listening than others in sales.

Failure to Listen

Unfortunately, not all organizations listen. A recent Australian study examined organizations in Australia, the United Kingdom and the United States and found that many customer relationship plans forget the essential listening component. Jim Macnamara of The University of Technology in Sydney claims most customer relationship programs are focused on selling additional products to customers, instead of listening to them.[63] He gives an example of an insurance company that claims it listens. A client had to make numerous calls over a three week time period to get his claim approved. Ironically, the client received a request for feedback of their service. However, the survey only asked one question, allowing only one employee to be evaluated and the answer was skewed to get a "met expectations" answer. The company obviously didn't want answers that were contrary to what they wanted to hear. That's not listening. In order to be a listening organization, the company has to be open to all information.

When organizations don't maintain two-way symmetrical relationships with their publics, just like humans, they are subject to experiencing communication failure. Miscommunication or communication failure can be caused by a range of problems such as failure to receive the message, failure to understand the message, or failure to receive all or part of the message. Any of these problems can have a profound impact on an organization's relationships with its employees and customers. A brief look at miscommunication will help us better understand this problematic occurrence and its impact on listening at the organizational level.

Research on miscommunication has focused on interpersonal communication. However, we can find a number of parallels between the way organizations communicate with their receivers and the way people interact. Early research identified two types of communication failures: input and model.[64] **Input failures** involve incorrectly perceiving or interpreting information. When an organization misreads market research, feedback from employees, or other important parties, the organization suffers from input failure. **Model failure** occurs when the incoming information fails to fit with expectations or fit into the listener's existing schema. When this happens, the listener may make inappropriate inferences or reach the wrong conclusions about the information. On an organizational level, model failure can occur if an organization focuses more on their own ideas of product needs than they do on changing trends. For example, when the automotive industry continues to manufacture large SUVs rather than smaller, more fuel-efficient vehicles when gasoline prices skyrocket, they are exhibiting model failure. News that gas prices were increasing and consumers were concerned didn't fit with their expectations.

Miscommunication can also occur in cross-cultural settings. In order for organizations to be successful when they do business in other countries, they must shift their models to incorporate cultural concerns. One reason international companies like BMW, Mercedes, Toyota, Honda, and Hyundai are so successful in their US manufacturing plants is they took the time to study US expectations and customs. They knew that simply importing their business models to the US wouldn't work so they were smart enough to incorporate US business models into their US-based companies while maintaining key components of their own organizational models. As we saw in our previous case study, Mr. Goleman certainly hopes that S&K follows the example of other international firms.

Research on miscommunication shows we understand or interpret actions and discourse by making inferences about the goals we think the other party has and the plans they have for attaining those goals.[65] As listeners, organizations also attempt to understand their relevant publics by interpreting actions and feedback. They make inferences about their customers' goals and the goals of other important groups. When an organization practices two-way symmetrical communication, or actually listens to their publics, they are much more likely to make smart business decisions. Those organizations that fail to listen will be more likely to make decisions that alienate their customers and employees, and more likely to get embroiled in conflict.

Becoming a Listening Organization

Several times in this chapter we have utilized Seattle's Pikes Fish Market as an organization that practices listening. The Fish Market is a small company in an area where other vendors also sell fish. However, this particular market sets itself apart by the effort it puts into listening to its customers. In fact, this small company is the model for a series of books on customer service and motivation (as seen in our use of earlier examples). The owner of the market, John Yokoyama, suggests that one of the elements that make the market so famous and so popular is that the organization is built on being a listening organization. The following is a summary of how Yokoyama and the fish market became a listening organization.[66]

The transformation began when all of the employees of the market defined their vision to become world famous. Yokoyama had to make a decision to be open to employee ideas. In essence he had to listen to them and their ideas. As a listening leader, he had to listen to more than just the words, he had to listen to the entire message, whether he agreed with it or not. He had to, and continues to, work on suspending judgment and remaining open to ideas, which have ranged from reducing the number of hours in a work week to installing a webcam in the market.

This transformation called for speaking and listening responsibly. In essence, this means everyone who works there has to take responsibility for his own experience and perceptions, and be able, and willing, to recognize the difference between blame and personal responsibility. In a regular organization, we might expect to hear employees playing the blame game. If anything goes wrong, it must be someone's fault (usually someone else's or another department's). In a listening organization, each person takes personal responsibility to address problems and challenges. This certainly doesn't mean that every employee has to "fix" the problem; it means they have to be committed to working as a team member toward the team's efforts. In order for this to happen, employees have to be willing to express their frustrations and make it safe for everyone to say anything they feel needs to be said. They have to have a listening "safe zone." Certainly, they can become upset by some of the things that are said. However, they have to commit to being quiet and to listening. The listener has to take responsibility for his own reactions and feelings.

A listener who takes responsibility for his/her own reactions as a listener must have a high level of emotional maturity, and be of high emotional intelligence. As they listen to a fellow worker, they understand that they, as a listener, are attaching emotional energy to the words in the message. This emotional energy has a direct impact on how they react. They also realize that individuals may hear the same words, but they often make different choices about how to react to those words. An emotionally mature crew in an organization like the fish market takes control of their emotional reactions. So, when a customer (or fellow crew member), is having a bad day and takes his or her frustration out on the crew, they are able to create a safe listening zone in the workplace. As a result, they are less likely to get defensive when a customer gets angry or unpleasant. They know that the more they listen, the sooner the other person will become calmer.

An emotionally mature listener can, in turn, become a more responsible speaker. So instead of using blaming language when discussing a problem or a reaction to something, the emotionally mature speaker takes responsibility for his or her reactions. **Blaming language** is language that focuses the blame and responsibility on the other person. Phrases like "you make me so mad," is an example of this type of language. Such phrases suggest that the other person has "power" over the speaker. As a good listener, you should try to communicate in a less threatening and more emotionally mature way. So you would use a phrase like, "I perceive your comment in this way and I feel this way about it. I'm expressing this to you because it is hindering my working effectively with you."

However, before organizations can build empathic relationships with customers, they need to have systems in place to listen to the customer. Marketing scholars Berry and Parasuraman suggest organizations need to listen to three categories of customers: external, internal, and competitors' customers.[67] The listening system should be able to get a picture of these groups and their needs from numerous perspectives.

An example of a listening organization that has excellent customer relations is Virgin Atlantic Airways. One of the few financially successful airlines in the world, this company listens to the needs of its customers. By empathizing with customers, Sir Richard Branson has built an airline that provides little extras that keep customers coming back. For example, knowing how uncomfortable it can be to be strapped into a seat for a long time, Virgin Atlantic Airways instituted stand-up bars in their cabins. Additionally, they offer nail treatments and massages on board long flights. The airline was also the first to offer seatback videos so that flyers could watch movies they wanted to watch, when they wanted to watch them.[68] How did all these innovations occur?

Any organizational listening system should allow an organization's managers to get involved with customers in such a way they can get valuable information from the customers' perspective. To do this, an organization should gather information that is relevant, precise, useful, credible, understandable, and timely. Today, organizations listen to their customers by conducting focus groups or surveys, monitoring calls and emails to their customer service centers, establishing chat rooms and blogs for real-time interaction with customers, using Twitter and monitoring other social media sites where their company is being discussed. Getting the information isn't enough to improve customer relationships, however. Organizations must respond appropriately in a timely manner and address challenges while they are still important and before they morph into something more serious. Being responsive to customer needs directly impacts the customer, and hopefully leads to increased satisfaction. However, additional benefits are increased employee morale and good public relations. Responsive companies get noticed, whether by word of mouth or some other type of public recognition. So, good listening can lead to good news, and good news can lead to increased profits – a win–win situation for an organization and all of its publics.

Summary

This chapter has looked at how organizations listen. Just as listening is a critical competency for an individual communicator, it is a critical aspect of being a successful business.

Intelligent organizations listen to the needs of their employees and have lower turnover rates and better overall morale. Likewise, companies that listen to their customers build stronger relationships and achieve higher satisfaction ratings. Listening isn't just a human skill, it is also a critical business skill.

Although this chapter focuses on organizations as the listening entity, we can learn to be better listeners by using a listening organization as a model. We offer the following three suggestions:

* Within ourselves, we need to develop a sense of deep inquiry. That requires us not just to acknowledge what the other person is saying by giving appropriate feedback, it requires us to ask the right questions. A joking response that is often used when something happens is, "be careful what you ask for, you might just get it." Well, a deep inquirer will craft questions to get exactly what he or she needs to know. So the questions will go beyond the superficial and "socially rote."

- In addition, the questions will be accompanied with a calm and receptive mindset that is indicative of deep listening. Suspending judgment and bias are critical competencies used by the listening leader.
- Listen to the whole message. Whether we are serving a customer or not, the people to whom we are listening want to say what they want to say. If we interrupt them or finish ideas for them, or zone out because we think we know what they are going to say, we provide a disservice and won't be able to meet their needs.

Key Concepts

Organization
Mission statement
Organizational Cognition
Organizational Culture
Culture Gaps
Organizational Climate
    Alignment
    Collaboration
Organizational Social Support
    Action facilitating
    Instrumental
    Informational
    Nurturing
Inquiry
Organizational Listening
Two-way Symbolic Model of Public Relations
Publics
Listening Organization
Organizational Structure
Systemic Changes
Listening Safe Zones
Objective Issues
Personal Issues
Input Failure
Model Failure
Blaming Language

Discussion Questions

1. Think of two incidents where you had a negative experience with a company – one where the ultimate outcome was negative and one where it ended more positively. What occurred? What differentiated the two outcomes? The two companies? Did you feel listened to by both companies? Why or Why not? What type of listening occurred (red, yellow, or green)?
2. Think of a recent place you have worked. Would you describe the company or organization as having a listening culture or climate? Why or Why not?

3.   Keeping in mind our description of organizational climate, culture, etc., describe the "perfect company" that you would like to work for. How does your description explicitly or implicitly focus on listening?

Listening Activities

1.   Check out paper or online job listings for customer service representatives. How do they (or don't they) emphasize listening skills?
2.   In groups of three to four individuals, identify three to four companies that have "good" or positive public images. What makes you identify them as "good" companies? What characteristics do they share? Do these characteristics suggest they value organizational listening? Are these characteristics reflected in the company mission statements?
3.   During the recent Gulf Oil spill, British Petroleum (BP) received a lot of negative publicity for how they handled the disaster. In groups of three to four individuals, review some of the negative stories associated with the disaster. What do they suggest about input or model failure on the part of BP?

Notes

1 Shockley-Zalabak, 2006
2 Bryson, 2011
3 Hull, 2013
4 Ford Motor Company, 2007; The Ford standards of corporate conduct are updated periodically but still rely on the 2007 document as a base.
5 Ford Motor Company, 2007
6 Littlejohn & Foss, 2011
7 Schein, 2010
8 Eisenberg, Goodall, & Trethewey, 2010.
9 Maxfield, 2016
10 Glazer, 2015
11 Wells Fargo, 2016
12 Maxfield, 2016
13 Rockoff, Radnofsky, & Hernandez, 2016
14 Furnham & Goodstein, 1997
15 Ashforth, 1985
16 Van Maanen & Schein, 1979
17 Freedman, 2011
18 Koles & Kondath, 2015
19 Johnston & Johnston, 2005
20 Eisenberg, et al., 2010, p. 213
21 Albrecht & Goldsmith, 2003
22 duPre, 2013
23 Fortune, 2017
24 Burleson, 1994
25 Hrywna, 2016
26 Segedin, 2016, p. 6
27 Janusik & Wolvin, 2006
28 Yokoyama & Michelli, 2004, p. 87
29 Witt, 2017

30 Gardner et al., 2010
31 Breen, 2005
32 Sharf, 2016
33 Walters, 2005
34 Ledingham & Brunig, 1998
35 Burnside-Lawry, 2012
36 Shockley-Zalabak, 2006
37 Grunig & Hunt, 1984
38 Simpson, 2014
39 Grunig, Grunig, & Ehling, 1992; Grunig, Grunig, & Dozier, 2002
40 Ledingham, Bruning, & Wilson, 1999; Grunig, 1993
41 Grunig, et al., 1992
42 O'Keeffe, 2002; Serenko, Bontins, & Hardie, 2007; Wang & Ahmed, 2003
43 Salovey, Mayer, Caruso, & Lopes, 2003
44 Harvey, Cambron-McCabe, Cunningham, & Koff, 2013
45 Jones, 2015; US Bureau of Statistics, 2016
46 Reaney, 2012
47 Allen, Golden, & Shockley, 2015
48 Rosenfeld, Richman, & May, 2004
49 Lipsky, Seeber, & Fincher, 2003
50 IBEW (International Brotherhood of Electrical Workers), 2004
51 PECO, 2017
52 Van Slyke, 1999, pp. 98–99
53 Van Slyke, 1999
54 Van Slyke, 1999, p. 101
55 Bannon, 2003
56 Tschohl, 1994
57 McCormick, 1984
58 Kriegel & Brandt, 1996
59 Motley, 2005
60 Yokoyama & Michelli, 2004, pp. 98–99
61 Malshe & Pryor, 2004; Ramsey & Sohi, 1997
62 Nichols, 2006
63 Macnamara, 2015
64 Ringle & Bruce, 1980
65 Berger, 2001
66 Yokoyama & Michelli, 2004
67 Berry & Parasuraman,1997
68 Conley, 2005

Additional Readings

Dwyer, J. (2012). *Business communication handbook* (9th ed.). Frenchs Forest, NSW: Pearson Australia.

Guffey, M. E., Rhodes, K., & Rogin, P. (2006). Workplace listening and nonverbal communication (pp. 50–67). In *Business communication: Process & product*. Toronto, Ontario: Nelson Education.

Macnamara, J. (2015, May). Creating an 'architecture of listening' in organizations: The basis of engagement, trust, healthy democracy, social equity, and business sustainability. Sydney, NSW: University of Technology Sydney. Retrieved from www.uts.edu.au/sites/default/files/fass-organizational-listening-report.pdf.

Nohria, N., & Khurana, R. (Eds.). (2010). *Handbook of leadership theory and practice.* Boston: Harvard Business School.

References

Albrecht, T. L., & Goldsmith, D. J. (2003). Social support, social networks, and health. In A. Marshall, K. I. Miller, R. Parrott, & T. L. Thompson (Eds.), *Handbook of health communication* (pp. 263–284). Hillsdale, NJ: LEA.

Allen, T., Golden, T., & Shockley, K. (2015). How effective is telecommuting? Assessing the status of our scientific findings. *Psychological Science in the Public Interest, 16*, 40–68.

American Cancer Society. (2017). Mission statement. Retrieved from www.cancer.org/about-us/who-we-are/mission-statements.html.

Ashforth, B. E. (1985). Climate formation: Issues and extensions. *Academy of Management Review, 10*, 837–847.

Bannon, J. (2003, Oct.). Anger at work: Whether it's others' or your own, here's how to deal with it. *Talent Development, 57*, 64–65.

Berger, C. R. (2001). Miscommunication and communication failure. In W. P. Robinson & H. Giles (Eds.), *The new handbook of language and social psychology* (pp. 177–192). Chichester, UK: Wiley.

Berry, L. L., & Parasuraman, A. (1997), Listening to the customer: The concept of a service-quality information system. *Sloan Management Review, 38*, 65–76.

Breen, B. (2005, December 1). The Seoul of design. *Fast company.* Retrieved from www.fastcompany.com/magazine/101/samsung.html.

Bryson, J. (2011). *Strategic planning for public and nonprofit organizations* (4th ed.). San Francisco, CA: Jossey Bass.

Burleson, B. R. (1994). Comforting messages: Features, functions, and outcomes. In J. A. Daly & J. M. Wiemann (Eds.), *Strategic interpersonal communication* (pp. 135–161). Hillsdale, NJ: Erlbaum.

Burnside-Lawry, J. (2012). Listening and participatory communication: A model to assess organizational listening competency. *The International Journal of Listening, 26*, 102–121.

Conley, L. (2005, October 1). Profitable player runner-up: Virgin Atlantic. *Fast Company.* Retrieved from www.fastcompany.com/magazine/99/open_customer-virgin.html?

du Pre, A. (2013). *Communicating about health: Current issues and perspectives* (4th ed.). New York: Oxford.

Eisenberg, E. M., Goodall, H. L., Jr., & Trethewey, A. (2010). *Organizational communication: Balancing creativity and constraint* (6th ed.). New York: Bedford/St. Martin's Press.

Ford Motor Company. (2007). Ford standards of corporate conduct. Retrieved from http://corporate.ford.com/microsites/sustainability-report-2015-16/doc/sr15-code-of-conduct.pdf.

Fortune. (2017). The 100 best companies to work for. Retrieved from http://beta.fortune.com/best-companies.

Freedman, J. (2011, June 9). Case study: Emotional intelligence at the Sheraton Studio City Hotel. Six Seconds Institute for Organizational Performance. Retrieved from www.6seconds.org/2011/06/09/case-eq-sheraton.

Furnham, A., & Goodstein, L. (1997). The organizational climate questionnaire (OCQ). *The 1997 Annual: Volume 2, Consulting,* (pp. 163–181). San Francisco, CA: Jossey-Bass.

Gardner, W. L., Lowe, K. B., Moss, T. W., Mahoney, K. T., & Cogliser, C. C. (2010). Scholarly leadership of the study of leadership: A review of *The Leadership Quarterly's* second decade, 2000–2009. *Leadership Quarterly, 21*, 922–958.

Glazer, E. (2015) At Wells Fargo, how far did bank's sales culture go? *The Wall Street Journal.* Retrieved from www.wsj.com/articles/at-wells-fargo-how-far-did-banks-sales-culture-go-1448879643.

Grunig, J. E. (1993). On the effects of marketing, media relations, and public relations: Images, agendas, and relationships. In W. Armbrecht, H. Avenarius, & U. Zabel (Eds.), *Image und PR* (pp. 263–295). Opladen, Germany: Westdeutscher Verlag.

Grunig, L. A., Grunig, J. E., & Dozier, D. M. (2002). *Excellent public relations and effective organizations: A study of communication management in three countries.* Mahwah, NJ: LEA.

Grunig, L. A., Grunig, J. E., & Ehling, W. P. (1992). What is an effective organization? In J. E. Grunig (Ed.), *Excellence in public relations and communication management* (pp. 65–90). Hillsdale, NJ: LEA.

Grunig, J. E., & Hunt, T. (1984). *Managing public relations.* New York: Holt, Rinehart & Winston.

Harvey, J., Cambron-McCabe, N., Cunningham, L. L., & Koff, R. H. (2013). *The superintendent's fieldbook: A guide for leaders of learning* (2nd ed.). Thousand Oaks, CA: Corwin.

Hull, P. (2013, January 10). Answer 4 questions to get a great mission statement. *Forbes.* Retrieved from www.forbes.com/sites/patrickhull/2013/01/10/answer-4-questions-to-get-a-great-mission-statement/#50c5878067f5.

Hrywna, M. (2016, April 1). 2016 NPT best nonprofits to work. *The NonProfit Times.* Retrieved from www.thenonprofittimes.com/wp-content/uploads/2016/04/4-1-16_SR_BestNonprofits.pdf.

IBEW (International Brotherhood of Electrical Workers). (2004, July 27). IBEW wins big at PECO... again! Retrieved from www.ibew.org/articles/04daily/0407/040727_peco.htm.

Janusik, L. A., & Wolvin, A. D. (2006). 24 hours in a day: A listening update to the time studies. *International Journal of Listening, 23*, 104–120.

Johnston, A., & Johnston, L. (2005). The relationship between organizational climate, occupational type and workaholism. *Journal of Psychology, 34*, 181–188.

Jones, J. M. (2015, August 19). In US, telecommuting climes to 37%. Gallop. Retrieved from www.gallup.com/poll/184649/telecommuting-work-climbs.aspx.

Koles, B., & Kondath, B. (2015). Organizational climate in Hungary, Portugal, and India: A cultural perspective. *AI & Society, 30*, 251–259.

Kriegel, R., & Brandt, D. (1996). *Sacred cows make the best burgers.* New York: Warner.

Ledingham, J. A., & Bruning, S. D. (1998). Relationship management in public relations: Dimensions of an organization–public relationship. *Public Relations Review, 24*, 55–65.

Ledingham, J. A., Bruning, S. D., & Wilson, L. J. (1999). Time as an indicator of the perceptions and behavior of members of a key public: Monitoring and predicting organization – Public relationships. *Journal of Public Relations Research, 11*, 167–183.

Littlejohn, S. W., & Foss, K. A. (2011). *Theories of human communication* (10th ed.). Belmont, CA: Wadsworth.

Lipsky, D. B., Seeber, R. L., & Fincher, R. (2003). *Emerging systems for managing workplace conflict.* San Francisco, CA: Jossey-Bass.

McCormick, M. (1984). *What they don't teach you at Harvard business school: Notes from a street-smart executive.* New York: Bantam.

Macnamara, J. (2015, May). Creating an 'architecture of listening' in organizations: The basis of engagement, trust, healthy democracy, social equity, and business sustainability. Sydney: University of Technology. Retrieved from www.uts.edu.au/sites/default/files/fass-organizational-listening-report.pdf.

Malshe, A., & Pryor, S. (2004). Relational listening and impression management in salesperson-customer relationships. *Advances in consumer research, 31*, 447–448.

Maxfield, J. (2016, December 30). Wells Fargo fake accounts scandal is still having a big impact on business. *Business Insider.* Retrieved from www.businessinsider.com/wells-fargo-fake-accounts-scandal-impact-on-business-2016-12.

Motley, L. B. (2005, October). The benefits of listening to customers. *ABA Bank Marketing, 37*, 43.

Nichols, M. (2006, September 14). Listen up for better sales. *Bloomberg Businessweek.* Retrieved from www.businessweek.com.

O'Keeffe, T. (2002). Organizational learning: A new perspective. *Journal of European Industrial Training, 26*, 130–141.

PECO. (2017). Leadership & values. Retrieved from www.peco.com/AboutUs/Pages/LeadershipValues.aspx.

Ramsey, R. P., & Sohi, R. A. (1997). Listening to your customers: The impact of perceived salesperson listening behavior on relational outcomes. *Journal of the Academy of Marketing Science, 25*, 127–137.

Reaney, P. (2012, January 24). About one in five workers worldwide telecommute: poll. *Reuters Technology News.* Retrieved from www.reuters.com/article/us-telecommuting-idUSTRE80N1IL20120124.

Ringle, M. H., & Bruce, B. C. (1980). Conversation failure. In W. G. Lehnert & M. H. Ringle (Eds.), *Strategies for natural language processing* (pp. 203–221). Hillsdale, NJ: LEA.

Rockoff, J. D., Radnofsky, L., & Harnandez, D. (2016, September 22). Mylan CEO faces tough questioning in congressional Epipen hearing. *The Wall Street Journal.* Retrieved from www.wsj.com/articles/mylan-ceo-to-shift-blame-on-epipen-pricing-at-house-hearing-1474466910.

Rosenfeld, L. B., Richman, J. M., & May, S. K. (2004). Information adequacy, job satisfaction, and organizational culture in a dispersed-network organization. *Journal of Applied Communication Research, 32,* 28–54.

Salovey, P., Mayer, J. D., Caruso, D., & Lopes, P. N. (2003). In S. J. Lopez & C. R. Snyder (Ed.), *Positive psychological assessment: A handbook of models and measures.* (pp. 251–265). Washington, DC: APA.

Schein, E. (2010). *Organizational culture and leadership* (4rd ed.). San Francisco, CA: Jossey-Bass.

Segedin, A. (2016, April 1). Best large organizations: Making sure staff members aren't just numbers. *The NonProfit Times.* Retrieved from www.thenonprofittimes.com/wp-content/uploads/2016/04/4-1-16_SR_BestNonprofits.pdf.

Serenko, A., Bontis, N., & Hardie, T. (2007). Organizational size and knowledge flow: A proposed theoretical link. *Journal of Intellectual Capital, 8,* 610–627.

Sharf, S. (2016, May 26). The world's largest tech companies 2016: Apple bests Samsung, Microsoft and alphabet. *Forbes.* Retrieved from www.forbes.com/sites/samanthasharf/2016/05/26/the-worlds-largest-tech-companies-2016-apple-bests-samsung-microsoft-and-alphabet/#68a630bcb661.

Shockley-Zalabak, P. (2006) *Essentials of organizational communication* (6th ed.) Boston: Allen & Bacon.

Simpson, E. (2014). The four models in Grunig's and Hunt's PR theories. LinkedIn. Retrieved from www.linkedin.com/pulse/20140611205435-83891954-the-four-models-in-grunig-s-and-hunt-s-pr-theories.

The Coca-Cola Company. (2017). Mission, vision & values. Retrieved from www.coca-colacompany.com/our-company/mission-vision-values.

The Ritz-Carlton Hotel Company, LLC. (2017). The credo. Retrieved from www.ritzcarlton.com/en/about/gold-standards.

Tschohl, J. (1994). *Achieving excellence through customer service.* Englewood Cliffs, NJ: Prentice-Hall.

US Bureau of Statistics. (2016, July 8). 24% of employed people did some or all of their work from home. *TED: The Economics Daily.* Retrieved from www.bls.gov/opub/ted/2016/24-percent-of-employed-people-did-some-or-all-of-their-work-at-home-in-2015.htm.

Van Maanen, J., & Schein, E. H. (1979). Toward a theory of organizational socialization. In B. Staw (Ed.), *Research in organizational behavior* (Vol. 1, pp. 209–264). Greenwich: JAI.

Van Slyke, E. (1999). *Listening to conflict: Finding constructive solutions to workplace disputes.* New York: AMACOM.

Walmart. (2017). Our history. Retrieved from http://corporate.walmart.com/our-story/our-history.

Walters, J. (2005). Fostering a culture of deep inquiry and listening. *Journal for Quality & Participation, 28,* 4–7.

Wang, C. L., & Ahmed, P. K. (2003). Organizational learning: A critical review. *The learning organization, 10,* 8–17.

Wells Fargo. (2017). Our values. Retrieved from www.wellsfargo.com/about/corporate/vision-and-values/our-values.

Witt, C. (2017). The listening leader. Witt Communications. Retrieved from http://wittcom.com/the-listening-leader.

Yokoyama, J. & Michelli, J. (2004). *When fish fly: Lessons for creating a vital and energized workplace.* New York: Hyperion.

11 Listening and Health

Psychological and Physical Realities

Case Study 11.1 The Physician's Office

This discussion takes place in an examination room at a doctor's office. NaMii Kim's grandmother hasn't been feeling well, so she has gone to see her primary care physician, Dr. Julia Moore.

Dr. Moore: *Hello, Mrs. Kim, what seems to be wrong today?*

Mrs. Kim: *I haven't been feeling very good lately, it seems, uh, it seems that …*

Dr. Moore is looking at her chart and interrupts Mrs. Kim: *Hmmmm, I see your temperature is okay and your blood pressure has stabilized. The medicine we have you on seems to be doing the trick. Is something else bothering you today?*

Mrs. Kim: *I just don't feel good and I don't … uh … my back hurts some … and*

Dr. Moore: *Well, let's draw some blood and run some tests. It's been a while since we've done that. Let's see what it tells us. After the nurse takes the blood, make an appointment to come back next week to get the test results. Talk to you soon.*

The most recent data available, a 2012 National Ambulatory Medical Care Survey by the Centers for Disease Control, reports that 928.6 million medical visits occurred that year.[1] Unfortunately, many of these visits likely reflected the type of interaction presented in the case study above. Mrs. Kim's interaction illustrates several common patient experiences. An early study by medical researchers Howard Beckman and Richard Frankel found that doctors tend to only let their patients talk for an average of *18 seconds* before interrupting them. The longest time any doctor in their study listened was 2.5 minutes.[2] Follow-up research, done over a decade later, found that the amount of time physicians let their patients talk before interrupting them had increased to a whopping *23 seconds*.[3] In related research, Frankel found that 15 out of 16 patients who were interrupted failed to resume what they were talking about after they were interrupted.[4] Dr. Herbert Fred, associate editor for the *Texas Heart Institute Journal* put the challenge in these words, "The disease of not listening strikes everyone from time to time. Although this malady is prevalent in medical practice today, it rarely receives the attention it deserves."[5]

Good communication affects our health both psychologically and physically. As the above example shows, listening plays a critical role in our health care. In the context of provider–patient interactions, active, mindful listening has been described as transformative.[6] Nirmal Joshi, chief medical officer for Pinnacle Health System, emphasized the point in a recent *New York Times* op-ed article, when he wrote "A good bedside manner is simply good medicine."[7]

In this chapter, we look at the impact of listening on health. We first examine the general importance of listening to your physical and psychological health. We then examine patient–health provider communication, including tips that will help improve communication with your own health care professionals.

The Importance of Health Communication

Communication is central to successful health care encounters.[8] We have to be able to communicate our symptoms and physical ailments. Research in this area has consistently found that good communication with health providers promotes trust in a doctor's diagnosis, increases patient compliance with treatment plans, leads to improved symptoms, and improved management of chronic diseases.[9] For example, studies conducted at the University of California at Irvine show that good doctor–patient communication leads to lower blood sugar levels in people with diabetes and lower blood pressure in hypertensive patients.[10] Our overall satisfaction with both the people and the process of health care delivery is directly related to good communication.

Satisfaction, in turn, affects a number of patient to doctor communication factors. Important factors include the level of respect and trust we feel toward health professionals as well as the level of openness we will have with them. This communication is even more important for the estimated 77 million individuals with basic or low health literacy – those who have difficulty reading medical directions, following directions on a prescription bottle, or using other health information.[11] The financial impact of low health literacy is estimated to range between $106 and $238 billion in health expenses each year.[12] **Health literacy** involves more than the ability to read and write; it includes having both access to health information as well as the willingness to research and use it effectively. Athena Du Pré argues that effective interpersonal communication can help these patients avoid costly medical errors and delays as well as the associated pain and loss of quality of life that may occur. In short, good listening is critical in compensating for the impact of low health literacy.

Social changes have affected how we approach health care and have resulted in major changes in how health care is managed. By the early 2000s, 88% of US physicians were associated with some type of managed health care system.[13] One of the results is that doctors and other health care providers become responsible for seeing many more patients, as many as 15–20 in an hour if not more. Obviously, such a schedule creates problems for providers and patients who want to listen and communicate well with one another.[14]

Social changes have also affected our perceptions of physicians. At the beginning of the 20th century, doctors were viewed as "all-knowing" individuals who dispensed good health. This **paternalist** approach affected the doctor–patient relationship in many ways. For example, good patients did not question their physicians and they were expected to do as they were told. During the 1970s, 1980s, and 1990s, the attitude toward doctors shifted as did their relationships with patients. Many patients and doctors developed and expected a more **consumeristic** approach. As consumers of medicine, patients were expected to actively participate in their health. Today, patients and physicians are encouraged to take a more **collaborative** approach – jointly working toward good health.

The increasing emphasis on collaborative communication reflects a growing interest in patient–health care provider communication. An interest that is further reflected in the research published in medical, nursing, and other allied health journals, which increasingly addresses the importance of listening and communicating well in health care contexts.[15]

Listening and Psychological Wellbeing

While listening is important in any health-related encounter, it can be critical to those who work in the helping or therapeutic professions (e.g., psychiatrists, psychologists, social workers, marriage and family therapists). As psychologists and counselors Steven Graybar and Leah Leonard write, "If the foundation of successful psychotherapy is the therapeutic relationship, then the mortar of the therapeutic relationship is listening."[16]

We introduced therapeutic and relational listening and social support in Chapter 2. Here, we expand on these types of listening examining them in the context of psychological and psychiatric counseling. The most prevalent approach to counseling today is the patient or client-centered approach.[17] This approach focuses upon the client as the primary source of identifying means to solve his or her problem. With the counselor's help, patients and clients can arrive at a solution that is the most workable for them.

The quality of the relationship between patients and their counselor/therapist is important. In fact, one study found it to be the strongest predictor of a positive outcome for the patient, no matter the treatment regimen.[18] Graybar and Leonard argue that listening is the foundation of psychotherapy. They note that, "listening and being listened to are the cornerstones of psychological development, psychological relatedness, and psychological treatment."[19] They go on to assert that people who see therapists often do so because they "have been listened to far too little in their lives."[20] This statement poignantly illustrates the importance of listening to our lives. But, sometimes we need to be listened to by someone who is separate from our daily lives – who can listen compassionately, but also in a way that allows us to assess relationships, situations, or events more objectively and effectively. Through listening, counselors and therapists can help identify the underlying problems a patient or client may have and empower them to address their problems meaningfully.

Elements of Reflective Listening

All therapists use important communication skills, most of which are related to relational listening. A key element, **reflective listening**, was introduced by early psychologist Carl Rogers.[21] These skills include asking questions, reflection, selective reflection, empathy building, and checking for understanding. Questions, particularly *open-ended questions*, are quite important. They allow us to expand on our story or comments, and encourage us to continue speaking. *Reflection*, also known as echoing, includes restatement and paraphrasing. This type of repetition is important in counseling sessions because it not only signals that the counselor is listening, it also acts as a verbal prompt encouraging the individual to continue speaking. *Selective reflection* is a more refined type of reflection. Counselors use this technique to identify information that the client appears to be emphasizing or that is emotionally charged.[22] *Empathy building statements* allow therapists to acknowledge their client's feelings and indicate they understand those feelings. This aspect of counseling can be quite important, especially if the person is from cultures such as the United States or England where people are typically taught that they are supposed to control their feelings. *Checking for understanding* can be an important method of ensuring accuracy. It is not unusual in counseling sessions for patients to quickly introduce a number of topics into a discussion. As a result, counselors may want to do a verbal check to determine if they have identified the primary issues troubling a person. This technique is also used by counselors to review topics that have been covered over the course of a session.

Think on it: Think back on the last time a friend came to you with a personal crisis. How did you help them? Did you engage in any of the communication skills therapists' use? How might you use the advice presented here in a similar situation in the future?

What sets the best therapists apart? According to Swiss psychologists Daniel Gassmann and Klaus Grawe, they are able to assess their clients' strengths and abilities.[23] As they assist their clients in recognizing and accepting their problems, they remind clients of their strong points, while at the same time pointing out the support available to them. Importantly, they use this technique throughout the counseling session – not just at the end. It is no surprise, then, that effective listening is an important skill for those in the helping professions – professionals and volunteers. Another important quality is **empathy** – empathic concern and empathic understanding.

The importance of empathy and empathic listening can be seen in the findings of a study at a mental health facility in Hong Kong.[24] This research found that psychiatric inpatients were more likely to have a positive perception of being physically restrained if the staff displayed concern for them, actively listened to them, and provided information about the restraint while it was in use.

As you can see, listening is fundamental to the work of mental health professionals. In the next section, we'll discover that it is just as important to our physical health.

Listening and Physical Wellbeing

There are times when we get sick and have to see a health professional. Our illness may be as simple as a cold, or as complex as a chronic or terminal illness. In this section we address communication issues between health providers and patients – highlighting the importance of listening on both sides of the health team. The negative outcomes for poor listening can range from mild to severe. For instance, as a patient, you may take food with your medicine (when you shouldn't have) and end up with a stomach ache. Consider the following real-life example. Mason worked at a manufacturing plant. One day he pulled a muscle while repairing a piece of equipment. His supervisor sent him to visit the company doctor. At the office, Mason told both the nurse *and* the doctor that he was severely allergic to aspirin. The doctor gave him samples of medication along with a prescription. On his way home (a 30 minute drive), Mason decided to wait to take the medicine because he did not have anything in the car to drink. As soon as he got home, he took the pills and immediately knew it included aspirin and that he was in trouble. He also knew better than to wait for an ambulance. His wife drove him to the hospital, running red lights on the way. By the time they arrived at the emergency room, Mason had stopped breathing. Mason was luckier than some patients – he lived and suffered no ill effects from the incident.

Unfortunately, Mason's experience isn't unique. This event represents only one of the many medical errors estimated to occur every day in this country. Errors are produced by combinations of human factors as well as system factors. Changing definitions and methods of data gathering have led to estimates that vary widely. One early report by the Institute of Medicine found that as many as 98,000 people die yearly from medical errors, while a more recent review published in the *Journal of Patient Safety* suggests there may be upwards of 400,000 deaths a year.[25] (Importantly, these figures only address errors associated with hospital care.) Further, the majority of these mistakes are attributed to communication errors of some type, including poor listening.[26]

In this book we have covered a number of aspects of listening that have implications for your health-related interactions. For instance, in Chapter 1, we discussed the role of recall as an important aspect of why Listening MATERRS. The type of information we receive appears to affect our ability to recall it. For example, patients seem to recall information about their medication better than other information (e.g., how to wrap a bandage, what to eat or avoid eating). In addition, the more information provided, the greater the chance for information overload and the less a patient will remember. Of course, the more serious the illness, the more likely a patient will be overwhelmed and misunderstand or simply not process the physician's message.

Your schema about physicians will also affect how you interact with your doctors. For example, if you believe that physicians hold a higher status than you, you may feel at a disadvantage when interacting with them. Keep in mind, while they know a lot about medicine, you know your body and your illness – you are both experts in your own way! Combining your expertise can lead to better health for you.

Another important schema is the one we hold for our personal health. Do you view yourself as a "healthy" person? Would you describe your health as excellent, great, good, poor? What happens if you are diagnosed with a chronic illness (e.g., allergies, asthma, cystic fibrosis, sickle-cell anemia)? What if it is an acute illness (e.g., cold, flu, sprained ankle)? The schemas we hold for ourselves are important ones and they are difficult to change. Like all schemas, they have a way of shaping how we listen to information. If you consider yourself to be healthy, you will probably expect to hear that whatever is bothering you is temporary, that it will soon end. You may have difficulty listening to anything to the contrary.

Factors Affecting Patient–Provider Interactions

In addition to our health schemas, a number of other factors can influence how patients communicate with health care providers. We touch on several of these below.

Nature of the Visit

Why you are visiting your doctor and the diagnosis you receive can affect how you listen.[27] If you have a general check-up and the physician says all is fine, then you may not pay much attention to her directions to cut down on fatty foods in your diet because of a slightly elevated cholesterol level. If, on the other hand, she tells you that you have a chronic kidney disease, you may find it difficult to process the rest of the conversation. Such a message creates anxiety and fear, both of which interfere with your ability to attend to the message. While many studies have reported that patients tend to be passive and deferential when interacting with medical experts, a recent study in the *Journal of Health Communication* suggests that context matters. Professors Wayne Beach and David Dozier found that new cancer patients were more communicatively active when meeting with their oncologists, asking more questions and expressing fears as they attempted to manage the uncertainties associated with their disease.[28]

Patient Sex

Men and women differ in their use of the medical system and views of health care. For example, women are more likely to go see their physicians and see them more often than do men.[29] At least one study suggests that women's greater contact with health providers and the health system may lead them to develop a more consumeristic approach to patient–provider interactions.[30] Case Study 11.2 illustrates this tendency.

Case Study 11.2 Deena's Story

When I was 29 I had a cousin die of skin cancer – melanoma. He had felt a lump under his arm, but didn't think too much about it. When it got uncomfortable, he finally went to the doctor to have it checked on. It was too late. Surgery removed much of his chest wall, lymph nodes and shoulder. The chemo was awful. He died six months after he was diagnosed.

Pretty much everyone in the family went to be checked out by their dermatologist, including myself. After I got back to the exam room, I told Dr. "Smith" what happened. I also told him about how different skin cancers seem to run in the family. Both my mother and grandmother were diagnosed with basal cell and squamous cell (skin) cancer. Several years back I had two moles removed because they had changed in size and after testing we found out they were pre-cancerous.

After giving him all this history, basically all he did was do a cursory check of a few of my visible moles and told me everything would be fine. What he didn't know and still doesn't know is that I am an informed patient. I know what a full body check is. (It is when the dermatologist physically checks every inch of your skin and charts all skin characteristics.) My mom has one done every year. I felt that I had reached the age where I needed to have one to establish a baseline for future changes in my skin. I suggested this to Dr. "Smith, but he didn't agree. He didn't act concerned at all. I felt like a child who was being petted on the head and being told, "There, there, now." Upon hearing about my cousin, it was clear that this doctor had decided I was a hysterical female who was simply overreacting or running scared.

I could have forced the issue and insisted on a full body check. But why bother? I never wanted to see him again and couldn't get out of the office fast enough! Although it is inconvenient and almost an hour drive, I now go to my mother's dermatologist. He takes me seriously!

As you can see, Deena felt she was not being listened to by this physician. In fact, based on her description, it would appear that Deena preferred to be very active in her medical encounters. Unfortunately, her doctor was unable to meet her dual needs for involvement and control in her personal health care. Patient satisfaction is only one of the outcomes that may be affected by poor communication with health providers.

Impact of Culture

Culture is another factor that has an impact on how we view health and illness. Désirée Lie, clinical professor of family medicine at the Keck School of Medicine, writes "Cultural differences may arise between those with different race or ethnicity, primary language preference, ancestry, age, religion, sexual preference or identity, physical ability, and across the socio-economic and educational spectrum."[31] Misunderstandings can also occur when people have "different ideas about the nature of disease, how people are supposed to act in health care situations, and how illness reflects on people in the community."[32] For example, people from Eastern cultures often refuse to acknowledge mental illness; in Malawi, women who openly discuss sex are seen as bad mannered and promiscuous; and in other parts of the world, men and women must see physicians of the same sex, a major difficulty when physicians of any gender are in short supply.

Different cultures also view health differently. For example, many Western societies have adopted an **organic or biomedical** view of health. Based on this view, health providers seek to identify signs of ill health (e.g., fever, bacteria, rash). Health is seen more in terms of "health versus illness." If you don't have the signs or symptoms, then you are assumed to be in good health. Of course, you know that some days you feel better than others, you know that some colds are worse than others (even though the symptoms can be exactly the same), and you know that some sprained ankles are more severe than others. Thus, health (and illness) is on a continuum. However, the organic model does not do a good job of addressing this "continuum." This model is evidence based. If you lack evidence of being sick, then you must be well. What is observable is what is important.

Other cultures take a more **holistic approach** conceptualizing "health as harmony."[33] Health incorporates more than just signs and symptoms of illness. It is based on a combination of our physical, social and psychological wellbeing. Thus, the next time you are ill, your Asian friends may tell you that you need to focus on your Qi (pronounced chee). Qi refers to the life force or energy that resides within the body. Health is related to life energy, life rhythms, and maintaining a balance within one's body. Importantly, this perspective actually emphasizes strong communication between patient and provider. Through communication and listening, the caregiver can identify what area of the patient's life is "out of balance." While some providers have incorporated aspects of the harmony perspective into their practice, it is more commonly found in practices of alternative medical specialists.[34]

> ***Think on it:*** What are the implications of the biomedical and holistic views of health to patient–provider interactions? What is emphasized? Or de-emphasized? What are the implications for listening? Rapport building, etc.?

Differences can be compounded for individuals who are not native English speakers (or speak it poorly). Not surprisingly, language differences can lead to avoidance, misdiagnoses, improper treatment, and lower patient satisfaction.[35] For example, a study by Donald Rubin and his colleagues found that the accent and ethnicity of the physician can affect how North American patients respond to physicians of non-Western ethno-linguistic backgrounds (e.g., Turkish, Chinese, Indian).[36] One recent survey found that one in four visits to office-based physicians were to international medical graduates.[37] Thus, the odds of a North American patient coming in contact with a non-native physician at some point in his or her life are fairly high.

Not surprisingly, language proficiency can affect patient compliance – it is difficult to follow instructions that you do not understand. However, there is some question about whether stereotyping on the part of the patient may affect his or her listening ability.[38] For example, one recent study found that participants rated the Anglo physician (who spoke standard American English) higher in interpersonal attractiveness than his Asian counterpart. Intuitively, it would seem that interpersonal attractiveness (i.e., overall likeability) could affect patient health care interactions. Likeability is a component of source credibility and we are less likely to question the recommendations of someone who we find interpersonally attractive.

Age

Understanding health issues related to older adults is of increasing importance. According to the US Administration on Aging, by 2050 25% of the US population will be over the age of 65.[39] Not everyone, including many of those who will be in this cohort, see this as a positive event. Just as people can be discriminated against because of their race or gender, they can also be discriminated against because of their age. Many Americans hold negative views of the elderly, which are, unfortunately, frequently reinforced by media portrayals.[40] Overall, these negative stereotypes tend to present older individuals as cranky and dour, often lonely and unhappy. Additionally, these individuals often believe the elderly are commonly ill and befuddled. As a result, providers may treat their elderly clients as if they cannot care for themselves, or that they are not interested in or cannot understand health information.[41] Studies of the communication patterns between physicians and older patients have found that providers ask older patients fewer questions, provide less information, and ignore patient concerns associated with psychosocial issues, such as depression and relationships.[42]

One way this is often manifested is through "elderspeak." **Elderspeak** occurs when people use terms like "sweetie" and "dear" or when they talk slower to someone just because the person is older.[43] Many older people find it demeaning and upsetting, in part, because it suggests they are incompetent. Kristine Williams, a nurse gerontologist at the University of Kansas's School of Nursing, notes that health care workers are often among the worst offenders.

Communication patterns between the older patient and health providers can be affected by several other factors.[44] It is not unusual for the older patient to be "sidelined" while the family member and provider converse. In fact, some physicians perceive the patient's companion as a "patient substitute," who provides biomedical information about the patient.[45] While there does not appear to be major differences in what is discussed during the visit, older patients are often implicitly excluded from the conversation, are referred to as "she" or "he, and are left feeling that they aren't being listened to."[46]

Problems associated with caring for elderly patients are exacerbated when the patient is also chronically ill. Obviously then, it is important that these patients follow their treatment plans and take their medications correctly. But without good communication, there is less chance the older patient will comply.[47] Doctors can increase the probability of compliance by providing more information about the medication and its purpose. When physicians listen, treatment programs can be adapted to important aspects of the elderly patients' lives such as their cognitive and physical abilities, daily schedules, and living arrangements. Case Study 11.3 illustrates this challenge as Radley's family tries to make sure that his grandmother received the best care possible.

Case Study 11.3 Helping Nana

Hey, Radley, we missed you at our last meeting. Is your grandmother okay?

Thanks for asking, Tamarah. My Nana likes for me to help her when I can since I'm her oldest grandchild. Nana's visit with Dr. Cessanie was good. She really listened to her. Nana is in the early stages of dementia so she gets confused occasionally. The Doc understood that and was real patient with her. The last doctor I took her to was just the opposite and Nana refused to go back to her.

Is she in assisted living?

No, fortunately she can stay at home. We have a service that helps us. We all try to spend a much time with her as we can, but none of us live in her town. Fortunately, she's only about 35 miles away from me...

What You Can do as a Patient

As you have seen in previous sections of this chapter, many factors impact health communication. You can improve your communication with providers. To be effective, however, you have to believe that your opinion matters and that shared decision-making is valued and valuable to better health care.[48]

Enhancing Communication

To enhance your listening effectiveness in future health care encounters, try the following tips.

First, **be aware of your schemas**: about the physician–patient relationship, your attitude toward health care, the illness you are diagnosed with. Remember we process information via our mental schemas, and as result they can have a major impact on our interpretation of information and our interactions with health care providers.

Second, **come prepared**. Write down your symptoms or any questions you may have. It's easy to get distracted at the doctor's office, so a list of simple notes can help keep you on track. Most health providers will not mind and are actually pleased when you do so. They take it as a sign you want to follow their instructions. Having questions also makes you appear more competent, which in turn has a positive impact on other aspects of the interaction such as history-taking.[49] However, if you have a lot of questions or concerns, you may need to consider making more than one appointment.

Of course, if you do not understand something, then you cannot follow instructions. So the third thing you should do is **be assertive**. Ask that terms be explained, be direct in stating your symptoms and in asking your questions. Many patients ask indirect questions – questions that are disguised as statements. If you've ever told your physician, "I think my stomach is always upset because of the stress I'm under," you are using an indirect question. The problem with these types of questions is that your physician may not recognize them for what they are – an indirect way of seeking information. We often use this technique because we don't want to appear foolish or ignorant, but it's more effective to take the plunge and be direct.[50]

The fourth way to have a better health encounter is to **make sure you have the physician's complete attention**. In the United States, eye contact is a good check on this final suggestion. Doctors may turn away to wash hands, be typing on their computer or tablet, come in making notes, or even speak to nurses or other office personnel. However, to make an accurate diagnosis, your caregiver needs to do more than hear you; he or she needs to really listen. If you are unsure if you have his or her full attention, pause. Most of us tend to look at someone who unexpectedly stops talking in order to determine what's going on.

Finally, **use the information-verifying skills** you've learned. Double check your information by using restatements, summaries, and paraphrases. Personally summarize the information. It will help you in recalling it later. If your caregiver does not have a convenient information brochure on your condition or the treatment regimen that she suggests, write down the information and review it with her. This can save you an extra call to the office asking for clarification and it can save you further illness or aggravation because you did not follow the treatment plan like you should have. If you want to be a cooperative patient, one who is active in caring for your health, you have to not only be willing to comply with the doctor's suggestions, but you have to have the correct information in the first place and be able to recall it – information-verifying skills allow you to do this.

Think on it: Looking at the above suggestions, what advice would you give to Deena (in Case Study 11.2) the next time she visits her physician. What could she have done differently in her visit with the dermatologist?

Of course when assessing these suggestions keep in mind that they are based on and are most appropriate for health providers in Western cultures, and may need to be adapted if you are in other parts of the world. Ultimately, you and your caregiver are responsible for working together to achieve your good health. If you feel that you are doing everything you can to reach that goal, but that your relationship with the health professional is not helping you to achieve that end, then perhaps you should seek advice elsewhere. Such a decision does not imply that you believe that your physician is incompetent, but may simply be a sign that the two of you approach your health in different ways. Some individuals want a physician who is efficient, direct, and to the point, while others want someone who spends more time with them and expresses greater empathy.

Remember Mason, Nana, and Deena above? Clearly they varied in their ability to act as their own advocate. Remember, you are your own best advocate. Openly communicate with your providers and expect the same from them. When you begin taking the steps necessary to be your own advocate, you empower yourself in a way that significantly impacts your life. Our interview with cardiologist Dr. Allan Schwadron emphasizes the importance of patients participating in their own health care. Dr. Schwadron spent quite a bit of time as a patient in his battle with cancer. He was asked about how he had changed as a physician following his experience.

Doctor as Patient: Listening Lessons

Allan Schwadron, MD, FACC, FCCP, FSCAI,
Auburn, AL

What changed was that I found patients really need to be their own advocates. Avoid being the person who asks no questions and follows every piece of advice blindly. You don't have to accept everything told to you. Asking for a second opinion and asking questions about how your case may be different (or not) from the usual case benefits the overall care of the patient.

Today with the internet, you have access to sites like WEBMD where you can find a little bit about what may be going on. Or, if you get a diagnosis, you can look it up to learn some basic information without medical jargon. Ask about tests or medications that you've heard about.

But, be careful of the friend, neighbor, or family member who tries to tell you that they had something similar and everything they went through. Also be careful of some sites on the internet.

Talk to the nurses in the doctor's office. They can prep a patient about the kind of questions the physician is going to ask and things he or she might need to know. The patient can be thinking about the answers to those questions.

My experience helped me be more patient and understanding with patients who are uncertain about undergoing something or reluctant to proceed in a direction I want them to go. Also, I learned that I need to be more of a patient advocate.

Provider Communication and Listening

The importance of listening to medicine is not a new idea. Sir William Osler, sometimes called the Father of Modern Medicine, was famous for having said that "if you listen to the patient, he will give you his diagnosis."[51] Interviews with leading physicians today find that they recognize the importance of listening to understanding and treating their patients.[52] A study of nurses found that how a nurse listens affects his or her ability to identify patients who've been victims of domestic abuse.[53]

In recent years, medical schools and health communication experts have attempted to identify the key communication skills associated with each function of the medical interview. Table 11.1 presents several of these functions and their related communication goals and skills.[54] You'll notice that listening is explicitly or implicitly a part of the communication skills associated with the functions of a medical interview.

Table 11.1 Communication Goals and Skills in the Medical Interview

Medical Interview Functions	Physician Responsibilities	Communication-related Skills
Relationship-building Goal: Establish Partnership	Build rapport & trust Express compassion & commitment Discuss mutual roles & responsibilities Demonstrate respect	Greet patient appropriately Maintain eye contact Listen actively Use appropriate language Encourage patient participation Show interest in the patient as a person
Information Gathering Goal: Understand Purpose of Visit	Understand physical ailments/issues Explore related social and emotional factors	Utilize open-ended questions Avoid interruptions Listen actively Encourage full disclosure (e.g., concerns, effect of illness, perspective on the problem/illness, additional concerns). Review, clarify & summarize information

(continued)

Table 11.1 (Cont.)

Medical Interview Functions	Physician Responsibilities	Communication-related Skills
Information Providing Goal: Patient Understanding	Facilitate understanding (e.g., identify informational needs; provide information) Identify & address barriers to understanding (e.g., language, health literacy, hearing, numeracy) Provide information resources and assist in reviewing and using them	Explain nature of problem and approach to diagnosis, treatment Give uncomplicated explanations and instructions Avoid jargon and complexity Encourage questions and check understanding Emphasize key messages
Decision-making Goal: Patient Investment in Personal Care	Outline treatment plan(s) Foster treatment decisions	Encourage participation in treatment decisions by reviewing choices and exploring preferences and understanding Reach mutual agreement Identify and enlist resources and support Discuss follow-up and plan for unexpected outcomes
Treatment Promotion Goal: Patient Participation	Assess interest in and ability to manage personal care Facilitate success (e.g., additional informational needs, need for support, strategies for success, etc.) Collaborate on upcoming steps Encourage autonomy and self-management Act as health system advocate	Evaluate willingness to modify health behaviors Elicit goals, ideas, and decisions
Emotional Responsiveness Goal: Psychological Support	Provide emotional support	Acknowledge and explore emotions Express empathy, sympathy, and reassurance Provide help in dealing with emotions Assess psychological distress

Adapted from King & Hoppe (2013)

Think on it: King and Hoppe explicitly list listening in the first two functions of the medical interview. Do you agree? Does listening play a significant role in the remaining functions? What other important communication behaviors or skills should be included with each function? From the patient's viewpoint, would the goal, purpose, communication skills of the medical interview outlined in Table 11.1 hold true for patients?

As you learned in Chapter 1, many of us are poor listeners. Health providers are no exception to this. We have all experienced medical interviews that were less than optimal. Case Study 11.4 illustrates one such example.

Case Study 11.4 NaMii's Story

NaMii has been concerned because she has experienced what she calls a racing heart a couple of times over the last month. She decided that she needed to be checked out and so she made an appointment at the Student Health Center. The Student Health Center is a large clinic with 6 doctors and 8 nurses and other support staff.

Prior to meeting her doctor, NaMii filled out a number of insurance forms and medical background forms. She waited approximately 45 minutes to meet the doctor.

Doctor Holmes enters the exam room. He says hello to NaMii and asks how she is. Overhead, the intercom calls Doctor Holmes' name. He excuses himself, only to return 15 minutes later. He looks at the chart and says, *"So you're in for a physical. Let's get started."* So far, NaMii has only said hello. Dr. Holmes asks NaMii how she is doing. NaMii says, *"My heart races sometimes. I don't know if it's really anything, but…"* Dr. Holmes interrupts, *"Let's see what your physical tells us."*

As the interview continues, Dr. Holmes asks NaMii about her physical activity, vices and habits (i.e., smoking, drinking, etc.), medications, etc. He gives her a prescription for an allergy medication. NaMii responds to all the questions. *"I run two miles a day, lift weights three times a week." "I don't smoke." "I was diagnosed with seasonal allergies five years ago."*

Finally, as the interview ends, while he is entering notes on NaMii's chart, Dr. Holmes asks, *"Is there anything else?"* NaMii again mentions her racing heart. Doctor Holmes interrupts and notes that everything seems fine with her physical, *"You're probably just overdoing it. Students tend to burn the candle at both ends. Eventually it catches up with you. Make sure you're eating and sleeping the way you ought to. (Laughing) Don't wait till the last minute to do your assignments like I used to do."*

NaMii doesn't tell Dr. Holmes that she doesn't wait to till the night before to write her papers or study for an exam. Overall, she was not satisfied with Dr. Holmes' response, but did not say anything. She took her prescription, and left.

As we see in the case study, Dr. Holmes was not very responsive to NaMii's concerns. At the same time, however, NaMii did not assert herself. As we mentioned at the beginning of this chapter, patient–caregiver communication is transactional in nature. However, neither NaMii nor Dr. Holmes were aware of the influence they had on the other's responses.

Factors Influencing Providers

While Case Study 11.4 illustrates a number of things that can affect our attitude toward health professionals and the health care process, caregivers are also influenced by other factors. One important factor may be the process of medical school which affects providers' schemas of health care practice and patients.[55] While schools in some health areas, such as nursing, operate from more of a patient-centered perspective,[56] others generally do not (e.g., medical, dentistry) or do so minimally (e.g., physical, occupational, speech therapy).[57] In addition, few curricula, particularly medical schools, provide in-depth training in patient–provider communication.[58] At the same time, future providers undergo an intense socialization process.

Medical socialization encourages caregivers to become data driven. In other words, they rely on the results of physical exams and other medical tests. As a result, they come to use and depend on what Howard Waitzken calls the **"voice of medicine."**[59] Oftentimes, caregivers become so comfortable with this "voice" (i.e., discussing symptoms, test results, medications, and treatment options) that they are unwilling to listen to the "**voice of the lifeworld**" from their patients (e.g., personal or family issues, fears). Care providers may feel these concerns, such as those associated with family and friends, are not relevant to the patient's condition or that they are out of the caregiver's control and so they ignore them or turn the discussion back to topics where they feel greater control.

Medical socialization can also lead future health providers, particularly physicians, to see themselves as authorities, whose opinions should not be questioned. In addition, the stress of medical school may actually lead medical students to engage in listening avoidance![60] Listening takes time and energy – medical students have relatively little of both as they pursue their goals of becoming doctors, nurses, or other allied health professionals.

As noted earlier, physicians get little **communication training**. One survey found that 75% of the surveyed physicians had never been exposed to a communication class of any type.[61] Those who were exposed to communication training most often learned about listening, observing patients, and interviewing. This lack of training is reflected in findings showing that while approximately one-third of a medical encounter focuses on the physician providing information and instructions, general practitioners almost never attempt to determine their patients' viewpoints or opinions either prior to or after providing medical information.[62]

Not surprisingly, most physicians tend to engage in **physician-centered talk**.[63] This "I'm in charge" communication approach has the provider doing the majority of the talking, controlling what gets discussed (topics), and determining when the interaction ends.[64] In addition, doctors tend to be assertive, interrupting more, using touch more, asking questions more, but answering questions less.[65] Roughly 91% of questions during a health interview are asked by physicians.[66] As we saw in NaMii's story, Dr. Holmes engaged in a number of physician-centered behaviors. Unfortunately, most of these behaviors (i.e., interrupting, stereotyping her as a college student, etc.) send clear signals to NaMii that Dr. Holmes is not really listening to her concerns.

Part of the problem that physicians face is that they have to balance two roles – one, technical, the other, interpersonal.[67] During their information interview, or history taking, with a patient, the primary task is generally gathering evidence about the illness (e.g., date of onset, symptoms). However, it is mediated by the interpersonal role adopted by the doctor. This role is based on the overall communication style of the physician. Researchers and writers suggest that in meeting the demands of these two roles it is almost as if physicians should use one ear to listen to a patient's biomedical information, while the other attends to a patient's psychosocial information.[68]

It is important to note that when providers adopt a "person-centered" approach, they are more open to the listener's needs. Caregivers adopting this approach are more likely to self-disclose to their patients, and are more likely to express empathy to them. Physicians of this type are also more likely to provide desired information and discuss treatment regimens.[69] The patient-centered approach has other important implications for physicians. Doctors who develop ongoing relationships with their patients have higher job satisfaction, feel more valued, and are less likely to experience job burn-out.[70] Also, they are less likely to be sued. Other researchers actually argue that primary care physicians who are unable or unwilling to take the time to develop quality patient–provider relationships should consider areas where long-term patient–caregiver relationships are unlikely (i.e., emergency medicine or anesthesiology).[71] Finally, one Swedish study indicated that a patient-centered consultation style (e.g., listening to patients, providing information, and discussing treatment effects) may be related to fewer unnecessary antibiotic prescriptions.[72]

Patient Outcomes: Satisfaction and Compliance

Research indicates that patients value good communication skills as much as they value good clinical skills, and that patient satisfaction is more dependent on provider communication skills than on their clinical skills.[73] It is important to note that patients can be satisfied with their care, but actually dissatisfied with the communication that occurs during the office visit. Professor of ophthalmology Calvin W. Roberts argues that "the quest for satisfaction begins with listening." As a physician, he notes that he actively works to create an office environment "that enhances communications and fosters satisfaction."[74] In his practice he follows, what he calls the **QuEST** model to address patient dissatisfaction. This model reflects a patient-centered approach in that it suggests that physicians, "**Qu**estion and acknowledge, **E**valuate, **S**et a course of action, and **T**alk and discuss" patient concerns and problems. He goes on to say that an open dialogue with patients allows them at least to have an opportunity to express their needs and concerns, and the physician to validate the patient's feelings. A pragmatic man, Dr. Roberts notes that not only are satisfied patients more likely to follow treatment plans, but they are more likely to return for follow-up care, and more likely to refer their family and friends.

Communication skills that appear to positively influence patient satisfaction include overall friendliness of the communication, increased interpersonal involvement, low communicative dominance, less interrupting, focused active listening, clear detailed explanations, acknowledging patient concerns, avoiding technical jargon, and maintaining eye contact.[75] While you may think these skills are self-evident, the fact is that numerous studies indicate that health care providers, especially doctors, do not use them.[76]

A recent review of health communication literature identified a number of important communication factors associated with patient satisfaction, including "a caring and understanding manner on the part of the health care provider... a balanced inquiry into psychosocial and biomedical concerns... and the expression of patient and provider expectations."[77] Of course, factors such as medical competency also factor into patient satisfaction. In addition, immediacy behaviors (i.e., smiling, eye contact, reduced physical distance) and perceived listening are positively related to patient satisfaction with care and with provider communication.[78]

> **Think on it:** Probably a few of you reading this book have been hospitalized or have had a relative hospitalized. Think back on that experience. What was the most memorable positive and negative experience you had? Was it related to your communication with health care workers?

How do patients express their dissatisfaction? They often will change physicians. One study found that 20% of newly established patients (i.e., they had been seeing their physician for one year or less) indicated they changed physicians because they were unhappy with their previous doctor.[79] Interestingly, of these patients almost 30% indicated they were dissatisfied with the attitude or personality of their previous physician, while approximately 25% indicated they changed physicians due to dissatisfaction with their previous treatment regimen. Three communication factors – empathic communication, listening, and immediacy – seem to predict patient satisfaction with, not only their doctors, but also with nurses and other hospital staff.[80] These behaviors help reduce the uncertainty and relieve the anxiety often associated with hospital stays.

Clearly, listening and communication skills positively affect the patient–provider relationship. For example, in one nursing home, residents reported higher levels of satisfaction with nursing home assistants after the assistants participated in a listening training program.[81] Residents reported improvements in several areas including increased eye contact, increased personal self-disclosures, positive use of silence, positive feedback, and reduced advice-giving.

Tips for Health Workers and Volunteers

As you have learned, empathy and empathic listening are important to our overall wellbeing. Careful active listening is an important component of the patient–provider encounter, not only for the patient's satisfaction and health, but also for the wellbeing of the provider. While much work remains, medical, nursing, and pharmaceutical schools as well as hospital and hospice

"It's nothing to worry about nurse. It's only teeth bites on your tongue. Lots of good listeners have them."

volunteer programs are increasingly providing interpersonal training.[82] While still a medical student, Dr. Shinya Amano recognized the importance of listening, advising other medical students "to take full advantage of this opportunity to help patients by listening to their stories... [because]... it has everything to do with being a good doctor."[83]

Those of you who are contemplating either volunteering with or entering a health care profession, should keep in mind that the following advice is designed to convey one important thing to patients (and their families) – **respect**. While a number of factors are related to building respect, arguably the most important is establishing trust. **Trust** is strongly associated with patient reports of improved health as well as overall satisfaction with doctors, willingness to disclose sensitive information, and willingness to stick to a treatment program.[84] For adults, a trusted physician is seen as competent, honest, and committed to maintaining confidentiality. Adolescents respond to physicians in much the same way as their parents do. They describe trusted physicians as someone they respect, who is honest, and who knows what they are doing. However, one significant difference between adults and adolescents is that adolescents are more likely to stress the importance of confidentiality of health and personal information.[85] One reason for this concern is that adolescents may be uncertain about what physicians can and/or will tell their parents or guardians. Adolescents worried about confidentiality concerns may not fully inform their physician about their symptoms or may not fully comply with treatment because they do not want to miss out on activities such as Friday night's dance or a double-date with friends.

How can you build trust? First, **be aware of personal schemas.** This piece of advice echoes what we suggested to you as patients. For example, physicians sometimes focus so much on one illness that another unrelated illness is ignored or goes undiagnosed. In addition, just like everyone else, health providers are "touchy" about some topics. Imagine a hospice volunteer facing the family member of someone whose mother has just died, when his own mother had passed away recently. Knowing yourself means you'll be aware of issues that may inadvertently affect your relationship with others. There are many ways to volunteer at hospitals and with hospices. The volunteer in the previous example might be more effective answering phones or running errands until he is able to fully deal with his grief.

Related to this, be aware of *and* wary of **context cues.** On one hand, physicians use any number of cues to help them to learn about and understand their patients. However, when a cue triggers a schema, that schema has the potential to hinder the health interaction. Doctors Saul Weiner and Alan Schwartz suggest that we should listen for what matters.[86] In other words, we need to listen beyond these types of cues and the schemas they trigger. If we don't, we may ignore important cues and/or stereotype others, which can result in errors in health care. For example, Dr. Richard Garcia describes how assumptions about a patient's race (African-American) led to a significant delay in diagnosis of cystic fibrosis.[87] You see, this disease most often occurs in white populations. As Dr. Garcia describes, it wasn't until a radiologist, who had no knowledge of the patient's race, glanced at her lung x-ray and asked, "Who's the kid with CF?" After years of hospital and doctor visits, her illness was finally identified and properly diagnosed; she was eight years old. Contextual cues also include those things "outside the patient's skin" that are relevant to their care. As Doctors Weiner and Schwartz note in their book, *Listening for What Matters*, when health providers listen, when they attend to patient context, they are taking into account "what might or might not be going on in the life and in the mind of the person" they are caring for. Thus, it is important that health professionals "read between the lines" in order to learn that a patient's weight loss is mostly like due to depression from a recent divorce, that repeatedly missing dialysis appointments is due to transportation problems, or that bad teeth is due to a profound fear of needles. How do you learn about these types of issues? Engagement – closely attending to the conversations and nonverbal communication of patients and clients. As one of Dr. Weiner's interns put it, "You mean you talk to patients like you talk to people?"[88] Why yes, you do. And, it makes a difference – for you and for them.

> ***Think on it:*** How is the "voice of the life world" and listening for "contextual cues" similar? Different?

Second, **look interested (utilize immediacy behaviors)**. Generally speaking, patients respond better when those in health care settings appear interested in and supportive of what they say. For example, patients are more likely to speak freely and disclose when physicians and nurses maintain eye contact with them.[89] Other nonverbal behaviors associated with active listening include an open posture, confirming head nods, interested facial expressions, and appropriate gestures and touch. Nonverbal communication (i.e., immediacy behaviors) is one technique caregivers can use to validate a patient's experiences and confirm that they understand the patient's needs.[90]

Health workers can also **listen for distress markers**. While nonverbals can tell us much about how others are feeling, nonfluencies can tell us a lot as well. For example, patients may stutter or stammer, have extensive pauses while they build up to making an important disclosure."[91] Health communication scholar Athena du Pre suggests that caregivers avoid changing topics until they can determine what the disclosure addresses. Another strategy is to **use silence (carefully)**. Silence can be golden when used positively. It opens space for someone to think and express an idea. However, silence can be quite negative as well. Oftentimes disapproval is tied to silence. Have you ever had a parent or friend offer silence as a response to something you said or did? If so, you know what we are talking about.

You'll want to **avoid abruptly changing topics**. Changing topics quickly, as our Dr. Holmes did in Case Study 11.4, can make patients feel out of control. It certainly is not a way to encourage peer-oriented, collaborative communication, and is unlikely to lead to a trusting relationship.

As we noted earlier in the book and in this chapter, **be empathic**. Empathy and empathic understanding have been discussed in detail elsewhere in this text. In the health care setting, empathy has been described as a primary dimension of developing a caring relationship, which is based on acceptance and respect for the patient.[92] Obviously, based on this description, collaborative, or patient-centered communication, must necessarily involve empathic understanding – the attempt to understand health and illness from the patient's perspective. Engaging in empathic communication is especially important when working with children and elderly patients. Caregivers should strive to establish a supportive environment that empowers patients. This involves several factors including acknowledging patients as individuals (at a level they can understand), being aware of their values and beliefs, and working with family members and significant others in assisting the patient in meeting a mutually agreed upon treatment plan.

Of course it is important to **listen more than you talk**. We're not suggesting this just because you are reading a listening text. Remember that physicians, on average, interrupt their patients within 18 seconds of beginning their health interview.[93] It's no wonder 75% of patients say they did not tell their physician everything they planned to tell them. Interestingly, patients who are allowed to finish speaking tend to only speak for about two minutes. As we noted earlier, patients sometimes use indirect questions when they want to avoid appearing ignorant or foolish. It is important to "listen between the lines" of these types of requests for information as they are an important part of hearing a patient's voice of the lifeworld. When health care providers put themselves in the "background," they allow the patient's narrative to be heard.[94] Volunteers need to be particularly good listeners. As a volunteer, you may interact with physicians, nurses, orderlies, family members, and of course, the patient. They all have different needs and concerns and it may sometimes be difficult to sort through conflicting information.

Much of this chapter's discussion boils down to control issues during the health interview. Questions are a "mainstay" of the health care interview; however, "health professionals should be cautious so as not to control interviews through the use of questions."[95] **Allowing patients some control** (i.e., allowing them to talk) during the interview emphasizes the responsibility that both parties have in receiving and disclosing information as well as in requesting and providing information. Nurse Catherine Reynolds relates how asking a patient an open-ended question, "So, what brings you here?" led to a fascinating and insightful conversation with a World War II veteran.[96] Yes, he came in because he was ill, but importantly, he saw the reason why he was in the hospital as the result of his war experiences, which left him with severe anxiety and memory problems. As seen here, a simple open-ended question became an important means of learning about related contextual cues that gave insight into his illness and his behaviors. When providers engage in collaborative communication, patient contributions to their own health care are highlighted and emphasized.[97] When this is done, providers legitimize the voice of the lifeworld and acknowledge the important contributions patients make to their own care. We're more likely to be open with people who treat us as equals.

It always helps to **take steps to ensure understanding.** Ensuring understanding is particularly important because medical interactions often include medical jargon, which may be incomprehensible to patients and their families. As you learned earlier in the text, asking for feedback is an important way of ensuring that others understand us. It is also a method of empowering patients. When patients share in health decision-making, they not only feel respect, but they see themselves as a partner who can make meaningful contributions to their health care and treatment decisions.[98] As you learned, paraphrasing and restating information are also an excellent method of ensuring that you (and others) have heard and fully understood the other's message.

Summary

While it is beyond the scope of this chapter, you should be aware that listening in the medical context goes beyond the relationship we have with our providers, whether physician or nurse, laboratory technician or radiologist, therapist or volunteer. In other chapters we discuss the importance of social support systems, listening across the life-span, and listening and the media. All of these areas have important implications for how we interact with health care professionals. In addition, how doctors, nurses, social workers, and other health professionals interact and work together can have a significant impact on a person's health. Health care activities have to be coordinated, multiple physicians and support staffs may be involved. Subsequently, developing cooperative relationships between all these health care "players" is important in achieving the goal of patient comfort and health. Patients and family members may turn to online social support groups, such as cancer caregiver groups and Alcoholics Anonymous, which allow them to share information and gain emotional support. If you are interested in learning more about health communication, check out the additional readings listed below.

Key Concepts

Health Literacy
Health Approaches
    Paternalistic Approach
    Consumeristic Approach
    Collaborative Approach
Elements of Reflective Listening
    Open-ended Question
    Reflection (echoing)
    Selective Reflection
    Empathy Building
    Checking for Understanding
    Empathy
Patient–Provider Interaction Factors
    Nature of the Visit
    Patient Sex
    Culture
        Biomedical view of medicine
        Holistic view of medicine
    Race/Ethnicity
    Age
    Elderspeak
Tips for Patients
    Be Aware of Personal Schemas
    Be Prepared
    Be Assertive
    Ensure Physician Attention
    Use Information-verification
Factors Affecting Providers
    Medical Socialization
    Voice of Medicine
    Voice of Lifeworld
    Communication Training
    Physician-centered Talk
QuEST Model
Tips for Providers
    Respect
    Trust
    Be Aware of Personal Schemas
    Context Cues
    Immediacy
    Distress Markers
    Silence
    Changing Topics
    Empathy
    Listen More

Allow Control
Ensure Understanding

Discussion Questions

1. This chapter discusses the importance of listening for both the patient and the health care provider. Is it more important for the health care provider to be a good listener or the patient? Why?
2. Do you have more of a paternalistic or consumeristic approach to health care? What makes you think so? What are the advantages and disadvantages of each approach?
3. Do you think your approach to health care changes with context? For example, would you interact with your health care provider differently if you had a clear-cut problem, like a broken leg, as opposed to something more ambiguous, like unexplained abdominal pain? What about something more serious, like lupus?

Listening Activities

1. Visit three to four different medical school websites. If available, check out their mission statements. Do these statements address patient–provider communication in any way? If so, how? Now look at course offerings, course descriptions, etc. Do they offer communication skill building classes to students? Are they required or electives? If required, how many are students required to take. If there are no required classes, do course descriptions suggest they touch on communication issues? You might also consider doing the same for other medical schools (e.g., nursing schools, dental schools).
2. Doctor–patient interactions (as well as nurse–patient interactions) are portrayed in many prime time dramas, soap operas, and comedies. Choose two different types of shows (a comedy and drama, drama and soap, etc.). Watch an episode of each. Do they portray patient–provider interactions similarly or not? Looking at what we've covered in this chapter, which does the best job of illustrating good listening? How? If you were to rewrite a scene from one of the shows you watched to better exemplify the advice in this chapter, what would it look like? What would you want to emphasize or do differently? Why?
3. We've provided you with several suggestions for communicating with patients (and their families). Based on what you've read elsewhere in the text, what other suggestions would you make? Develop a list of four to six additional tips, providing a justification for why each should be included, and giving an example to illustrate each.

Notes

1 Centers for Disease Control and Prevention, 2012; Downloadable files and other related information can be found at: www.cdc.gov/nchs/fastats/physician-visits.htm
2 Beckman & Frankel, 1984
3 Levine, 2004
4 Frankel, 1990; Dyche & Swiderski, 2005; see also Li, Krysko, Desroches & Deagle, 2004
5 Fred, 2014; see also, Rousseau, 2014
6 Branch, 2014
7 Joshi, 2015
8 King & Hoppe, 2013

 9 See, for example, Brody, Miller, Lerman, Smith, & Caputo, 1989; Burgoon, Birk, & Hall, 1991; Frankel, 1990; Greenfield, Kaplan, Ware, Yano, & Haskard & DiMatteo, 2009; King & Hoppe, 2013

10 Levine, 2004, provides an easy to read summary of select research findings on the impact of doctor–patient communication on patient health, medical risks, and malpractice.

11 US Department of Health and Human Services, 2008

12 National Network of Libraries of Medicine, 2017

13 Kaiser Family Foundation, 2004

14 Ly & Glied, 2013

15 See, for example, Denning, 2001; Dennis, 2004; Dykes, 2004; Lloyd, 2003; Lundkvist, Åkerlind, Borgquist, & Mölstad, 2002; Roberts, 2004

16 Graybar & Leonard, 2005, p. 2

17 Burnard, 1997; Cooper, Watson, & Hoeldampf, 2010.

18 Krupnick et al., 1996

19 Graybar & Leonard, 2005, p. 3

20 Graybar & Leonard, 2005

21 Arnold, 2014, provides an excellent review of the role of reflective listening in the work of Carl Rogers.

22 Arnold, 2014

23 Gassmann & Grawe, 2006

24 Chien, Chan, Lam, & Kam, 2005

25 Institute of Medicine, 2000; James, 2013

26 James, 2013;

27 Robinson, 2003

28 Beach & Dozier, 2015.

29 Nussbaum, Ragan, & Whaley, 2003

30 See Nussbaum et al. (2003) for a review of the impact of gender on patient–provider interactions.

31 Lie, 2014

32 du Pré, 2010, p. 203

33 du Pré, 2010

34 du Pré, 2010

35 Weech-Maldonado et al., 2003; Flores et al., 1998

36 Rubin, Healy, Gardiner, Zath, & Moore, 1997

37 Hing & Lin, 2009; McCabe (2012) presents a nice summary of the nature and ways that foreign-born workers contribute to our current and future health care fields.

38 Ray & Bostrom, 1990

39 See "Aging Statistics," (Department of Health and Human Services Administration on Aging, 2010) for additional aging statistics visit the department's web site (www.aoa.gov/AoARoot/Aging_Statistics/index.aspx)

40 Mulac & Giles, 1996; Nussbaum, Thompson, & Robinson, 1989

41 Baltes & Wahl, 1996

42 See Harwood, 2007, for a review

43 Leland, 2008

44 Greene & Adelman, 2001; Nussbaum et al., 1989; Nussbaum et al., 2003

45 Hasselkus, 1992

46 Greene & Adelman, 2001

47 Beisecker & Thompson, 1995; McLane, Zyzanski, & Flocke, 1995

48 Street, 2007

49 Cegala, Gade, Broz, & McClure, 2004

50 Cegala, 1997; Frankel, 1990

51 Silverman, Murray, & Bryan, 2003, p. 98

52 Meldrum, 2011

53 Chapin, Froats, & Hudspeth, 2013

54 Adapted from King & Hoppe, 2013

55 du Pré, 2010

56 Drass, 1988; Robertson, 1996
57 Bryan, 1991; du Pré, 2010
58 Bryan, 1991
59 Waitzken, 1991
60 Watson, Lazarus, & Thomas, 1999
61 Zimmerman & Arnold, 1990
62 Goss, Mazzi, Del Piccolo, Rimondini, & Zimmermann, 2005
63 du Pré, 2010
64 Arnold & Shirreffs, 1998, p. 3
65 Cegala, 1997; du Pré, 2010; Goss et al., 2005
66 West, 1993
67 Ong, de Haes, Hoos, & Lammes, 1995
68 Arnold & Shirreffs, 1998
69 Kinnersley, Stott, Petters, & Harvey, 1999
70 Brown, Stewart, & Ryan, 2003; Dykes, 2004
71 Gray et al., 2003
72 Lundkvist et al., 2002
73 Tarrant, Windridge, Boulton, Baker, & Freeman, 2003
74 Roberts, 2004, p. 64
75 Conlee, Olvera, & Vagim, 1993; Grant, Cissna, & Rosenfeld, 2000; Jadad & Rizo, 2003; Williams, 1997
76 Bowman & Ruben, 1986; Ruben, 1989; Welch, 2010
77 Brown et al., 2003
78 Wanzer, Booth-Butterfield, & Gruber, 2004
79 Weiss & Blustein, 1996
80 Wanzer, et al., 2004
81 Trahan & Rockwell, 1999
82 Bowles, McIntosh, & Torn, 2001; Chambers-Evans, Stelling, & Godin, 1999; Garcia de Lucio, et al., 2000; Ito & Lambert, 2002; Rogan & Timmins, 2004; Roter, 2000
83 Amano, 2014, p. 574
84 See, for example, Huynh, Sweeny, & Miller, in press; Mechanic & Meyer, 2000; Rosser & Kasperski, 2001
85 Klostermann, Slap, Nebrig, Tivorsak, & Britto, 2005. This finding appears to hold true in other Western-based cultures, see Farrant & Watson, 2004
86 Weiner & Schwartz, 2016
87 Garcia, 2003
88 Weiner & Schwartz, 2016, p. 20
89 Bensing, Kerssens, & van der Pasch, 1995; Burnard, 1997; Sidell, 2001
90 Wanzer et al., 2004
91 du Pré, 2010, p. 70
92 Brown et al., 2003; Corbett, 2001
93 Beckman & Frankel, 1984
94 Delbene, 2015
95 Northouse & Northouse, 1992, p. 167
96 Reynolds, 2012
97 du Pré, 2001
98 Rogan & Timmins, 2004; Edwards, Elwyn, Smith, Williams, & Thornton, 2001

Additional Readings

Martin, L. R., & DiMatteo, M. R. (Eds.). (2014). *The Oxford handbook of health communication, behavior change, and treatment adherence.* New York: Oxford.

Rupert, D. J., Dillon, E. D., Teitelbaum, A. S., & Ray, S. E. (2016). Succeeding as a master's degree health communication professional: Six key skills and characteristics. *Journal of Communication in Healthcare,* *9*, 146–152.

Sparks, L., & Villagran, M. (2010). *Patient and provider interaction: A global health communication perspective.* Malden, MA: Polity.

Weiner, S. J., & Schwartz, A. (2016). *Listening for what matters.* New York: Oxford.

References

Amano, S. U. (2014). Therapeutic listening. *Texas Heart Institute Journal, 41*, 573–574.

Arnold, K. (2014). Behind the mirror: Reflective listening and its tain in the work of Carl Rogers. *The Humanistic Psychologist, 42*, 354–369.

Arnold, W. E., & Shirreffs, J. H. (1998). Patient perceptions of patient-physician communication with allopathic and naturopathic physicians. *International Journal of Listening, 12*, 1–11.

Baltes, M. M., & Wahl, H. (1996). Patterns of communication in old age: The dependence-support and independence-ignore script. *Health Communication, 8*, 217–231.

Beach, W. A., & Dozier, D. M. (2015). Fears, uncertainties, and hopes: Patient-initiated actions and doctors' responses during oncology interviews. *Journal of Health Communication, 20*, 1–12.

Beckman, H. B. & Frankel, R. M. (1984). The effect of physician behavior on the collection of data. *Annals of Internal Medicine, 101*, 692–696.

Beisecker, A. E., & Thompson, T. L. (1995). The elderly patient–physician interaction. In J. F. Nussbaum & J. Coupland (Eds.), *Handbook of communication and aging research* (pp. 397–416). Mahwah, NJ: LEA.

Bensing, J. M., Kerssens, J. J., & van der Pasch, M. (1995). Patient-directed gaze as a tool for discovering and handling psychosocial problems in general practice. *Journal of Nonverbal Behavior, 19*, 223–242.

Bowles, N., Mackintosh, C., & Torn, A. (2001). Nurses' communication skills: An evaluation of the impact of solution-focused communication training. *Journal of Advanced Nursing, 36*, 347–354.

Bowman, J. C., & Ruben, B. D. (1986). Patient satisfaction: Critical issues in the implementation and evaluation of patient relations training. *Journal of Healthcare Education and Training, 1*, 24–27.

Branch, W. T., Jr. (2014). Treating the whole patient: Passing time-honored skills for building doctor-patient relationship on to generations of doctors. *Medical Education, 48*, 67–74.

Brody, D. S., Miller, S. M., Lerman, C. E., Smith, D. G., & Caputo, G. C. (1989). Patient perception of involvement in medical care: Relationship to illness attitudes and outcomes. *Journal of General Internal Medicine, 4*, 506–511.

Brown, J. B., Stewart, M., & Ryan, B. L. (2003). Outcomes of patient-provider interaction. In T. L. Thompson, A. M. Dorsey, K. I. Miller, & R. Parrott (Eds.), *Handbook of health communication* (pp. 141–161). Mahwah, NJ: LEA.

Bryan, G. T. (1991). Physicians and medical education. *Journal of the American Medical Association, 266*, 1407–1408.

Burgoon, M., Birk, T. S., & Hall, J. R. (1991). Compliance and satisfaction with physician-patient communication. *Health Communication Research, 18*, 177–208.

Burnard, P. (1997). *Effective communication skills for health professionals* (2nd ed.). New York: Chapman & Hall.

Cegala, D. J. (1997). A study of doctors' and patients' communication during a primary care consultation: Implications for communication training. *Journal of Health Communication, 2*, 169–194.

Cegala, D. J., Gade, C., Broz, S. L., & McClure, L. (2004). Physicians' and patients' perceptions of patients' communication competence in a primary care medical interview. *Health Communication, 16*, 289–304.

Centers for Disease Control and Prevention. (2012). National ambulatory medical care survey. National Center for Health Statistics. Retrieved from www.cdc.gov/nchs/data/ahcd/namcs_summary/2012_namcs_web_tables.pdf.

Chambers-Evans, J., Stelling, J. & Godin, M. (1999). Learning to listen: Serendipitous outcomes of a research training experience. *Journal of Advanced Nursing, 26,* 1421–1426.

Chapin, J., Froats, T., Jr., & Hudspeth, T. (2013). Who's listening to victims? Nurses' listening. styles and domestic violence screening. *International Journal of Listening, 27,* 2–12.

Chien, W. T., Chan, C. H. H., Lam, L. W., & Kam, C.W. (2005). Psychiatric inpatients' perceptions of positive and negative aspects of physical restraint. *Patient Education and Counseling, 59,* 80–86.

Conlee, C. J., Olvera, J., & Vagim, N. N. (1993). The relationships among physician nonverbal immediacy and measures of patient satisfaction with physician care. *Communication Reports, 6,* 25–33.

Cooper, M., Watson, J. C., & Hoeldampf, D. (2010). *Person-centered and experiential therapies work: A review of the research on counseling, psychotherapy and related practices.* Ross-on-Wye, UK: PCCS Books.

Corbett, T. (2001). The nurse as a professional career. In R. B. Ellis, J. Gates, & N. Kenworthy (Eds.), *Interpersonal communication in nursing: Theory and practice* (pp. 91–105). London: Churchill Livingstone.

Delbene, R. (2015). Listening to "How the patient presents herself": A case study of a doctor–patient interaction in an emergency room. *Journal of Education and Training Studies, 3.* Retrieved from http://dx.doi.org/10.11114/jets.v3i2.498.

Denning, J. J. (2001). How to improve your listening skills, avoid mix-ups. *Ophthalmology Times, 26,* 28.

Dennis, S. (2004). Active listening is key to client-centered care, but how often do we make the effort? *Nursing Standard, 19,* 22–23.

Department of Health and Human Services Administration on Aging. (2010). Aging statistics. Retrieved from www.aoa.gov/AoARoot/Aging_Statistics/index.aspx.

Drass, K. A. (1988). Discourse and occupational perspective: A comparison of nurse practitioners and physician assistants. *Discourse Processes, 11,* 163–181.

du Pré, A. (2001). Accomplishing the impossible: Talking about body and soul and mind during a medical visit. *Health Communication, 14,* 1–22.

du Pré, A. (2010). *Communicating about health: Current issues and perspectives* (3rd ed.). New York: Oxford.

Dyche, L., & Swiderski, D. (2005). The effect of physician solicitation approaches on ability to identify patient concerns. *Journal of General Internal Medicine, 20,* 267–270.

Dykes, J. R. (2004, September). Making time to listen. *Family Practice Medicine.* Retrieved from www.aafp.org/fpm.

Edwards, E., Elwyn, G., Smith, C., Williams, S., & Thornton, H. (2001). Consumers' views of quality in the consultation and their relevance to 'shared decision-making' approaches. *Health Expectations, 4,* 151–161.

Farrant, B., & Watson, P. D. (2004). Health care delivery: Perspectives of young people with chronic illness and their parents. *Journal of Paediatrics and Child Health, 40,* 175–179.

Flores, G., Abreu, M., Olivar, M. A., & Kastner, B. (1998). Access barriers to health care for Latino children. *Archives of Pediatric & Adolescent Medicine, 152,* 1119–1125.

Frankel, R. (1990). Talking in interviews: A dispreference for patient-initiated questions in physician-patient encounters. In G. Psathas (Ed.), *Interaction competence* (pp. 231–262). Washington, DC: International Institute for Ethnomethodology and Conversation Analysis and University Press of America.

Fred, H. L. (2014, December 1). Editor's commentary: Deaf to the patient. *The Heart Institute of Texas Journal, 41*(6), 574.

Garcia, R. (2003, May 9). The misuse of race in medical diagnosis. *Chronicle of Higher Education,* B15.

Garcia de Lucio, L., Garcia Lopez, F. J., Marin Lopez, M. T., Hesse, B. M., & Caamano Vaz, M. D. (2000). Training programme in techniques of self-control and communication skills to improve nurses' relationships with relatives of seriously ill patients: A randomized controlled study. *Journal of Advanced Nursing, 32,* 425–431.

Gassmann, D., & Grawe, K. (2006). General change mechanisms: The relation between problem activation and resource activation in successful and unsuccessful therapeutic interactions. *Journal of Clinical Psychology and Psychotherapy, 13,* 1–11.

Goss, C., Mazzi, M. A., Del Piccolo, L., Rimondini, M., & Zimmermann, C. (2005). Information-giving sequences in general practice consultations. *Journal of Evaluation in Clinical Practice, 11,* 339–349.

Grant, C. J., III, Cissna, K. N., & Rosenfeld, L. B. (2000). Patients' perceptions of physicians' communication and outcomes of the accrual to trial process. *Health Communication, 12*, 23–39.

Gray, D., Evans, P., Sweeney, K., Lings, P., Seamark, D., Seamark, C., Dixon, M., & Bradley, M. (2003). Towards a theory of continuity of care. *Journal of Royal Society of Medicine, 96*, 160–166.

Graybar, S. R., & Leonard, L. M. (2005). In defense of listening. *American Journal of Psychotherapy, 59*, 1–18.

Greene, M. G., & Adelman, R. D. (2001). In M. L. Hummert, & J. F. Nussbaum (Eds.), *Aging, communication, & health* (pp. 101–120). Mahwah, NJ: LEA.

Harwood, J. (2007). *Understanding communication and aging: developing knowledge and awareness.* Thousand Oaks, CA: Sage.

Haskard, K. B. Z., & DiMatteo, M. R. (2009). Physician communication skills and patient adherence to treatment: A meta-analysis. *Medical Care, 47*, 826–834.

Hasselkus, B. R. (1992). Physician and family caregivers in the medical setting? Negotiation of care? *Journal of Aging Studies, 6*, 67–80.

Hing E., & Lin S. (2009). *Role of international medical school graduates in providing office-based medical care: United States, 2005–2006.* (NCHS data brief no. 13). Hyattsville, MD: National Center for Health Statistics. Retrieved from www.cdc.gov/nchs/data/databriefs/db13.htm.

Huynh, H. P., Sweeny, K., & Miller, T. (in press). Transformational leadership in primary care: Clinicians' patterned approaches to care predict patient satisfaction and health expectations. *Journal of Health Psychology.*

Institute of Medicine. (2000). *To err is human—Building a safer health system.* Washington, DC: The National Academies Press.

Ito, M., & Lambert, V. (2002). Communication effectiveness of nurses working in a variety of settings within one large university teaching hospital in western Japan. *Nursing and Health Sciences, 4*, 149–153.

Jadad, A. R., & Rizo, C. A. (2003). I am a good patient believe it or not. *British Medical Journal, 326*, 1293–1294.

James, J. T. (2013). A new, evidence-based estimate of patient harms associated with hospital care. *Journal of Patient Safety, 9*, 122–128.

Joshi, N. (2015, January 5). Doctor, shut up and listen. *The New York Times*, p. A17. Retrieved from www.nytimes.com/2015/01/05/opinion/doctor-shut-up-and-listen.html.

Kaiser Family Foundation. (2004). Trends and indicators in the changing healthcare marketplace. Health Insurances/Costs. Retrieved from www.kff.org/insurance/7031/print-sec5.cfm.

King, A., & Hoppe, R. B. (2013). "Best Practice" for patient-centered communication: A narrative review. *Journal of Graduate Medical Education, 5*, 385–393.

Kinnersley, P., Stott, N., Peters, T. J., & Harvey, I. (1999). The patient-centeredness of consultations and outcome in primary care. *British Journal of General Practice, 49*, 711–716.

Klostermann, B. K., Slap, G. B., Nebrig, D. M., Tivorsak, T. L., & Britto, M. T. (2005). Earning trust and losing it: Adolescents' views of trusting physicians. *The Journal of Family Practice, 54*, 679–687.

Krupnick, J. L., Sotsky, S. M., Simmens, S., Moyer, J., Elkin, I., Watkins, J., & Pilkonis, P. (1996). The role of the therapeutic alliance in psychotherapy and pharmacotherapy outcome: Findings in the National Institute of Mental Health Treatment of Depression collaborative research program. *Journal of Consulting and Clinical Psychology, 64*, 532–549.

Lie, D. (2014). Cultural differences. In T. L. Thompson (Ed.), *Encyclopedia of health communication* (pp. 278–280). Thousand Oaks, CA: Sage.

Leland, J. (2008, October 7). In "Sweetie" and "Dear," a hurt for the elderly. *New York Times online.* Retrieved from www.nytimes.com.

Levine, M. (June 1, 2004). Tell the doctor all your problems, but keep it to less than a minute. *The New York Times Online.* Retrieved from www.nytimes.com.

Li, H. Z., Krysko, M., Desroches, N. G., & Deagle, G. (2004). Reconceptualizing interruptions in physician-patient interviews: Cooperative and intrusive. *Communication & Medicine, 1*, 145–157.

Lloyd, R. C. (2003). Improving ambulatory care through better listening. *Journal of Ambulatory Care Management, 26*, 100–109.

Lundkvist, J., Åkerlind, B., & Mölstad, S. (2002). The more time spent on listening, the less time spent on prescribing antibiotics in general practice. *Family Practice, 19*, 638–640.

Ly, D. P., & Glied, S. A. (2013). The impact of managed care contracting on physicians. *Journal of General Internal Medicine, 29*, 237–42.

McCabe, K. (2012, June 27). Foreign-born health care workers in the United States. Migration Policy Institute. Retrieved from www.migrationpolicy.org/article/foreign-born-health-care-workers-united-states#4.

McLane, C. G., Zyzanski, S. J., & Flocke, S. A. (1995). Factors associated with medication noncompliance in rural elderly hypertensive patients. *American Journal of Hypertension, 8*, 206–209.

Mechanic, D., & Meyer, S. (2000). Concepts of trust among patients with serious illness. *Social Science Medicine, 51*, 657–668;

Meldrum, H. (2011). Listening practices of exemplary physicians. *International Journal of Listening, 25*, 145–160.

Mulac, A., & Giles, H. (1996). "You're only as old as you sound": Perceived vocal age and social meanings. *Health Communication, 8*, 199–215.

National Network of Libraries of Medicine. (2017). Health literacy. Department of Health and Human Services, National Institutes of Health, National Library of Medicine. Retrieved from https://nnlm.gov/professional-development/topics/health-literacy.

Northouse, P. G., & Northouse, L. L. (1992). *Health communication: Strategies for health professionals.* Norwalk, CT: Appleton & Lange.

Nussbaum, J. F., Ragan, S., & Whaley, B. (2003). Children, older adults, and women: Impact on provider-patient interaction. In T. L. Thompson, A. M. Dorsey, K. I. Miller, & R. Parrott (Eds.), *Handbook of health communication* (pp. 183–204). Mahwah, NJ: LEA.

Nussbaum, J. F., Thompson, T., & Robinson, J. D. (1989). *Communication and aging.* Cambridge, MA: Harper & Row.

Ong, L. M. L., de Haes, J. C. J. M., Hoos, A. M., & Lammes, F. B. (1995). Doctor–patient communication: A review of the literature. *Social Science and Medicine, 40*, 903–918.

Ray, E. B., & Bostrom, R. N. (1990). Listening in medical messages: The relationship of physician gender, patient gender, and seriousness of illness on short- and long-term recall. In R. Bostrom (Ed.), *Listening behavior: Measurement and applications* (pp. 128–143). New York: Guilford.

Reynolds, C. M. (2012). Visit with a veteran: A lesson in open listening. *Patient Education and Counseling, 88*.

Roberts, C. (2004). 'Only connect': The centrality of doctor–patient relationships in primary care. *Family Practice, 21*, 232–233.

Roberts, C. W. (2004, October). The QuEST for satisfaction begins with listening. *Review of Ophthalmology, 11*(10), 64–68.

Robertson, D. W. (1996). Ethical theory, ethnography, and differences between doctors and nurses in approaches to patient care. *Journal of Medical Ethics, 22*, 292–299.

Robinson, J. D. (2003). An international structure of medical activities during acute visits and its implications for patients' participation. *Health Communication, 15*, 27–58.

Rogan, F. C., & Timmins, F. (2004). Improving communication in day surgery settings. *Nursing Standard, 19*, 37–42.

Rosser, W. W., & Kasperski, J. (2001). The benefits of a trusting physician-patient relationship. *Journal of Family Practice, 50*, 329–330.

Roter, D. (2000). The medical visit context of treatment decision-making and the therapeutic relationship. *Health Expectations, 3*, 17–25.

Rousseau, P. C. (2014). Begging to be heard. *Journal of Palliative Medicine, 17*, 751–752.

Ruben, B. D. (1989). The health caregiver–patient relationship: Pathology, etiology, treatment. In E. B. Ray & L. Donohew (Eds.), *Communication and health: Systems and applications* (pp. 51–68). Hillsdale, NJ: LEA.

Rubin, D. L., Healy, P. Gardiner, T. C., Zath, R. C., & Moore, C. P. (1997). Nonnative physicians as message sources: Effects of accent and ethnicity on patients' responses to AIDS prevention counseling. *Health Communication, 9*, 351–368.

Sidell, M. (2001). Supporting individuals and facilitation change: The role of counseling skills. In J. Katz, A. Peberdy, & J. Douglas (Eds.), *Promoting health: Knowledge and practice* (2nd ed.). London: Palgrave.

Silverman, M., Murray, T. J., & Bryan, C. S. (Eds.). (2003). *The quotable Osler.* Philadelphia, PA: American College of Physicians.

Street, R. L., Jr. (2007). Aiding medical decision-making: A communication perspective. *Medical Decision-making, 10,* 550–553.

Tarrant, C., Windridge, K., Boulton, J., Baker, R., & Freeman, G. (2003, June 14). How important is personal care in general practice? *British Medical Journal (Clinical Research Edition), 326,* 1310.

Trahan, B. C., & Rockwell, P. (1999). The effects of listening training on nursing home assistants: Residents' satisfaction with and perceptions of assistants' listening behavior. *International Journal of Listening, 13,* 62–74.

US Department of Health and Human Services. (2008).America's health literacy: Why we need accessible health information. Retrieved from https://health.gov/communication/literacy/issuebrief.

Waitzken, H. (1991). *The politics of medical encounters: How patients and doctors deal with social problems.* New Haven, CT: Yale University Press.

Wanzer, M. B., Booth-Butterfield, M., & Gruber, K. (2004). Perceptions of health care providers' communication: Relationships between patient-centered communication and satisfaction. *Health Communication, 16,* 363–384.

Watson, K. W., Lazarus, C. J., & Thomas, T. (1999). First-year medical students' listener preferences: A longitudinal study. *International Journal of Listening, 13,* 1–11.

Weech-Maldonado, R., Morales, L. S., Elliott, M., Spritzer, K. L., Marshall, G., & Hays, R. D. (2003). Race/ethnicity, language and patients' assessments of care in Medicaid managed care. *Health Services Research, 38,* 789–808.

Weiner, S. J., & Schwartz, A. (2016). *Listening for what matters.* New York: Oxford.

Weiss, L. J., & Blustein, J. (1996). Faithful patients: The effect of long-term physician-patient relationships on the costs and use of health care by older Americans. *American Journal of Public Health, 86,* 1742–1747.

Welch, S. J. (2010). Twenty years of patient satisfaction research applied to the emergency department: A qualitative review. *American Journal of Medical Quality, 25,* 64–72.

West, C. (1993). "Ask me no questions…" – An analysis of queries and replies in physician–patient dialogues. In A. D. Todd & S. Fisher (Eds.), *The social organization of doctor-patient communication* (2nd ed., pp. 127–157). Norwood, NJ: Ablex.

Williams, S. A. (1997, June). The relationship of patients' perceptions of holistic nursing caring to satisfaction with nursing care. *Journal of Nursing Care Quality, 11,* 15–29.

Zimmerman, R., & Arnold, W. E. (1990). Physicians' and patients' perceptions of actual versus ideal physician communications and listening behaviors. *Journal of the International Listening Association, 4,* 143–164.

12   Listening in Legal Contexts

Case Study 12.1 Shooting at Merc's Department Store

Hey, Radley, is your mom's station going to cover any of that woman's trial? You know the one accused of shoplifting from Merc's Department store and then shooting the security guard? My mom is going to be one of the witnesses. She saw the whole thing and gave statements to the police right after it happened. And, Tamarah was the 911 operator who took the initial call from Merc's.

Wow, I didn't realize we were so connected to that shooting. I'm pretty sure the station will cover the story, NaMii, but mom hasn't mentioned anything about working on that particular one. But then again, she doesn't always tell me what stories she's working on. Is your mom nervous about being a witness? I wonder if the lawyer will rough her up like in the trial scenes on crime shows.

Oh, Radley, my dad has to work with his company's legal counsels all of the time and he says they are easy to work with. And, my mom said the officer who took her statement was really nice. He asked clear questions and listened to what she had to say. I think he is also going to be a witness. I wonder who will end up on the jury.

As we begin this chapter, we offer the following caveat. We address this listening context from the perspective of the US legal system. Later in the chapter, you'll find an interview with listening and legal scholar Tuula-Riitta Välikoski, who provides you with a glimpse of the changing legal landscape in Finland.

To begin, when you think about listening in a legal context, what springs to mind? A courtroom like Radley thought of in the case above? A police interrogation? We take a very broad approach to listening in the legal context. While we do talk about listening in law enforcement and the courtroom, we also address mediation, a type of alternative dispute resolution. We examine interactions between a variety of individuals who work in legal contexts including attorneys, jurors, negotiators, mediators, law enforcement, 911 operators, emergency medical technicians (EMTs) and the general public. If you think there is the potential overlap between each of these areas, you are right. Take the scenario in Case Study 12.2.

Case Study 12.2 To Catch a Vandal

Wendell called 911 to report that his car had been vandalized. He told the operator he had seen a man, about 5'10" wearing a yellow jacket in his front yard. The hood of the jacket was up, so he hadn't been able to see the man's face. A few minutes later, Jeff, a young man walking in the neighborhood and wearing a yellow jacket was stopped and detained by police officer Frank Long. After speaking with Jeff, Officer Long was suspicious and asked Jeff to go to the station with him. Upon their arrival, Jeff called his attorney, Joe Pritchard, who met him at the police station.

Think of all the areas where listening occurs during this brief scenario – the 911 operator listens to Wendell, Wendell listens and answers the operator's questions, Officer Long listens to his dispatcher and to Jeff, Jeff's attorney listens to both the officer and to Jeff. All of these listening opportunities occur and Jeff hasn't even been formally charged with a crime! Regardless of whether Jeff simply wore the wrong color jacket at the wrong time, or is accused of and tried for the vandalism, there will be many more listening opportunities before the situation is resolved. Let's take a look at some of the possible listening situations.

Public Safety Officials

Law Enforcement Officers

Often the first legal related person we have contact with is a police officer. Most police officers undergo an average of 21 weeks of training to learn their job.[1] This training includes a significant communication component including mediation training which typically includes a great deal of listening training. Clearly, an officer's duties are more than crime prosecutions and prevention, maintaining order (e.g., traffic flow and violations, maintaining the peace), and other services (e.g., medical, missing persons, assisting motorists, etc.) The following sections demonstrate how listening plays a key role in the field of law enforcement. Importantly, many of these skills can be applied to similar contexts in other fields.

Investigative Interviewing. Law enforcement officers work with members of the public in many ways. When you watch a crime drama, you often see an officer interviewing an eyewitness about the particulars of a crime, as is the case with NaMii's mother in the case at the beginning of the chapter. This type of situation involves both the listening of the officer as well as the observation skills of the witness. Eyewitnesses face a number of challenges. The account in Case Study 12.3 of an office invasion witnessed by Dr. Worthington illustrates several problems.

Case Study 12.3 Office Invasion

A friend and I were working on a Saturday evening in my office. As we sat in my office (with the door open), a young man came out of the instructional resource center (IRC) across the hall. First, I was greatly surprised, then I tried to figure out who he was. I did not recognize him as a graduate student and knew he was not related to any of our faculty. He headed for the front door of the building, opened it, and let someone else in. I stopped him in the hall and asked him what he was doing. He said he and his friend were going to study. (His friend was standing behind him.) When I asked him why he was in the IRC, he said he came through an open window to get to the front door to let his friend in (the front doors were locked). Obviously, all kinds of warning bells were going off in my head. As I was telling him that the building was off limits to students on the weekend and that he had to leave, I was trying to memorize everything I could about him. I've studied problems with eyewitness testimony and know how events can affect our memory. For the first time, I experienced them. While I can remember the one "dark-haired" student-type, I can't remember anything about his friend except that he was about 5'10" and had sandy-colored hair.

Two weeks later the department was burglarized. Was it the same young men? We don't know. However, as seen here, events typically happen within minutes, if not seconds, adrenaline is coursing your system, and as seen with Professor Worthington's account, you often center your attention on just a few things. Keep in mind that what happened to Dr. Worthington is not particularly shocking or unusual. Witnessing an actual assault, robbery, or severe car accident is traumatic for everyone involved. Consequently, the observation and attending skills of any witness are tested to their limits. To complicate matters, witnesses often focus on different things, causing police officers to interview as many different people at the scene of an accident as they can. Therefore, an officer has to be particularly careful as both a listener and a questioner.

How an investigator asks a question can shape the response of the witness. Therefore, a witness like Mrs. Kim in Case Study 12.1 should carefully listen to the question and be mindful of the potential impact of the wording of that question. Research indicates that listeners often integrate into their own memories what officers, other witnesses, and other parties involved with a case say to them. Elizabeth Loftus, a highly respected cognitive psychologist, and others have found that if a questioner introduces the existence of an object (that was not at the original scene), the eyewitness will integrated the information into his or her memory of events. As an example, if the police officer had asked Dr. Worthington in the situation mentioned earlier, "And, what color was the young man's baseball cap," she might have added the presence of the baseball cap to her memory of events that night. Fortunately, the police officer who interviewed her simply asked, "What can you tell me," thus allowed for a free flowing response, and hopefully more accurate recall on her part. The lesson here for law enforcement officials is to *listen and not lead the other person* – less talking and more listening aids a witness's ability to recall events and details accurately. In these types of situations, comprehensive listening allows officers to gain accurate understanding of what occurred, building a picture of events leading to the incident. Critical listening helps witnesses separate what they remember from anything that might be included in a question. Officer Natalie McKinley offers additional advice in her interview later in this chapter.

Much of the research on eye witness testimony focuses on two types of information: estimator variables and system variables.[2] **Estimator variables** are elements not under our control but directly related to the crime events. Examples of estimator variables include the type and severity of crime, complexity of the event, familiarity with surroundings, available lighting as well as the race, attractiveness, sex, and age of the accused. As we discussed earlier in the text, any of these factors can impact how we perceive both auditory and visual information. In the example at the beginning of the chapter, Mrs. Kim's answers to the officer's question would have been influenced by the fact the crimes took place in her place of employment, a department store, her relationship with the guard who was shot, and her perceptions of the accused.

System variables, in contrast, are related to events within the criminal justice system. They include factors such as the time lapse between when someone witnesses the event and the eventual testimony, interviewer question structure, and police line-up instructions. For example, one early study in this area found that when recalling a filmed murder, witnesses are 91% accurate when they are allowed to elaborate their recall of the event freely without any questions. When an interviewer used open-ended questions the accuracy dropped to 83%. Accuracy dropped even more to 72% when the witness responded to leading questions.[3] This research illustrates the power of simply listening. Fewer questions can lead to greater (and more accurate) recall.

Like witnesses, officials also use a variety of types of listening. For example, following an accident or crime, people are naturally shaken by events. It is important that officers take time to engage in empathic listening to calm witnesses. In Case Study 12.1, Mrs. Kim witnessed a coworker get shot. Chances are she was very upset by what she had seen. Therefore, a good police officer would recognize her heightened emotional state and work to calm her before asking questions. People who are calm (or at least somewhat calmer) are more likely to recall events and recall them more accurately. Of course, officers also use their critical listening skills to assess the veracity of a witness's statement as well identify any missing information. This combination of empathic and critical listening not only helps the officer get the information, it will also help him or her during the testimony phase of the trial if the situation ends up in court.

Crisis Negotiation

As the previous section indicates, there are many ways that listening is important to the jobs of those involved in public safety. A specific area where listening is critical is in a crisis situation. Today, the National Council of Negotiation Associations, composed of agencies at the local, state, and federal level, lists strong interpersonal and listening skills in their guidelines for selecting negotiation team members. The role of listening is also included in the required initial training for negotiators, and when negotiating, it is recommended that negotiators engage in "non-threatening, nonjudgmental communication to include active listening skills… with the goal of de-escalating and defusing the incident."[4]

Learn more about it: Over 40 years ago, New York City led the way in developing hostage negotiation. In 1973, they were the first law enforcement agency to develop a dedicated hostage negotiation team. They responded to over 400 incidents in 2012.

Members of the New York Police Department's hostage negotiation team discuss the importance of active listening to hostage negotiations in the following YouTube video: http://bit.ly/NYPDHNT.

You can learn more about their approach to listening at the following website: http://nypdnews.com/activelistening.

Fortunately, law enforcement officers now receive substantial training in crisis negotiation. Examples of crisis negotiations include hostage taking, some instances of domestic violence, suicide attempts, and stand-offs. Arthur Slatkin, a police and criminal psychologist, notes that today's negotiators have psychology and counseling backgrounds and strong communication skills.[5] Research shows that FBI agents trained in hostage negotiation have stronger active listening skills and a lower tendency to engage in counterproductive behaviors such as problem-solving.[6]

Problem solving is problematic if someone jumps to solving the situation before listening to all sides of the issue. Slatkin acknowledges the fundamental role listening plays in these types of negotiations when he writes,

> at the heart of negotiation and negotiator trained skills is "active listening," a way in which a listener communicates demonstrably that he is listening... that he acknowledges the other person, is taking in what is being said, is trying to understand what is being said, and cares about the person saying it.[7]

The crisis negotiator uses her training to connect with persons in crisis in order to bring them to a more balanced state with the expectation of bringing the crisis to a conclusion that will preserve some of the individual's self-respect. This suggests that relational listening is an important part of what crisis negotiators do. Through relational listening, crisis negotiators make connection with the party in crisis using specific techniques. A negotiator's communication techniques can be broken down into three categories: listening, action, and sharing.[8] You are already familiar with the basic *listening techniques* – clarification, paraphrasing, reflection, and summarizing. *Action techniques* involve probing, confrontation, interpretation, and information-giving, and instructions. Finally, *sharing responses*, which reflect relational listening, include self-disclosure, immediacy, and reinforcement.

> ***Think on it:*** Even as a student you sometimes talk with people who are experiencing a crisis. Sometimes these crises are romances that break up, family upheavals, or negative medical news. How can you use crisis negotiation listening in such situations?

Most of these techniques appear self-evident. However, they are specially adapted to crisis negotiations. For example, **confrontation** is used in a very specific manner to address inconsistencies or discrepancies in a person's statements, in behaviors, or between statements and behaviors (i.e., "You say you don't want to hurt anyone, but you shot out the window twice."). Similarly, when a negotiator engages in **self-disclosure** it is strategically done so as to further the negotiations. Thus, the negotiation may model personal disclosure in order to encourage someone threatening suicide to disclose back. Earlier in this book we discussed the reciprocal nature of self-disclosure and the societal pressure we may feel to respond in similar manner. Thus, when an officer discloses seemingly personal information, the other person may feel like they should as well, without fully realizing why. Such information may give the officer important insight into the person and the situation.

Immediacy responses involve statements of the negotiators feeling about the individual, at that particular time. For example, one of the characters we have followed throughout this book, Tamarah Jackson, works as a 911 operator in public safety. If Tamarah receives a call from someone who is reporting a break-in she might say something like the following to someone who has stopped talking on the phone, "Do you know that when you stop talking to me, I think that something has happened." **Reinforcement**, on the other hand, encourages someone to start or continue with a behavior (e.g., "You really showed good faith when you released that hostage"). As you can see, one of the primary ways in which negotiators attempt to diffuse a crisis situation is by connecting with the individual. As we learned earlier, we all want to feel that we are valued, respected, and important. People in crisis are no different. Of course, the ultimate goal of every negotiator is to end the crisis safely for everyone involved and their listening and communication reflect that goal.

If You Are a Witness: Listening Lessons

Natalie Blackstock
Patrol Officer, Crisis Negotiator, & D.A.R.E. School Resource Officer
LaGrange Police Department
LaGrange, GA, USA

Police officers have to listen very carefully. We listen for tone, inflection and try to determine if someone is lying to us or not. In hostage negotiations, we listen to everything, including background noise! Over my career, I've learned that close listening encourages people to talk. And, the more people talk, the more they may reveal.

What is the most significant piece of advice I can offer to the public? When you are in an emergency – *slow down*. People tend to talk very fast and their words come out in a rush when they are excited, scared, mad, etc. It can be hard, but if you take a few deep breaths before explaining something, it can actually speed up the interview process! A deep breath gives you time to collect and organize your thoughts, and to determine what you really need to say. This means we may not have to ask so many questions and can address your emergency even more quickly.

Attorney–Client Communication

While not all of you will have contact with someone in public safety, the odds are that at some point in your life you will have contact with others in the legal field. In addition to attorneys, jurors and judges, there are bailiffs, court reporters, paralegals, jury consultants, project managers, and court interpreters, to name a few. In this section, we focus on attorney–client communication. You may want to have a will drawn up, a contract reviewed, or get divorced. Good listening skills – on both your and your attorney's part – result in a more effective and satisfactory relationship.

Certainly, it is important for an attorney to know the law; however, communication is central to almost all attorney tasks. Until recently attorney–client relationships received little, if any, formal attention in law schools. As a result, younger attorneys often failed to recognize the importance of listening.[9] Consequently, attorneys fresh from law school were often less people-oriented and more law and research focused. As they matured as lawyers, they learned the importance of good communication and strong listening skills in gaining and maintaining their client relationships.

Fortunately, law schools, attorneys, and other legal professionals today have come to recognize the importance of establishing and maintaining a quality relationship with their clients.[10] Organizations like the Law Society of British Columbia, Canada have developed communication short courses with the goal of improving attorney communication skills.[11] There are educational blogs like *Listen like a Lawyer* that address the importance of, and provides tips for, improving attorney listening. Jennifer Romig, an instructor at Emory University Law School, began the blog because she felt that good listening makes for good lawyering.[12] She agrees with us that listening is a central communication skill in attorney–client relations. In fact, active listening is the guiding force behind effective communication between attorneys and their clients.

The following sections are designed to look at listening and communication skills and behavior for both attorneys and clients.

Advice for Attorneys

For those of you who think you want to become lawyers, below are suggestions for developing your listening skills. The rest of you will find the suggestions applicable to most professional settings and interactions. We have organized our advice around the three stages of an attorney interview – developing rapport, gathering information, and counseling. You will notice that attorneys tend to begin the interview using relational listening then move to comprehensive listening and finishing with critical listening.

Interviewing – Stage One. The initial contact between attorneys and their clients and witnesses is very important.[13] It is here the interview focuses on establishing a relationship, while later stages address understanding and assessing a client's case. The primary purpose of this first stage of the interviewing process is to **establish rapport** with clients.[14] If clients feel that the attorney is unresponsive or indifferent about their case, it is unlikely they will remain clients for very long. Thus, it is important that attorneys help clients relax and establish a supportive communication climate. Attorneys must assess the merits of a case and the needs of the client during the initial stages of the interview. In an effort to get adequate and accurate information, attorneys attempt to establish rapport by doing the following:

- *Putting clients at ease by presenting a professional image and keeping distractions to a minimum.* Inappropriate clothing, ringing phones, loud conversations and other external noises can interfere with a quality interview. Earlier in the book, we discussed the impact of these types of stimuli on information processing. Most attorneys begin a visit by using ice breakers such as a warm welcome and a few minor personal questions (e.g., "Is this your first time visiting an attorney?" "did you find the office okay?" "I hope you didn't have to wait too long"). This social exchange sets the tone for the rest of the interview.
- *Allowing the client to direct the initial part of the interview.* This lets them establish their comfort zone. The attorney should focus on active listening and asking open-ended questions that encourage the client to talk. Of course an attorney who is listening to the client will let the other person talk use these types of question sparingly since they tend to interrupt the flow of information. While some visits may be straightforward (e.g., reviewing a business contract), other cases may be more volatile, the attorney interview is the first time the client has been able to purge the emotions associated with the case, whether it is a divorce, an arrest for driving under the influence (DUI), or a wrongful death. At this stage, the primary goal is to "build empathic identification and rapport."[15]
- *Engaging in relational listening.* Depending on the type of case, attorneys can find themselves playing the role of counselor.[16] It is easy to see how divorce or child custody cases require lawyers to focus on the emotional impact on their client as well as attempting to gather information about the case. It is no surprise that in these types of cases clients experience great emotional distress, and lawyers must be able to address this distress. However, other more common

types of cases (e.g., contract disputes, personal injury, or bankruptcy) can be emotionally upsetting as well. When emotions run high, a good listener will use empathic silence. Head nods and other nonverbals assure clients that the lawyer is listening, while silence encourages them to continue speaking. Of course, a good listening attorney will be attuned to when the client has truly finished talking, is uncomfortable opening up, or expects him or her to direct the interview. As you can see, empathic or therapeutic listening is an important part of attorney–client interviews. Attorney Merit Bennett encourages his clients to "talk themselves out." He finds that not only does he learn about the events surrounding the case, but he often can learn what type of outcome they will be satisfied with.[17] Other attorneys also note the importance of expressing empathy while engaging in active listening. Through paraphrasing and direct assertions of empathy, lawyers can not only acknowledge the content of the client's communication, but the underlying emotions as well.[18] As Lauren Howe, a student at the University of Huddersfield Law School (United Kingdom), wrote, "Communication and the ability to encourage a client to confide in you is one of the most important parts of being a lawyer…"[19]

Interviewing – Stage Two. The next stage of the attorney–client interview focuses on **information gathering.** Here, comprehensive and critical listening are most useful. Comprehensive listening is central to translating or interpreting a client's communication and is necessary for fully understanding the client's needs. An easy pitfall at this stage is premature counseling or problem solving. Counseling, or giving advice too soon, can prevent an attorney from getting needed facts. Problem solving, or listening in the yellow fix-it mode discussed in Chapter 2, can be viewed as an indication that the attorney is more focused on his or her assessment than on the client's information. Critical listening is important in this stage so lawyers can evaluate the information and ask for needed clarification. The following suggestions will help attorneys and others maximize listening.

- *Briefly outline the purpose and goals of the interview.* By letting the client know what to expect in the interview, the attorney helps establish a framework from which the client can listen and process the information. Most clients, particularly first time ones, have only media portrayals to shape their expectations of the process, and such portrayals are generally inaccurate. For example, if our friend Radley who has watched too many courtroom dramas, were to be interviewed by a lawyer, his expectation of being "grilled by the attorney" might make him defensive. So, an outline of what to expect would help Radley relax and listen to the questions. The overview also provides a good transition from relational to comprehensive and critical listening. Of course, attorneys should use everyday language and avoid "legalese" as they address information gathered from the client's narration of events and ask for further clarification or expansion. A good listener will use summary statements and paraphrasing to ensure full understanding of the client's needs.
- *Ask questions.* While asking questions is important, the wording of the questions is critical. As you recall from earlier in the chapter, leading questions could predispose the client to answer in a particular way. For example, "Isn't it true that John played high stakes poker regularly?" versus "Did John like to gamble?" carry different implications and will consequently get different responses. Probing questions don't have to lead the client to answer in a specific manner. Asking someone to elaborate or complete his or her thoughts opens the door for more accurate information. Whatever the type of question or technique, the primary function is to keep the discussion moving in order to gather necessary information. Consequently, as in all listening situations, attorneys should keep interruptions to a minimum. The client has the information the attorney needs, and allowing him or her to talk freely will oftentimes help the attorney identify important topics to explore later.

- *Take brief notes (if necessary)*, but avoid writing large amounts of information down. Clients may slow their narrative to match the speed of note taking, or start wondering about what is being written – either way, it can become a distraction.
- *Be respectful.* While this isn't a listening skill per se, being respectful helps an attorney (and others) establish a climate in which the client is able to give the information necessary, regardless of how painful it may be. Because the topic may be very emotional, both attorneys and clients may need to take a break to gather themselves emotionally. Margaret Fitch-Hauser once gave a lengthy deposition as an expert witness to an attorney who tended to become angry when he didn't get the answer he wanted. Fortunately, he was professional enough to realize when he needed to take a break so he wouldn't say anything that would be harmful. Being respectful also includes being polite to clients. People want to be acknowledged as respected individuals.[20] Saying, "please," apologizing for delays, and giving full attention to the client when listening are just a few ways of achieving this goal.
- *Listen for truthfulness, accuracy, omissions and contradictions.* Clients need to feel comfortable enough to disclose their case with all its "negatives." However, clients do forget, misremember, and occasionally outright lie. As attorney Merit Bennett notes, omitted information is potentially detrimental to a client's case.[21] For example, if an attorney finds out in court that his client has previously been ticketed for driving under the influence, it may lead jurors to question his or the client's credibility. The attorney who knows possibly negative information in advance can plan for it and deal with it accordingly. Through active listening, attorneys can better assess the strengths (and weaknesses) of a client's story, and identify and address any contradictions.
- *Avoid prejudging.* Attorneys, like all of us, have biases that can affect the interpretation of messages. Few attorneys have the option of only working with clients they approve of. Even if they do, they will be required to interview other individuals, work with other attorneys, or have cases tried before judges they simply do not like. Consequently, it is important for attorneys to assess their biases and determine if they can listen without prejudice and effectively handle the case.[22] If they cannot, the ethical attorney will refer the case to a colleague. In addition, attorneys need to be aware of the effect of cultural differences on communication and their assessment of the case. As law professor Susan Bryant notes, "all lawyering is cross cultural," requiring a non-judgmental approach to the attorney–client relationship. One way to achieve this is by focusing on the facts of the case, not the judgment of the client.[23] Thus, it is important for attorneys to recognize the impact of their own schemas on their perceptions and listening when they start a relationship with a new client.

Interviewing – Stage Three. The final stage of the attorney–client interview involves **counseling** the client. It is here that attorneys move from comprehensive listener to advisor and problem solver. Please note, however, this does not mean they stop listening, they simply listen differently.

- Perhaps the most important aspect of this stage is *evaluating the facts of the case.* First, the attorney must use critical and comprehensive listening to assess whether the situation should go into the legal system at all, and if so, is it one that is "provable," and worth pursuing. For example, in Chapter 11 we describe Mason's experience with medical malpractice. The doctor who prescribed the incorrect medication came to visit Mason, took personal responsibility for what happened, and apologized. Because he was the company physician, all medical bills were paid, and he received full pay while recuperating. He suffered no lasting physical or neurological damage. If he had chosen to sue, it is unlikely an attorney would take the case. One attorney friend calls these types of incidents – "no harm; no foul" cases. They take time and money to pursue, and are unlikely to result in a monetary return that makes it worth everyone's time and effort.

- Counseling a client also entails *assessing viable courses of action open to the client.* Through active listening and closely watching the client's nonverbals, an attorney can better assess client responses to the different options and resulting scenarios (e.g., best case versus worst case scenario). Attorneys use their listening and related observation skills as well as their knowledge of the legal system to realistically analyze risks, costs, time, effort, and other realities of taking a case to court (or negotiations). Once attorneys make this assessment, they then present the information to the client in such a way the client can listen and absorb the truth of that assessment even when the client doesn't want to hear it. Attorney Lucinda Jesson notes the importance of managing client expectations so that clients clearly understand the possible *realistic* outcomes of their case.[24] A good attorney will do his or her best, but none promise a win.

Think on it: While the above suggestions were applied to attorney–client interviews, how might the advice be applied to other interviewing contexts?

Advice for Clients

Many more of you will be clients than attorneys. Listening will be just as important for you as it is for the attorney. Like the attorney, you will want to set the stage for effective listening by being prepared. This will include having all pertinent documents organized and with you when you meet. The more accurate and in depth the information you provide, the better attorneys will be able to do their job.[25] It will also be helpful if you create an outline of the situation to help you remember and to present a balanced overview of the situation. Here are a few other suggestions that will help you be a better client:

- *Recognize your own biases and the strength of your emotions.* In other words, be as accurate and objective as you can as you present information about your case to the attorney. Being objective also means trying to keep emotions from clouding your description of events. The attorney is not there to judge you, but to determine your needs, and to present viable options. If you are not honest or misrepresent facts, then he cannot properly do his job.[26]
- *Look for an attorney who listens.* A lawyer who does not fully understand the situation cannot offer you adequate advice or appropriate legal options. If you are continually interrupted by staff and phone calls, if your attorney spends all the time talking, then you may want to think twice about using her as your representative.
- *Engage in comprehensive and critical listening.* After listening to your information, your attorney will generally offer you advice on how to proceed. You will need to understand and evaluate the relative merits of each option.
- *Fully understand the attorney retainer and fee agreement.* When you are under stress or emotionally charged, as people often are when they talk with attorneys, it is easy to "zone out" on information that doesn't specifically address the case, such as information about fee agreements. One friend was rudely awakened when she discovered the emotional purging she engaged in while on the telephone with her attorney cost her several hundred dollars – the attorney was charging her an hourly rate for each call. Her attorney was an excellent, relational listener and offered great emotional support, but it came at a price.

Think on it: How does the advice for clients apply to interactions you may have with either professionals or situations you are currently facing. For example, how can you use this information when you apply for a job or when you talk with one of your instructors?

If the attorney takes your case, you have several means of resolving it. You may end up litigating it (going to trial), or you may engage in one of several types of alternative dispute resolution (ADR) methods. We start our discussion looking at the role listening plays in the courtroom context.

Listening Challenges of the Jury

The Jury as Audience

The jury process begins with jury selection or **voir dire**. Every jurisdiction has what is commonly called a venire, or jury pool. The jury pool is composed of individuals from the community and the actual jury is selected from this pool. During voir dire the attorneys, clients, and judge meet potential jurors. Generally, potential jurors are questioned in an open courtroom about their backgrounds, attitudes, and other experiences related to the case. Listening on the part of attorneys and potential jurors is very important during this process.

Voir dire is more than just selecting who will actually serve on a jury. Attorneys also use it to build or establish their case, introduce case themes, and to introduce their clients favorably. The goal of both sides is to impanel jurors who will be the least biased against their cases. Therefore, attorneys listen for any information which might indicate a potential bias or predisposition against their client. Jaine Fraser, a jury consultant and trial psychologist, suggests that attorneys use the **80–20 rule of listening** during voir dire: listen 80% of the time, and talk 20% of the time. New Mexico attorney Randi McGinn offers even more specific advice.[27] She tells attorneys that they should ask open-ended questions, avoid speaking legalese, avoid being judgmental. Most importantly, she tells attorneys they should listen – allowing jurors to talk – and avoiding note-taking while jurors are speaking.

Listening and Voir Dire

If you are ever called for juror duty, our first suggestion is to go! It's a fascinating look at our legal system at work. Just keep in mind that you bear the responsibility of listening carefully so you can reach a fair decision. Here are some suggestions that can help you be a better listener:

- *Use comprehensive listening.* During jury selection, the judge and attorneys will introduce the case, general background, and primary players. You need to pay close attention at this time for at least two reasons. First, there may be a legitimate reason for you to be excused (i.e., you were cited for driving under the influence, you were the victim of a robbery, or you know one of the individuals involved). Second, this information provides you with background on the case if you are actually picked for jury duty.
- *Be aware of potential biases and schemas.* Remember that the attorneys are introducing their case and trying to influence how you interpret evidence. After all, attorneys do have an obligation to put their client's case in the best light possible. Of course you will also want to be honest about your own biases and the experiences that may have caused you to have these biases. For example, if Tamarah had a good friend killed by a drunk driver. She would be the first to

admit that she has no tolerance for driving under the influence. Consequently, she would not be the best candidate to serve as a juror on a DUI case.

- *Stay focused.* The voir dire process is full of distractions. You may wonder why the person next to you was dismissed or what the judge and bailiff are discussing. Like most listening situations, it takes concentration to stay focused on the task at hand. Active listening will help you to answer questions accurately and can help you learn even more about a case.

- *Ask for clarification.* Keep in mind that responding is an important part of listening. If during the voir dire, you don't understand what the question is asking or a word being used, ask for clarification. Judges and attorneys are so used to using legal language that they sometimes forget that most of us are not familiar with those terms. Since you can't evaluate and respond to a judge's or attorney's questions without first understanding it, it's okay to say, "I'm not sure what that word means" or "Could you rephrase that; I don't understand." Odds are others in the jury pool could use the clarification as well.

- *Volunteer information if it is needed.* If you are asked a question, be direct in answering it. However, as a comprehensive and critical listener, you may recognize that the question requires more than the obvious answer. For example, if asked "What do you do for a living," we would most likely respond that we are college professors. However, we also do some litigation consulting. Professor Fitch-Hauser has worked as an expert witness on several cases and Professor Worthington assists in witness preparation and is an active member of the American Society of Trial Consultants. So, we would need to reveal that activity in our responses to the question.

Law and Culture: Listening Lessons

Tuula-Riitta Välikoski
Adjunct Professor, Communication Sciences
University of Tampere
Finland

Approximately 15 years ago the criminal trial procedures in Finland changed. Previously, judicial decisions were based upon written arguments. Today, verdict is based on orally presented material. This change means that the role of listening during trials has also changed.

Effective listening is especially crucial for prosecutors because they have to hear, understand and critically evaluate information as it is presented. At the same time, they must keep their own case goals clearly in mind as they have to be ready to present when the judge signals it is their turn.

One of the most demanding phases of a trial procedure for the prosecutor is the witness hearing. It can involve both critical and supportive listening. Prosecutors must be especially attentive and prepared to respond, particularly given that unexpected testimony can occur. At the same time, they must be aware of the anxiety that a witness may be feeling as it can negatively affect his or her testimony.

Courtroom Context

If you are selected to serve on a jury, once the trial begins you will want to be prepared to listen to the different stages of the trial. Attorney and litigation consultant, Richard Waites, argued that "Listening in the courtroom is critical to the process of communication and persuasion."[28] In the following sections, we focus on stages of the trial where juror listening is critical: attorney opening statements and closing arguments, witness examination, judicial instructions, and jury deliberations.

Opening Statements

Each side starts the trial by presenting opening statements or arguments. You will probably be motivated to listen because of your curiosity about the case. As a responsible listener, you will want to use this motivation to focus on the schema formation aspect of the opening statements. Attorneys typically strategically organized their openings in a narrative format because they believed that a strong story had the greatest potential for influencing juror decisions. By presenting an overview of the case and introducing the story, or theory of the case, opening statements provide a framework through which later evidence and information is interpreted.[29] Researchers in trial advocacy agree that opening statements can have a great influence on the jury.[30]

Schema activation naturally occurs during opening statements. They affect what information we attend to, what meaning we assign to incoming information, how we draw inferences (i.e., connect information or fill in gaps), and how we organize and store information in memory. If you think about the Listening MATERRS Model presented in Chapter 1, it becomes clear that the listeners will look for motivation to listen to the testimony as well as begin putting schemas in place that will help them translate and evaluate it. How attorneys frame their opening statements has a significant impact on how jurors listen to their cases.

The Importance of Stories and Schemas. Listeners' use of schemas continues throughout the testimony phase of a trial. The **story model of jury decision-making** helps us understand how jurors process information during the pre-deliberation stage of the trial.[31] Why are stories so important? For listeners, stories provide a way to keep track of and make sense of all the information in the trial. Attorney Richard Waites also notes that the underlying themes in a story, "help jurors organize case information along the lines that the [attorney] wishes, and help them to overcome disputes or conflicts with specific evidence."[32]

Unfortunately, not all information in a trial is presented "in order." The story then helps listeners reorder the information they receive into an easier to understand narrative format. Years of research reveal that when we hear information "out of order" we naturally reorder it into a standard story format.[33] In general, storing things in our memory as a narrative makes it easier for us to remember, and what we remember will impact the decisions we make as a jury.

These stories become very helpful when the jurors go into deliberation after they have heard the evidence. Deliberation is often a process of constructing the most plausible story that fits the case facts and explains case events. And, as psychologists Patricia Devine and Thomas Ostrom note, memory of information can be quite important because verdicts are primarily based on the jurors' shared recollections of trial events.[34] Stories help us identify and process important information (such as motives or means) and pay less attention to background or less important information (what the defendant and the victim ate for dinner at the restaurant).

At the heart of every story are themes. In a trial, these are called case themes. Waites argues that compelling themes "are at least as important as the key facts of the case."[35] In general, we can classify case themes as **evaluative** (characterizing character traits, behaviors and motivations) or **more powerful than fact** (characterizing the evidence).[36] Powerful stories include the most powerful themes and evidence in a way that coincides with juror life experiences. Whether the theme is taken from a fairy tale (The Boy Who Called Wolf), a biblical story (David versus Goliath), or a historical event (Rosa Parks), it should be "easy to remember, appeal to common sense, [be] in accord with jurors' concepts of fairness and justice, and [be] consistent with the evidence."[37]

As you can see, using stories actually aids the listening process. We find it easier to remember trial evidence when it is organized narratively. In fact, trial simulations suggest that jurors take the many bits and pieces of the trial (evidence and testimony), and construct their own stories. In addition, attorneys will attempt to "prime" the schemas we draw upon to process and evaluate trial evidence. In other words, if one attorney's version (story) of events is more compelling, we will likely engage and use schemas that are in keeping with that story. Thus, we may pay greater attention to some evidence and testimony than others. We may also work harder to make that evidence fit with that story, dismissing any that doesn't fit.

Testimony

After the opening statements, each side presents the evidence supporting their case. As you know from watching movie and television court scenes, this evidence takes many forms (photographs, diagrams, physical evidence, and so forth). The most influential is witness testimony, especially when it is live testimony rather than written or taped. Eye witnesses recount events, identify suspects, and provide important background information. Listening to testimony can teach us many lessons about critical listening. Jurors, as they listen to both sides, need to evaluate all of the testimony, especially when it is contradictory. They have to assess witness credibility, by following the attorney questions and evaluating witness responses, all while closely watching the witness's nonverbal. As you can see in the silicone breast implant case study, in addition to factual contradictions, jurors also often have to deal with emotional conflicts as well. Imagine the listening challenges of balancing and evaluating all of the contradictory information!

Case Study: 12.4 Silicone Breast Implant

During the testimony phase of a class action law suit against silicone breast implant makers, women testified that their implants had leaked or burst. They alleged the silicone had traveled in their bodies and caused a host of illnesses and autoimmune disorders such as chronic fatigue syndrome, depression, fibromyalgia, and other ailments. These witnesses had clearly suffered emotional and physical trauma. Their emotional trauma was further supported by psychologists who testified about psychological effects of removing the implants. On the other hand, the companies being sued presented experts who countered the alleged victims' claims. They had research scientists testify about the causes of autoimmune diseases and statisticians testify about the probabilities of developing specific symptoms or diseases.

Of the evidence described above, descriptions of trauma, research reports, and statistics, which do you believe would be most influential? Why? How does it fit in with our previous discussion of listening and storytelling?

(For a description of the SBI controversy, check out the following *Forbes* magazine article: http://bit.ly/ForbesSBI.)

Closing Arguments

Just as opening statements are influential in their ability to frame a dispute, closing arguments are influential in their ability to synthesize trial information and remind jurors of evidence deemed important to an advocate's case. Here, attorneys openly attempt to affect attitude change. Good listening jurors will want to listen closely (and be aware of) attorney attempts to the persuade them to adopt a certain version of the case facts. Closings allow attorneys to highlight key elements of their case and reinforce case themes and theory. Attorney John Crawford suggests that strategic "planned redundancy" during a closing aids jurors' memories during deliberation.[38]

Jury Deliberations

After all of the testimony and closing arguments, judges give juries instructions for deliberation and decision-making and the jurors retire to deliberate. By this point of the trial, jurors' energy level is typically pretty low. After all, they have been listening for a long time and listening takes a lot of energy. However, it is important to engage in close comprehensive listening as the judge's instructions ultimately guide jury deliberations and affect the type of verdict juries reach.

The fact that jurors get to talk for the first time in the trial process can sometimes cause them to focus on talking rather than discussing and listening. However, our experience as researchers (and as actual jurors) suggests that people work hard to be fair during jury deliberations. In the next few paragraphs we offer suggestions for enhancing listening during the deliberation process. Drawn from the work of Aubrey Fisher, as an added bonus, these suggestions can be adapted to other problem-solving groups, whose members initially do not know one another very well.[39]

Fisher's Phases. If not appointed, the first thing a jury does after retiring to the jury room is to select a foreperson. This individual typically helps facilitate the discussion and will ultimately deliver the jury's verdict to the court official (a bailiff). Once this is done, the deliberation begins. However, jurors should avoid jumping into immediate discussions about the case. During this initial **orientation phase**, they need a few minutes to decompress from the events of the trial and get to know one another a bit. And as in any setting, it is more comfortable talking with and listening to people who we know at least a little bit about. One way to break the ice is to have each person introduce themselves and tell everyone what they would be doing if they were not jurors that day.

Jury deliberation can involve conflict and debate. At the early stages of deliberation, people are uncomfortable engaging in this type of exchange. Consequently, during the **conflict phase** juries should *avoid early votes*. In fact, judges will often tell you *not* to take an early vote, but to discuss the evidence first. This is excellent advice for several reasons. First, since the jury members aren't ready to engage in a debate about the evidence, they may be too influenced by others in the group before they make up their own minds. This, in turn, can prevent them from listening with an open mind to what others have to say. You can see this happen in the movie, *Twelve Angry Men*, when the group takes a vote (for the death penalty) as soon as they sit down. Hands slowly go up around the table. It is clear that some individuals are unsure, but they almost vote to send the young man to the electric chair anyway. If it were not for Henry Fonda (in the original film version), the group would have reached what is called a *false consensus* (i.e., group members think they agree, when in actuality, they don't), and the defendant would have received the death penalty.

Second, early votes often can have a polarizing effect on jury decision-making.[40] Individual jurors know where everyone stands, but have no clue why. They haven't had a chance to find out. Since the act of publicly committing to a position can have a detrimental effect on discussion, they may never learn why. People do not want to appear indecisive or "wishy-washy" and so they may become firmly committed to their publicly stated position, and be less willing to listen to others. When they do listen it is often to listen selectively for information that supports their position. As a result, they ignore important ideas and evidence. Juries who reach decisions in this manner are labeled **verdict driven**.

Listening juries are **evidence driven**. Here, jurors actively listen to one another, openly debating the validity of the evidence and how it fits with the judge's instructions. Not surprisingly, active listening techniques are important to this type of jury as is critical listening. This type of jury *focuses on the evidence* and engages in **substantive conflict** or debating over ideas and avoids **affective conflict** which focuses on personality differences. Members are careful to avoid pre-judging either ideas or the jury member who is delivering the idea. They are able to do so because they know the important work of the group is to deliver a fair verdict. Consequently, they listen carefully to the points made regardless of who originates the idea. Of course, it is important for all members of the jury to participate. An observant listener will listen for what's not being said as well as to what is being said. For example, if a juror notices someone rolling his or her eyes and looking out the window, the juror should follow-up to find out what their counterpart is thinking.

Jury deliberation can be tense and emotionally taxing. Therefore, it's important for the group to *take breaks when necessary*, particularly if emotions are running high because of heated debate. It's difficult to listen when we are upset or angry. Taking a break, getting a soft drink, or engaging in some other activity may help everyone relax and lead to better listening and group decision-making.

The behaviors that are appropriate for any group discussion are even more important during jury deliberation. Most juries will eventually enter an **emergence phase.** At this time, jurors will begin to "emerge" from conflict. One way jurors can determine if they are emerging from conflict is to listen for *preludes to agreement.* People seldom abruptly change their position during deliberations. Usually, they provide both verbal and nonverbal indications that they are moving toward the opposing position. They might nod their head at an opposing point, shrug to indicate they are unsure, or they may say something like, "I can see your point," or "I haven't thought about it that way before." These types of ambiguous statements allow jurors to change their minds, but in a way that helps them "save face." It is also important for jurors to demonstrate they are listening by engaging in nonverbal behaviors that show they are being attentive. These behaviors may include such things as leaning forward, nodding in agreement, or in some other manner acknowledging the points of other jurors.

Another good listening behavior (throughout deliberations) that enhances the jury experience is to *avoid interrupting.* As trial consultants, we see jurors in simulated trials do this frequently. They are so intent on presenting their own position that they interrupt or cut off what others are saying. Verdicts are a joint decision. Interruptions disrupt listening and inhibit the ability to fully understand and evaluate what is being said. Eventually, most juries will reach a verdict. An important aspect of the **reinforcement phase** is acknowledging and bonding over the decision that has been reached. Here, jurors will complement each other for a job well done and recognize the hard work they've accomplished. It's important, when possible, for jurors to engage in this type of supportive listening as it increases satisfaction with the verdict that was made and with the overall legal and jury process.

Being on a jury is a unique opportunity to actively participate in the American legal system. If called, serve! Every case allows you to offer your personal contribution in rendering justice in a criminal case or resolving a civil dispute. However, as we mentioned earlier, litigation is only one method of resolving disputes. In reality, most cases never reach the courtroom. People can resolve conflicts through several other alternative dispute methods in the legal system. Next, we introduce you to other alternative methods of resolving disputes. Because many of the listening skills hold true across the varying methods, we will focus on listening in one particular method – mediation.

Alternative Dispute Resolution

Alternative dispute resolution (ADR) is the phrase used to describe a number of methods of resolving disputes without litigation. The two major approaches used are mediation and binding arbitration.[41] Other approaches include mediation-arbitration, non-binding arbitration, mini-trials, partnering, and early neutral evaluation. The greatest differences in these methods are the amount of input and freedom in participation and outcomes. Figure 12.1 illustrates the level of outcome control associated with each type of ADR and litigation.

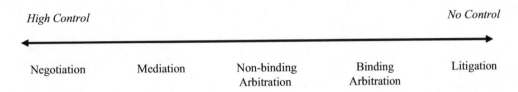

Figure 12.1 Level of Outcome Control and Alternative Dispute Resolution Type

Types of Disputes

The choice of which ADR method to use should be based on the type of dispute. Three broad areas or disputes are issue oriented, emotion oriented, or a blend of the two.[42] **Issue-oriented** dispute resolution is connected to rules, regulations, or the guidelines we follow in everyday life. It is not unusual for judges and arbitrators or your boss, principal, or teacher to take on the role of an evaluator in these instances. When there is a school fight, the teacher or principal steps in; when we have a significant on-the-job dispute, the boss may be called in to decide; if a neighbor is shooting off late night fireworks, we call the police. Whoever is called upon to resolve the dispute, that person relies on listening to all sides being fair, unemotional, and objective when deciding the outcome.

Emotionally oriented dispute resolution calls on professionals such as counselors, psychologists, social workers, ministers, or others in the helping professions to assist in resolving the dispute. These helping professionals are trained in therapeutic, empathic and other types of listening needed to resolve these very personal disputes. A primary focus of the problem in these types of disputes is the emotions involved. Thus, a marriage counselor may mediate for a distressed couple, coaches may work with the disappointment of the loss of a state championship, or grief counselors may be called in when a student dies in a car accident. In these cases, emphasis is placed on the emotions themselves.

Issue-emotion dispute resolution addresses both issues and emotions. In this type of dispute there is something about the dispute that makes it difficult for parties to address their problems. Consequently a neutral third party (e.g., mediators, professional negotiators and other professionals) is needed to help individuals to resolve their differences. Usually the neutral third party aids in facilitating an open dialogue between those involved, while at the same time ensuring the discussion is fair and balanced. Ideally, the process allows everyone an equal input into discussion and equal input into mutually agreeable resolution options. Of course equal input calls for equal listening!

We summarize the different types of resolution in Table 12.1.

Table 12.1 Issues, Emotions, and Dispute Resolution

Type of Dispute	Examples of Professional Roles	Primary Attributes
Issue-oriented	Judge, Arbitrator, Supervisor	Focus is on rules, gathering evidence, being objective, maintaining social order.
Emotion-oriented	Counselor, Social Worker, Psychologist	Focus is on understanding the emotional climate, stabilizing emotions, neutralizing negative emotions and/or other emotional impediments to resolution. Mediator will personally intervene as needed.
Issue & Emotion-oriented	Mediator, Diplomat, Intermediary, Negotiator	Conducted by a neutral third party, ensures equitable discussions stressing fairness and mutual areas of interest. Identifies and addresses issue-oriented and emotion-oriented topics. Defuses or neutralizes emotions impeding resolution. Mediator may personally intervene.

Adapted from Ladd, 2005, p. 5.

Listening and Alternative Dispute Resolution

Professional mediator Louis Phipps Senft argues that listening is a fundamental component of mediation, arguing that "listening is more important... than speaking."[43] However, she argues that not only are mediators responsible for engaging in good listening skills, but so should clients and the attorneys who represent them. She notes that in many cases the parties come to negotiations and mediation are so focused on proving their point that they fail to listen to the other side or the mediator. She asserts that it is through listening that parties are able reach a fair and workable solution. Individuals become people instead of being viewed as the enemy. Mediator William Logue agrees by suggesting that when listening is evident, the parties involved feel acknowledged and that their beliefs and feelings have been accepted, creativity is boosted, and the number of emotional outbursts are reduced.[44]

Mediation

In this type of ADR, a neutral third party – a mediator – facilitates negotiations between two (or more) parties in hopes of reaching a mutually satisfactory resolution. Disputes that revolve around conflicts of interest are particularly appropriate for mediation. These conflicts typically stem from a situation of scarcity. Both parties want the same thing, but there is not enough of it to be had. Thus, someone wants more money for a property than you want to pay, you disagree with your insurance agent about how much they should pay for the damage to your car, and so forth. These types of conflict are particularly prone to compromise, in part because bargaining is not associated with deep-seated values (ethical, moral, or religious differences). Cases that focus on the "principle of the matter" are usually over values and are consequently difficult to settle. We don't want to look like we are willing to compromise our principles. An illustration of the difference in issue-oriented and principle-based approach can be seen in a divorce case. If the parties are issue oriented, not focused on the "morality" of the behavior that led to the divorce, they can focus on interests of dividing the estate fairly. If they focus on the "morality" aspect of the situation, they will more than likely get bogged down in the blame game and fail to listen to the needs of the other party in such a way a fair settlement can be reached.

Mediation differs from other types of legal and alternative dispute resolution methods in that while there is a mediator who helps to facilitate negotiations, the mediator is not charged with imposing a solution on the disputing parties. Mediators play an important role in helping each party to step outside of their "schemas." In other words, a skilled mediator has the ability to get the parties involved to see beyond the events leading up to the mediation (e.g., who breached the contract first, how much damage a company suffered), to develop creative solutions to the problem(s) for a win-win situation for everyone involved. The example in Case Study 12.5 does an excellent job of distinguished mediation from other types of ADR:[45]

Case Study 12.5 Kathryn and Indigo's Problem

Kathryn and her cousin Indigo are arguing over the last orange in the basket on the kitchen table. Indigo's mom, Sydney, hearing the argument tells the children they know the importance of being able to share, so she carefully slices the orange giving half to each child. The children were not any happier. Imagine for a moment that a mediator had handled the situation. The mediator would have first asked the children, "Why do you want the orange?" Kathryn, the cook in the family, wants to make marmalade, while Indigo is thirsty. With this information, the mediator suggests that Indigo juice the orange, then give the rind and pulp to Kathryn – a win-win situation for both young girls.

Why do People Choose Mediation? Generally, mediation follows a failed attempt at direct, unassisted negotiations.[46] Sometimes the failure is due to poor listening by one or both parties. In these cases, a mediator steps in to listen to both sides and assist them in reaching a mutually agreeable outcome. It is also often used in a variety of other types of disputes where one or both parties want to avoid the high costs of going to trial, wish to maintain confidentiality and/or avoid publicity, need to continue a working relationship with the other party, know that litigation will not fully address the issues, and/or recognize that those involved are so emotional that it is doubtful that they could negotiate a settlement on their own. Mediators do not "decide what is best" for the disputing parties, nor do they attempt to impose a resolution.[47] They do, however, assist those involved in reaching a mutually agreeable outcome.

Most importantly, mediation works.[48] While success rates vary with the context, research suggests that overall mediation leads to between 40% and 70% of disputes reaching a lasting, formal agreement. The parties tend to be more satisfied, and believe the agreements are fairer, in part because both parties have contributed to the outcome and solution. As a result, they are more likely to comply with the settlement terms.

What Makes Mediation Work? Fundamentally, the introduction of a neutral third party who listens changes the communication between the disputing parties.[49] Civility is usually a ground rule

of discussions. Mediators are better able to see the bigger picture, including aspects of the conflict that go beyond legal issues to underlying areas of interest to both parties. Because mediators **listen to both sides**, they are often in the best position not only to identify barriers to resolution but to recognize the "blinders" parties to a dispute may have. Mediators point out unrecognized areas of interest, barriers to resolution, and other perceptual stumbling blocks; both parties can address these areas in open discussion.

The best mediators are impartial, supportive, active listeners who utilize an array of skills, including paraphrasing, reframing, and reviewing.[50] However, these skills are necessary for effective listening between competing parties. As you can see, these skills are basic to and reflect good listening. ***Paraphrasing*** is important because it allows the mediator essentially to pause the mediation process and sum up and point out the primary points in a concise manner. Professor Peter Ladd notes that it is especially useful when the involved parties become overly emotional or communication between the parties begins to stall. By providing a summary of what has occurred or the agreed upon main points, mediators can provide a sense of forward motion, simultaneously conveying what has been covered as well as pointing out continued areas of difference. ***Reframing*** is necessary when disputants use language or messages that could potentially inflame the discussion or lead to a breakdown in the dialogue. Generally, the mediator attempts to reframe the message so that it is more acceptable for the opposing party, thus allowing the mediation to continue. For example, if Tori claims, "You promised you would fix my computer. You worked on it and now it does not run at all! You cheated me out of $200." If you were mediating between Tori and Jameth, you might tell Jameth, "Tori is trying to say that it was her understanding that the work you did on her computer was guaranteed, but that the guarantee has not been honored." Finally, ***reviewing*** goes beyond a general paraphrasing of issues. Mediators tend to use the technique when an extended silence occurs during discussion. Essentially, you review the major issues or themes that have been discussed. Reviews such as these help identify new topic areas as well as help put discussion back on track.

If you ever find yourself in a mediation situation, you should keep in mind that the best mediators work hard to help both sides reach an amicable and hopefully long-term agreement.

> ***Think on it:*** Do you know someone who seems to be a "natural" mediator? Which of the characteristics and skills described here are reflected in his or her behaviors?

Summary

This chapter has examined how listening plays a critical role in several legal contexts. Not surprisingly, listening is critical in law enforcement, all phases of a trial as well as in alternative dispute resolution situations. So, whether you talk with someone in public safety, an attorney, a judge, or a mediator you will notice that listening plays a critical role in the success of that interaction. If you plan to go into law enforcement or become an attorney, listening will be a critical communication competency for you. Importantly, however, many of the skills discussed in this chapter go beyond the legal context to other professional encounters. Whether working in a small group, attending a professional seminar, or listening to a workplace dispute, a clear understanding of listening in legal contexts can aid your comprehension, assist in evaluating information, and enhance group problem solving.

Key Concepts

Eye Witness Testimony
Estimator and System variables
Negotiator Communication Techniques
Attorney Interview Stages
Advice for Clients

Advice for Jurors
80–20 Rule
Voir dire
Opening Statements
Story model
Trial Themes
Jury Deliberation
    Fisher's Phases
    Evidence versus Verdict Driven Juries
Alternative Dispute Resolution
    Issue-oriented disputes
    Emotional-oriented disputes
    Issue-emotion disputes
Mediation

Discussion Questions

In 2007, 911 dispatcher Theresa Parker disappeared from LaFayette, Georgia. A year later, her husband Sam, a former police officer, was arrested. At the time he was arrested, her body had not been found (it wasn't found until 2010). Imagine that he has come to trial and you have been hired as a communication consultant by his defense attorney. Address the following questions based on the material covered in the chapter.

1. What type of biases would you want to explore during voir dire? Rank order them from most important to least important. Why did you choose these biases and why did you rank them this way? How could such biases affect juror listening during the trial or juror decision-making during deliberations?
2. What type of story or theme(s) might you develop to help aid jurors while listening during the trial? How might different themes address different issues (or biases) associated with the trial (e.g., death penalty, no body has been located).
3. How comfortable would you be aiding in the defense of Mr. Parker? If you are uncomfortable, how might that affect your ability to listen to him fully? To provide him with solid/effective advice?

Listening Activities

1. View a movie or television program portraying courtroom communication (e.g., *Class Action*, *A Few Good Men*, *Law & Order*, *Chicago Justice*). Drawing on material from this and earlier chapters of the book, which of the characters presented portrayed the best listening skills? The worst? As a listening expert, what advice would you give to improve the listening of characters portraying poor listening skills?
2. Using the same video material from above, what biases do you see evidenced by the judge, attorneys, witnesses or jurors? How might such biases impact the testimony of a witness? The rulings by a judge? Questioning by an attorney? Verdict discussions of a juror?
3. Write a one to two page description of your current schema of courtrooms and what occurs within them. Next, watch actual trial proceedings by going to the local courthouse or, if

you're unable to view an actual trial, try viewing trial proceedings on television channels such as truTV. Does what you observe match up with your original schema? How was your schema confirmed? What did you find surprising?

4. Watch the movie *Twelve Angry Men*. Does the group follow the decision-making process described by Fisher? Do they go through each of the four phases? What actions, behaviors, comments, etc. by the characters support your claims? Would you say they were an evidence-driven jury? What could they have done differently to improve their decision-making process? To improve individual and group listening?

Notes

1 Bureau of Justice Statistics, 2016
2 Wells, 1987, 2008
3 See Wells, 1987; Pansky, Koriat, & Goldsmith, 2005; and Steblay & Loftus (2012) for a review of related research on eyewitness recall and testimony.
4 National Council of Negotiation Associations, 2009
5 Slatkin, 2010
6 Van Hasselt et al., 2006
7 Slatkin, 2010, p. xi
8 Slatkin, 2010, Chapter 2
9 Seckler, 2008
10 Arenson, 2002
11 Law Society Online Learning Centre, 2015
12 Romig, 2017
13 Dinerstein, Ellmann, Gunning, & Shalleck, 2004
14 Post, 2009
15 Matlon, 1988, p. 25
16 Bayles, 2002
17 Keeva, 2011
18 Dinerstein et al., 2004
19 Howe, 2017
20 Lore, 2005
21 Keeva, 2011
22 Keeva, 2011
23 Bryant, 2001
24 Lore, 2005
25 Contra Costa County Bar Association, 2016
26 Contra Costa County Bar Association, 2016
27 McGinn, 2005
28 Waites, 2003, p. 21
29 Frederick, 2012; Spiecker & Worthington, 2003, 2008
30 Spiecker & Worthington, 2008
31 Pennington & Hastie, 1992; See also Williams & Jones, 2005, for a brief review of trial strategy and tactics.
32 Waites, 2003, p. 139
33 For an early summary of this research see Fitch-Hauser, 1990
34 Devine & Ostrom, 1985
35 Waites, 2003, p. 139
36 Waites, 2003
37 Waites, 2003, p. 140

38 As cited in Waites, 2003

39 Littlejohn, Foss, & Oetzel, 2017; Adapted from Fisher's (1970) decision-making model, these suggestions are based on newly formed groups in which members have had little or no previous prior contact.

40 Hastie, Penrod & Pennington, 1983; Levett, Danielsen, Kovera, & Cutler, 2005

41 Picker, 2004

42 Ladd, 2005

43 Senft, 2005

44 Logue, 2003

45 Adapted from Picker (2004), who attributes it to Fisher & Ury (1981) in *Getting to yes: Negotiating agreement without giving in.*

46 Picker, 2004

47 Mayer, 2012

48 Mayer, 2012; Spangle & Isenhart, 2003

49 Lewicki, Hiam, & Olander 1996; Mayer, 2012; Spangle & Isenhart, 2003

50 Teply, 2015

Additional Readings

Brewer, N., & Williams, K. D. (2005). *Psychology and law: An empirical perspective.* New York: Guildford.

McMains, M. J., & Mullins, W. C. (2013). *Crisis negotiations: Managing critical incidents and hostage situations in law enforcement and correction* (3rd ed.). Cincinnati, OH: Anderson.

McCorkle, S., & Rees, M. J. (2015). *Mediation theory and practice.* Thousand Oaks, CA: Sage.

Silkenat, J. R., Aresty, J. M., & Klosek, J. (Eds.). (2009). *ABA guide to international business negotiations: A comparison of cross-cultural issues and successful approaches* (3rd ed.). Chicago: American Bar Association.

Motley, M. T. (Ed.). (2012). *Forensic communication: Application of communication science to courtroom litigation.* Cresskill, NJ: Hampton Press.

References

Arenson, K. W. (2002, January 13). The fine art of listening. *New York Times*, Section 4A, Education Life Supplement, p. 34.

Bayles, F. (2002, July 31). Abuse victims flock to lawyers. *USA Today*, p. D1.

Bryant, S. (2001). The five habits: Building cross-cultural competence in lawyers. *Clinical Law Review, 8,* 33–107.

Bureau of Justice Statistics. (2016, July). State and local law enforcement training academies, 2013. (Report No. NCJ249784). Retrieved from www.bjs.gov/content/pub/pdf/slleta13_sum.pdf.

Contra Costa County Bar Association. (2016). Get prepared for your 30-minute consultation. Retrieved from www.cccba.org/community/find-a-lawyer/get-prepared.php.

Devine, P. G., & Ostrom, T. M. (1985). Cognitive mediation of inconsistency discounting. *Journal of Personality and Social Psychology, 49,* 5–21.

Dinerstein, R., Ellmann, S., Gunning, I., & Shalleck, A. (2004). Connection, capacity and morality in lawyer-client relationships: Dialogues and commentary *Clinical Law Review, 10,* 755–804.

Fisher, B. A. (1970). Decision emergence: Phases in group decision making. *Speech Monographs, 37,* 53–66.

Fisher, R., & Ury, W. (1981). *Getting to yes: Negotiating agreement without giving in* (1st ed.). New York: Penguin.

Fitch-Hauser, M. (1990). Making sense of data: Constructs, schemas, and concepts. In R. N. Bostrom (Ed.), *Listening behavior: Measurement and application.* New York: Guilford.

Frederick, J. T. (2012). *Mastering voir dire and jury selection.* (3rd ed.). Chicago, IL: American Bar Association.

Hastie, R., Penrod, S. D., & Pennington, N. (1983). *Inside the jury.* Cambridge, MA: Harvard University Press.

Howe, L. (2017). Student views. The Client Interviewing Competition. Retrieved from www.clientinterviewing.com/student-views.html.

Keeva, S. (2011). *Transforming practices: Finding joy and satisfaction in the legal life.* Chicago: American Bar Association.

Ladd, P. D. (2005). *Mediation, conciliation, and emotions: A practitioner's guide for understanding emotions in dispute resolution.* Lanham, MD: University Press of America.

Law Society Online Learning Centre. (2015). Communication toolkit. Law Society Communication Toolkit Course. British Columbia, Canada: The Law Society of British Columbia. Retrieved from https://learn-lsbc.ca/node/487.

Levett, L. M., Danielsen, E. M., Kovera, M. B., & Cutler, B. L. (2005). The psychology of jury and juror decision making. In N. Brewer & K. D. Williams, *Psychology and law: An empirical perspective.* New York: Guilford.

Lewicki, R., Hiam, A., & Olander K. W. (1996). *Think before you speak: A complete guide to strategic negotiation.* New York: John Wiley.

Littlejohn, S., Foss, K. A., & Oetzel, J. G. (2017). *Theories of human communication* (11th ed.). Long Grove, IL: Waveland.

Logue, W. D. (2003, March 24). What's it worth? Listen and learn. *Connecticut Law Tribune.* Retrieved from www.law.com/jsp/article.jsp?id=900005382952.

Lore, M. (2005, October 17). Legal professionals offer advice on how to maintain good relations with clients. *The Minnesota Lawyer.* Retrieved from www.minnlawyer.com/article.cfm?recid=73599.

McGinn, R. (2005). *Cause strikes: How to discover jurors' true beliefs and eliminate those who deny justice.* ATLA Toronto 2005 Annual Convention Papers.

Matlon, R. J. (1988). *Communication in the legal process.* New York: Holt, Rinehart, & Winston.

Mayer, B. (2012). *The dynamics of conflict: A guide to engagement and intervention.* San Francisco, CA: Jossey-Bass.

National Council of Negotiation Associations. (2009). Recommended negotiation guidelines and policies. Retrieved from www.ncna.us/default.aspx?MenuItemID=96&MenuGroup=Home.

Pansky, A., Koriat, A., & Goldsmith, M. (2005). Eyewitness recall and testimony. In N. Brewer & K. Williams (Eds.), *Psychology and law: An empirical perspective* (pp. 93–150). New York: Guilford.

Pennington, N., & Hastie, R. (1992). Explaining the evidence: Tests of the story model for juror decision making. *Journal of Personality and Social Psychology, 62,* 189–206.

Picker, B. G. (2004). *Mediation practice guide: A handbook for resolving business disputes.* (2nd ed.). Washington, DC: American Bar Association Section of Dispute Resolution.

Post, A. J. (2009, December 7). Advice for your first client interview. *Law Trends & News Practice Area Newsletter, 6.* Retrieved from www.americanbar.org/newsletter/publications/law_trends_news_practice_area_e_newsletter_home/09_fall_yl_feat2.html.

Romig, J. M. (2017). About: Listen like a lawyer. Retrieved from https://listenlikealawyer.com/about.

Seckler, S. (2008). Questions to ask when it's time to listen. *BCG Attorney Search Newsletter.* Retrieved from www.bcgsearch.com.

Senft, L. P. (2005, March 11). Commentary: The negotiation table – Turning problems into opportunities: Listening, mediator style. *The Baltimore Daily Record.* Retrieved from http://findarticles.com/p/articles/mi_qn4183/is_20050311/ai_n12946511/? tag=content;col1.

Slatkin, A. A. (2010). *Communication in crisis and hostage negotiations.* (2nd ed). Springfield, IL: Charles C. Tomas.

Spangle, M. L., & Isenhart, M. W. (2003). *Negotiation: Communication for diverse settings.* Thousand Oaks, CA: Sage.

Spiecker, S. C., & Worthington, D. L. (2003). The influence of opening statement and closing argument organizational strategy on juror decision-making. *Law and Human Behavior*, *27*, 437–456.

Spiecker, S., & Worthington, D. L. (2008). Explorations of juror reasoning: The influence of attorney opening statement/closing argument organizational strategy. *Communication Law Review*, *8*, 52–63. Retrieved from http://commlawreview.org.

Steblay, N. M., & Loftus, E. F. (2012). Eyewitness memory and the legal system. In E. Shafir (Ed.), *The behavioural foundations of public policy* (pp. 145–162). Princeton, NJ: Princeton University Press.

Teply, L. L. (2015). *Legal negotiation in a nutshell* (3rd ed.). St. Paul, MN: West.

Van Hasselt, V. B., Baker, M. T., Romano, S. J., Schlessinger, K. M., Zucker, M., Dragone, R., & Perera, A. L. (2006). Crisis (hostage) negotiation training. *Criminal Justice and Behavior*, *33*, 56–69.

Waites, R. C. (2003). *Courtroom psychology and trial advocacy.* New York: ALM.

Wells, G. (1987). Applied eyewitness-testimony research: System variables and estimator variables. In L. S. Wrightsman, C. E. Willis, & S. M. Kassin (Eds.), *On the witness stand.* Newbury, CA: Sage.

Wells, G. (2008). Estimator and system variables in eyewitness identification. In B. L. Cutler (Ed.), *Encyclopedia of psychology and law*, pp. 257–258. Thousand Oaks, CA: Sage.

Williams, K. & Jones, A. (2005). Trial strategies and tactics. In N. Brewer & K. D. Williams (Eds.), *Psychology and law* (pp. 276–322). New York: Guilford.

Part IV

Listening

New Frontiers

13 Transforming Listening

Future Directions

Case Study 13.1 Looking Back. Looking Forward.

Nolvia: *Can you believe our class is almost over. Only one more week!*

Ben: *Yeah, just our group presentation tomorrow and the final exam. It seems like we just started the semester.*

Nolvia: *It's been fun. I really liked the family listening diary that we did.*

Ben: *Well, I liked the personality profiles we filled out. I'm minoring in psychology and I'd never thought about how my personality could affect how I listen.*

Nolvia: *I liked learning about Grice's Maxims and how they affect our conversations. They help explain why some of my conversations with my cousin Abelson seem awkward. He's constantly breaking the conversational rules. At least now I know what part of the problem is. What about you Tamarah?*

Tamarah: *I don't know if I can pick out one thing. I knew listening was important before I got here. My job and people's lives depend on it. I also liked the material on social support. What makes for good support and bad support. Looking back to some of my arguments with my family, I know there have been times when I wasn't always being as supportive as I should have been or could have been. What about you, Ben? Do you feel like you're a better listener now?*

Ben: *Yes and no. I know a lot more about listening and all the distractions that are out there. If anything, I know how bad I can be at it sometimes. It's really hard work to truly listen to others. Of course, I pay a lot more attention to how I listen and how others listen as well. I'd like to think I'm a better listener now.*

Nolvia: *I feel the same way. Carter and I were working together last night and I found my attention wandering. I just winced and said to myself, Nolvia, focus!*

Ben: *I know exactly what you mean. I think I've got a better handle on one of my really bad habits – interrupting. It can be really hard, but I keep working at not interrupting others unless I absolutely have to. I've found that if I keep my mouth shut I learn a lot more about people and I think I help them more too.*

Nolvia: *Hey, that's like that NCIS episode we watched in class where Gibbs didn't say a word during his entire conversation with Abby. She gave him that big hug and told him how great he was at helping her out with her problem. I had basically the same thing happen with my friend Shelly last weekend. It was weird having watched the show. Sometimes you really can be a better friend if you just listen and stop trying to solve the other person's problems.*

> Tamarah: *Yeah, I know one thing. I'll never think of listening the same way again… and I'll work hard to be a better listener too.*
>
> Ben: *Speaking of solving problems, this looks like the rest of the group headed this way. We need to iron out the last of our presentation. Hey, Radley!*

The goal of this book has been to introduce you to the importance of listening in our everyday lives. Over the course of this text, you've learned about important underlying features that may affect how we listen and you've learned about aspects of listening in specific contexts such as the workplace and the classroom.

Our understanding of listening continues to change, in part because of new and exciting research that is being conducted by prominent listening scholars. As we noted in Chapter 1, listening is a relatively new area of study. As a result, theory and conceptual development lag behind those of other more established areas of communication study (e.g., interpersonal, persuasion, health communication).[1] As more listening research is conducted and as new technologies emerge, our notion of what it means "to listen" has and will likely change significantly. This chapter will look at a few directions in listening research that we believe will set the tone for the next generation of research in this vital area.

Let's start by looking at the aural component of listening. Aural listening requires ability. Thus, we need a better understanding of the **physiology of listening**. Listening disabilities can be caused by both physiological and neurological dysfunctions with the auditory system. In addition to the traditional hearing loss discussed in earlier chapters, there are auditory processing disorders and language processing disorders. These types of disabilities can occur at any age and are often quite difficult to diagnose, but they can have devastating results. Even a small hearing loss can affect the language development in children and lead to feelings of social isolation in adults. In addition, it may affect a child's ability to learn to read and write and how they interact with others. Young adults with auditory processing problems may find their career choices limited and often experience additional workplace problems.

Our understanding, however, must go beyond the physical make-up of the ear and related auditory reception to include what happens in the brain once we have received a message stimulus. What elements affect the way information is recorded? How does the *temporal lobe*, the auditory area of the brain, effectively retrieve and retain a message in a coordinated way?[2] What factors affect the physiology of listening? Obviously, factors such as hearing loss or brain damage can affect how we translate and process incoming messages. What is unclear is what additional physiological features impact our listening behaviors. There are many unanswered questions. Fortunately, new research methodologies are helping us learn more about this area of listening and how it impacts how we listen to and process incoming messages. Thus, we begin this chapter with a brief examination of an emerging research method, fMRI. We then move on to examine emerging research in music and architecture.

Functional Magnetic Resonance Imaging

One new research method is beginning to reveal much about how we listen. **Functional magnetic resonance imaging**, or fMRI, is a non-invasive test that creates detailed images of the brain (and the rest of the body) using a strong magnetic field and radio waves to track brain activity from blood flow in the brain. Basically, when we activate a section of the brain, blood begins to flow

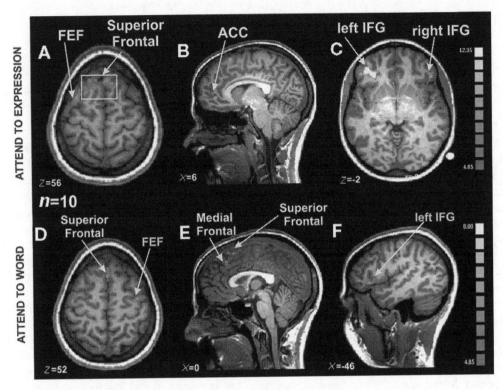

Figure 13.1 fMRI Image of Brain
Source: S. Ovaysikia, K. A. Tahir, J. L. Chan & J. F. X. DeSouza

to that area. This research method has the potential to tell us much about how our brains work when listening.

While fMRI shows great promise, we would be remiss if we did not mention some of the problems with this emerging research methodology. While there are several issues with this method, we touch on only two here: **noise** and **realism**. First, if you've ever had a traditional MRI, you know that they can be quite physically noisy. But, other types of "noise" exist for this type of sensitive research. Other examples of fMRI *noise* include head movement, fidgeting, and even breathing, all of which can affect fMRI results. *Realism* addresses validity. Can we take the results and apply them to our daily lives? fMRI research often involves **dichotic listening. Dichotic listening** involves being scanned while hearing a sound in one ear or the other. Needless to say, such studies lack *mundane realism*. They do not reflect real life.

Understanding its limitations, many listening-related areas have positively benefited from fMRI and other brain research methods (e.g., magnetoencephalography (MEG), electroencephalography (EEG) or functional near-infrared spectroscopy (fNIRS)). For example, recent research using fMRI suggests that the "reward" sections of our brain are activated when we judge someone as actively listening.[3] Related research has examined people's reactions when listening to stories, and found that narratives are more likely to engage large sections of the brain, and that listeners often "sync" their brains with the storyteller. In other words, the same sections of the brain are activated in both the storyteller and the listener. This finding suggests that narratives possess great persuasive strength. Consider, for example, the implications of these findings to the importance of attorneys developing a coherent narrative when defending their clients in court.

> ***Learn more about it:*** You can learn more about the effect of storytelling on brain processes in the following Ted Talk by Princeton neurobiologist, Professor Uri Hasson: http://bit.ly/UHTedTalk.

What we listen to also has implications for how we feel and behave. Doctors Mark Waldman and Andrew Newberg reviewed findings of fMRI research examining the effect of negativity on brain and other physiological functions.[4] Interestingly, when we voice negative thoughts and feelings, our brain releases stress chemicals, which can interrupt normal brain functions, negatively affect our ability to reason logically, and impair language and communication. In some cases, these results were stimulated by simply uttering the word "No." Just as interesting, the research also indicates that upon hearing our negative message, the same chemicals are released into the listener's brain. Listeners may become more irritable and anxious and less cooperative. Further, repeated exposure to negative messages increased prejudice toward others. fMRI research has demonstrated the power of the word "No."

Referencing back to our Listening MATERRS Model, fMRI research is often directed at attentional processes and memory.[5] Much of the early research focused on examining areas of the brain associated with hearing and listening. Have you ever been at a large party and heard someone say your name? You tune out the sounds around you to focus on how and why you're suddenly a part of this conversation across the room. Known as the **cocktail party effect**, this phenomenon is selective listening in action.[6] Selective attention has been researched for quite some time, but with an fMRI we can now "see" the sections of the brain at work when we perceive a sound, process it, and move to store it in our working memory. We can also see what sections of the brain are associated with different kinds of memory (e.g., aural, visual).

For instance, one study examining the physical changes when forming memories illustrates how incredibly efficient the brain is at developing and storing memories.[7] When we retrieve a memory such as that of your first car (Nissan Juke), favorite vacation spot (Austin, Texas), close friend (Audrey), or worst gift (luggage), only a few neurons are activated. In some instances, this selective activation holds true for letter strings (i.e., reading your father's name triggers the same brain areas as viewing a photograph of him). The good news is that we have approximately *100 billion* neurons in our brain and a memory storage capacity around *2.5 petabytes* (or a million gigabytes). We need all of this to maintain the millions of memories we form over a life time. As psychology professor Paul Reber explains,

> For comparison, if your brain worked like a digital video recorder in a television, 2.5 petabytes would be enough to hold three million hours of TV shows. You would have to leave the TV running continuously for more than 300 years to use up all that storage.[8]

Other brain research illustrates the connection between sleep, listening and memory formation. There is some evidence that during deep sleep our minds sort through our memories. Even more intriguing, it appears that we can bolster an existing memory during sleep.[9] In a study published in *Nature Neuroscience*, scientists utilized a technique called **targeted memory reactivation**. They first taught study participants to play two songs on a keyboard. Afterwards, the participants took a 90 minute nap. When they reached the deepest stages of sleep, the research team played one of the songs over and over. After participants awoke from their naps, they were asked to play the songs. Participants were consistently better at recalling and playing the targeted song they had heard while they slept. Other studies support these initial findings.[10] This research has interesting implications for listening. First, if the findings hold true, they suggest that in the future we may be able to develop programs to extend our learning time into the late night hours. Perhaps future teachers will provide recordings for students to listen to overnight to enhance what has been learned that day in class. These findings also give rise to scientific and philosophical questions about what it means to listen. Do we describe listening based on the role of intentionality? As the conscious process by which we intentionally focus on a message?

As seen from our brief review here, brain research has much to offer to our understanding of listening, and reinforces how much we still have to learn. We next turn to our expanding understanding of the musical brain.

The Musical Brain

We discussed some aspects of music earlier in the text. Here, we focus on how brain researchers are exploring how we listen to and process music. Charles Limb, a professor at Johns Hopkins University, noted that musical experience, musical exposure, and musical training changes our brain processing. You've experienced some of these effects when you used melodies to learn your ABCs, to help you remember the elements of the periodic table or state capitals.

Think on it: Make a list of the mnemonic songs you have used to learn basic information (e.g., the alphabet song, periodic table jingle, school house rock songs). Which songs do you remember best? Can you still sing them? Do you remember some songs better than others? What makes them more successful for you? Do they share any commonalties?

Psychology professor Daniel Levitin studies the neuroscience of music. In a recent interview, he noted that the "structures that respond to music in the brain evolved earlier than the structures that respond to language" (suggesting that humans used music in some way to communicate before developing language).[11] These structures are one reason why that we fall prey to ear worms. **Ear worms** are those songs or snippets of songs that seemingly get stuck in our heads. Dr. Levitin says it's as if our neural circuits get stuck in a repeating play loop. We can try getting rid of an ear worm by listening to a different song, which hopefully will cancel the first song out and not just replace it with another. Our personal suggestion is to make the second song radically different (e.g., Bohemian Rhapsody versus You are My Sunshine).

Other research has discovered that when listening to music, neurons are activated throughout the brain, including in the cognitive, motor and limbic brain regions.[12] Listening to music also changes the way in which our left and right hemisphere are connected and work together.[13] The effect on this connectivity is further enhanced if you learned to play an instrument, particularly the piano (as opposed to stringed instruments like the violin). It seems that practice emphasizes the pattern and order of notes; the more you practice, the stronger these connections become.

We may also be able to use music to encourage cooperation. Aniruddh Patel, a psychology professor at Tufts University, studies the connections between music, language, and the brain.

Discussing the impact of music on the brain, he noted that humans are the only primates that can actually move to a beat, likely because our brains are organized differently than apes and other close species. It is hypothesized that music may have played a role in early social bonding.[14] Think of social and group activities associated with music (e.g., group dancing, soldiers marching to a beat). Group dance songs have a long history and include moves like conga lines, line dancing, the Wobble, and the Cupid Shuffle. Notably, there are studies that suggest that when we move together to a beat, we increase our tendency to cooperate with one another versus when we participate in non-musical tasks.[15] While the research is ongoing, it suggests that teachers, trainers and others may want to consider building in classroom tasks and activities with a musical component to them.

As you know, people respond to music differently. For example, when listening to a "bouncy" tune, some people can't help moving extensively to the beat, others will tap a foot, while still others may not respond at all. People can also be **musically tone deaf**. While we may label ourselves as tone deaf because we don't sing well, Dr. Patel uses the phrase a bit differently.[16] True, people who are tone deaf often can't sing in tune because they can't tell when they are out of tune, but they also won't be able to tell if someone else is singing out of tune. In addition, people who are tone deaf in this sense would not be able to "name that tune." In other words, they have difficulty or may not be able to recognize music without the accompanying words. If we mention Beethoven's Fifth to you, many of you are familiar with and can hum the opening notes to this well-known symphony. Even if you don't know the title, if you heard the notes played, you will likely recognize this iconic classical melody. People who are tone deaf, however, will be unable to recognize the melody of this or other culturally relevant songs. (If you're not into classical music, try inserting the Sesame Street theme song, *Somewhere over the Rainbow*, or *Amazing Grace* into the above conversation.) Tone deafness appears to be a genetically based neurological disorder.

Learn more: You can listen to the first movement of Beethoven's Fifth Symphony at the following link: http://bit.ly/B5symphony.

Professor Daniel Levitin also discusses a number of other factors associated with listening to music. For example, pitch is the primary means by which "musical emotions" are conveyed. We vary our pitch when we ask questions.[17] In most cultures, the intonation rises as speakers get to the end of the statement, indicating to the listener that they are actually asking a question. Interestingly, when we listen to a particular pitch or tone (e.g., 440 Hertz), our brain's auditory cortex will basically fire at the same frequency (e.g., 440 Hertz). Thus, our brain is essentially in sync with what we hear. Other researchers argue that a similar type of **neural coupling** occurs between a speaker and listener and underlies successful communication.[18]

Notably, we have schemas for music, just as we do for other things in our lives.[19] As Professor Levitin points out, Western music relies on knowledge of how scales are typically used. It is one of the reasons that music from other cultures, such as India, may sound strange the first time we hear it. If you grew up in India (or had a broad musical upbringing), this music sounds normal to you. Children develop musical schemas over time, even while in the womb. By the time they are five years old, children can recognize chord progressions of their culture. Our music schemas continue to develop throughout our lives as we continue to listen and experience other music. We have schemas for various genres and styles of music, such as opera, hip hop, and indie. As we noted in

Chapter 2, our schemas can bias us. When this occurs, we run the risk of rejecting a musician or song outright. We may not consider ourselves a fan of, for instance, country music, but still can identify some country songs that we like and appreciate.

Learn more: What does 440 Hertz sound like? For musicians, this is musical note A above middle C.

Figure 13.2 Musical note A

You can listen to this note at the following link: http://bit.ly/440_Hz.

At the same time, violations of our musical schemas often make a particular song stand out. Research in this area suggests that songs that violate our expectations in some way (i.e., of a scale, melody, etc.) are the ones that we continue to listen to even years later. The violation we hear provides us with a musical "surprise" each time we hear it and, apparently, our brains like this feeling. Examples of artists who have done this include Steely Dan, Miles Davis, the Beatles, and Rachmaninoff; songs include *Somewhere over the Rainbow*, originally sung by Judy Garland, the Beatle's *Yesterday*, Sting's *Roxanne*, and Beethoven's *Ode to Joy*.[20] In his book, *This is Your Brain on Music*, Professor Levitin explains in detail the musical deviations at work in these songs and the unconventional techniques used by these and other artists.

Research in music has also extended our understanding of memory. When you sing a favorite song, you rely on your memory, not just for the lyrics, but also of pitch. Most all of us, when asked to sing our favorite song, can sing at, or at least near, perfect pitch. But, we can do more than just match the pitch of the song. We are also good at singing it at the original tempo. These two findings suggest that we are amazingly accurate in our memory of music. An old game show, *Name That Tune*, took advantage of this memory. Contestants would listen to the beginning notes of a song and then name its title. Some contestants could successfully do so after hearing as few as two notes. Our memories are enhanced when we like the music and when vocals accompany the music (versus instrumental music).[21] As researchers Stephanie Stalinski and Glenn Schellenberg found, "...listeners tend to like music that they remember and to remember music that they like."[22]

Our discussion of musical memory also contributes to our previous discussion of ear worms. Interestingly, musicians appear to be more susceptible to earworms than non-musicians. An earworm, as we noted above, is often composed of a snippet of a song, rather than the entire song. Further research has found that these snippets are typically about 15–30 seconds long – the same length of time or duration that has previously been associated with echoic or short-term auditory memory.[23]

Other research suggests there are connections between music and language. In many ways, music and language are comparable. They are both forms of expression that can be used to convey emotion, and each follow their own set of rules, reflecting the culture they are a part of.

Effects of Listening to Music

Another context that will be familiar to you is listening to music. While we touched on this topic in Chapters 2 and 5, we introduce several additional areas of study here. Research into the psychology of listening to music suggests that listening to music at work positively affects work performance, and importantly tends to put us in a good mood.[24] What type of music do you think is the most beneficial? Classical is often what springs to mind. You may have heard or read something about the "Mozart Effect." The **Mozart Effect** is a popular phrase to describe supposed increases in intelligence following listening to Mozart's sonatas. Unfortunately, the effect isn't that clear cut (or we'd all be listening to Mozart). Overall, this research suggests that, at best, there may be some very short-term gains in spatial-temporal reasoning, although more recent studies dispute even these findings.[25]

Other research suggests that listening to upbeat music is the key. Generally, such music positively affects individual mood.[26] As genres, Rap and Hip Hop often get a bad "rap" and likely unfairly. While the music videos may sometimes give older adults pause, much of the music has positive or at least neutral messages. However, it is true that some music does deserve at least part of its negative reputation. Many music lyrics advocate violence (particularly toward women), drug usage, and similar counter culture behavior. There is some evidence that listening to this type of the music does affect individual cognitions and perceptions, increasing hostile or aggressive thoughts and actions.[27] Whether listening to it leads to negative, antisocial behavior is less clear.

If you listen to music at all, you probably have developed one, if not multiple, **playlists**. Research conducted at the Brain Music Treatment Center suggests that we can develop playlists to help us reach specific goals. As we noted in Chapter 5, listening to certain types of music can reduce pain and help patients with neurological disorders increase control over their physical movements. Neuropsychiatrist Galina Mindlin suggests that listening to particular songs or music can increase your productivity, reduce anxiety, and improve concentration.[28] However, there's a catch. The songs must be carefully selected, and they must be listened to over and over again. It appears that repetition is a key part of the equation. Essentially, you're conditioning your mind (and body) to respond in a particular way when it hears the songs from your playlist. How does this work? First, consider your goal – are you trying to add energy to your work day? Calm yourself after an argument? Decrease feelings of anxiety while at the dentist?

Second, consider your favorite genres of music. Which piece(s) energize you? Which calm you? Next, you need to play and replay the music until you determine if it is having the effect that you seek. Dr. Mindlin admits that this may take some time, but she believes it is well worth it. She also notes that our musical tastes are constantly changing. Thus, our playlists will change over time. Once you've constructed your initial playlist, start listening (repeatedly). If a song doesn't have the effect you'd like, change it out.

There are other positive gains from listening to music. Several studies suggest there are direct positive benefits to listening to music with prosocial messages.[29] Psychologist Dr. Tobias Greitemeyer reported that students who listened to **prosocial music** were more likely to engage in helping behaviors.[30] What types of music did the students listen to? Michael Jackson's, *Heal the World*; the Beatles', *Help*; and, Liveaid's, *We are the World.*

Think on it: Dr. Greitemeyer's study suggests there is a direct relationship between what we listen to and how we behave. What do you think? Make a list of your five favorite songs and get the lyrics of each. Examining the lyrics, how might what you listen to affect your own behavior?

Drawing on this and other research on emotional intelligence, music professor Susan Kenney argues that music can also help teach children **delayed gratification.** She suggests that songs like "Patty Cake" use actions and rhyme to teach children anticipation, and the importance of waiting for the climax of a song.[31] Earlier research in emotional intelligence provides tangential support for her claim. In his book *Emotional Intelligence*, Daniel Goleman reports results of a longitudinal study (a study that lasts over several years) that found that children who were able to delay gratification at age four tended to become adolescents who exhibited better coping skills and conflict resolution skills, and who were more self-assertive and who had higher self-esteem. Unfortunately, no one has directly tested the relationship between listening to the types of childhood music mentioned by Dr. Kenney and an increased ability to delay gratification as adults. However, her ideas provide an intriguing topic for future listening study.

Aural Architecture (and More)

While listening to music is often an individual activity (i.e., earbuds, etc.), sometimes it is a public activity. We listen to music in concert halls, at open-air concerts, in restaurants and in elevators. Authors Barry Blesser and Linda-Ruth Salter explore the idea of aural architecture in their book, *Spaces Speak, Are You Listening?*[32] We became interested in this topic after attending a reception at a local museum. Visually, the reception hall is a stunningly beautiful room, with a domed ceiling, polished marble walls on one side, and windows soaring two stories on the other. Acoustically, the room is a disaster. It echoes. As more and more people came into the room, it became more and more difficult to hear. One attendee, who experiences tinnitus, said the noise was too much and left the reception early. The museum understanding this acoustical problem recently renovated the room to address it.

There is an entire science associated with aural designs for theatres, concert halls and similar spaces. However, rather than exploring the physical and mathematical properties of soundwaves and how they affect, for instance, the aural experience of concert goers at a particular concert hall, Blesser and Salter approach the phenomenon more broadly as they explore "the experience of space by attentive listening."[33] Their approach is unique because it acknowledges that listening involves more than soundwaves hitting our eardrums. It includes a host of other factors, such as acoustic cues (objects and surfaces), social meaning (i.e., a room that seems inviting versus one that seems cold), visual experiences (a cathedral versus a chapel), and the internal experiences of the receiver (schemas, culture, mood, etc.).

Aural architecture, then, goes beyond acoustic architecture, which focuses on the sound physics of a space. Aural architecture addresses the emotional, behavioral, and instinctive response that those within that space experience. Applied to our example above, a seemingly elegant reception space was ruined by its acoustics. People within it were functionally deaf, unable to communicate with one another.

Blesser's ideas are not new, but his interdisciplinary approach is – the bringing together of literature in art, space, culture, and technology. In terms of music, he notes that early composers purposely composed their music to fit the space where it was to be played, whether it was chamber music played at a royal palace or music meant to be performed in a large symphony hall. To understand how this approach can be applied to your own life, consider a space you spend a lot of time in. It could be a study area at the student union, your living room, your workplace. Now, consider the space itself. Is there thick carpet on the floor, which deadens sound? Or, is it tile, which amplifies it. Is the furniture inviting? Does the layout encourage or discourage social gatherings? What about the walls and artwork? What is your reaction to the space? Do you consider it warm and inviting, or cold and utilitarian? The physicality of the space as well as our reactions to it affect our listening. Similarly, the architecture of buildings affect our listening when outdoors. In a large city, tall, slick, glass-walled buildings result in sound that bounces around and off the buildings. In contrast, older buildings with decorative gables, overhanging eaves, carved works and other architectural features, can actually help mute sound for pedestrians.

Learn more: If you are unfamiliar with sound art, we introduce you to Janet Cardiff, a world renowned sound artist. The following YouTube video presents several of her works http://bit.ly/JanetCardiffinterview. This second video features an audio walk of her work – 40 Part Motet http://bit.ly/audiowalk40PM. For this sound installation, 40 individual speakers are set up in a large circle pointing inward, with each speaker delivering the voice of a single individual who participated in the recording. Listeners can approach a single speaker and hear a unique voice or they may sit or stand in the center and listen to the synthesis of all 40 voices.

The idea of an expanded concept of listening is growing, as researchers in engineering, like Blesser, and other fields, such as human geography, art, and landscaping, expand our notions of listening beyond hearing (vibration on our eardrum) to include the kinetic and spatial qualities of sound.[34]

Listening and Technology

One of the most significant changes between the first and second editions of this book was the addition of a stand-alone chapter on mediated listening. We're sure that when it comes to revising this text in the future, this new chapter will require significant updating. In many ways, research in this area is just getting started. As we pointed out in Chapter 5, relatively few studies have specifically focused on the technology user as listener. Mediated listening crosses over into many of the contexts we have examined in this book.

For example, **online social support** is becoming more and more common. It provides a means for people with a wide variety of health-related needs to learn more about their conditions and to gain needed emotional support. Similar social support groups exist for friends and family members. Antonina Bambina, who studies the interconnections between social networks and computer-mediated communication, advocates for social support groups that include in-person and online participants.[35] Similar to online classes and business meetings, participants both near and far can interact with one another. These types of groups would be especially useful for individuals experiencing suppressed immune systems, anxiety disorders, or who are too ill to travel. Online members can gain the support they need until they are willing and/or able to attend in person. We do offer the following caveat. Some research indicates that face-to-face communication may not always offer the best medium for offering social support. Like many things in life, it depends on the circumstances and the individuals. Some individuals who are hesitant to disclose personal information in a face-to-face setting will do so to an online support group.[36]

Research in when, where, how, and why we use computer, tablets, and other mobile devices will continue to grow, reflecting the changing face of business, medicine, education and our personal lives. Professor Worthington is only one of many researchers exploring this area from a cross-cultural perspective. She and her co-authors have examined the use of mobile phones and how their use varies with individual differences in privacy management behaviors and noise sensitivity across multiple countries (e.g., Finland, Germany, and the USA).[37] Other work addresses mobile phone addiction and its impact on user behaviors. Some compelling questions are: How aware are users of those around them? Do they use their devices in socially inappropriate ways? At socially inappropriate times? Are there cultural differences in how people use their devices?

Other research use computers and mobile technologies to study listening and/or assist in listening processes. For example, several studies have utilized mobile apps to gather data. Using the app, My Social Ties, one group of researchers collected data from almost 500 conversations.[38] One of the more interesting findings was that people tended to enjoy conversations more when they spoke less. These findings provide insight into our everyday social interactions.

Apps can also be beneficial in other ways. Psychiatrist John Pestian developed an app that tracks vocal distress patterns called **thought markers.** Thought markers provide insight into a person's state of mind. The software tracks *vowel space* (i.e., how we pronounce and articulate words). Depression influences our motor control functions in a number of areas, but particularly in speech production. Even therapists who listen really well will have difficulty identifying the most subtle of depressive thought markers. This app shows promise as an important "listening" tool for therapists.

Exploring Listening and Conversations

The social support groups mentioned above are one area of listening study associated with health outcomes. Another area addresses informal helping conversations. These types of conversations are often associated with troubles talk. **Troubles talk** occurs when we disclose our stress to others.[39] Ideally, these conversations reduce our distress, strengthen our relationships, and improve our physical and mental health. However, most of us have experienced times when we've tried discussing negative events or other stressful moments with someone and we actually end up feeling worse after the conversation than before it. What distinguishes helpful troubles talk from one which is harmful is the quality of enacted support.[40]

Think on it: Think back on a recent troubles talk you had with a friend. Were you satisfied with the support you received? Why or Why not? Are some of your friends more skilled at providing support? If so, what do they say or do that sets them apart? Do you go to some friends for some types of trouble and others for other types of trouble? What does this tell you about the nature of stress and social support?

As we discussed earlier in the text, active listening has long been identified as a therapeutic tool in the health professions.[41] Current investigations are focusing on what is the nature and form of the best of these informal helping conversations, particularly in terms of active listening.[42] Initial findings suggest that active listening does contribute to feelings of support (e.g., paraphrasing, asking questions, checking understanding). For instance, for many years, we've been told that the "best" paraphrasing occurs when the listener is able to capture the whole meaning of the speaker's message (i.e., their emotions and message content). Recent research suggests that this aspect of active listening is more nuanced. Listening scholar Graham Bodie and his colleagues tested four types of paraphrasing – event, durative descriptive, evaluative, and adequate. Each type focuses on an element of a speaker's message. An **event** is the thing or trigger behind the story (e.g., breaking up with your significant other; a colleague presents your ideas as his or her own). A **durative description** includes typical story elements (e.g., context, setting, individuals who were involved). **Evaluative information** focuses on the feelings that are expressed, so that the listener can identify the most important parts of the story (e.g., finding "love note" texts on your now ex's phone). A successful **adequate paraphrase** will encompass all of these elements.

A closer look, however, suggests that these elements are not created equal. Results of the Bodie study found that speakers preferred adequate and durative descriptive paraphrasing over event and evaluative information paraphrasing. While it makes sense that adequate paraphrasing was rated favorably, why was durative descriptive paraphrasing rated more highly than the other two? Bodie and his colleagues believe that durative descriptive information relays several important features, such as: 1) story elements that help us understand why we should listen to the story; 2) necessary background information; and 3) reasons for disclosing the information (i.e., why we should listen). Note, however, that findings are not "one size fits all," and can vary with the individuals involved and the situation. Their study points out the need for listening scholars to test other long-held assumptions.

Exploring Listening and Education

The good news, bad news is that after taking a listening class, you tend to have much more realistic perceptions of the quality of your own listening. If you were asked to rate your listening competency at the beginning of this semester, many of you may have rated yourself as a fairly competent listener. However, following a listening class it is not unusual for students to actually rate their listening competency lower! We see this evidenced in Ben's comments in the case study at the beginning of this chapter. This decline in your perception of your listening competency is due to your greater understanding of what goes into being an effective listener.[43]

As we noted at the beginning of this text, few of you had the opportunity to take listening classes prior to the one you are currently enrolled in. In addition, listening training was probably not available and was seldom if ever emphasized in your other classes. Our text has sought to offer you a taste of our current understanding of the art and science of listening. We also hope your experience with this book and your listening class has improved your **metacognitive listening strategies** – a listener's awareness of, skill at, and ability to regulate his or her own listening comprehension processes.[44] In other words, if you face a listening problem, you'll be able to recognize the source of the problem and determine a means of addressing it.

As you can see in our discussion above and elsewhere in the text, research in listening is at a new and exciting nexus. Young scholars are expanding our knowledge of what it means to listen, which in turn will shape what is taught in the listening class in the future. Organizations such as the International Listening Association and the National Communication Association provide forums to introduce emerging listening research to new and established listening scholars, many of whom are teaching classes similar to the one you are currently enrolled in.

One proposed strategy for increasing listening performance is **Listening Across the Curriculum.** Many colleges and university have writing across the curriculum and oral communication across the curriculum programs. These programs were developed to help students hone their communication skills so that they will be effective communicators when they enter the workplace.[45] Such programs encourage or require instructors across disciplines to include writing or speaking assignments in their classes in order to improve students' skills in these areas. Unfortunately, few institutions have incorporated listening across the curriculum programs.[46]

Professor Janice Newton of Canada's York University believes that listening education should go beyond a single class.[47] She argues that in order to truly master listening skills they need to be taught in university core classes. Assigned to teach in two different departments, Dr. Newton has personal experience doing just this. She includes listening activities and skills practice in both her political science and her women's studies courses. Listening and critical thinking are closely related. Ideally, improving your listening skills will assist your critical thinking and ultimately your classroom performance.

Instituting Dr. Newton's suggestion represents an ideal for educators who value listening. However, there are a number of challenges that face listening classes included in current, more traditional communication curriculum. For example, the majority of listening classes are taught at the junior and senior college level.[48] While it's good to have the benefit of listening training prior to graduation and beginning your career, wouldn't it be nice to have the benefit of such training throughout your college career? As we discussed earlier in Chapter 9, improved listening has been associated with improved classroom performance.

Think on it: What might be some of the difficulties in instituting Dr. Newton's suggestion for a listening across the curriculum program? What challenges might be faced by faculty? By students?

An additional issue in listening education addresses the **role of the college textbook**. Researchers differ in the underlying goal that a college textbook should serve – to help produce additional knowledge of a field *or* to present what is known and proven about a field.[49] As listening scholar Laura Janusik notes, either of these views assumes that the material presented in the textbook is accurate, based on solid research. Unfortunately, the listening chapters presented in many communication textbooks (e.g., public speaking, small group communication, health communication, etc.) are not supported by research.[50] Most instructors trust the quality of the material being presented in these chapters and so few review the research presented in them. Writers of listening textbooks also experience problems. We are often faced with a lack of research or with conflicting research from various disciplines. Psychologists study listening as related to counseling and witness examination. Political scientists study the impact of listening on mediation and arbitration. Medical researchers study listening in doctor–patient interviews. And, of course, communication scholars study the impact of listening in all of these areas and more. Laura Janusik best sums up the relationship between the teaching and research of listening when she writes, "Thus, as a field, we have approached a crossroads because much of what we have believed to be true about listening is not supported, and without supported knowledge, new knowledge cannot be created."[51] She argues that we need to focus greater attention on researching listening, what it is and how it works.

Scholars both in the USA and abroad are accepting Janusik's charge. Findings from their recent studies are presented throughout this book. We have worked hard to bring you research by scholars from a variety of disciplines and have drawn on established research wherever possible. We have extensively reviewed listening research with the goal of providing you with knowledge of the current state of the field, while at the same time synthesizing research from areas outside of communication. From the beginning, we hoped to broaden your understanding of listening and to provide you with the means of improving your own listening skills.

Concluding Thoughts

Is it Listening?

We've touched on this topic now and again throughout the text. When you receive a message via email or a text are you reading or listening? Obviously when using programs like Zoom, Skype or FaceTime, you engage in computer-mediated F2F conversation and you use the same listening skill as any other F2F interaction. But, what about asynchronous text-based interaction like an online class chat room or text messaging? Interestingly, you call upon listening-based behavior when you actively participate in those discussions.

Researchers Alyssa Wise, Simone Hauskneckt, and Yuting Zhao of Simone Fraser University coined the term **online listening**.[52] They argue that listening in both an aural and written context are fundamentally alike. As we have discussed before, listening is a complex cognitive process which involves numerous decisions.

In the Listening MATERRS Model we presented some of those decisions. Based on a review of listening-related research, Professors Wise, Hauskuecht, and Zhao drew the following parallels between listening aurally and online.

- Listening is an active process – we must process someone else's ideas.
- Prior experiences (think schemata and biases) affect how an individual translates the message, thus, different people perceive different meanings from the same message.
- Listening connotes a certain openness to considering a variety of ideas.
- Listening is part of a larger process of give and take of ideas, including the critical examination, challenging and building on the ideas.

In summary, participating in an online discussion involves the same process as F2F discussions.

- You must be **M**otivated to participate.
- You become **A**ware and pay attention to the message.
- You **T**ranslate and interpret what the person means.
- You **E**valuate the message as you cognitively process it.
- You **R**ecall what the other people in the discussion "said."
- You **R**espond to the discussion with your ideas, opinions and questions.
- You **S**tay connected and motivated throughout the discussion.

Listening and what it means to listen continues to change. Do you "listen" to your "inner voice," to those conversations you have with yourself? Some listening scholars suggest that when you attend to these conversations that you are "listening."[53] Similarly, the development of interactive media has led the act of listening to be transformed into a metaphor to describe these other communication activities. For example, do you consider yourself "listening" to text messages? When you read your email? When Tweeting (or reading Tweets)? In these contexts, listening has become a metaphor used to describe our act of paying attention to online communication.[54] Kate Crawford, a professor at the University of New South Wales in Sydney, Australia, specializes in research addressing the technologies of listening. She argues that the metaphor of listening is useful for describing how we receive and process online interactions, such as those associated with various social media and Twitter. It is true that how we pay attention and what we pay attention to evolves in response to social and technological changes.[55] Yet, the use of this metaphor is problematic.

How does it "muddy" our understanding of listening? Of course, this begs the question as to how we should reference these types of online communication. If we call them conversations, then the language associated with descriptions of conversations is naturally engaged (e.g., talk, listen, etc.). However, when we equate listening to "paying attention," we ignore what makes listening a unique aspect of communication. So, we conclude this book with one last call to *Think on it*: Should we use the metaphor of listening when referencing how we pay attention to electronic communication? To our inner voice? If not, why not? If yes, why?

Key Concepts

> Physiology of Listening
> Temporal Lobe
> Functional Magnetic Resonance Imaging
> > Noise
> > Mundane realism
> Cocktail Party Effect
> Targeted Memory Reactivation
> Ear worms
> Musically Tone Deaf
> Neural Coupling
> Mozart Effect
> Playlists
> Prosocial Music
> Delayed Gratification
> Aural Architecture
> Online Social Support
> Thought Markers
> > Vowel space
> Troubles Talk
> > Event
> > Durative description
> > Evaluative information
> > Adequate paraphrase
> Metacognitive Listening Strategies
> Listening Across the Curriculum
> Role of Textbooks
> Online Listening

Discussion Questions

1. Dr. Blesser comes from an engineering background. Based on the courses you've taken thus far in your academic career, what additional elements would you suggest he consider?

2. Blesser and others argue that our conceptual view of listening should be expanded. Do you agree? If so, what should be considered parts of our listening "soundscape?" Just elements of architecture? What about landscaping? What of your beating heart? Do we only focus on sounds that hit our ears? Should we include vibrations or frequencies that we may not be able to hear aurally, but instead can only feel?

3. We are familiar with many musical artists, but other artists have been "playing" with sound for centuries. Check out the following recent examples: Carsten Nicolai's reflektor distortion (https://vimeo.com/168672417); Thessia Machado's rec/play (https://vimeo.com/88451951); and Christine Sun Kim's Game of Skill 2.0 (https://vimeo.com/142659892). Headphones may help you to fully hear the finer sounds of some of these works. What is your reaction to these artistic pieces?
4. We discussed reading, writing, and listening across the curriculum programs. If you could institute only one of these three programs, which would you institute first? Second? Why?
5. We introduced you to several new listening measures of the course of the text. In your opinion, which of the measurements appear to have the greatest ability to help us learn more about how people listen and process information?

Listening Activities

1. Blesser believes that we can act as aural architects because we can create and influence our personal sonic experience by manipulating relevant properties in our environment. Things to consider when addressing the aural architecture of your own spaces include:
    *   how many people will be using a space
    *   the choice of furniture
    *   windows and doors (open versus closed, window coverings)
    *   floor coverings (polished concrete, wood floors, area rugs)
    *   selecting which kind of sonic events are to be encouraged (e.g., conversational groupings, selecting and positioning loudspeakers in a home theatre, etc.).
    Imagine that you are redesigning your living space. First, identify the sonic event(s) you would like to emphasize. What factors would you need to consider that might be challenges to your redesign (e.g., size and shape of the room, etc.)? How can you address them? What factors listed above would you need to consider? Are there other elements of the environment that should be addressed?
2. Working in a small group of four to five individuals, choose a song and develop a dance to accompany it. Teach the rest of the class your dance moves. Why did your group choose the music it did? How did you develop your moves? How did working on this activity compare or differ from other small group assignments you've worked on this semester? What was the mood of the class during and after the activity?
3. Pick a television or online educational program designed for preschool children. When and where do you hear music during the program? What role do you believe music plays in helping children learn?
4. Listening across the curriculum programs provide listening training and activities in classes from all areas and majors. In groups of three to four individuals, develop an outline of a program for your college or university. You should include ideas for sample assignments, identify the primary classes that should be included, and develop a one to two page justification for the program you design.

Notes

1 Bodie, 2011, 2009, 2008
2 See Wolvin, 2010, Chapter 1, for a fuller discussion of physiological processes of listening
3 Kawamichi et al., 2015

4 Waldman & Newberg, 2013
5 Worthington, 2017, provides a review of research methods used to examine cognitive processes of listening, including fMRI.
6 Cherry, 1953
7 Gross et al., 2013
8 Reber, 2010
9 Antony, Gobel, O'Hare, Reber, & Paller, 2012
10 Cousins et al., 2014
11 As quoted in Landau, 2012
12 Alluri et al., 2012
13 Burunat et al., 2015
14 Landau, 2012
15 Landau, 2012
16 Patel, 2008
17 Saindon, Trehub, Schellenberg, & van Lieshout, 2017
18 Stephens, Silbert, & Hasson, 2010
19 Levitin, 2007
20 Levitin, 2007
21 Weiss, Schellenberg, & Trehub, 2017
22 Stalinski & Schellenberg, 2013
23 Levitin, 2007
24 Lesiuk, 2005
25 See Schellenberg, 2012 for a review
26 Thompson, Husain, & Schellenberg, 2001
27 See Timmerman, Allen, Jorgensen, Herrett-Skjellum, Kramer, & Ryan, 2008 for a meta-analysis of related studies.
28 Mindlin, Durousseau, & Cardillo, 2012
29 Böhm, Ruch, & Schramm, 2016; Greitemeyer, 2009
30 Greitemeyer, 2009
31 Kenney, 2009
32 Blesser & Salter, 2006
33 Blesser & Salter, 2007
34 Gallagher, Kanngieser, & Prior, 2016 provide a review. Their article is available online and includes embedded audio links illustrating many of the concepts they discuss relevant to human geography.
35 Bambina, 2007
36 Rains, Brunner, Akers, Pavlich, & Tsetsi, 2016
37 Worthington, Keaton, Imhof, & Välikoski, 2016
38 Sandstrom et al., 2016
39 Rimé, 2009
40 Goldsmith, 2004
41 See Bodie, Vickery, Cannava, & Jones, 2015 for a review; Bodie et al., 2016
42 See, for example, Bodie, Vickery, Cannava, & Jones, 2015; Vickery, Keaton, & Bodie, 2015
43 Ford, Wolvin, & Chung, 2000
44 Goh, 2008; Vandergrift, Goh, Mareschal, & Tafaghodtari, 2006 Janusik & Keaton, 2011, 2015
45 Helsel & Hogg, 2006
46 One notable exception is Alverno Collego. For a full description of Alverno's Integrated Listening Model, see Thompson, Leintz, Nevers, & Witkowski, 2010.
47 Newton, 2010
48 Janusik, 2010
49 Alfred & Thelen, 1993; Connors, 1986
50 Janusik & Wolvin, 2002

51 Janusik, 2010
52 Wise, Hausknecht, & Zhao, 2014
53 Robson & Young, 2007
54 Crawford, 2009
55 Crary, 1999

Additional Readings

Beard, D., & Bodie, G. D. (2014). Listening research in the Communication discipline. In P. J. Gehrke & W. M. Keith (Eds.), *The unfinished conversation: 100 years of Communication Studies.* New York: Routledge.

Bodie, G. D. (2016, August). Listening. *Oxford Research Encyclopedia of Communication.* Retrieved from http://communication.oxfordre.com/view/10.1093/acrefore/9780190228613.001.0001/acrefore-9780190228613-e-279?rskey=H6zL87&result=1.

Wolvin, A. D. (2010). *Listening and human communication in the 21st century.* New York: Wiley.

Kuhl, B. A., & Chun, M. M. (2014). Memory and attention. In A. C. Nobre & S. Kastner (Eds.), *The Oxford handbook of attention* (pp. 806–836). Oxford: Oxford Library of Psychology.

Worthington, D. L., & Bodie, G. D. (2017). *The sourcebook of listening research: Methodology and measures.* Malden, MA: Wiley.

References

Alfred, G. J., & Thelen, E. A. (1993). Are textbooks contributions to scholarship? *College Composition and Communication, 44,* 466–477.

Antony, J. W., Gobel, E. W., O'Hare, J. K, Reber, P. J., & Paller, K. A. (2012). Cued memory reactivation during sleep influences skill learning. *Nature Neuroscience, 15,* 1114–1116.

Alluri, V., Toiviainen, P., Jääskeläinen, I. P., Glerean, E., Sams, M., & Brattico, E. (2012). Large-scale brain networks emerge from dynamic processing of musical timbre, key and rhythm. *NeuroImage, 59,* 3677–3689.

Bambina, A. (2007). *Online social support.* Youngstown, NY: Cambria.

Blesser, B., & Salter, L.-R. (2006). *Space speak, are you listening?* Cambridge, MA: MIT Press.

Blesser, B., & Salter, L.-R. (2007, Winter). Aural architecture. *Research-Design Connections.* Retrieved from www.blesser.net/downloads/RDC%20Article.pdf.

Bodie, G. D. (2011). The understudied nature of listening in interpersonal communication research: Introduction to a special issue. *International Journal of Listening, 29,* 1–9.

Bodie, G. D. (2009). Evaluating listening theory: Development and illustration of five criteria. *International Journal of Listening, 23,* 81–103.

Bodie, G. D. (2008, March). *The concept of theory in listening: What is it and how can we tell if we have one?* Paper presented at the annual convention of the International Listening Association, Portland, ME.

Bodie, G. D., Cannava, K., & Vickery, A. J. (2016). Supportive communication and the adequate paraphrase. *Communication Research Reports, 33,* 166–172.

Bodie, G. D., Vickery, A. J., Cannava, K., & Jones, S. M. (2015). The role of "active listening" in informal helping conversations: Impact on perceptions of listener helpfulness, sensitivity, and supportiveness and discloser emotional improvement. *Western Journal of Communication, 79,* 151–173.

Böhm, T., Ruth, N., & Schramm, H. (2016). "Count on me" – The influence of music with prosocial lyrics on cognitive and affective aggression. *Psychomusicology: Music, Mind, and Brain, 26,* 279–283.

Burunat, I., Brattico, E., Puoliväli, T., Ristaniemi, T., Sams, M., & Toiviainen, P. (2015). Action in perception: Prominent visuo-motor functional symmetry in musicians during music listening. *PLoS ONE, 10*(9), e0138238.

Cherry, E. C. (1953). Some experiments on the recognition of speech, with one and with two ears. *The Journal of the Acoustical Society of America, 25,* 975–979.

Connors, R. J. (1986). Textbooks and the evolution of the discipline. *College Composition and Communication, 37*, 178–194.

Cousins, J. N., El-Deredy, W., Parkes, L. M., Hennies, N., & Lewis, P. A. (2014). Cued memory reactivation during slow-wave sleep promotes explicit knowledge of a motor sequence. *Journal of Neuroscience, 34*, 15870–15876.

Crary, J. (1999). *Suspensions of perception: Attention, spectacle, and modern culture*. Cambridge, MA: MIT Press.

Crawford, K. (2009). Following you: Disciplines of listening in social media. *Continuum: Journal of Media & Cultural Studies, 23*, 525–535.

Ford, W. Z., Wolvin, A. D., & Chung, S. (2000). Students' self-perceived listening competencies. *International Journal of Listening, 14*, 1–13.

Gallagher, M., Kanngieser, A., & Prior, J. (2016). Listening geographies: Landscape, affect and geotechnologies. *Progress in Human Geography*. Retrieved from http://journals.sagepub.com/doi/pdf/10.1177/0309132516652952.

Goh, C. M. (2008). Metacognitive instruction for second language listening development: Theory, practice and research implications. *RELC Journal, 39*, 188–213.

Goldsmith, D. J. (2004). Problematizing provider/recipient roles in troubles talk. In D. J. Goldsmith (Ed.), *Communicating social support series: Advances in personal relationships* (pp. 116–148). New York: Cambridge University Press.

Greitemeyer, T. (2009). Effects of songs with prosocial lyrics on prosocial behavior: Further evidence and a mediating mechanism. *PSPB, 35*, 1500–1511.

Gross, G. G., Junge, J. A., Mora, R. J., Kwon, H-B., Olson, C. A., Takahashi, T. T., & Arnold, D. B. (2013). Recombinant probes for visualizing endogenous synaptic proteins in living neurons. *Neuron, 78*, 971–985.

Helsel, C. R., & Hogg, M. C. (2006). Assessing communication proficiency in higher education. Speaking labs offer possibilities. *International Journal of Listening, 20*, 29–54.

Janusik, L. A. (2010). Listening pedagogy: Where do we go from here? In A. D. Wolvin (Ed.), *Listening and human communication in the 21st century* (pp. 193–224). Malden, MA: Wiley-Blackwell.

Janusik, L., & Keaton, S. A. (2011). Listening metacognitions: Another key to teaching listening? *Listening Education, 3*, 33–42.

Janusik, L., & Keaton, S. A. (2015). Towards developing a cross-cultural metacognition listening instrument for listening in first language (L1) contexts: The (Janusik–Keaton) metacognitive listening instrument. *Journal of Intercultural Communication Research, 44*, 288–306.

Janusik, L. A., & Wolvin, A. (2002). Listening treatment in the basic communication course text. In D. Sellnow (Ed.), *Basic communication course annual, 14* (pp. 164–210). Boston: American Press.

Kawamichi, H., Yoshihara, K. Sasaki, A. T., Sugawara, S. K., Tanabe, H. C., Shinohara, R., ... & Sadato, N. (2015). Perceiving active listening activates the reward system and improves the impression of relevant experiences. *Social Neurosciences, 10*, 16–26.

Kenney, S. (2009). A marshmallow and a song. *General Music Today, 22*, 27–29.

Landau, E. (2012). Music: It's in your head, changing your brain. CNN. Retrieved from www.cnn.com/2012/05/26/health/mental-health/music-brain-science/index.html.

Lesiuk, T. (2005). The effect of music listening on work performance. *Psychology of Music, 33*, 173–191.

Levitin, D. J. (2007). *This is your brain on music*. New York: Plume.

Mindlin, G., Durousseau, D., & Cardillo, J. (2012). *Your playlist can change your life*. Naperville, IL: Sourcebooks.

Newton, J. (2010, March). *Listening across disciplines: How do we teach it?* Paper presented at the International Listening Association convention, Albuquerque, NM.

Patel, A. D. (2008, November 7). *The music of language and the language of music*. Library of Congress Podcast. Retrieved from www.loc.gov/podcasts/musicandthebrain/podcast_aniruddhpatel.html.

Rains, S. A., Brunner, S. R., Akers, C., Pavlich, C. A., & Tsetsi, E. (2016). The implications of computer-mediated communication (CMC) for social support message processing and outcomes: When and why are the effects of support messages strengthened during CMC? *Human Communication Research, 42*, 553–576.

Reber, P. (2010, May 1). What is the memory capacity of the human brain? *Scientific American.* Retrieved from www.scientificamerican.com/article/what-is-the-memory-capacity.

Rimé, B. (2009). Emotion elicits the social sharing of emotion: Theory and empirical review. *Emotion Review, 1,* 60–85.

Robson, D. C., & Young, R. (2007). Listening to inner speech: Can students listen to themselves think? *International Journal of Listening, 21,* 1–13.

Sandstrom, G. M., Tseng, V. W., Costa, J., Okeke, F., Choudhury, T., & Dunn, E. W. (2016). Talking less during social interactions predicts enjoyment: A mobile sensing pilot study. *PLoS One, 20,* 11(7):e0158834.

Saindon, M. R., Trehub, S. E., Schellenberg, E. G., & van Lieshout, P. H. H. M. (2017). When is a question a question for children and adults? Advance online publication. *Language Learning and Development.* Retrieved from http://dx.doi.org/10.1080/15475441.2016.1252681.

Schellenberg, E. G. (2012). Cognitive performance after music listening: A review of the Mozart effect. In R. A. R. MacDonald, G. Kreutz, & L. Mitchell (Eds.), *Music, health and wellbeing* (pp. 324–338). Oxford, UK: Oxford.

Stalinski, S. M., & Schellenberg, E. G. (2013). Listeners remember music they like. *Journal of Experimental Psychology: Learning, Memory, and Cognition, 39,* 700–716.

Stephens, G. J., Silbert L. J., & Hasson, U. (2010). Speaker–listener neural coupling underlies successful communication. *Proceedings of the National Academy of Science, 107,* 14425–14430.

Thompson, W. F., Husain, G., & Schellenberg, G. (2001). Arousal, mood, and the Mozart effect. *Psychological Science, 12,* 248–251.

Thompson, K., Leintz, P., Nevers, B., & Witkowski, S. (2010). The integrated listening model: An approach to teaching and learning listening. In A. D. Wolvin (Ed.), *Listening and human communication in the 21st century* (pp. 266–286). Malden, MA: Wiley-Blackwell.

Timmerman, L., Allen, M., Jorgensen, J., Herrett-Skjellum, J., Kramer, M., & Ryan, D. (2008). A review and meta-analysis examining the relationship of music content with sex, race, priming, and attitudes. *Communication Quarterly, 56,* 303–324.

Vandergrift, L., Goh, C. C., Mareschal, C. J., & Tafaghodtari, M. H. (2006). The metacognitive awareness listening questionnaire: Development and validation. *Language Learning, 56,* 431–462.

Waldman, M. R., & Newberg, A. (2013). *Words can change your brain.* New York: Plume.

Vickery, A. J., Keaton, S. A., & Bodie, G. D. (2015). An examination of imagined interactions features and active empathic listening behaviors. *Southern Communication Journal, 80,* 20–38.

Weiss, M. W., Schellenberg, E. G., & Trehub, S. E. (2017). Generality of the memory advantage for vocal melodies. *Music Perception, 34,* 313–318.

Wise, A. F., Hausknecht, S., N., & Zhao, Y. (2014). Attending to others' posts in asynchronous discussions: Learners' online "listening" and its relationship to speaking. *International Journal of Computer-Supported Collaborative Learning, 9,* 185–209.

Worthington, D. L. (2017). Modeling & measuring cognitive components of listening. In D. L. Worthington & G. Bodie (Eds.), *The sourcebook of listening research: Methodology and measures* (Chapter 4). Malden, MA: Wiley.

Worthington, D. L., Keaton, S., Imhof, M., & Valikoski, T.-R. (2016). Impact of noise sensitivity on mobile phone attitudes and behaviors. *Mobile Media and Communication, 4,* 3–18.

Wolvin, A. D. (2010). Listening engagement: Intersecting theoretical perspectives. In A. D. Wolvin (Ed.), *Listening and human communication in the 21st century* (pp. 7–30). Malden, MA: Wiley.

Index

 Taylor & Francis eBooks

Helping you to choose the right eBooks for your Library

Add Routledge titles to your library's digital collection today. Taylor and Francis ebooks contains over 50,000 titles in the Humanities, Social Sciences, Behavioural Sciences, Built Environment and Law.

Choose from a range of subject packages or create your own!

Benefits for you

» Free MARC records
» COUNTER-compliant usage statistics
» Flexible purchase and pricing options
» All titles DRM-free.

Benefits for your user

» Off-site, anytime access via Athens or referring URL
» Print or copy pages or chapters
» Full content search
» Bookmark, highlight and annotate text
» Access to thousands of pages of quality research at the click of a button.

REQUEST YOUR FREE INSTITUTIONAL TRIAL TODAY

Free Trials Available
We offer free trials to qualifying academic, corporate and government customers.

eCollections – Choose from over 30 subject eCollections, including:

Archaeology	Language Learning
Architecture	Law
Asian Studies	Literature
Business & Management	Media & Communication
Classical Studies	Middle East Studies
Construction	Music
Creative & Media Arts	Philosophy
Criminology & Criminal Justice	Planning
Economics	Politics
Education	Psychology & Mental Health
Energy	Religion
Engineering	Security
English Language & Linguistics	Social Work
Environment & Sustainability	Sociology
Geography	Sport
Health Studies	Theatre & Performance
History	Tourism, Hospitality & Events

For more information, pricing enquiries or to order a free trial, please contact your local sales team: **www.tandfebooks.com/page/sales**

 Routledge
Taylor & Francis Group

The home of
Routledge books

www.tandfebooks.com